MW00560317

Dear John,

It's a pleasure & an honor
to be linked to you also this
way, through Richard —
all sacred, nothing sinister!

David.

Dear John,

You taught me about the red
and the black and so much else
— small wonder that I moved to
the sacred and the sinister!

Richard

THE SACRED AND THE SINISTER

THE SACRED AND THE SINISTER

STUDIES IN MEDIEVAL RELIGION AND MAGIC

Edited by
David J. Collins, S.J.

THE PENNSYLVANIA STATE UNIVERSITY PRESS
UNIVERSITY PARK, PENNSYLVANIA

Library of Congress Cataloging-in-Publication Data

Names: Collins, David J., 1965– editor.
Title: The sacred and the sinister : studies in medieval religion and magic / edited by
    David J. Collins, S.J.
Description: University Park, Pennsylvania : The Pennsylvania State University
    Press, [2019] | Includes bibliographical references and index.
Summary: "A collection of essays focusing on the relationship between concepts of
    the holy and the unholy in western European medieval culture. Demonstrates
    how religion, magic, and science were all modes of engagement with a natural
    world that was understood to be divinely created and infused with mysterious
    power"—Provided by publisher.
Identifiers: LCCN 2018053167 | ISBN 9780271082400 (cloth : alk. paper)
Subjects: LCSH: Good and evil—History—To 1500. | Europe—Church history—
    600–1500. | Magic—Europe—History—To 1500.
Classification: LCC BJ1401.S23 2019 | DDC 200.94/0902—dc23
LC record available at https://lccn.loc.gov/2018053167

Copyright © 2019 The Pennsylvania State University
All rights reserved
Printed in the United States of America
Published by The Pennsylvania State University Press,
University Park, PA 16802–1003

The Pennsylvania State University Press is a member of the Association of
University Presses.

It is the policy of The Pennsylvania State University Press to use acid-free paper.
Publications on uncoated stock satisfy the minimum requirements of American
National Standard for Information Sciences—Permanence of Paper for Printed
Library Material, ANSI Z39.48–1992.

CONTENTS

ACKNOWLEDGMENTS

This volume of collected scholarship is a group effort in every respect. The editor wishes to acknowledge gratefully the many whose generous participation brought it into existence. All the contributors provided abundant evidence to contradict the conventional wisdom that coordinating academics in such a project is as frustrating as herding hoopoes. From the beginning, Michael Bailey and Claire Fanger offered the editor invaluable advice on how to organize and direct the project and many tips on how to present the project persuasively to the press. More recently, Maeve Callan generously stepped in to organize the ceremonial conclusion to the project. Barbara Newman provided encouragement throughout and, very crucially, kept the dedicatee distracted from our efforts. Several colleagues at Georgetown and other universities graciously reviewed chapters in draft and provided much useful feedback. The anonymous reviewers later provided by the press could not have fulfilled their duties with greater diligence. Eleanor Goodman and her assistant Hannah Hebert were our thoughtful, thorough, patient, supportive, and amiable partners at the press. Finally, with all those who have worked over the last four years on this project (and done such a good job at keeping it a secret), I offer an enthusiastic and heartfelt word of thanks to the one whose scholarship, example, and mentoring over nearly a half century are the ultimate inspiration for the volume:

Richardo Kieckhefer
doctori collegae amico
hoc opus dedicant eius
discipuli collegae amici.

David J. Collins, S.J.
Washington, D.C.
November 30, 2018

INTRODUCTION:

FLIRTING BETWEEN HEAVEN AND HELL

David J. Collins, S.J.

Richard Kieckhefer began his 1994 article "The Holy and the Unholy: Saint-hood, Witchcraft, and Magic in Late Medieval Europe" with a literary compari-son. He used the novelistic treatments of two historical personalities—Dorothea von Montau (1347–1394) in Günter Grass's novel *Der Butt* (1977) and Gilles de Rais (1405–1440) in J. K. Huysmans's novel *Là-bas* (1891)—to reflect on the rela-tionship of holy to unholy in medieval culture. In the former work, Grass portrayed an ambivalence in how contemporaries identified Dorothea: some-times as a saint, sometimes as a witch. In the latter, Huysmans insinuated an ambiguity in Gilles's self-understanding as a necromancer derived from a doubt over whether the origin of his experiences is divine or satanic. While discounting the historical pretensions of both works, Kieckhefer endorsed a historical insight from each: First, sainthood and witchcraft were ascribed roles that could indeed occasion among medieval observers competing identi-fications, from which could emerge an ambivalence over who was what. And second, a participant's own understanding of the spiritual powers he or she was communing with could be ambiguous, with the effect that the divine and the demonic were allowed to enter into "a rare and fascinating alliance." By Kieckhefer's lights, appreciations of ambivalence, as in Dorothea's case, and ambiguity, as in Gilles's, open to the modern-day researcher understandings of medieval culture not apprehensible if opposition between the holy and the unholy is taken as self-evident and necessary. With an eye to the historical implications, Kieckhefer concluded, "Both the ambivalence in the one case and the ambiguity in the other were deeply disturbing [in the Middle Ages]: . . . orthodox observers understandably felt threatened by such flirtation between heaven and hell."[1]

The aim of this volume, *The Sacred and the Sinister*, is to advance our under-standing of that flirtation, and it is much inspired by Kieckhefer's career-long

efforts at figuring out how the difference between holy and unholy was understood in medieval culture—where that frontier was less clear-cut and more
permeable than is conventionally imagined—and why the difference mattered.
The aim of this initial chapter is to introduce the full volume *The Sacred and
the Sinister* in three steps: first, with a brief overview of the recent and interdisciplinary origins of the pairing of holy and unholy as an object of scholarly
analysis, especially in the history of medieval Christianity; second, with a
sketch of Kieckhefer's own contribution to framing the questions and shedding
light on the problems; and third, with an outline of the volume at hand, which
has been organized as a tribute to Richard Kieckhefer on the occasion of his
retirement and as an effort to advance the scholarly agenda his work lays out.

Sacred and Profane, an Interdisciplinary Development

Today it is often taken as axiomatic by scholars of medieval culture that postu-
lating the strict opposition between the holy and the unholy is an unwise starting point. Instead, scrutinizing the historical materials for indecision over and
conflict between these beguilingly self-evident opposites holds out the greater
promise for insight into medieval religious culture. The latter approach requires
both the careful selection of tools to interrogate the sources and purposefulness in aggregating the relevant evidence. Kieckhefer's 1994 article makes precisely this point: assembling a coherent body of evidence and applying to it the
proper analytical tools are preconditions for ascertaining the complex historical associations (and distinctions) between witch and saint, demonic *fascinatio*
and mystical *ecstasia*, or exorcism and conjuration. Kieckhefer likewise challenged the modern-day historical researcher to keep in mind who the participants are to whom these associations and differences matter. Indeed, there are
several kinds of participants, and they need not, as groups, agree: the historical
participants themselves; those who observed, interacted with, and evaluated
the direct participants; and the historical researcher today. Each of these interested parties has, of course, specific ways of understanding the problems. Once
mindful of this range of distinctions and approaches, one can undertake what
Kieckhefer held out as the historian's proper tasks: to strive to draw out the
coherent from the seemingly incoherent and, at the very least, to explain the
changes through time, the consistencies and variations between and across
cultures, and the distinctive perspectives across social strata.

This approach to the historical materials has its own history, a brief review
of which will provide helpful background to the structure and content of this
volume. A status quo ante can be determined in the scholarly activities of the

early twentieth century. At this point saints were not studied in conjunction with witches, nor seers with mystics, nor exorcists with necromancers. It may be illustrative to imagine an encounter—because none occurred—between two esteemed and representative historians of the period, the early twentieth-century Belgian scholar of sainthood Hippolyte Delehaye (1859–1941) and the German historian of witchcraft and heresy Joseph Hansen (1862–1943). Both were respected scholars in their particular specializations, produced seminal monographs, and were prolific editors of historical texts.[2] Both were also deeply committed to principles of a scientific history whose truth claims could be derived from and tested against historical documents. Yet despite drawing from the same well of methodological presupposition and expertise and even sharing an obvious, if incongruous, interest in the West's ecclesiastical past, their research was not mutually informing. One never cited the other, and there was never any scholarly collaboration. Delehaye's saints dwelled in holy isolation from Hansen's heretics.

The roots of the transformation from isolation to discourse can also be traced to this period, and even further back. They were nurtured by the diverse historians who constituted the early phases of cultural history and developed new ways of handling familiar sources to arrive at fresh historical insight. Study of the very centuries under closest scrutiny in this volume also proved themselves fertile for exactly these historiographical developments. Jacob Burckhardt (1818–1897) and Johan Huizinga (1872–1945), usually brought out to represent opposing views of the fifteenth century, were in fact both central figures in the "classic phase" of cultural history. They can be referred to here in conjunction because of the ways in which they examined a wide range of sources, restlessly looking across disciplinary frontiers, to draw conclusions about the condition—political, theological, social, and cultural—of medieval society. Decisive accomplishments of the "classic phase" pertinent to this volume include searching for social attitudes and values apart from the more common political historical narratives; removing the necessity of finding explanations for given social phenomena in contemporaneous learned understandings; searching for explanation in such alternative, indirect sources as art and ritual; and being no minder of disciplinary division.[3]

Developments in other fields, indeed in new disciplines altogether, also prompted historians to think beyond the categories derived from Christian theology and Enlightenment philosophy. The contributions of early anthropology, psychology, and sociology to understanding magic in relation to religion and science laid the groundwork for later reevaluations. Anthropological approaches to magic and especially witchcraft and their implications for historical research have been evaluated in detail elsewhere and so will not be repeated here.[4] Suffice it here to highlight, first, the early attempts of such figures as James George Frazer (1854–1941), who strove to comprehend the human efforts to gain advantage from supernatural interventions in the natural world, and Émile Durkheim (1858–1917), whose ideas about the sacred and the profane became the foundation for later analysis of the holy and unholy in societies in and beyond the West. It is also in these earliest generations of sociology and anthropology that a triad was sketched out among magic, science, and religion, which were identified as sustained and systematic ways humans engaged with the sacred and the profane in a world assumed to be supernaturally created. The links among the three were, especially under the branding of functional structuralism, made evolutionary. The analysis claimed a decreasing persuasive power of supernatural explanations for natural phenomena correlating to expanding powers of human rationality even though there was not clear unanimity in the sequencing of religion and magic as antecedent to science.

Evolutionary hypotheses inspired criticism and the formulation of alternatives. Bronisław Malinowski (1884–1942) and Claude Lévi-Strauss (1908–2009) were leaders among those who reacted skeptically to evolutionary understandings of the three conceptual fields and corresponding practices. Malinowski rejected, for example, the idea that magic was proto- or pseudo-science, arguing that the savage readily distinguishes natural causes from sympathy, similarity, synecdoche, contagion, and other forms of magical causation. Rather, magic would be better understood as religion's competitor. Lévi-Strauss argued for blurred lines between the natural and supernatural orders, and he rejected the cultural possibility of mutually exclusive and clean-cut religion or magic.[5] In any event, it was often wondered whether such a concept as the supernatural existed outside of the West. By the late twentieth century, historians of medieval religion and magic, while still making extensive use of anthropological models and theories, were similarly worrying that these tools neglected too much local variation and subtlety of change over time.[6] Kieckhefer's ruminations on "holy" and "unholy" in 1994 reflect both the debt of historical religious studies to more than a century of anthropological reflection as well as a concern that social scientific models, not unlike the theologically informed perspectives of an earlier age, could mislead.

The encouragement to acknowledge ambiguity and ambivalence in the relationship between the holy and the unholy could be taken as a call to abandon the attempt to figure out the difference altogether. Ambiguity and ambivalence could be understood as but one step away from incoherence. This, however, was not at all what Kieckhefer had in mind. To the contrary, the difference between holiness and unholiness mattered to the medieval and early modern European. He clarified this dimension of the historiographical challenge in another seminal article appearing in the same year, "The Specific Rationality of Medieval Magic." Not only was it presumed in the medieval and early modern periods, he argued, that magic worked—that is, effected real change in the created world, including human society—but "its workings were governed by principles that could be coherently articulated" as well.[7] Consequently, it becomes incumbent on the historian to figure out an internal logic, or the specific rationality, of a culture that, in this instance, intuited a difference between witchcraft and sainthood even as it sometimes struggled to discern the distinction in the concrete.

On Their Own Terms, Holy and Unholy: Kieckhefer's Scholarship

Kieckhefer's skill at reframing questions considered settled and proposing compelling new understandings of fundamental aspects of medieval religious culture extends beyond distinguishing between saints and witches. He founds his scholarship on the close reading of historical documents that are aggregated with a skeptical eye toward the conventional categories, placed in careful historical context, and interpreted sympathetically before they are criticized. How this approach itself emerged can be conveniently traced through his five scholarly monographs and his textbook on magic.

The first two monographs built on research he undertook as a doctoral student under the direction of John T. Ferguson at the University of Texas at Austin and the guidance of Alexander Patschovsky at the Monumenta Germaniae Historica in the early 1970s. The research strategy leading to *European Witch Trials: Their Foundations in Popular and Learned Culture, 1300–1500* (1976) was as simple as looking for the intellectual and social antecedents of events in one period in the previous one. To figure out the theological, philosophical, and jurisprudential thinking that sustained the early modern witch craze, he turned to the fourteenth and fifteenth centuries. There he found—crucially—what others had not; and, by testing what was commonly but uncritically repeated, he forced wider reevaluations throughout the field of witchcraft studies. A first seminal insight in *European Witch Trials* had to do with his organization of multiple interacting layers of medieval society—distinguished as "popular" and "learned"—and how the latter's concern for diabolization transformed more benign popular understandings of magic with horrific consequences.

A second was an inspired skepticism toward nineteenth-century scholarship on the witch craze. His testing of the work of Étienne-Léon de Lamothe-Langon (1786–1864), *Histoire de l'Inquisition en France*, devastated certain widely held conventions about medieval ecclesiastical inquisition. Supposedly taken from secret archives in the diocese of Toulouse, the blood-curdling accounts of the *Histoire* had become a major source for popular as well as scholarly understandings of heresy tribunals, judicial procedure and the forensic use of torture, and the prosecution of witchcraft and heresy as crimes. Even Joseph Hansen repeated from it uncritically in his *Quellen und Untersuchungen*. But Lamothe-Langon had forged his sources, and it was not until Kieckhefer (and independently and concurrently Norman Cohn) attempted to track down the footnotes that the forgery was exposed.[8]

Kieckhefer used a similar approach to trailblazing effect in *Repression of Heresy in Medieval Germany* (1979). Once again he looked into materials supporting a conclusion taken as foregone and ascertained instead an egregiously faulty interpolation. In this instance, he was able to conclude that medieval heresy tribunals, though numerous, did not constitute an "Inquisition." The term—singular and capitalized—had to be, in contradiction to Henry Charles Lea and so many subsequent historians of "the Inquisition," abandoned. Rejecting other, often materialist and reductionist speculations, Kieckhefer further proposed that the religious motive for the heresy prosecutions was not only adequate but foundational: "the high valuation that medieval society placed on religious orthodoxy" suffices to explain the phenomenon, and indeed explains the endurance and effectiveness of the method through multiple centuries.[9]

Fourteenth-century saints might not appear to have a natural connection to fifteenth-century inquisitors. Nonetheless, Kieckhefer developed insights taken from study of the later in his study of the former in his third monograph, *Unquiet Souls: Fourteenth-Century Saints and Their Religious Milieu* (1984). His by-this-point–hallmark scholarly sympathy for the objects of his analysis came to the fore again, as he took what appears to be pious frenzy and turned it into theological vision. This work, like his others, eschews any easy caricature of medieval religious expression. When, for example, he analyzed the conflicting perceptions of sanctity and insanity in the same saint, he built on the theoretical groundwork laid in the two 1994 articles. He strove, in the first instance, to understand the historical figures on their own terms and with a respect for the sources at his disposal. The result is not a whitewashing of medieval peculiarities, but a nuanced evaluation. Kieckhefer identified in the prayers, visions, and penances of the "unquiet souls" clear strains of Saint Augustine—yearnings, searchings, strong affective movements oriented interiorly toward the divine—but noted, too, an absence of the Augustine who was restrained, controlled, and self-critical. It is the Augustine who is passionate and impassioned that Dorothea von Montau and the others channel, but without the sober one. The work moves from text to context as Kieckhefer attempts to account for this uneven Augustinian reception by locating these historical figures in their religious milieu, one shaped in the fourteenth century by, for example, burgeoning literacy and new, unsettling forms of religious and semi-religious life. Like two other works on sainthood appearing at roughly the same time—André Vauchez's *La sainteté en Occident* (1981) and Donald Weinstein and Rudolph Bell's *Saints and Society* (1982)—*Unquiet Souls* was an effort to move a scholarly conversation forward in the field of religious culture and the saints by drawing on advances developed across the humanities and the social sciences. Unlike other pathbreaking historians, Kieckhefer focused in his trademark way on a discrete set of texts that he determined to be emblematic. He exploited these texts for their significance through close reading and careful placement in historical contexts.[10]

Kieckhefer turned to the basics in what is his best-known and most-read volume, *Magic in the Middle Ages* (first edition, 1989; latest printing, 2014). Although the abundance of eye-catching examples and poignant quotations reliably captures the attention of an undergraduate readership and there is a satisfying clarity to the chronological structure and analytical framework, to suggest that the book, labeled a textbook by the publisher, is conventionally propaedeutical undervalues its originality and depth and sells short its service as a catalytic agent for new scholarship on magic. The book proposes a way to understand magic in Western history: what "it" was and how it related to other modes of engagement with a rational and created world. Rationally created, this world lent itself to being known by humans and also to being engaged with by them. Magic was one mode of accomplishing these ends, along with, as the early social theorists had themselves already tried to make clear, science and religion. Kieckhefer needed to engage in the terms of the conversation that stretched back to the nineteenth-century figures we sketched above, and beyond. He argued for the impossibility of isolating magic as a perspective on the world and the powers afoot in it. Rather, magic was a perspective that—in different ways, changing over time and different across cultures and demographic strata—was best understood in conjunction with the religious and with the scientific. His earlier thinking on the differences between popular and elite magic was replaced with a distinction between "common magic," practiced across medieval society, and "learned," practiced especially in schools, religious houses, and courts. He located specific developments of the later Middle Ages, such as the emergence of a concern about diabolized witchcraft as representing a breakdown of distinctions once holding consensus across stratified medieval society. In the final analysis, Kieckhefer situated magic at the intersection of religion, science, and culture.[11]

Kieckhefer pushed his case for the ambivalence between holy and unholy yet further in his next monograph, *Forbidden Rites: A Necromancer's Manual of the Fifteenth Century* (1998). He had elsewhere and en passant already drawn attention to a clerical underworld as the principal milieu for the practice of necromancy, that is, conjuring the dead. His meticulous analysis of the fifteenth-century necromancer's manual from the Bavarian State Library made the case by tracing out the startling but extensive parallels between its rituals and those of sacramental exorcism. As in his previous work, *Forbidden Rites* demonstrates the promise of the search for the internal logic and contextual relevance of the bizarre and contradictory. It exemplifies again his reverence for the overlooked and the disdained. The analysis required negotiating the natures of and boundaries between the sacred and sinister, the practical and theoretical in ritual (whether divinely ordered or demonically), and social and intellectual history. The inadequacies of facile binaries imposed on the past are laid bare.

Forbidden Rites includes an edition of the manual itself. With mischievous satisfaction Kieckhefer has related the bump in the road of international publishing that this caused, as lawyers negotiated across the Atlantic how liability would be distributed should harm come from using the recipes in the book. The story highlights a dimension of Kieckhefer's tenacity regarding historical documents and especially "the book." The identification and reliance on sources are, of course, something close to the heart of any serious historian. Kieckhefer, in his appreciation not only of manuscript research but also of manuscript editions, shares something with a distinguished class of historian who values direct contact with the evidence as well as the form that it comes in; who loves languages, those that manuscripts are written in and that they are translated into; and who appreciates the need for and the influence of editions in the contemporary scholarly community.

Two additional works appearing in the last decade attest yet further to his commitment to primary materials and their accessibility to scholars and students. The most recent is his translation of two significant fifteenth-century works on magic, Johannes Hartlieb's *Book of All Forbidden Arts* and Ulrich Molitoris's *On Witches and Pythonesses*.[12] The other, slightly earlier editing project began with his Schickelesque stumbling across a cycle of theological poems on a quire hidden between the pages of an unrelated book he had purchased online from an antiquarian book dealer in England. His careful identification and editing of the singular manuscript and the astute commentary he provided the edition, published under the title *There Once Was a Serpent*, constitute another case in point.[13]

In Kieckhefer's most recent monograph, *Theology in Stone: Church Architecture from Byzantium to Berkeley* (2004), there is little sinister, unholy, or even profane. It would seem to mark a significant change in course. This is not the case. In fact, if one focuses on analytical framework and overarching question, then one finds in *Theology in Stone* the other side of the diptych begun with *Forbidden Rites*. The underlying curiosity sustaining both works has to do with how ritual connects human beings to sentience and power beyond themselves. As in *Forbidden Rites*, he grappled with the problem of how ritual works. Moving beyond *Forbidden Rites*, he interrogated the physical spaces in which these rituals take place and the shaping of those spaces according to theological insight and the users' yearnings for spiritual experience. Architectural style, theological expression, and communal expectations change through time; so, too, then, do the sacred spaces that communities construct for their rituals, taking place in time, space, and culture and negotiating the relationship between transcendent and immanent. Kieckhefer demonstrated the dependence of any architectural program on that religious purpose. The dependence creates ambiguity across time, space, and culture: one person's church is another's barn; that person's church is the other one's powder room. Kieckhefer's basic questions thus sustain this work no less than the others. The fundamentals are evident throughout. The questions are ultimately simple, even obvious. Kieckhefer, however, actually poses them and explores the rich infrastructure of ideas and aspirations to which they point.

Sacred and Sinister: Advancing the Program

This volume, *The Sacred and the Sinister*, is devoted to advancing our understanding of the interplay between holy and unholy, sacred and profane, and supernatural and natural in the history of "Old Europe." The chronological scope encompasses the Middle Ages and the early modern period and concentrates on the fifteenth and sixteenth centuries; the geographical and cultural scope encompasses the Latin West. Limited attention—for Kieckhefer's liking, surely too little—extends to the larger Mediterranean world. The ideas sketched above provide the two principles inspiring the chapters that follow, as well as axes along which they can be plotted. The first of the principles is that holy and unholy admit of ambivalence and ambiguity in their imputation to phenomena in the medieval and early modern world; the second, that it behooves the modern historian to assume an internal logic and to discern it, as far as is possible, from the sources. The first of the axes allows for a plotting of holy and unholy, sacred and profane, supernatural and natural. The second offers a scale of the social dimension—that is, where what we are analyzing belongs within medieval society. Kieckhefer first proposed in *European Witch*

Trials that the distinction lay between popular and elite and later, in *Magic in the Middle Ages*, between common and elite. Along both axes, however, the search for interactions is as important, if not more so, as the determination of position. Movement and the absence of clear plotting points are exactly the way to avoid the problem of binaries and capture the ambiguities and ambivalences that are, by Kieckhefer's lights, so much a part of medieval religious culture.

The volume is divided into four parts. The first two chapters examine holiness in a traditional form, in the cult of the saints and the attempt to articulate holiness in the *vitae sanctorum*. Christina Mirabilis (1150–1224) and Margherita Colonna (1255–1280) could scarcely have taken more divergent routes to sainthood, the former starting as the sickly youngest sister in a family of modest means in the Lowlands, the latter as a privileged daughter of a Roman aristocratic family. The vitae written to demonstrate their closeness to God likewise make that point quite differently. Claire Fanger's meticulous examination of the hagiographical materials about Christina demonstrates that as bizarre and extreme as her behavior seemed to her near contemporaries, as to readers today, the structure and content of hagiographer Thomas of Cantimpré's (1201–1272) famous vita of Christina sanctifies the extremes by highlighting their similarity to a seemingly more mainstream saint, Francis of Assisi (1181/82–1226). In contrast (and as indicated by Sean L. Field in his contribution), the vita of Margherita by one of the saint's early followers, Stefania, argues for her holiness from an opposing vantage: rather than taking what was known through the other sources and arguing for their correspondence to real saintly holiness, the hagiographer adds and subtracts with a heavy editorial hand to the body of sources to create a saint in conformity to an established type, the wealthy female foundress. From opposite directions, Fanger and Field have discovered a common hagiographical endpoint, the thirteenth century's unquiet soul.

In the second section, the unholy manifests itself, and ambiguity and ambivalence take center stage. Kristi Woodward Bain examines the conflict between monks and parishioners over control of a church building in Wymondham, Norfolk. Conflicts over ecclesiastical property in medieval history are hardly unusual, but Bain adds to her study a much broader framework of time, demonstrating not only how mercurial the relationship between religious and laity was but also how simultaneously unstable and determined memories of historical events can be in forming community identities, in this case even to the present. In chapter 4, Elizabeth Casteen draws our attention to a single word, *raptus*, that acquired opposing connotations with highly gendered implications: on the one hand, suggesting sexual assault; on the other, mystical union.

The connotations and their implications likewise shift over time. She argues that, by the later fourteenth century, *raptus* became increasingly ambiguous in the law and increasingly eroticized in mystical and chivalric texts. The conceptual overlap that had characterized thirteenth-century hagiography faded as the semantic range of *raptus* grew wider and more slippery. In chapter 5, Maeve Callan examines the history of *syneisaktism*—intimate yet platonic partnerships between unrelated men and women, dedicated in religious life to Christ—and analyzes, to the extent the sources allow, the range of forms these partnerships took and the theological reflection, sometimes sympathetic, usually hostile, that the partnerships, real or imagined, inspired in learned writings of the day.

The volume's third section looks to areas where the power of the sacred seems most challenged and that of the sinister most conspicuous. Michael Bailey draws us into these issues in his chapter, which examines the frontier between magic and religion, a frontier that vexed thinkers in the Middle Ages as much as historians today. Bailey develops a framework for his analysis of the problem from Herbert Grundmann and explores whether magic can be fruitfully, if counterintuitively, understood as itself a religious movement. In chapter 7, Katelyn Mesler examines the jurisdictional challenge of determining the circumstances under which the unbaptized might fall under the authority of an inquisitor. It was the Jew whose ambiguity in this regard most disquieted arch-inquisitor Nicholas Eymeric and inspired his treatise "On Infidels Invoking Demons," which Mesler presents in edition and makes the object of her analysis. And in chapter 8, Anne Koenig considers another question that vexed some of the same inquisitors Bailey and Mesler allude to and examines magic as the muddled alternative to medical diagnosis. Her chapter evaluates intersections of medicine and magic to explore the rationality of medieval explanations of madness in fifteenth-century Germany, and she maps out the landscape of beliefs about magic's role in causing and curing insanity.

The last two chapters build on the preceding ones as they look to the ambiguities and ambivalences in medieval links between magic and celestial knowledge. In chapter 9, Sophie Page sketches the range of cosmologies that captured the medieval imagination, some with more, some with less reference to Aristotle as enthusiasm for his thought gained from the twelfth century onward. She explores the often confused and usually permeable boundaries between philosophical and popular cosmologies and thus sheds light on the perennially intriguing question of how and whether scientific reflections inform popular convictions. In the final chapter, David Collins likewise turns to the Scholastics' embrace of Aristotelian astronomy and looks for it in later medieval biblical commentaries on Matthew 2, the story of the magi and the star of

Bethlehem. Scholastics, Albert the Great in particular, brought the latest natural-philosophical tools and insights to the biblical passage. The result was commentary that was new not because the Scholastics had new theological ideas, but because, thanks to Aristotle and subsequent Mediterranean commentators, they were challenged to transform their conventional explanations for the Nativity accordingly.

By way of conclusion, a story. This one is factual rather than literary and takes place in an office so gabled and nooked as to make Hogwarts seem Bauhaus by comparison. There Richard Kieckhefer offered words of encouragement to a prospective graduate student who was unquieted over how the same historian could write both on fourteenth-century saints and fifteenth-century necromancers, the subjects of his most recent scholarly works: "My scholarship," he replied, "has a right hand and a left one." Aside from being an understated summary of a scholarly range that instead requires Kaliesque imagery, Kieckhefer's metaphor indirectly raises a full range of problems pertinent to his research and to this volume. Most obviously, the offhand response addressed and resolved a seeming contradiction within his research. The metaphor allows for the obvious differences between his interests in late medieval saints and in necromancers, yet rejects a mutual exclusivity and hints at a cooperative interdependence. The full range of his scholarship from European witch trials to sacral architecture bears this out, even if the discrete topics of the research seem to beg the question: If not mutually exclusive and incoherent, then what form of relationship does the study of saints and necromancers, of the sacred and the profane, and of the ecstatic and the demonic take? The ambiguities have been a lifetime's project for Richard Kieckhefer. It is this project the volume hopes to advance.

NOTES

1. Richard Kieckhefer, "The Holy and the Unholy: Sainthood, Witchcraft, and Magic in Late Medieval Europe," *Journal of Medieval and Renaissance Studies* 24 (1994): 55–85.

2. Compare, for example, Hippolyte Delehaye, *The Legends of the Saints* (Portland: Four Courts Press, 1998); Joseph Hansen, *Zauberwahn, Inquisition und Hexenprozess im Mittelalter, und die Entstehung der Grossen Hexenverfolgung* (Aalen: Scientia, 1964). Also, Delehaye participated in editing the November volumes 2, 3, and 4 as well as the Propyleum for December of the *Acta sanctorum* (Brussels: Société des Bollandistes, 1894–1940), whereas Hansen edited *Quellen und Untersuchungen zur Geschichte des Hexenwahns und der Hexenverfolgung im Mittelalter* (Bonn: C. Georgi, 1901). Hansen's contribution to German scholarship also includes his translation of works by eminent nineteenth-century U.S. historian of witchcraft and inquisition Henry Charles Lea. Henry Charles Lea, *Materials Toward a History of Witchcraft*, 3 vols. (New York: AMS Press, 1986); Lea, *A History of the Inquisition of Spain*, 4 vols. (New York: AMS Press, 1988).

3. For a review of the characteristics of the earlier cultural history and its relevance to the newer, see Peter Burke, *What Is Cultural History?* (Cambridge: Polity Press, 2004), 6–19.

4. David J. Collins, "Introduction: The History and Historiography of Magic," in *The Cambridge History of Magic and Witchcraft in the West: From Antiquity to the Present*, ed. David J. Collins (Cambridge: Cambridge University Press, 2015), 1–14.

5. Nevill Drury, "Modern Western Magic and Altered States of Consciousness," in *Handbook of Religion and the Authority of Science*, ed. James R. Lewis and Olav Hammer (Leiden: Brill, 2011), 715–17.

6. E.g., Michael Bailey's rationale for the founding of an interdisciplinary journal on magic in 2006: Michael D. Bailey, "The Meanings of Magic," *Magic, Ritual, and Witchcraft* 1 (2006): 1–23.

7. Richard Kieckhefer, "The Specific Rationality of Medieval Magic," *American Historical Review* 99 (1994): 814.

8. Étienne-Léon de Lamothe-Langon, *Histoire de l'Inquisition en France, depuis son établissement au XIIIᵉ siècle, à la suite de la croisade contre les Albigeois, jusqu'en 1772, époque définitive de sa suppression* (Paris: J.-G. Dentu, 1829); Hansen, *Quellen und Untersuchungen*. See Richard Kieckhefer, *European Witch Trials: Their Foundations in Popular and Learned Culture, 1300–1500* (Berkeley: University of California Press, 1976); see also Norman Cohn, "Three Forgeries: Myths and Hoaxes of European Demonology," *Encounter* 44 (1975): 11–24.

9. Richard Kieckhefer, *European Witch Trials: Their Foundations in Popular and Learned Culture, 1300–1500* (Berkeley: University of California Press, 1976); Kieckhefer, *Repression of Heresy in Medieval Germany*, The Middle Ages Series (Philadelphia: University of Pennsylvania Press, 1979).

10. Both works were exciting experiments with new modes of quantification in historical analysis. A sharper grasp of quantifications, possibilities, and limits was achieved thanks to both works. Criticism of *Saints and Society* along these lines often neglects its innovative aspect. With Kieckhefer's strong encouragement, Cambridge University Press finally published an English translation of Vauchez's work sixteen years after its initial publication in French. Donald Weinstein and Rudolph M. Bell, *Saints and Society: The Two Worlds of Western Christendom, 1000–1700* (Chicago: University of Chicago Press, 1982); André Vauchez, *Sainthood in the Later Middle Ages*, trans. Jean Birell (Cambridge: Cambridge University Press, 1997).

11. Richard Kieckhefer, *Magic in the Middle Ages* (Cambridge: Cambridge University Press, 2014).

12. Richard Kieckhefer, ed., *Hazards of the Dark Arts: Advice for Medieval Princes on Witchcraft and Magic*, Magic in History Sourcebooks (University Park: Pennsylvania State University Press, 2017).

13. Richard Kieckhefer, ed., *There Once Was a Serpent* (Winchester, U.K.: O Books, 2010).

Part 1 | TRADITIONAL HOLINESS

1

EXTREME SANCTITY AT THE TURN OF THE THIRTEENTH CENTURY
THE METAMORPHOSIS OF BODY AND COMMUNITY IN THE VITAE
OF CHRISTINA MIRABILIS AND FRANCIS OF ASSISI

Claire Fanger

Richard Kieckhefer's *Unquiet Souls* (1984) looked at fourteenth-century saints known for the most radical acts of self-mortification. In making a theme of saintly disquiet, he reflects on the ways that extreme mortification embodies the yearning for heaven; the saint's miracles of heroic asceticism are about relative values of heaven and earth, not meant to be imitable so much as memorable. He does not suggest that the fourteenth century presents any kind of novelty in the depiction of extreme sanctity (extreme feats indeed were always the stock in trade of hagiography), but just that there is more of it present in that period. He thus focuses on what the extremism of these vitae have in common with each other, and does not treat any of his cases as exceptional.

My aim here is similarly to articulate some aspects of the theological vision implicit in the vitae of two people, one Umbrian and one Fleming, Francis of Assisi and Christina Mirabilis, who died about two years apart at the end of the first quarter of the thirteenth century. Like the fourteenth-century saints discussed in *Unquiet Souls*, both of my protagonists are known for extreme acts of bodily mortification. As I will argue, however, the lives of both Christina and Francis are exceptional, less for the degree of their self-mortification (though that is certainly remarkable) than for the novel insights into God's dispensation that their vitae manifest. The point of taking these two examples as my focus is that each of them uniquely exemplifies a clear, immediate theological vision of what, at its best, the relation between the body's material plasticity and God's shaping hand actually looks like. Both vitae show in different but related ways how completely the plastic body can be rendered biddable to the creator via the obedient soul bent under God's yoke. In turn, this makes it possible to render palpable the wonders of the soul's afterlife, to realize the near possibility of, or imminent approach of, the restoration of paradise. Perhaps all hagiography tends in this direction, but these two stories are exceptional in ways that I hope will become clear in what follows. Each of them, in a singular way, generates alterations in the stakes and mythological shape of the hagiographic tradition. One might suggest that the lives of both individuals force their biographers to reinvent the genre of the saintly vita, or at least to adapt it to new circumstances.

My focus will principally be on two representations: first, on Christina as depicted in the full span between her first and last death in the vita by Thomas of Cantimpré, and second, on Francis as depicted in the two years after his stigmatization in part 2 of the *Vita Prima* by Thomas of Celano. In the exposition of these stories, I trace how the hagiographers see God interacting with the world through the human person. Both Christina and Francis are depicted in a state of suspension between death and the afterlife, in a slow or stalled process of dying, the better to allow us to witness their bodily expressions of the will of God. In the stories told about them, especially as they enter and exit their extended or multiple deaths, this world and the afterworlds become visible as one thing, one unified dispensational process, through the increasingly transparent window of the saint's body.

Christina

Christina, in striking contrast to Francis, offers the hagiographer little by way of biographical documentation. Her sole vita was written by a man, Thomas of Cantimpré, who had never met her and claims to have collated a dossier of witnesses into the vita. The events of her life are freakish enough that it would be pardonable to wonder if Thomas hadn't made them up out of whole cloth but for the fact that she crops up in connection to other historical personages in the area, including Lutgard of Aywières, whom Christina had apparently counseled about her spiritual life.[1] Prior to Thomas's research, Jacques de Vitry (bishop of Liège from 1216) had described Christina, writing about her as one of the notable holy women pursuing the apostolic life in that time period in the diocese of Liège.[2] Whatever the truth status of the more incredible events of her vita, there is little doubt that Christina was a real person who made a strong impression on those who met her.

Recent interpreters of Christina's life have carefully examined the likely moral and rhetorical purposes her hagiographer had in presenting her life as he did; some have used this labor as well to pry out facts or at least speculations about the circumstances and motivations of Christina the human woman. Margot King maps her three deaths onto stages of mystical ascent, understanding her vita as recording a kind of reified visionary experience.[3] Robert Sweet-man attends to the specifics by which her biographer presented her real life as a living sermon (in this way indeed it shares features with the vitae of Francis of Assisi).[4] Barbara Newman attempts to get at the understratum of the vita by suggesting that Christina's career may have begun as a more ordinary case of demonic possession, transformed in part by the care of others, in part by the agency of her hagiographers, to a holy woman.[5] Anke Passenier, similarly con-cerned with how the "real" Christina seems to be hidden under the exagger-ated deeds of power, suggests that her biographer emphasized the weirdness of her miracles deliberately with the aim of "stylizing a specifically female apos-tolate," simultaneously marginalizing her real charisma and real ministry.[6] Most readings that have taken the vita of Christina Mirabilis seriously have thus to some extent also normalized her story by emphasizing its moral or doctrinal purpose, or by seeking a way to locate in it contextual clues to aspects of the real Christina. This is inevitable and necessary in the process of mediat-ing the alterity of the more extreme aspects of medieval religion; however, my reading here will aim not to normalize the story. Rather, I would like to focus on the ways the vita of Christina deviates from every kind of medieval narra-tive it might be expected to replicate.

Jacques de Vitry transmitted the first skeletal outline of Christina's story, which Thomas references, closely quoting Jacques in his prologue:

> After she had lain dead a long time—but before her body was buried in the ground—her soul returned to her body and she lived again. She obtained from the Lord that she would endure purgatory, living in this world in her body. It was for this reason she was afflicted for a long time by the Lord, so that sometimes she rolled herself in the fire, and some-times in winter she remained for lengthy periods in the icy water and at other times she was driven to enter the tombs of the dead. But after she had performed penance in so many ways, she lived in peace and merited grace from the Lord and many times, rapt in spirit, she led the souls of the dead as far as purgatory, or through purgatory as far as the kingdom of heaven, without any harm to herself.[7]

Writing some eight years after Christina's death, Thomas explains that he has filled out her life history from other eyewitness accounts after consulting people who had known her well while she was alive in the area around Sint-Truiden; he says that much of his information came from a recluse named Jutta with whom Christina had lived for nine years.[8] However, Thomas is doing more than fill-ing out the narrative sketch given above by Jacques de Vitry, who suggested the purgatorial penance Christina undergoes is for *her own* sin; as Jacques put it, God granted that "she would endure purgatory, living in this world in her body," and "it was for this reason she was afflicted for a long time by the Lord." Only after she had purified her soul by performing this penance did she achieve "peace" and the grace that enabled her to lead others into the afterworlds.

If Christina were simply a person performing her own purgatory on earth, this would make her relation to the afterworlds more fluid than usual, though it would hardly be unheard of; purgatory is after all commutable with penance in this world. But Thomas goes further than this: by his account, Christina is carried by angels to look into Hell and Purgatory; after this, she is carried before the throne of God. There, God tells her that she may remain with him in Paradise if she chooses, but since she had such compassion for the purgatorial souls, she may choose instead to return to earth," there to undergo the punishment of an immortal soul in a mortal body without damage to it, and by these your sufferings to deliver all those souls on whom you had compassion in that place of purgatory, and by the example of your suffering and your way of life to convert the living to me and make them turn aside from their sins."[9] In other words, according to Thomas, Christina, once back on earth, has no need to do penance on her own behalf; she has truly died and knows she is among the elect. She chooses to return solely in order to help others, and for this purpose she is given a body that can feel pain, but not be permanently damaged or die—as Barbara Newman has called it, a "resurrection body."[10] And by the sufferings of her now infinitely renewable body she performs a penance of which she has herself has no need, and knows it.

These doings take her further outside the literary forms as well as the theological norms of hagiography; for whatever deeds the saints may do, and however much they perform miraculous phenomena through their intimacy with God (of course all the saints whose lives are told by Thomas do remarkable deeds of power), saints' vitae are typically of people in their first life and not their second. Christina, as Thomas makes clearer than Jacques, is already living in a state of suspension between this world and the next; her body is not a normal body, and she does not inhabit it in a normal way.

Her deeds of penitential self-torment, already shadowed by Jacques de Vitry, range from the incredible to the macabre and show a heroic penance that appears impossible, and it is clearly meant to appear so: her feats include spending extended periods in hot ovens without burning up, residing for an unusual time under water without drowning, and suspending herself between criminals on the gallows also without dying, much of the time screaming in pain.[11] Her body is also abnormally plastic: she is said in her ecstasy of contemplation to melt into a ball like hot wax "so that all that could be perceived of her was a round mass" and then to unroll herself like a hedgehog, and when she hears (from God) of someone being damned, she has the habit of bending her arms and fingers "as though her limbs had no bones."[12] Her body is thus always partly expository of her relation to the divine; she is simultaneously a denizen of heaven and of earth, making visible how fully she inhabits her material form through the unusual bodily changes and the extreme discomfort she experiences in her embodied state.

The Abnormal Absence of Demons in Her Vita

Remarkable though her heroic feats are, the abnormality of her embodied situation is perhaps more clearly shown by what is absent from her vita than by what is present in it. Demons are so common in hagiographic narratives from St. Anthony onward that their presence can be regarded as a standard feature of the genre; yet once Christina has had her view of the afterworlds in the narrative of her first death, she encounters no demons at all.

As foils for the normal saint's heroic activity, demons serve several functions. In the lives of desert saints, following the model of the monks of Egypt and St. Anthony, demons typically mount specific assaults on those who are working hardest to rise above earthly concerns; for this reason demons are more active around dedicated monks, virgins, and ascetics than ordinary householders. They distract, disturb, frighten, and tempt such people, and they tend to do so more strongly the more holy the life sought by the person in question is. St. Anthony offers a paradigm of this type: living in the wilderness, he is subjected to multiple attacks of demons in the form of ferocious animals; demons also tempt him to sloth, lust, and avarice, for an important job of demons in hagiography is stimulating earthly appetites of those who would be athletes of Christ.

In a similar way, and clearly under the influence of Anthony, Christina's contemporary Marie of Oignies fights the noonday demon and battles with and on behalf of a virginal companion with a demonically induced fear and despair.[13] Demonic work may also be recognized by saints in the lives of others, thus proving the saint's prophetic or clairvoyant powers, and demons may even come to the saint and confess an evil deed, as happens in Thomas of Cantimpré's vita of Lutgard.[14] Lutgard also releases a woman from the temptations of an incubus,[15] and demons appeared to her regularly for more pernicious reasons—to make lying announcements of calamitous happenings—but Lutgard is said to have spit on them, driving them away easily.[16] The triumphant victory over besieging demons is a standard narrative element in the lives of medieval holy women, and many more examples of this kind could be adduced.

Christina's vita, by contrast, is abnormally free of demonic attacks. While there is worry expressed repeatedly by her sisters and friends that she might be thought of as a demoniac herself (by those who do not understand her divine acts and ecstasies), her biographer takes no advantage of this possibility in his story. That is, he never suggests that her difficulties are actually demonic *battles* (such as we see in the lives of both Lutgard and Marie). Indeed Thomas ascribes to Christina no fleshly temptations at all. Sloth, lust, and avarice seem to have no purchase on her. She does not predict the presence of demons nor see them in action. Perhaps it is simply that there is nothing she can learn from demons that God has not already told her; there is really very little for demons to do in relation to the perfect. If demons could have had any place in Christina's vita, their role could have been only what it was in relation to souls in purgatory—to torture, not to tempt. But Christina looks after her own self-torture with a zest that renders them redundant. We do not even see her banishing or spitting on demons; they simply leave her alone.

Her Antisocial Tendencies and Flight Behaviors

The absence of demons may be the more remarkable given how much time she spends in the wilderness—a place where demons are well known to lurk, waiting to tempt athletes of Christ. However, the wilderness itself has a paradoxical sense in her vita: it is not the background of an ascetic life or a place she goes to confront greater hardship away from human comforts. Rather, it appears instead to be a shelter from the hardship of normal human congress.

For the most visible of her disabilities is that she is not easily socialized; she hates to be enclosed and has trouble waiting on or even remaining in close proximity to the human community that she serves. Even when things are going well she is often moved to dash for the wilderness suddenly and without explanation. She always seems to be on the point of flight, sometimes literally; for beyond the difficulty of normal converse with other humans, she has a problem just staying on the ground. The light and subtle nature of her material body is stressed throughout the narrative and is repeatedly linked to her flight behavior. Thomas says that "her body was so subtle and light that she walked on dizzy heights and, like a sparrow, hung suspended from branches of trees."[17] She stood on fence palings to pray, "for it was very painful for her to touch the ground while she was praying."[18] And her lightness of body was listed as one reason for fears about her being or appearing to be demonically possessed, "especially because Christina, fleeing the presence of humans, would ascend into lofty places like a bird and linger long in the waters like a fish."[19]

While flight behavior, in both senses, is certainly not unique in hagiography (levitation is also attributed to Lutgard of Aywières, whereas Marie of Oignies also occasionally runs off into the fields and thickets[20]), flight is a theme that informs Christina's vita more deeply and fully than it does others. In her difficulty staying on the ground, her levitations to the tops of fences, trees, and buildings, as well as her sudden dashes for the wilderness, she seems to struggle with her human role.[21] Her odd, antisocial, and self-injurious behaviors prompt attempts to keep her shut up, but these backfire. Embarrassed by the thought that she might be suspected of demonic possessions, her friends pay a strong man to capture her. He ends up breaking her leg. She is shut up in a locked cellar, treated for her injuries by a physician, and chained to a pillar. That she is confined by chains as well as a locked door, despite the broken leg, suggests that a more-than-human strength must have been suspected. Indeed it is not easy to keep her shut up. According to Thomas, God soon heals her injuries and undoes her chains; Christina does a brief victory dance, and then "in an impassioned spirit [*in spiritu vehementi*], she perforated the wall with a stone seized from the cellar floor. To use an analogy, just as an arrow is the more forcefully released the more strongly the bow is bent, so Christina's spirit, which had been restrained [*arctatus*] more than was just, flew through the empty air like a bird, carrying with it the fleshy weight of her body."[22] The ethical underpinning of this explanation is Christian, but the physical logic is Aristotelian. The forcible spirit can propel a connected body further when it has been shut up, and the connected body in Christina's case, as Thomas often tells us, is itself very light, thus more easily commanded by the spirit within. Though in accordance with the laws of nature, her extreme bodily lightness makes human laws and customs more difficult to observe: her levity puts her perpetually at odds with the gravity required for social behavior that would seem more "natural" according to human convention.

After repeated attempts to keep her forcibly restrained fail, her family decides to set her free, though they remain concerned for her safety on account of her elopements, her mendicant habits, and her penchant for drawing crowds during her ecstasies. Begging her to behave more normally, they pray to God that her extreme sanctity may manifest itself in less troubling ways.[23] Their prayers are answered in due course, for in this period Christina, said to be "violently stirred by a spirit [*agitata a spiritu vehementissime*]," took refuge in a church in the village of Wellen, "and coming upon an uncovered baptismal font, completely immersed herself in it. It is said that after she had done this, her manner of life was more moderate with regard to society, and she behaved more calmly and was more able to endure the smell of men, and live among them."[24] Note that this is the second instance where the *vehemence* of her spiritual stirring is mentioned; the first was on the occasion of her escape from prison, where the spirit in question is read by Thomas as both divine and natural, but not demonic. Elsewhere in the vita, *vehementia* is used to describe Christina's ecstatic states, in which she whirls around until her body loses its perceptible form (§35), as well as the cries of her companion Beatrice, who calls her back from the dead for a second time (§52). Thus, generally speaking, in the context supplied by the uses of this word elsewhere, a stirring by a vehement spirit is unlikely to mean a malign spirit. One is compelled to read the vehement spirit more simply as an index of profound desire, a desperate request for divine assistance in learning to live with "the smell of men."

Her Interstitial Status

Christina's distaste for "the smell of men" comes up very early in the narrative, in the description of her funeral, where her initial birdlike levitation kicks the story off: "while her requiem mass was being performed, suddenly the disturbed body stirred on the bier and rose up and, like a bird, immediately ascended to the rafters of the church. All those present fled and only her older sister remained behind fearfully. Christina was immovable until mass was finished, when constrained by the priest with the sacrament of the church, she was forced to descend. Some say the subtlety of her spirit was revolted by the smell of human bodies."[25] Such behavior in a corpse might have been seen prima facie to indicate a revenant, a corpse animated, often, in folklore, by its own departed soul, and in more theologically conscious sources by a demon.[26] Winston Black suggests that the tendency to understand the animating energy as demonic comes rather late in the evolution of these stories, concretizing with the development of Aristotelian ideas about relations between matter and spirit in the thirteenth century; at the same time he stresses how, even where demons animate the corpse, they seem to do so where the person has lived an unsalubrious life, so that there is an implicit kind of continuity of person with body even in cases of demonic animation: only the bodies of evildoers tend to come back to life.[27]

Thomas of Cantimpré is obviously familiar with this genre of story as he relates anecdotes about demonically animated corpses elsewhere in his oeuvre. Two instances are pointed out by Nancy Caciola: in one, Ida of Nivelles battles a demonically animated corpse in a church; in another, the demonically animated corpse of a knight asks a former servant to remove the point of the lance that killed him.[28] It is clear that Thomas does not intend to cast Christina in this light. In the first place, he makes clear that Christina was not a bad person while she lived. Her first death he attributes to weakness brought on by excess of contemplative practice;[29] faith in Christina's essential goodness is demonstrated by her older sister, the only one besides the priest to remain in the church, albeit fearfully. In the second place, Thomas rescues the reader quickly from suspicion that she is a revenant by reading the levitation in the light of her later flight behavior, mentioning her "distaste for the smell of human bodies." Thomas does not commit himself to this interpretation; it is adduced here as an observation of others, a thing that "some people say." However, the statement serves here to make a connection between Christina's mobile corpse and her later flight behavior. The distaste for human "smell" is so much of a piece with Christina's ambivalence about human closeness and companionship in general that it works as a sensory metonymy of her awkward relation to earthly human society.

But Christina, rather than being a reensouled corpse, is something perhaps even stranger: a soul that has been reembodied. She is most strongly repelled from the living human world when she is nearest to an experience of heaven. As we have seen, there is a certain alleviation of her antisocial behavior after her immersion in the baptismal font, which takes place some time after her first death. She evidently succeeds for a while in making a friend of the recluse Jutta, the nuns at nearby St. Catherine's, and even the Count of Looz, who becomes very attached to her. However, her ability to socialize, hard won in the first place, is also tenuous and suffers attrition as she furthers the job she is actually there to do.

In the last year of her life, according to Thomas, Christina suffers more and more for the condition of those in the world whose actions are leading them to damnation, and whose fate she is doomed to know in advance by the increasing activation of her prophetic spirit. After the death of the Count of Looz, we see her take on his pains in purgatory;[30] tormented by turns with burning smoke and freezing cold, she is a visible index both of his postmortem suffering and his spirit's nearness to her. Her difficulty with the proximity of other human beings is in part a function of the fate that makes it necessary not only to know their sins but to suffer for them: because of her role in the economy of human salvation, her divine knowledge of their sin is immediate, visceral, and physically uncomfortable. She endures a compassionate excess that distances her from the companionship of others for the very reason that what she shares with them imprints their eventual afterlife torments directly on her body.

The year before she dies her penultimate and final deaths, she spends almost all her time in the wilderness. Her flights cannot be restrained, and when she emerges her appearance grows increasingly spectral; she hardly touches the ground when she walks. "No one dared greet her, no one dared ask her anything. Once she returned at vespers and passed above the ground right through the middle of a house like a spirit."[31] Thomas, once again quoting others, suggests there was a commonly perceived connection between her divine knowledge of others' sin and the increase in her wild flights: "[she] would eat only a scrap of food and sleep only a little before midnight and then go into the wilderness. In those days, no one ever saw a smile on her lips: she was like one who has gone mad from excessive sorrow. She would wander around praying, weeping and mourning, and for this reason, some people believed that the Lord had shown her even more than usual about the condition and malice of the world."[32] This last sentence, again introduced by the formula "some people believed," attests to the basic goodwill of those watching her; it suggests that to her friends, Christina's scarce and difficult connection with other humans would have appeared unavoidable insofar as she was doomed to take on the malady of sin and to heal it by her suffering.

When the time comes for her to pass on, she approaches the moment in an "unbroken grace of contemplation " that leaves her with no attention to spare for anything else.[33] She dies quietly but to her great annoyance is almost immediately called back to life by the petition of her friend Beatrice, a nun at St. Catherine's, who wants her to answer one last question. "O Christina!" Beatrice pleads, "You were ever obedient to me in life! I now therefore beseech you and admonish you earnestly through the Lord Jesus Christ, whom you loved with ardent desire while you lived, that you obey me even now. For you are powerfully able, through him to whom you are now joined, to do whatever you want. So return to life and tell me what I begged you to reveal to me with great desire while you were alive."[34] Thus conjured in the name of Christ, Christina returns to her body one last time. She begs Beatrice to be quick. As she speaks, the room fills with the other nuns who gather to receive her final blessing. Having been blocked in her last flight, as she had been in earlier ones, by the social needs of the living, she is finally allowed to give herself to her third death, surrounded by the people she sought to avoid, bringing to a close the miracle she had prayed would not accompany her passing.[35]

There are several kinds of story that Christina's vita evokes without quite replicating. Clearly, apparitions of the dead increasingly being linked to purgatory give a broader playing field for interactions with the spirits of the dead on earth, and stories about them influence Christina's vita. Thomas's contemporary William of Auvergne argues that purgatory has in fact an earthly location, both because it is theologically an extension of earthly penance and because the frequent apparitions of the purgatorial dead on earth make this seem likely.[36] We see aspects of this idea, too, in the life of Marie of Oignies, who is troubled by apparitions of disembodied hands, culminating in the actual sensation of hands clutching at her garments as she walks; though at first disturbed, her distress turns to sweetness when a prayer for illumination establishes that these are only souls in purgatory trying to beg for her prayers.[37]

But Marie herself is a living woman. Christina is different, and her story is different, too; it is neither a normal story of a purgatorial ghost, nor is it a normal saintly tale of penance and redemption. Twice returned from the dead, she does not evoke the normal story of a revenant either. The unique flavor of this vita comes from how it refuses to fit into the available templates. Christina was an actual sainted and elect spirit returning from heaven in an ultralight resurrection body that is very much hers (pain and all), but which she inhabits like an alien. As with St. Francis also, the vita makes manifest how passible flesh in extremis (in every sense), obeying a divine mission with single-minded dedication, can come more and more to reveal things outside and beyond this world.

Francis

In interpreting the stigmatization of Francis and focusing on part 2 of the *Vita Prima*, I will be attending to aspects of the episode that comparison with Christina's vita helps make meaningful: the way extreme penitential obedience is linked to miraculous transformation of the body, which in turn is revelatory of God's power to transform the world. The saintly body in both lives is a visible interface between heaven and earth, revealing the will of God by its metamorphosis under the shaping will of the perfectly obedient soul. In both cases there is a connection between the passible saintly subjects, their extreme compassion, and what God does with, to, and through their dead or dying bodies. The extraordinary events described in the vitae in both cases make manifest in a visible and tangible way what the presence of God on earth may actually look like.

There are differences, of course. Unlike Christina, Francis is a person still living his first life, striving for a full and complete obedience to the rules of apostolic life, but for him, the desires of the flesh still exist; demons do have a role to play in Francis's story, and like most holy men and women, he drives them away, is tempted by them, and argues with them. However, like Christina, the primary message of his gospel is to do penance. Like Christina, too, perhaps more unusually for a male agent, his gospel is represented importantly as practical and performative—a gospel of doing rather than saying. If Thomas of Celano was trying to write the biography of a saint who is in some respects like other saints (only better, stronger, newer, perhaps), pressing against this work is the perceived emergence under his hand of a new gospel about a new Christ he already sees as transforming the world in a new way. The understanding of Francis as an *alter Christus* is something that becomes more pronounced in some later writings about Francis;[38] however, I would like to uncover some of the ways the radical nature of this story is already visible in the *Vita Prima*.

Faith and Doubt

Paradoxically, in a saint known for the large-scale public and performative nature of his deeds, the most iconic incident in the life of Francis, his reception of the stigmata, was a private event. The actual stigmatization had no witnesses, and the wounds after the event had hardly any. Francis is said to have done his best while he lived to conceal them even from his followers, and to those who noticed, he protested that he did not want them spoken of to anyone. This unwonted will to privacy has certainly occasioned some problems with the interpretation of this aspect of his vita. If the wounds were generally unobserved, how can anyone know they persisted from the time they were said to have been received until his death? It is hardly surprising that the event in Francis's life most cherished by his followers also had many skeptics in the period immediately following his death.

Scanty as the evidence may be, historians, too, have cared a great deal about possible realities behind the stigmata. If this is in part because the evidence teases us, it is also in part because the wounds are not all that improbable as hysterical symptoms: real wounds may have developed on Francis's body and been seen by someone. This puts more stress on the miraculous nature of the event than in the case of more obviously impossible things. Scholars have considered at length the primary sources that discuss Francis's stigmata, their reliability, and their discrepancies of description,[39] as well as attempts to discredit the miracle by detractors.[40] They have treated the prior traditions of stigmatic thought and behavior in which the incident is embedded (including that of fakery),[41] and the descriptions of Francis's wounds have been compared to many subsequent cases of stigmatization.[42] Since the time they were first reported, it has been possible to argue both that the wounds were fictional, part of the Franciscan or public imaginary, and also that they were created by the natural power of Francis's imagination on Francis's body, so that, while not fictional, they were not really very miraculous at all.

However, the extent to which the wounds are an article of faith from an early period is an important feature of their status in the traditions about Francis. In order for faith to be possible, doubt must also be possible. In Thomas of Celano's treatise on the miracles of Francis (finished in 1252, a little over twenty years after his *Vita Prima*), he briefly recapitulated the miracle of the stigmata, following this with a suite of miracles about people who doubted their truth. In one tale, a cleric called Ruggiero, wondering if the stigmata might have been no more than a deception invented by the brothers, receives a sudden fiery and bloody wound in the palm of his left hand. The wound occurs under a glove, and without damage to it, thus proving that the wound had no material agency.[43] In another tale, a woman meditating before a painted image of Francis realizes the marks of stigmata had been left out by the painter; looking carefully for them, she sees the marks suddenly appear. Now she begins to engage the opposite worry: had she simply missed them at first? She calls in a witness who attests that they had indeed not been there before. But she remains concerned that she might simply *not have seen them*; then the marks are again suddenly, mysteriously removed from the painting, and thus "the second sign became proof of the first," as Thomas puts it.[44] Another brother, "irritated by a scruple of doubt," has a vision of Francis in which the saint asks, "Why all these conflicting struggles in you? Why these filthy doubts? See my hands and my feet!" The poor brother is able to see the wounds in the hands clearly, but not the feet, because they are covered with mud. Francis says, "Remove the mud from my feet and examine the place of the nails"—this is done, and once he sees the wounds, the brother wakes up in tears.[45] The mud here is written into the parable as a figure for the doubt itself and what it has done to Francis.

These miracles may at first blush seem apologetic, but none of them is really about whether the event actually *happened*; they are rather about the importance of faith in its truth. Certainly the stories must have reflected doubts and worries that real people had about whether the story of the carefully concealed stigmata was true, or whether it meant what it was said to mean. If it were not true, or not meaningful, was it right to meditate on the wounds as if they were the wounds of Christ? Should they be depicted in paintings, or upheld as a part of the devotional iconography around Francis? The miraculous answers are unambiguous: it is not merely right to imagine the stigmatized body of Francis; it is wrong to doubt it. The many relics of the wounds and images of their reception guarded or produced since Francis's death provide further mnemonic aids to confirm the event in the public memory, as well as (for those who doubt) further reason to suspect confection of holy appearances.[46] However, the stakes are creedal; this is important in the way Thomas configures the bend in the Christian tradition.

A New Gospel

Much has been made of whether the stigmata really constitute a "new" miracle, as Thomas of Celano is the first to claim; in literal terms, this clearly is not the case.[47] However, within the *Vita Prima*, the idea of newness attaches to much more than the stigmata. In fact, the wounds are chiefly important because they are a metonymy of a much larger change understood to be expressed in the body of Francis and in the body of his followers. As will be shown below, the primary "novelty" in the life of Francis, as Thomas represents it, is the fact that the gospel preached by him is a matter of deeds (*opera*) rather than words. The reception of the stigmata is no more than the last episode in a life spent transforming the gospel into earthly action.

The word "new" (*novus*) and its compounds and derivatives (*novitas, innovare, renovare*) occur twenty-two times in part 2 of the *Vita*, clustering thickly in chapter 1 of this section, where Thomas reintroduces the saint, as though his life had not just been told:

> As the teachings of the gospel had declined seriously in practice—not just in some cases but in general everywhere—this man was sent from God so that everywhere throughout the whole world, after the example of the apostles, he might bear witness to the truth. . . . [I]n these last times (*novissimo tempore*), a new Evangelist (*novus Evangelista*) . . . preached the way of the Son of God and the teaching of truth in his deeds. In him and through him an unexpected joy and a holy newness (*sancta novitas*) came into the world: a shoot of the ancient religion suddenly renewed (*innovavit*) the old and decrepit. A new spirit (*spiritus novus*) was placed in the hearts of the elect and a holy anointing has been poured out into their midst. This holy servant of Christ, like one of the lights of heaven, shone from above with a new rite and new signs (*novo ritu & novis signis*). The ancient miracles have been renewed (*renovata sunt*) through him. In the desert of this world, a fruitful vine has been planted in a new Order [*ordine novo*], but in an ancient way.[48]

Clearly the primary novelty exposed here is the life of innovative, performative preaching. Francis's reception of the stigmata marks the exemplary denouement of this performative gospel; it perfects and epitomizes what Francis's entire life has already come to mean to his followers. Otherwise put, the only ending his story could have had, in a narrative sense, is by (Francis's performance of) a crucifixion. This is a tricky ending and is managed in a manner that is partly material and partly visionary. This makes a difference. If it boiled down simply to God's agency—a set of material marks made on Francis's body to indicate God's approval of his life and message—it would indeed be possible to read it as a mark of the Lord upon his servant. But this is not how it is described as happening.

Indeed this ending cannot just *happen* to anyone: here, it involved years of embodied training, years of Francis's tough love toward his body, which he called "Brother Donkey." So, in the telling of this part of the story, what is emphasized is the perfection of obedience in the formation of habit. In chapter 2, whose events take place an indeterminate amount of time before his experience on Mount Alverna, Francis, in quest of knowledge of God's will for him, lets the bible drop open and watches it fall three times on some depiction of the passion. Here he is not seeking knowledge of the future for its own sake but guidance for action; he prays "that at the first opening of the book he would be shown what was best for him to do, so that he could bring to complete fulfillment what he had earlier simply and devotedly begun."[49]

In a sense it is a divinatory question: Francis is asking how his life will end. But in the context of a life spent acting out gospel messages, the question is not really so much about how he will die but about how he must *perform* his death, how he will be able to shape its message for others to read. He applies to himself the image of the passion and is easily able to grasp that it means "he would have to enter into the kingdom of God through many trials, difficulties and struggles." The lesson he takes, we have to assume, is about patience, though Thomas does not state this explicitly; rather, he emphasizes that Francis is in no way cast down by the message and carries on cheerfully. Seeing himself suffering as Christ is not difficult for Francis; the allegory is easy to penetrate. Chapter 2 functions chiefly to concretize Francis's intent to live and die according to the will of God. If it is also prognostic of the reception of the stigmata in the next chapter, this is only because words, for Francis, especially scriptural ones, always get turned into actions eventually. The chapter ends with a moralizing reflection on the priority of works over words.[50]

Turning into God from the Inside Out

In chapter 3, whose events are set two years before his death, Francis famously sees, "in the vision of God, a man, having six wings like a Seraph, standing over him, arms extended and feet joined, affixed to a cross . . . the Seraph's beauty was beyond comprehension, but the fact that the Seraph was fixed to the cross and the bitter suffering of that passion thoroughly frightened him."[51] Who or what is the seraph? Its identity is carefully undefined. It is "a man" with "six wings like a Seraph" and later is called just a seraph that is "fixed to the cross." It is important to the story that its identity is not obvious to Francis, and it is reiterated several times that Francis has no clear perception of what the vision meant; "his spirit was anxious to discern a sensible meaning from the vision," but "he was unable to perceive anything clearly understandable."[52] A vision of a suffering Christ would be less difficult to interpret, one assumes, than a crucified seraph, and perhaps less frightening. The word "novelty" recurs again in this part, referencing *not* the stigmata here but the vision whose "newness very much pressed upon his heart."[53] And indeed a crucified seraph as such would be a theological novelty, if not a solecism (as Kleinberg notes, seraphs "have no body and are incapable of suffering"[54]).

While Francis, so far as we know, never himself interprets the image, the stigmatization follows the vision directly and makes its meaning clear; as the vision fades, but while Francis is still wondering about it, "Signs of the nails began to appear in his hands and feet, just as he had seen them a little while earlier on the crucified man hovering over him."[55] His body seems to be making its own remark: the message originally drawn from scripture, explicated through his vision, is transformed into an answer to his question. The suffering seraph is not Christ, but Francis himself.

If Francis never said this, the understanding that the seraph is (or needs to be interpreted as) Francis occurs to all his hagiographers starting with this first vita; indeed the obvious exegesis of the vision is that the six seraphic wings represent Francis's own burning love of God, the compassion that transforms his mind, and so the vision also collaborates on the divine transformation of Francis's body into God's likeness. This is Bonaventure's extrapolation at the beginning of the *Itinerarium mentis in Deum*, where he explains having traveled to Mount Alverna for a meditative writing retreat as he worked on a composition about ascent: "and remaining there, while turning over in my mind some mental ascents to God, among other things there occurred to me the miracle that had happened in the aforesaid place to the blessed Francis himself in the vision namely of a winged seraph in the likeness of a crucified man (or: of the Crucified). In considering this it seemed to me immediately that the vision showed the suspension of the blessed father in contemplation and the way it can be arrived at."[56] In this passage, as in Thomas's account above, the word "miracle" refers to the vision, not the stigmata. As in Thomas's account, too, Bonaventure leaves the crucified seraph of the initial vision ambiguously without a name ("crucifixi" here need not be Christ, though it often gets translated that way). However, he maps Francis wholly onto the crucified seraph in his subsequent suggestion that the winged figure represents Francis himself, "suspended in contemplation." There is a message about Francis understood to be encoded in the vision.

Despite the fact that the insight about Francis's seraphic wings is represented as a spontaneous gift of spirit on Mount Alverna, Bonaventure is basically following Thomas of Celano, who suggested at the end of chapter 9 that the seraph was a mirror of Francis and offers an exegesis in which the six wings represent his virtues.[57] A similar message, too, about Francis's body as a transparent image of his mind is laid bare in Thomas's account as it develops, but in Thomas's vita, the stigmatized flesh does not merely render visible the mind but runs ahead of it like an obedient dog. Thomas sums up the harmony of flesh with spirit in chapter 4, where he describes the virtue of habit:

> There was in him such harmony of flesh with spirit
> And such obedience that
> As the spirit strove to reach all holiness
> The flesh did not resist
> But even tried to run on ahead
> According to the saying
> For you my soul has thirsted;
> And my flesh in so many ways!
> Repeated, submission became spontaneous,
> As the flesh, yielding each day
> Reached a place of great virtue
> For habit often becomes nature.[58]

Francis's body here is shown to have been completely domesticated by Francis's will, which channels God's so completely that the work of his body is translated to something divine. I suggest that it is important that the seraph is not quite Christ, for it is that little bit of distance between Christ and the seraph that makes the mystery. After the seraphic vision, the spirit and the flesh no longer struggle in Francis. Demons do not come into this section of the vita at all. For Thomas of Celano, the stigmatization is for all practical purposes the beginning of the saint's long act of dying. The next three chapters compress the hiatus between the divine imprint and the final death of Francis into a single movement, at the end of which moment his body is rendered in its ultimate transparency.

In the description of his final illness, the word "novelty" occurs again, but as before, it is not the stigmata that constitute the "novelty" but Francis's sense of purpose (*propositum*). So in his illness, "He burned with a great desire to return to his earliest steps toward humility; rejoicing in hope because of his boundless love, although his body was now at its greatest extremity, he was thinking he could call it back to its original servitude. . . . He did not consider that he had already attained his goal, but tireless in pursuit of holy newness [*infatigabilis durans in sanctae novitatis proposito*] he constantly hoped to begin again."[59] Thomas points out that his dying is already a form of servitude, but it is not enough for him; he has given himself to the point where there is no further he can go, except down the road flagged by the stigmata.

By chapter 7 he is afflicted with graver illnesses, vomiting blood and unable to eat. Asked by a brother whether he would prefer a martyr's death to the suffering he was undergoing, he suggested that his pain was probably worse than martyrdom, though he insists he could never want otherwise for himself than God wanted for him.[60] Chapter 8 describes his dying, accompanied by the reading of a chapter from the Gospel of John about the events preceding Christ's death; the minister attending him had planned to read this before Francis asked for it, as it was "the passage that met his eye as he first opened the book."[61] Thus scripture continues to be divinatory of Francis's life.

Chapter 9 bears witness to the appearance of Francis's body after death; here Thomas does refer to the stigmatic marks when he speaks of the "novelty of the miracle" (*miraculi novitas*) turning the weeping of the mourners to jubilation.[62] However, it is important to see this manifestation of novelty in the context supplied by all the other instances of this idea: wrapped around this miracle is the larger context of Francis's ongoing living out of scriptural paradigms. Scripture at times seems to exist only to point the way to Francis's miracles.

In this aftermath of death, Francis might almost be directing from beyond the grave another phase of the story. Thomas of Celano depicts a moment around the dead saint when a crowd of followers comes to see the body; all are marveling because

> it seemed
> he had just been taken down from the cross,
> his hands and feet pierced by nails
> and his right side
> wounded by a lance.

> . . . All the people saw him glowing with remarkable beauty and his flesh even whiter than before. It was even more wonderful for them to see in the middle of his hands and feet not just the holes of the nails, but the nails themselves formed out of his own flesh and retaining the dark color of iron, and his right side reddened with blood. These signs of martyr-

dom did not provoke horror but added great beauty and grace, like little black stones in a white pavement.[63]

These words could describe a painting or pageant of the deposition of Christ. The wounds are part of the costume that was Francis's body, but the picture is now of a beautiful but static flesh, sloughed off by Francis, but draped becomingly, shining with the transmogrified ornaments of his compassion.

A Bend in the Tradition

The event of the stigmatization is what remains most iconic, iterated in paintings in different depictions with different emphases. Visualizing the scene is also a devotional act, an act of faith. The story has two parts, internal (the vision, the will and desire to subdue the body) and external (the wounds, the bodily transformations). It also shows how things internal become externally known: first Francis's internal mystification over the seraph is transformed into sensible, knowable marks by his external production of bodily wounds. Second, the wounds concealed from all but a few followers are transformed into a known fact to all faithful observers of his body after death. Third, faith in the disclosed wounds separates the inner circle of the faithful from the outer circle of those who doubt.

The event's visionary part is what has been called the "mystical" understanding of the incident by Davidson, who remarks that this has always been a little bit in tension with the reading of stigmata as a miracle, that is, as something wrought by God from without.[64] But mysticism is not the point of the internal part of the stigmata; it is an essential component of the miracle, in some spots the miracle itself. In fact the stigmata cannot be *merely* mystical any more than they can be *merely* miraculous, wrought by a God acting independently through Francis, since the human must be collaborative in the new order. What is seen in Francis, even as Thomas of Celano depicts it, is already a new divine *becoming*. The point of the story is that Francis turns into an imago Dei *from the inside out*, through habit and performance remaking Christianity in the process, as he also transforms scripture from the inside out. If his end in conformity with Christ is God's doing, it became possible only because Francis, too, bent his will to that becoming.

The bend in the tradition importantly occurs in Francis's body, just as the first bend that made Christianity out of Judaism occurred in the body of Jesus; but unlike Jesus, Francis is made and not born: he is a new thing, as much in this first telling as in later ones, and part of his mystery, like that of the stigmata itself, is that what he represents, as a person, is never fully disclosed. He may be something like a new Christ (but differently), or an angelified being previewing the perfection of the omega man, the actual triumph of spirit over flesh, the redemption of nature seeded in the human spirit in the last days.

The interpretation can be allowed to float seraphically, a figure for Christ that also a new thing, without resting on one or another, because it is just as important that Francis is himself *different* from Christ as it is important that he is divinely engaged in remaking Christianity. The parallel between Jesus and Francis is lodged in their revision of the traditions in which they were born (i.e., as Christianity is a revised Judaism, so the Franciscan order is a revised Christianity). The stigmata are important because they signify the collaborative divine-human expression of a new phase of the world.

Conclusion: Ways of Extreme Sanctity in the Thirteenth Century

In his biography of Francis, André Vauchez begins by setting the life of the saint in the context of the general eschatological expectations that marked the early thirteenth century. This is the context of Francis's preaching of penance, which is always coupled implicitly with the understanding, based in Matthew 4:17, that "the Kingdom of Heaven is at Hand." As Vauchez puts it, however, "the conversion to which [Francis and his followers] were inviting their listeners was not presented as a simple preparation or preliminary step that was necessary to pass through in order to attain perfection. It already included entry into this 'kingdom of heaven,' which it was helping to create here and now (*hic et nunc*)."[65] Francis's life becomes the paradigm case of this creation of a heaven on earth *hic et nunc*; it shows how a human body that has learned obedience may enable the opening of an earthly portal into paradise. Through the example of his own penitential metamorphosis, Francis demonstrates to his community of believers how to change the world.

However, his is not the only way of exposing a visibly divine structure in this world. Another important piece of the early thirteenth-century context can be seen in the life of Christina Mirabilis: the development of an idea of purgatory that is increasingly understood to be connected to this world. Christina's vita makes it possible to get a glimpse of the immediate fate of souls in their afterlives through her resurrection body and her vivid torments. Through her, too, we see how human beings can experience participation in God's work through penance. In both stories, penance is crucial—first, to the re-formation of the body, and second, to the reformation of the world immediately annexed to it. Penance brings the flesh to heel, and the social world follows.

It is clear that I disagree with many who have written about Christina in not seeing any of her tortures being intended by Thomas of Cantimpré to be envisioned as a result of a demonic struggle over her body.[66] It is true that some within the story are said to wonder if this may be the case, but what Thomas himself represents is rather the reverse: she has, with pure and divine volition, bent her body to a task, a task from which natural bodies recoil. This would be a wasted vita if the task she engaged were not wholly volitional. As the body learns compliance, the matter of which it is made also changes; it manifests as more transparent to God, subtler, but also on its own terms as more absolute. The absolute nature of her bodily obedience, resolutely embedded in a desire for God, is what she most powerfully has in common with Francis.

In her work on the resurrection of the body, Caroline Bynum, discussing the decades to either side of 1300, speaks to a kind of longing internal to the way the body is imagined in the theological system, wherein longing itself almost becomes an object:

> If assertion of wholeness replaced hope of reassemblage in the conception of resurrection in the early fourteenth century, it was because body had become so crucial to person that the line between form and matter, death and life, earth and eternity, fragment and whole, had almost disappeared.
>
> Yet resurrection was not merely the assertion of wholeness. It was also the object of desire. . . . By the late thirteenth century some mystics seemed to lodge desire not only before the resurrection in a soul that yearns for body as well as for God but also in a psychosomatic unity whose longing will not be sated for all eternity.[67]

The bodies of Christina and Francis as represented in these vitae—torn, bleeding, suffering, wasting away, disappearing and reappearing in the dreams of those who loved them—offer a positive shape and form for this longing, a confirmation of the personhood of the saint that also affirms the wholeness of the community surrounding them.

There are reasons for the form taken by this affirmation. It is the flesh that sits, often uncomfortably, between matter and spirit, a part of the self that is also a part of nature; it is thus transmutable by the will. Bodily transformations are part and parcel of mystical transports in both cases: they signify the way the flesh, perhaps matter itself, can be a plastic, obedient mirror of the soul in the flesh's ideal (paradisal) condition. The remaking of Francis's body into an image of a man crucified shows how a merely human body can mold itself to the Logos while remaining itself, bringing to life a new gospel, generative of new exegesis. Christina's metamorphosis (unrolling her body like a hedgehog, bending her arms as though she had no bones) provides a visible index of the unusual nature of her body, which (already in its afterlife) can suffer and bleed without dying. At the end, too, it renders more visible the afterlife of the others whose purgatorial penance she performs. In both stories, we see spirit acting on matter to transform the body and recreate the world, subjecting the body and the self to the needs of God's dispensation. In both cases, the role of the saints is importantly esoteric—partly disclosed, partly beyond knowing.

But this is so because heaven and earth are not distinct; they intersect and overlap, flowing in and out of each other. They affect each other; they are permeable. Human bodies, too, are permeable; they can be remade. Christina has a body remade by God, with her consent, to endure terrible suffering. Francis remakes his own body, with God's consent, through terrible suffering. Like God, too, the words of these saints are actions—as God's Logos brings world into being, so on a smaller scale Francis and Christina are depicted as God's word embodied, both reenactments and powerful new agencies, cosmic changes playing out in real time in semidivine, human bodies. If at times their more radical metamorphoses seem sinister, the goal of their hagiographers is in fact to demonstrate that they are true manifestations of the sacred and thus proper parts of the dispensation after all.

NOTES

1. For Christina's relation to Lutgard, see Thomas's *Life of Lutgard* in Margot King and Barbara Newman, *Thomas of Cantimpré: The Collected Saints' Lives* (Turnhout: Brepols, 2008), 237. All further references to Lutgard, as well as quotations from the text, are drawn from this edition.

2. Reference to Christina is in the prologue to Jacques's *Life of Marie of Oignies*; see the translation by Margot King, *The Life of Marie d'Oignies by Jacques de Vitry* (Toronto: Peregrina, 1993), §8, p. 42. All references to the *Life of Marie* will be to this translation.

3. Margot King, "The Sacramental Witness of Christina Mirabilis: the Mystic Growth of a Fool for Christ's Sake," *Medieval Religious Women* 2 (1987): 145–65.

4. Robert Sweetman, "Christine of St. Trond's Preaching Apostolate: Thomas of Cantimpre's Hagiographical Method Revisited," *Vox Benedictina* 9 (1992): 67–97.

5. Barbara Newman, "Possessed by the Spirit: Devout Women, Demoniacs, and the Apostolic Life in the Thirteenth Century," *Speculum* 73 (1998): 733–70.

6. Anke Passenier, "The Life of Christina Mirabilis, Miracles and the Construction of Marginality," in *Women and Miracle Stories: A Multidisciplinary Exploration*, ed. Anne-Marie Korte (Leiden: Brill, 2001), 177.

7. Quoted from Thomas in the prologue to the *Life of Christina* (but quite faithful to the identical passage from Jacques de Vitry) in the translation by King and Newman, *Thomas of Cantimpré*, 127–28. Translated quotations from Thomas's *Life of Christina* are drawn from this edition. Where noted, I have modified the English to suit the emphasis of my reading based on the Latin of *Vita de S. Christina Mirabili Virgine*, in *Acta sanctorum*, June 4 (Antwerp: Petrus Jacobs, 1707), 636–66.

8. *Life of Christina*, §38, p. 147.

9. Ibid., §7, p. 131.

10. Ibid., 133 n. 14.

11. Ibid., §§10–13, pp. 133–35.

12. Ibid., §16 and §26, pp. 136 and 142.

13. *Life of Marie*, §§30–31, pp. 60–62.

14. *Life of Lutgard*, chap. 10, p. 247.

15. Ibid., chap. 11, p. 249.

16. Ibid., chap. 16, p. 251.

17. *Life of Christina*, §15, p. 136.

18. Ibid., §16, p. 136.

19. Ibid., §17, p. 137.

20. For levitation, see the *Life of Lutgard*, chap. 10, p. 234; for flight into the fields, see the *Life of Marie*, §47, p. 78.

21. As noted by Elizabeth Casteen in her chapter in this volume, these signs are marks rapture in vitae of holy women. Christina's is perhaps more extreme but not atypical in other respects.

22. *Life of Christina*, §18, p. 137, translation modified.

23. Ibid., §20, p. 139.

24. Ibid., §21, p. 139. Barbara Newman suggests this is an example of Christina performing a "self-exorcism" and that the "vehement spirit" may be a demonic one; see Newman, "Possessed by Spirit," 763. As I try to show, I do not think this is a necessary conclusion.

25. Ibid., §5, p. 130, translation slightly modified.

26. See Winston Black, "Animated Corpses and Bodies with Power in the Scholastic Age," in, *Death in Medieval Europe: Death Scripted and Death Choreographed*, ed. Joelle Rollo-Koster (London: Routledge, 2016), 71–92.

27. For scholastic arguments about possibilities for corpse animation, see ibid., especially 88–92.

28. From Thomas's *Bonum Universale de Apibus* (Douai, 1597); the Ida of Nivelles incident at 2.57.8, pp. 541–42; the knight at 2.49.6, pp. 446–47; Caciola, *Afterlives: The Return of the Dead in the Middle Ages* (Ithaca: Cornell University Press, 2016), 288–91.

29. *Life of Christina*, §5, p. 130.

30. Ibid., §45, p. 150.

31. Ibid., §46, p. 150.

32. Ibid., §50, p. 152.

33. Ibid., §51, p. 152.

34. Ibid., §52, p. 153.

35. For Christina praying to avoid miracles, see ibid., §52; for the request that her death-bed be prepared "secretly," see §51.

36. As noted by Jacques Le Goff, *The Birth of Purgatory*, trans A. Goldhammer (Chicago: University of Chicago Press, 1984), 241. William writes on purgatory's location in *De universo*, *opera omnia*, 2 vols. (Paris, 1674; repr., Frankfurt: Minerva, 1963), vol. 1, chaps. 60–62, pp. 676–82. See also the account of William's understanding of purgatorial fire in Daniel Bornstein, "Esoteric Theology: William of Auvergne on the Fires of Hell and Purgatory," *Speculum* 57 (1982): 509–31.

37. *Life of Marie*, §27, p. 58.

38. E.g., see Aviad Kleinberg, *The Sensual God: How the Senses Make the Almighty Senseless* (New York: Columbia University Press, 2015), 140–42.

39. See Octavian Schmucki, *The Stigmata of St. Francis of Assisi: A Critical Investigation in the Light of Thirteenth-Century Sources* (St. Bonaventure, N.Y.: Franciscan Institute, 1991).

40. Beginning with André Vauchez, "Les stigmates de saint François et leurs détracteurs dans les derniers siècles du moyen âge," *Mélanges d'archéologie et d'histoire* 80, no. 2 (1968): 595–625. Cf. notes 41–43.

41. On prior traditions of stigmata, including fakery, see Richard C. Trexler, "The Stigmatized Body of Francis of Assisi: Conceived, Processed, Disappeared," in *Frömmigkeit im*

Mittelalter: Politisch-soziale Kontexte, visuelle Praxis, körperliche Ausdrucksformen, ed. Klaus Schreiner and Marc Müntz (Paderborn: Fink, 2002), 463–97, and Caroline Muessig, "Signs of Salvation: The Evolution of Stigmatic Spirituality before Francis of Assisi," *Church History* 82 (2013): 49–68; for the development of representation of Francis's wounds subsequent to his death, see Arnold Davidson, "Miracles of Bodily Transformation, or How St. Francis Received the Stigmata," *Critical Inquiry* 35, no. 3 (2009): 451–80.

42. Gábor Klaniczay, "Illness, Self-inflicted Body Pain and Supernatural Stigmata: Three Ways of Identification with the Suffering Body of Christ," in *Infirmity in Antiquity and the Middle Ages: Social and Cultural Approaches to Health, Weakness and Care*, ed. Christian Krötzl, Katariina Mustakallio, and Jenni Kuuliala (London: Routledge, 2016), 119–36.

43. Francis of Assisi, "Treatise on Miracles," in *Francis of Assisi, Early Documents*, vol. 2, *The Founder*, ed. Regis J. Armstrong, J. A. Wayne Hellmann, and William J. Short (New York: New City Press, 1999), 404–5.

44. Ibid., 406.

45. Ibid.

46. On relics, see Carla Salvati, "The Camoscio," in *The Stigmata of Francis of Assisi: New Studies, New Perspectives*, ed. Jacques Dalarun, Michael Cusato, and Carla Salvati (St. Bonaventure, N.Y.: Franciscan Institute, 2006), 79–99.

47. See especially Trexler, "Stigmatized Body," and Muessig, "Signs of Salvation."

48. Translation slightly modified (referencing *Vita prima, auctore Thoma de Celano, sancti discipulo*, in *Acta Sanctorum*, October 2 (Antwerp: Petrus Joannes vander Plassche, 1768), 683–723 from chapter 1, pp. 259–60 of *The Life of St. Francis by Thomas of Celano (1228–1229)*, in *Francis of Assisi, Early Documents*, vol. 1, ed. Regis J. Armstrong, J. A. Wayne Hellman, and William J. Short (New York: New City Press, 1999). Hereafter I abbreviate this translation as *ED* 1.

49. *ED* 1, chap. 2, p. 262.

50. Ibid., 263.

51. Ibid., chap. 3, p. 263.

52. Ibid., 264.

53. Ibid.

54. Kleinberg, *Sensual God*, 135.

55. *ED* 1, chap. 3, p. 264.

56. This is my translation, based on the Quaracchi edition, *Opera Omnia*, vol. 5 (Quaracchi: Collegii a S. Bonaventure, 1891). An English translation may be found in *Bonaventure: The Soul's Journey into God; The Tree of Life; The Life of St Francis*, trans. Ewert Cousins (Mahwah, N.J.: Paulist Press, 1978).

57. *ED* 1, chap. 9, pp. 282–283.

58. *ED* 1, chap. 4, p. 266.

59. *ED* 1, 273, translation modified.

60. *ED* 1, chap. 7, p. 275.

61. *ED* 1, chap. 8, p. 278.

62. *ED* 1, chap. 9, p. 280.

63. Ibid.

64. Davidson, "Miracles of Bodily Transformation," 477–78.

65. André Vauchez, *Francis of Assisi*, trans. Michael F. Cusato (New Haven: Yale University Press, 2012), 43. For another recent biography of Francis, see Augustine Thompson, *Francis of Assisi: A New Biography* (Ithaca: Cornell University Press, 2012).

66. Barbara Newman, e.g., suggests that she attempts "self-exorcism" at least twice ("Possessed by the Spirit," 763).

67. Caroline Walker Bynum, *Resurrection of the Body in Western Christianity, 200–1336* (New York: Columbia University Press, 1994), 328.

2

THE SOURCES AND SIGNIFICANCE OF STEFANIA'S *NEW STATEMENT* ON *MARGHERITA COLONNA'S PERFECTION OF THE VIRTUES*

Sean L. Field

Only a very small number of women wrote hagiographic works about other women in the thirteenth century.[1] Perhaps the least-known and least-studied text in this dossier is the hagiographic treatment of Margherita Colonna by a follower named Stefania. Margherita (ca. 1255–1280) was one of the thirteenth century's "unquiet souls,"[2] a determined laywoman living a life of visionary piety and Franciscan charity with the support of her powerful Roman family. Shortly after her death, her brother Giovanni Colonna, a layman and senator of Rome, wrote a first *Life* of Margherita. Just a few years later another brother, the Cardinal Giacomo Colonna, commissioned further recollections from Stefania. These two "lives" survive in a unique fourteenth-century manuscript that is today Rome, Biblioteca Casanatense MS 104. Although Margherita Colonna was beatified by the Catholic Church in 1847, these two works languished in near complete obscurity until they were edited by Livario Oliger in 1935.[3] Even then, neither Margherita Colonna nor the hagiographic texts written about her received much further attention.[4] Yet these texts are rich sources for many aspects of the way sanctity was imagined and constructed in Rome in the second half of the thirteenth century, and as such they are surely worthy of new study. Stefania's text, in particular, repays fresh textual attention. For example, a close reading demonstrates that while Oliger's edition was highly competent in most ways, it completely overlooked a number of wholesale borrowings employed by Stefania in composing and compiling her text. The present chapter therefore demonstrates and details these borrowings and assesses their significance for understanding this important female hagiographer and her work.[5]

I thank David J. Collins, S.J., for inviting and critiquing this essay; Anne Clark, Larry F. Field, and Lezlie S. Knox for insights and criticisms; and Richard Kieckhefer for many years of advice and encouragement.

Contextual Background: Margherita Colonna and Her *Lives*

Margherita Colonna was orphaned at a young age and grew up under her older brothers' tutelage. Around 1272, Giovanni Colonna (the layman and senator) sought a suitable husband for her, but Margherita preferred a chaste life devoted to Christ and so eventually fled to Castel San Pietro, the family compound atop Mount Prenestino overlooking the town of Palestrina in the Colonna heartlands to the east of Rome.[6] There Margherita assembled a group of pious followers as an informal, unenclosed community. At various points over the next few years Margherita pondered several different spiritual paths, including the possibility of becoming a nun at Santa Chiara in Assisi. But she instead adopted a pious life in the world and briefly moved with her followers to the church of Santa Maria in Vulturella (modern Mentorella), site of a famous Marian shrine. When the lord of the area proved hostile to this move, however, Margherita had to retreat, and she next briefly joined the household of "Lady Altruda of the Poor" (an intriguing but otherwise obscure figure) in Rome. There Margherita humbly performed household chores, but after "many days" her brothers convinced her to return to Mount Prenestino. With the support of her brother Giacomo (made cardinal in 1278), she spent the last years of her life in charitable work for the poor, before dying on December 30, 1280. Her body was buried in the church of San Pietro atop Mount Prenestino, and almost immediately (certainly before 1285) Giovanni Colonna composed her first hagiographic vita.

Margherita's followers at first continued to live some kind of communal life on Mount Prenestino. By September 1285, however, they had taken formal vows and professed the Rule of the Sorores minores inclusae (Enclosed Minor Sisters),[7] and Pope Honorius IV had given them the ancient Roman convent of San Silvestro in Capite, evidently at the urging of Cardinal Giacomo Colonna.[8] It was almost certainly at this time that Margherita's relics were transferred to San Silvestro, in the heart of the Colonna-dominated quarter of Rome.[9] Shortly afterward, Giacomo Colonna turned to Stefania to request a second hagiographic text on Margherita's saintly virtues. Because this text refers to Margherita's nephew Pietro Colonna as cardinal and Giovanni Colonna as still alive, it must have been written (or at least completed) between 1288 and 1292/94.

Textual Borrowing and Historical Context in Stefania's *Epistola*

One of the most informative elements in this hagiographic dossier is the dedicatory letter (labeled "*Epistola*" in the manuscript) with which Stefania's text commences. This letter contains some of the best evidence that helped Oliger to establish (quite correctly) that what he called the "First Life" had been written by Giovanni Colonna, and that the "Second Life" had been commissioned by Giacomo Colonna. Furthermore, this dedicatory letter is the only place where the author of the "Second Life" gives her name, and it includes her self-description as "presiding" over her band of sisters, a description that has generally been assumed to mean that Stefania occupied some kind of leadership position at San Silvestro in Capite. It is thus of considerable interest to note that nearly the entire *Epistola* is cobbled together from earlier sources. Identifying the nature and extent of this borrowing is crucial for understanding Stefania's writing process, as well as for reassessing how much authentic thirteenth-century historical information can be extracted from the letter.

The opening of the *Epistola* in fact draws heavily from the preface to the second part of the widely known *Collationes* by John Cassian (d. ca. 430), as the following table demonstrates:

Cassian:	Stefania:
Cum virtutem perfectionis vestrae, **qua velut magna quaedam** luminaria **in** hoc mundo **admirabili claritate fulgetis**, multi sanctorum qui vestro erudiuntur exemplo vix queant aemulari,	[**C**]**um virtutum perfeccionis** particulam, **qua** clare ac beate memorie Margarita **velud magna quedam** iubaria **in** presenti et futuro, **ammirabili claritate refulget**, nove edicionis eloquio, quamquam pollutalabiis [Isa 6:5] et arida lingua, coner depromere, insufficienciam meam et harencos loquele modulos ille compluat ymbre suo, qui moysaice virge gemine percussionis ictu in refocillacionem et haustum israelitici populi siccam rupem iuxit fluentes latices emanare [cf. Num 20:11], **tamen vos, o sanctissime** pater, **tanta sublimium** virtutum, **a quibus** ipsa soror per vestram doctrinam primitus extitit conducata, **laude flammamini, ut** me, licet immeritam, **ingenti** inopique sororum **cenobio presidentem; agrecacionem** mihi commissam **cotidiano** vestre **sancte conversacionis intuitu** desiderem **edoceri**.
tamen vos, o sancti fratres Honorate et Eucheri, **tanta** illorum **sublimium** virorum, **a quibus** prima anachoreseos instituta suscepimus, **laude flammamini, ut** unus quidem vestrum **ingenti** fratrum **coenobio praesidens congregationem** suam, quae **cotidiano sanctae conversationis** vestrae **docetur intuitu**.[10]	

Translated, Stefania's text reads as follows:

> Since I am attempting to set forth, with the declaration of a new state-
> ment, some part of the perfection of the virtues with which Margherita,
> of bright and blessed memory, blazes in astounding brilliance like a great
> beacon for the present and the future, although I am of *unclean lips* and
> parched tongue, may He who with two sharp blows from the *rod* of Moses
> forced the dry rock to give forth flowing drink for the refreshment and
> thirst of the people of Israel pour down his nourishing rain upon my
> inadequacy and upon this modest little oration! You, however, most holy
> father, burn with such praise for the noble virtues with which this same
> sister first stood forth, guided by your teaching, that I wish that I—who,
> though unworthy, am now presiding over our prodigious and impover-
> ished band of sisters and the whole gathering entrusted to me—could be
> taught by daily observation of your holy comportment.

Several points are immediately apparent from this comparison. First, the
author's borrowing is extensive, and yet Stefania has completely reshaped
much of the meaning, indicating her control of the material. For example,
whereas the point of Cassian's opening clause had been to say that even many
"holy persons" were not able to rival his recipients' perfections, Stefania has
altered the passage to indicate her own intention to give a new *eloquium*—
statement or declaration—concerning the way her subject's virtues shine forth.
Thus, the phrase "nove editionis eloquio" actually takes on additional significance when it is recognized as a conscious addition to the source text—in this
case, accurate identification of Stefania's borrowing clarifies her intentions.[11] In
fact, this clarification has seemed important enough to warrant calling the text
(untitled in the unique manuscript) the *New Statement on Margherita Colonna's Perfection of the Virtues*, in preference to the less specific "Second Life"
used by Oliger.

It is also apparent that the historical context of the *Epistola* can be analyzed
accurately only after identifying which passages are direct textual borrowings
and which are not. Thus, the changes introduced to Cassian's base text emphasize the fact that the author is writing to a "father" whose teachings led Margherita to the virtues. But this is clearly a *pater* in a spiritual sense, because
Margherita is also referred to as the dedicatee's *soror*. It is true that "sister"
could also be meant in a spiritual sense, but in light of other evidence (discussed below), the biological meaning seems strongly implied here. Thus, separating the borrowed passages from the original wording highlights the fact that
the dedicatee of this letter is an illustrious churchman who is also Margherita's

brother. Oliger was thus surely correct to identify him as Cardinal Giacomo Colonna, since the "First Life" makes it abundantly clear that Giacomo was Margherita's main spiritual guide.

But Oliger also took the phrase "sororum cenobio presidentem" as suggest- ing that Stefania might have been holding the office of "president," a unique official created by the Rule of the Sorores minores in order to assure continuity of leadership when an abbess was unable to fulfill her duties. Since it is now apparent that Cassian's "fratrum coenobio praesidens" was simply modified to "sororum cenobio presidentem," the participal *praesidens* probably cannot be understood in such a technical sense (since Cassian wrote centuries before the Rule of the Sorores minores existed).[12] The idea that Stefania was "president" of her monastery is thus unlikely. Yet at the same time, Stefania not only retained the overall formulation suggesting leadership, but modified "congregationem suam" to "agrecacionem mihi commissam," strongly emphasizing her claim to have had some kind of leadership entrusted personally to her. After 1285, reference to a group of "sisters" committed to following Margherita's example could really only mean the new community of San Silvestro in Capite. Thus it might seem logical to deduce that Stefania must have been abbess of San Silvestro at the time of her writing (another possibility raised by Oliger).

Unfortunately, no "Stefania" appears as abbess in the published records of San Silvestro. In fact, the only abbess known between 1285 and 1293 is "Herminia," who is documented in that office from 1285 to July 1288, and again in 1293.[13] Oliger therefore suggested that "Stefania" and "Herminia" might perhaps have been one and the same person. This hypothesis, however, seems unlikely since there is no evidence that the sisters of San Silvestro took on new names at the time of profession. Alternatively, perhaps Stefania was indeed abbess sometime between 1288 and 1292, the interval when no documentary evidence names an abbess and also exactly the window for the text's composition. Or Stefania's text might have been begun earlier than is usually supposed; if she wrote her dedicatory *Epistola* before 1285 (perhaps adding the later section of the text that mentions Cardinal Pietro Colonna only after 1288), then it might be possible to imagine that she was exercising informal leadership of Margherita's followers while they were still on Mount Prenestino. Or perhaps Stefania held no formal office at all, but as a senior figure among the sisters at San Silvestro, and as a woman who had been close to Margherita Colonna, she felt entitled to describe herself as entrusted with some kind of spiritual responsibility for the wider group. In support of this idea is the fact that Stefania was likely related to Margherita Colonna (as were a number of other early nuns of San Silvestro), and numerous episodes in her text reveal Stefania's privileged access to not only Margherita but also to her illustrious brothers.[14]

Most of the rest of the *Epistola* is then drawn from a letter that had supposedly been addressed by Abbot Odo of Cluny (d. 942) to Count Fulk of Anjou (d. 958) as part of the preface to a treatise "On the Return of the Blessed Martin to Burgundy."[15] Although modern scholars have identified the work as a twelfth-century forgery, Stefania apparently found pseudo-Odo's language useful in framing her own address to Giacomo Colonna. In the chart that follows, I have rearranged the text from pseudo-Odo's letter so as to match the order in which it was used by Stefania:

Pseudo-Odo of Cluny:

Siccine, comes **gloriosissime, neminem reperiebas, quem de virtute consuleres, et praecipue de** viro **virtutis** Martino, **nisi** tuum collactaneum Odonem? **Puto deerant praeclara** Francorum **ingenia, qui sublimem materiam sublimi aequipararent eloquentia?**

Cum in sublimi humilitas, et in magnis et multis negotiis occupato virtutis studium **reperitur, vere, fateor, illius opus est, qui potest** *de lapidibus suscitare filios* Abrabae. **Patet, credo, cur ista praemiserim. Ecce enim** *mundus in maligno totus positus est:* **nec tamen sibi vendicat generosissimum principem** Fulconem Bonum, **a quo tamen in parte non minima vendicatur.** Fulco Bonus, **utpote** comes **praepotens negotia tractat saecularia: sed hoc, ut perpendo,** specie tenus, **in divinis vero medullitus occupatur. Placet etiam in his immorari, et** Boni Fulconis **bonitatem exprimere: sed parco laudibus ne adulari videar,** et parco jussis, ne ingratus existam. **Hoc saltem unum me dixisse liceat,**

Stefania:

Siccine, gloriosissime pater, **neminem repperiebatis, quem de virtute consuleritis, et precipue de** muliere **virtutis** splendida Margarita, **nisi** vestram devotulam Stephaniam? **Puto deerant** vestri senioris fratris **preclara ingenia, qui sublimi eloquentia iam equiparavitmateriam tam sublimem.**

Et cum in multis et arduis negociis occupetur, tamen in eo virtutis emulacio **repperitur. Vere fateor, illius opus est, qui potest** *filios* Israel *de lapidibus suscitare* [Matt. 3:9]. **Patet, credo, cur ista premiserim. Ecce enim mundus in maligno totus est positus** [John 5:19] **nec tamen sibi generosissimum** Johannem **vendicat, a quo tamen in parte non minima vendicatur.** Ipse vero **ut prepotens negotia secularia tractat, sed hec, ut perpendo,** contracticitus, **in divinis vero medullitus occupatur. Placet equidem in hiis immorari et** eius **bonitatem exprimere, sed parco laudibus ne adulari videar** potius quam laudare. **Hoc saltem unum me dixisse liceat,**

rarum imo fere nullum reperiri,	**rarum immo fere nullum repperi,**
quem ita virtutis aemulatio saeculo	**quemita virtutis emulatio seculo**
subripiat, ut mancipet honestati.	**subripiat, mancipet honestati.**

Translated, Stefania's text reads as follows:

> Yet was it not the case, most glorious father, that you could find no one
> except your devoted little Stefania to ask about such virtue, and especially
> about that shining woman of virtue, Margherita? I suppose that you did
> not have access to the outstanding talents of your older brother, whose
> lofty eloquence is equal to such a lofty subject. Though he is busy with
> many serious endeavors, he embodies the emulation of virtue. In truth I
> confess that the task is one for him who *is able from these stones to raise up*
> *children* of Israel! It is obvious, I think, why I mention these things at the
> outset. For behold! *The whole world is seated in wickedness,* and yet does
> not claim as its own the most noble Giovanni, by whom in no small part
> it has been claimed. He truly deals with the business of this world as a
> man of power, but it seems to me he does this out of necessity, for at heart
> he is more occupied by divine matters. I am happy to dwell on such things
> and describe his goodness, but I am sparing in my praises, lest I seem to
> adulate rather than to praise. Yet perhaps I might be allowed to make this
> one remark—that rarely, if ever, is one found whom such an emulation of
> virtue steals away from this world to give over to honor and integrity.

Again, Stefania's changes and additions are what stand out. First and foremost, this passage is the only place where Stefania provides her own name. She
continues to address her recipient as "father," and the fact that he has an older
brother named John/Giovanni is now highlighted. This Giovanni is evidently a
man of the world, as was of course the senator of Rome (though anyone interested in the character of Giovanni Colonna should note that the language that
here seems to describe the hardheaded senator as most concerned with holy
things is in fact entirely taken from pseudo-Odo of Cluny.) Thus, even where
older phrases are being reused, there is still a clear sense that a churchman and
spiritual father has commissioned this work from Stefania in the absence of his
older brother "Giovanni," whose talents as a writer are already proven. Thus
highlighting the textual borrowings continues to emphasize, rather than
undermine, the basic historical context: Stefania is writing to Cardinal Giacomo Colonna, whose older brother Giovanni Colonna has already composed
a life of Margherita.

The last section of the *Epistola* continues to borrow long chunks from pseudo-Odo of Cluny.

Pseudo-Odo:

Sed esto, tibi pareo: **aggrediar** quod hortaris.

Sed, **ut sentio, quod** pace tua **dixerim, privatus amor claudit oculum mentis: plusque** tibi **placet** amici **rusticitas, quam ceterorum phalerata urbanitas.**

Sed quia, ut verum fatear, meipsum tibi debeo, **etiam ultra vires parere** tibi **non differam. Etsi enim inest ignorantia** quam **arguat praesumptio, vera tamen dilectio non horrescit. Parebo itaque non eloquens erudito, sed** ut amico amicissimus. **Plus verax, quam** eloquens, **inveniri conabor. Neque enim** nostra **patitur professio pompatici sermonis** affectare **gloriolas, studium est esse potius, quam videri.**

Verum quia nonnullis mos est scripta aliorum ad unguem elimare, cum ipsi lippientibus oculis, si qua forte ediderint, vix respectent, rogo **ut privata lectione conten-**

Stefania:

Sed necessario hoc mihi virtus caritatis extorsit, ut eorum aliqua, que pretermissa sunt a dissertissimo frater vestro, **aggrediar** et tam abruptum scribendi periculum non vitarim. Et licet in principio supra ipsius fundamentum aliquid videar fabricare, in subsequentibus evitabo. Et ut **sencio, quod** cum reverentia vestra **dixerim, privatus amor claudit oculum mentis, plusque** vobis **placet unius** muliercule **rusticitas, quam ceterorum urbanitas falerata. Sed quia, ut verum fatear, etiam ultra vires, vobis parere non differam; etsi enim inest ignorancia,** ipsa **arguat presumptio, vera tamen dilectio non horrescit. Parebo itaque, non ut eloquens erudito, sed ut** domino clientula, **plusque conabor verax, quam inveniri** facunda.[17] **Neque enim** mea **patitur** nec exigit **professio pompatici sermonis gloriolas,** quibus **studium est potius videri quam esse.** Si vero sanctam studii vestri sitim, etiam hi[18] furores quos, ut potui, pedaneo sermone digessi, non quiverint satiare, germanicam similaginem leccitetis, et desiderii vestri mirifice demulcebit ardorem.

Verum quia non nullis mos[19] est scripta aliorum ad unguem elimare, cum ipsi lippientibus oculis, si qua forte ediderint, vix respectent, supplico ut privata lectione

tus, et quae **privatim** dictavimus **privatim et ipse legas, ne si forte in manus** alienorum ipse **venero, discerpar ab eis, quos non vera, sed vana delectant.**[16]

contenti et que privatim intexui, **privatim ipsi legatis, ne si fortasse in manus devenero** detractorum, **ab eis, quos non vera, sed varia delectant,** dente[20] cinico dilaniar seu **discerpar.** Explicit epistula.[21]

Stefania's text, translated, reads as follows:

> Still, the force of pure love unavoidably compels me to deal with some of those things that were passed over by your most well-spoken brother, and I must not avoid the steep challenge of writing. Although at first I may seem to build on his foundation, I will avoid it in what follows. As I understand it, and I would say this with all due respect, personal love shuts the mind's eye, and thus the simplicity of a poor woman is more pleasing to you than the ornamented sophistication of others. But because, to speak truthfully, I will not hesitate to obey you, even if it is beyond my powers and even if some ignorance is involved (let that objection be assumed!), love does not shrink back. I will therefore comply, writing not as a gifted speaker to the learned but as a poor follower to her lord, and I will endeavor to be found truthful rather than eloquent. What I have to say neither allows nor requires the tinsel trapping of high-flown rhetoric, concerned with appearances rather than the essence of the matter. If, in truth, these flights of spirit that I have rendered in common prose are not able to satisfy the holy thirst of your zeal, then you may read over again your brother's composition, and it will soothe the passion of your longing in wondrous ways. Since it is the habit of some people to take a very sharp file to the writing of others, and yet, if they have published anything themselves, to hardly even run a bleary eye over it, I beg you to be content with reading this in private, so that what I have composed in private you may read in private. Otherwise, I might fall into the hands of critics and be mauled and torn apart by those who delight not in the truth but in the bizarre. Here ends the letter.

The main historical data are the reference, again, to the dedicatee's "most learned brother" and the existence of a "germanicam similaginem" that can be read and reread if the current text is not to the dedicatee's liking; the flowery phrase leaves some room for interpretation but can be reasonably translated as "similar text by your brother."

To sum up the analysis so far: Stefania's dedicatory *Epistola* is in very large measure drawn from two earlier texts. Highlighting the exact extent of her borrowings from these texts helps foreground some historical data, such as the author's name, the virtually certain fact of her dedicatee as Giacomo Colonna, and the several references to an earlier vita having been written by the dedicatee's brother Giovanni. At the same time, it also points away from other historical conclusions that might otherwise have seemed plausible, such as the idea that Stefania was "president" of San Silvestro in Capite.

Recycling Sanctity in Stefania's Statement

Chapters 2 through 9 (after the *Epistola*, considered as chap. 1) of Stefania's text are essentially a brief recap of some of the highlights of Margherita's saintly life and especially her death, intermixed with long passages of praise. Indeed, chapter 9 actually ends with an "amen" and then (in the unique manuscript) four blank lines at the bottom of a folio, underscoring a sense of internal completion before moving on to miracles and other recollections. In fact, the praises in this initial section turn out to be very largely adopted and adapted from earlier sources.

As one begins to read these chapters, the first impression is of a rather startling elevation of rhetoric as the text returns all the way to Creation and the fall of man, in order to set the context for Margherita Colonna's arrival on earth. This audacity actually results from the fact that the first two lengthy paragraphs of chapter 2 are taken directly from the opening of Gregory IX's bull *Gloriosus in majestate*, which had canonized Elizabeth of Hungary in 1235. In fact, the first borrowed section contains virtually no alterations of any kind.

Gregory IX:	Stefania:
Gloriosus in maiestate sua patris eterni filius redemptor noster dominus Jesus Christus de celorum summitate prospiciens conditionis humane gloriam multo concursu miserie, cui primi parentis culpa dedit initium, deformatam, ineffabili dispositione providit, ut et virtutem suam sedentibus in umbra mortis [Luke 1:79] exponeret, et in exilio	Gloriosus in magestate sua patris eterni filius redemptor noster dominus Jhesus Christus de celorum summitate prospiciens humanam gloriam multo concursu miserie, cui prime parentis culpa dedit initium, deformatam, ineffabili dispositione providit, ut et virtutem suam sedentibus in umbra mortis [Luke 1:79] exponeret, et in exilio positos ad lib-

positos ad libertatis patriam revocaret. Igitur quia nulli potius quam
sibi sue facture redemptio competebat, eo quod artifici sit et decens
et debitum, ut quocumque casu
depereat quod pulchrius finxisse
dinoscitur, in statum pristinum sue
virtutis studio restauretur, in exile
vasculum, si tamen sit exiguum,
quod recepit hospitem super omnia
spatiosum, scilicet in aulam virginis
refertam omni plenitudine sanctitatis, de regali throno se conferens,
opus inde cunctis visibile protulit,
per quod propulso tenebrarum principe de sui redemptione plasmatis triumphavit, certa relinquens instituta
fidelibus, per que ipsis ad patriam
redderetur transitus expeditus.

eratis patriam revocaret. Igitur quia
nulli potius quam sibi sue facture
redemptio competebat, eo quod artifici sit et decens et debitum, ut
quocumque casu depereat, quod pul-
crius finxisse dinoscitur, in statum
pristinum restauraret studio sue virtutis, in exile vasculum, si tamen
exiguum quod recepit hospitem
super omnia spatiosum, scilicet in
aulam virginis refertam omni plenitudine sanctitatis, de regali nature
throno se conferens, opus inde cunctis visibile protulit, per quod propulso tenebrarum principe de sui
redemptione plasmatis triumphavit,
certa relinquens instituta fidelibus,
per que ipsis redderetur ad patriam
transitus expeditus.[22]

Stefania's text reads as follows:

> Our redeemer, Lord Jesus Christ, Son of the Eternal Father, most glorious
> in his majesty, beholding from the height of heaven that human glory
> had been defiled by a great course of misery since the sin of Eve, pro-
> vided, through an ineffable plan, to show his virtue to those *sitting in the
> shadow of death*, and to recall to the homeland of freedom those now in
> exile. Accordingly, because the redemption of His creation pertained to
> no one more than to Himself, and insofar as it was right and proper for
> the Creator, through His power, to return to its original state what He is
> known to have created in more beautiful form (having been ruined by
> whatever happenstance), He took himself off the royal throne of nature
> into a small container that, however small it might have been, still
> received a guest of wider scope than all else: that is, into the hall of the
> Virgin replete with the fullness of sanctity. From there He brought forth
> a work that all could see and through which, having expelled the prince
> of darkness, He triumphed in the redemption of His creation, leaving
> secure instructions for believers by which an easy passage back to their
> homeland was restored.

But as Stefania continued to draw from the next section of the bull, some alteration was necessary as Gregory's bull began to discuss the specifics of Elizabeth's life:

Gregory:

Huiusmodi quidem pietatis seriem beata Elisabeth ex regali orta progenie et Thiringie lancravia gratiosa sollerti meditatione **considerans**

et iam dicta eligens instituta continius observare studiis, **ut dignam perceptione se** redderet **perpetue claritatis, quasi** *ab ortu vite usque ad occasum* [Ps. 49:1] **virtutum vacando cultui, numquam desiit in caritatis amplexibus delectari. Nam in confessione vere fidei menteque dedita sanctitati, celestis regine diligendo filium, per quem dulcedinem** consequi **posset celestium nuptiarum. Ita dilexit et proximum quod** amenum **sibi constituens** illorum **familiarem habere presentiam,** quam eorum inimica corruptio cunctis, suggerit effici peregrinam, se in multis sibi **reddidit inopem sollicitam fore pauperibus multipliciter affluentem**; quorum ab etate tenera tutrix esse desiderans et amatrix, **eo quod sciret perempnis vite premium dilectorum Deo acquiri meritis egenorum. Adeo conditionem ipsorum gratam sibi constituit, quam** naturaliter secularis **elatio vilipendit, quod etiam licitis sibi deliciis,** quas offerebat status excellentia coniugalis, deduc-

Stefania:

Huiusmodi quidem[24] pietatis seriem **considerans** virtutum emicans Margarita, que ex Columpnensium illustri prosapia genita, illustrioribus miraculis insignita, non solum penatibus, sed patrie indidit claritatem. **Et iam predicta eligens instituta continuis observare studiis, ut dignam perceptione se** traderet **perpetue claritatis, quasi** *ab ortu usque ad occasum* [Ps. 49:1] **virtutum vacando cultui, numquam desiit in caritatis amplexibus delectari. Nam in confessione vere fidei menteque dedita sanctitati, celestis regine filium diligendo, per quem dulcedinem posset** capescere **celestium nuptiarum. Ita dilexit et proximum quod** amenam **sibi constituens** pauperum **familiarem habere presentiam,**

eo quod sciret perempnis vite premium dilectorum Deo acquiri meritis egenorum. Adeo conditionem ipsorum gratam sibi constituit, quam naturalis elatio vilipendit, quod etiam licitis sibi delitiis se redidit inopem, sollicitam fore pauperibus multipliciter affluentem.

tis pluries in contemptum **corpus delicatum et tenerum reddebat assidue parsimonie studio** maceratum, **tanto sibi meriti quantitate proficiens, quanto quod sponte geritur maioris gratie premio muneratur. Quid ultra?**[23]

Et deducto mundo muliebri continue in contemptu **corpus delicatum et tenerum reddidit assidue parsimonie studio** laceratum, **tanto sibi meriti quantitate proficiens, quanto quod sponte geritur, maioris gratie premio muneratur. Quid ultra?**[25]

Stefania's text reads as follows:

> Giving thought therefore to the course of virtues of such piety, the sparkling Margherita, born to the renowned lineage of the Colonna, distinguished by even more renowned miracles, bestowed fame not only on her family but also on her country. She chose to follow the above mentioned teachings, with unremitting effort, in order to render herself worthy of the notice of eternal fame, as though *from the rising of the sun to the setting thereof.* Abandoning herself to the cultivation of virtues, she never ceased to find delight in the embraces of pure love, with a mind devoted to sanctity in profession of the true faith and by loving the Son of the Queen of Heaven, with whom she would be able to achieve the sweetness of a heavenly marriage. And she *loved* her *neighbor* so much that she established a household comprised of the poor, because she understood that the reward of eternal life comes from God through worthy service to the beloved poor. She held so dear their condition, which pride normally despises, that indulging her pleasure there she made herself penniless, abundantly and in many ways concerned for the poor. Withdrawn from the world of women that she held in contempt, she continuously beat down her delicately tender body by frugal self-denial, advancing so much in the scope of her merit that the more of it was of her own free will, the greater she was rewarded in grace. What more?

The details of Elizabeth's birth and family are of course altered to fit Margherita's case, and all reference to Elizabeth's marriage is omitted, since Margherita had never entered the married state. In small but interesting changes, the poverty of Margherita's spiritual family is emphasized, as are her miracles and her saving example to other women.

Thus, it is apparent that Stefania, searching out a model for a lay woman pursuing a life of poverty and charity in the world, hit upon the classic thirteenth-century example of this mode of life. Elizabeth of Hungary's canonization made her an ideal template for this kind of potentially controversial female sanctity outside a nunnery. By so heavily reusing the actual canonization bull for Elizabeth, Stefania was in a sense audaciously "pre-canonizing" her subject, simply attributing to her all of the praise that Gregory IX had heaped on this royal saint.

At this point, after a brief passage noting Giovanni Colonna's early attempt to arrange Margherita's marriage, Stefania suddenly begins to borrow heavily from another text, a letter "To G., a Nun" by the twelfth-century bishop Arnulf of Lisieux.

Arnulf:

... **dum illi sibi de humano coniugio nova amicitiarum federa compromittunt, et grata proventure sobolis pignora contemplantur, et humane quidem cogitationes ad humanos libere disponuntur affectus; sed omnis est inanis affectio, cui non** desideratos **divina bonitas largitur effectus. Dum enim thalamus illi nuptialis et coniugalis puelle maritales** destinantur **amplexus, quam nobilitas** generis, **quam forme gratia, quam denique** virginalis **commendabat** integritas, **divina** sepulchrum illi **dispositio preparabat, ut de flore iuventutis** in pulverem, de gloria pulchritudinis **et virtutis** in putredinem solveretur. **Felix** tu, **que corporales** aliquando sperasti **lascive voluptatis illecebras, quam ab eiusdemodi contactu zelus divine bonitatis conservavit intactam, ut, munere** tibi **perpetue virginitatis indulto,** *agnum* sequi *quocunque ierit* **[Apoc. 14:4],** et spirituale illud *canticum* possis **cum** assignatis milibus decantare. **Non ergo** tibi sublata sunt **sed** immutata

Stefania:

... **dum illi sibi de humano coniugio** amicitiarum federa compromittunt, congrata proventure sobolis pignora contemplantur, et humane quidem cogitationes ad humanos libere disponuntur affectus; sed omnis inanis est affectio, cui non divina bonitas largitur effectum. Dum enim** ille proconsul **nuptialem thalamum et coniugalis puelle maritales** concupiscit amplexus, **quam nobilitas, quam forme gratia, quam denique** virginitas **commendabat, divina** celibatum radianti Margarite **dispositio preparabat, ut** florem iuventutis conservaret in gloriam **pulcritudinis et virtutis.** Felix tamen ipsa, **que corporalis** superavit **lascivie et voluptatis illecebras, quam ab huiusmodi contactu celus divine bonitatis conservavit intactam, ut,** sibi **munere perpetue virginitatis indulto,** *agnum* sequi *quocumque ierit* **[Apoc. 14:4],** et novum illud *canticum* possit **cum** ceteris virginibus **decantare** [Apoc. 14:3]. **Non ergo** sibi **sublata** fuere, **sed** mutata

sponsalia, ut iam non homini sed
Deo spirituali copula coniungaris,
cuius desiderabilis te foveat et astrin-
gat amplexus, ut sit *leva eius sub
capite* tuo et *dextera* eius amplexetur
te [Song of Sol. 2:6].

sponsalia, ut iam non homini sed
Deo spirituali copula coniu[n]gatur,
cuius desiderabilis eam fovet et
astringit amplexus, ut sit *leva eius
sub capite* suo *et* eam *illius dextera
amplexetur* [Song of Sol. 2:6].

Stefania's text reads as follows:

> And while the men were drawing up the marriage agreements, mutu-
> ally pledging the amicable bonds that come from intermarriage, and
> looking to the guarantees of welcome future offspring, their human
> minds freely arranged these human affairs. But any such arrangement
> is in vain if divine goodness does not bring it about. For while that
> proconsul lusted for the marriage bed and for the conjugal embraces of
> that nubile girl whose high birth, striking beauty, and virginity so rec-
> ommended her, a heavenly arrangement was preparing celibacy for the
> glowing Margherita to preserve the flower of her youth in the glory of
> beauty and virtue. Happy is she whom heaven by the exercise of such
> blessed goodness preserves untouched, who rises above the wanton
> enticement of lust and pleasure so that, bolstered by the gift of eternal
> virginity, she may *follow the Lamb wherever he goes* and sing out that
> *new song* with the other virgins! Therefore the marriage vows were not
> forced upon her, but altered so that now she should be wed not to a man
> but in spiritual union to God, whose longed for embrace clasps and
> enfolds her so that *his left hand is under* her *head and his right hand
> embraces* her.

Besides changing second-person verbs into third-person ones, the main
shift is that the original text had addressed a woman who had been expecting
marriage, whereas Stefania now writes to describe a woman who had fled mat-
rimony. Thus, she changes the exhortation in her source text into claims about
actual behavior and attitude.

Stefania begins at this point at last to insert some of her own language into
the chapter (largely concerning Giacomo Colonna), but she concludes with a
few brief praises again drawn from Cassian.

Cassian:

... **tanta districtione omni aevo suo propositum** solitudinis **custodivit, ut nihil de praeteritae humilitatis tenore laxaverit** aut **de adiecto sibi honore blanditus** sit . . . [26]

Stefania:

... **tanta districtione omni evo suo** bonitatis integerrime illibatum **propositum custodivit, ut** numquam sibi fuerit **de adiecto honore blanditus et nichil de preterite humilitatis tenore laxaverit** quoquomodo.[27]

Stefania's text reads as follows:

> (Giacomo) . . . preserved the undiminished principle of most solid goodness throughout his life, so that he was never flattered by any rank that had accrued to him, and never abandoned in any way the humble character of his past.

Stefania's chapter 3 is then, for the most part, her original recollection of a conversation with Margherita concerning the propriety of fasting. But again, as though to punctuate the point, she returns to a direct use of Gregory IX's 1235 canonization bull for St. Elizabeth of Hungary.

Gregory:

O felix mulier, o matrona mirabilis, **o dulcis** Elisabeth dicta Dei saturitas, **que pro refectione pauperum** panem **meruit angelorum. O inclita** vidua **virtutum fecunda sobole, que studens ex** gratia **consequi,** quod a natura non peterat indulgeri, diris **anime** hostibus *per scutum fidei, loricam justitie, gladium spiritus, salutis galeam* [Eph. 6:16, 14, 17], **et astam perseverantie** debellatis . . .

Stefania:

O felix mulier, o dulcis Margarita, **que pro refectione pauperum** partem **meruit angelorum. O inclita** virgo, **virtutum fecunda sobole, que studens ex** gratiarum virtutibus **consequi** tante fortitudinis potestatem, ut diros hostes **anime** per *scutum fidei, loricam iustitie, gladium spiritus, salutis galeam* [Eph. 6:16, 14, 17], **et astam perseverantie** debellaret.[28]

Stefania's text reads as follows:

> Oh, happy woman! Oh sweet Margherita, who earned the angels' share for nourishing the poor! Oh famous virgin, fertile in virtues by lineage, who sought to attain the power of such courage from the virtues of grace

in order to conquer the formidable enemies of the soul with the *shield of faith*, the *breastplate of justice*, the *sword of the spirit*, *helmet of salvation*, and the spear of perseverance!

Again all references to marriage have been deleted, with "widow" changed to "virgin" as necessary.

Chapters 4 and 5 are Stefania's original work, with chapter 5 offering a particularly important account of one of Margherita's visions. But after this crucial moment, Stefania evidently again wished to draw her moral with gushing language fit for a saint and here made her most daring move. For chapter 6 is nothing other than a long passage drawn directly from Gregory IX's 1228 bull *Mira circa nos*, canonizing Francis of Assisi.

Gregory IX:

Mira circa nos **divinae pietatis dignatio, et inaestimabilis dilectio charitatis, qua filium pro servo tradit redimendo,** dona **suae miserationis non deserens, et vineam dextera ejus plantatam continua protectione conservans, in illam, qui salubriter ipsam excolant, evellentes sarculo, ac vomere,** quo Samgar sexcentos Philisthaeos percussit, **spinas et tribulos** [Heb. 6:8] **ex eadem. Operarios etiam in undicema hora transmittit, ut superfluitate palmitum resecata, et vitulaminibus spuriis radices altas non dantibus** [Wisd. 4:3], **necnon sentibus extirpatis, fructum suavem afferat, et jucundum; qui praelo patientiae defaecatus in aeternitatis cellarium transferatur: impietate profecto velut igne, succensa, et frigescente charitate multorum in ejusdem maceriam diruendam, irruentibus Philisthaeis potione terenae cadentibus volutatis.**

Stefania:

Mira circa humanum genus **divine pietatis** operatio et **inestimabilis dignatio caritatis, qua filium pro servo tradidit redimendo,** bona **sue miserationis non deserens et vineam**[30] **dextera eius plantatam** tam **continua protectione conservans, in illam** introducens **qui salubriter ipsam excolant sarculo ac vomere evellentes** *spinas* et *tribulos* [Heb. 6:8] **ex eadem. Operarios etiam in undecima hora transmittit, ut superfluitate palmitum resecata, et vitulaminibus spuriis** *radices altas non* **dantibus** [Wisd. 4:3] **necnon sentibus exstirpatis, fructum suavem afferant et iocundum, qui prelo patientie defecatus in eternitatis cellarium transferatur. Frigescente caritate multorum ac inpietate profecta, velud igni succensa, in eiusque maceriam diruendam irruentibus Philisteis, potione terrene cadentibus voluptatis.**

Ecce in hora undecima Dominus, qui cum diluvii aqua terram deleret, justum per lignum contemptibilem gubernavit; *super sortem justorum virgam* **peccantium** *non* **relinquens** [Ps. 124:3]**, excitavit** servum suum beatum Franciscum virum utique **secundum cor suum,** apud cogitationes divitum **lampadem quidem** contemptam, sed **paratam ad tempus statutum illam in vineam suam mittens** [Matt. 20:2]**, ut ex ipsa spinas, et vepres evelleret,** prostratis illam impugnantibus Philisthaeis, illuminando patriam et reconciliaret Deo exhortatione sedula commonendo.[29]

Ecce in hora undecima Dominus, qui cum per diluvii aquam terram deleret, *super sortem iustorum virgam* **peccantium** *non* **relinquens** [Ps. 124:3] **excitavit** mulierem **secundum cor suum,** fulgidam Margaritam, **lampadem quidem paratam tempore statuto** lucescere, repletam oleo sanctitatis. **Illam in vineam suam mittens** [Matt. 20:2]**, ut ex ipsa spinas et vepres evelleret**.et, **prostratis illam impugnantibus Philisteis, illuminando patriam et reconciliari Deo exhortatione sedula commonendo.**[31]

Stefania's text reads as follows:

> O wondrous working of divine piety for the human race! How boundless the worth of His love, by which He has given over His Son to redeem a slave! Not abandoning the good things of His mercy, and protecting with continual care the vineyard *which* His *right hand has planted*, He sends those to cultivate it healthfully with hoe and plowshare, rooting out the *thorns and briars*. Even *at the eleventh hour* He sends workers so that when the overgrowth has been cut back and the weak-rooted weeds and the thistles have been pulled up, they may gather the sweet and pleasant fruit. This fruit, when purged by the winepress of suffering, may be taken to the storehouse of eternity, even while the *charity of many grows cold* and impiety proceeds as though lit by fire, and the Philistines, overcome with the drink of earthly pleasure, rush in to demolish the garden wall. But behold! *At the eleventh hour,* God, who was destroying the earth with the water of the flood, *not leaving the rod of sinners upon the lot of the just,* raised up a woman *according to His own heart*, the resplendent Margherita. Indeed, she was a beacon made to shine forth at the appointed time, replete with the oil of holiness, sent *into His vineyard* to pluck up the thorns and nettles and, with the attacking Philistines laid low, to

reconcile people to God by illuminating our homeland and warning with earnest entreaty.

Whereas Elizabeth of Hungary seems a logical model for Margherita's pious life of poverty in the world, Francis of Assisi was a more surprising choice. If Stefania had wanted to draw on praise for a Franciscan saint, one might have expected her to choose the recently canonized Clare of Assisi. Of course, there the challenge would have been adapting Clare's professed and enclosed life to Margherita's circumstances. But in any case, this was not Stefania's preference. Instead, she looked directly to the founder of the Fratres minores and the thirteenth century's greatest model of apostolic simplicity. For Stefania, Margherita was, in a certain sense, an extension of Francis's model of sanctity.

Chapters 7 and 8 return to Stefania's prose, describing scenes as Margarita's death approached. Chapter 9 again utilizes a lengthy, wholesale borrowing from Elizabeth of Hungary's canonization bull to provide a conclusion.

Gregory IX:

Queque iura sanguinis in superne desiderium transferens voluptatis et imperfectum quid extimans, si iam viri destituta presidio sic residuum vite decurreret, quod se **ad iugum obedientie, cuius sub lege posita** maritali absque ipsius preiudicio amplexatrix extiterat, non artaret, **religionis habitum induit, sub quo dominice passionis in se celebrare misterium usque in diem ultimum non omisit ...**
sic amabilem immortali sponso se prebuit, sic regine virginum se dilectione continua colligavit suum deprimendo dominium in ancille humilis famulatum, sic sanctis Elisabeth **antique processibus conformem se reddidit, dum *in mandatis et iustificationibus Domini sine querela*** [Luke 1:6] sim-

Stefania:

Igitur Margarita **queque iura sanguinis in superne desiderium transferens voluptatis,** sic **ad iugum obedientie, cuius sub lege posita** se astrinxit, quod beatissime Clare **religionis habitum induit, sub quo dominice passionis in se celebrare misterium usque in diem ultimum non ommisit.**

Sic amabilem inmortalis sponso se prebuit, sic regine virginum se dilectione continua colligavit suum deprimendo dominium in anchille humilis famulatum, sic sanctis Margarite **antique processibus conformem se reddidit, dum *in mandatis et iustificationibus Domini sine querela*** [Luke 1:6] simpliciter ambulavit, Dei gratiam secreto mentis per affectum concipiens et eandem per effectum pariens ac nutriens assidue per profectum, quod salus *omnium in se sperantium* [Ps. 17:31] et exaltatio quorumlibet in humilitatis et innocentie vallibus positorum in promisse suis premia retributionis exurgens, ipsam mortis nexibus expeditam provexit ad solium luce inaccessibili luminosum de cuius stupenda et inexplicabili claritate procedit, quod illius spiritus et in superni fulgori abysso rutilat et in huius profundo caliginis multis coruscat miraculis gloriosis, quorum virtute catholicis fidei, spei et caritatis augmenta proveniunt, perfidis via veritatis exponitur et hereticis confusionis multe materia cumulatur, dum stuporis turbine obvoluti, quod dicte sancte meritis, que dum carnis clausa carcere teneretur, pauper spiritu, mitis mente, propria vel potius aliena peccata deplorans, *iustitiam sitiens* [Matt. 5:6], misericordie dedita, munda corde, vere pacifica, attrita persecutionibus et obprobriis extitit lacessita, vita mortuis, lumen cecis, auditus surdis, verbum mutis et gressus claudis celesti amplexibus cernunt multipliciter exultare.

De huiusmodi quidem et aliis eiusdem sancte miraculis . . . nos . . . dictam sanctam . . . sanctorum cathalogo ducimus ascribendam . . .

pliciter ambulavit, Dei gratiam secreto mentis per affectum concipiens et eandem[33] per effectum[34] pariens et nutriens assidue per profectum, quod salus *omnium in se sperantium* [Ps. 17:31] et ex alto quorumlibet in humilitatis et innocentie vallibus positorum in promisse suis premia retributionis exurgens, ipsam mortis nexibus expeditam provexit ad solum luce inaccessibili luminosum, de cuius stupenda et inexplicabili claritate procedit, quod spiritus eius et in superni fulgoris abbisso rutilat et in huius profundo caliginis multis corruscat miraculis gloriosis, quorum virtute catholicis fidei, spei et caritatis augmenta proveniunt, perfidis via veritatis exponitur et hereticis confusionis multa materia cumulatur, dum stuporis turbine obvoluti,[35] quod dicte Margarite miracula perhorrescunt. Que dum carnis clausa carcere teneretur, pauper spiritu, mitis mente, propria, vel potius aliena, peccata deplorans, *iustitiam sitiens* [Matt. 5:6] misericordie dedita, munda corde, vere pacifica, accepta persecutoribus, si persecutionum gladius affuisset, et lividi femoris, causa ulceris iugi cruciamine sauciata, sicut agna patiens *os suum non aperuit* ad lamentum [Isa. 53:7]. De huius quidem miraculis quandam materiam[36] huiusmodi semotim et breviter scriptitabo. Fuit itaque penultimo decembris mortis

quatinus XIII kal. **decembr**. die
videlicet, quo eadem **mortis
absoluta vinculis victura perempt-
niter ad fotenm superne prodiit
voluptatis**.[32]

**vinculis absoluta, victura
perempniter ad fontem superne
prodiit voluptatis**.[37]

Stefania's text reads as follows:

> Therefore Margherita, turning the rights of blood lineage into a longing
> for heavenly joy, bound herself to the yoke of obedience under whose law
> she was placed, because she put on the religious habit of the most blessed
> Clare, in which she unfailingly pursued the mystery of the Lord's passion
> until her final day. Thus she made herself beloved to her immortal Spouse;
> thus she bound herself in continual delight to the Queen of Virgins by
> reducing her noble status to that of a household servant; thus she attuned
> herself to the holy progress of the earlier Margherita while she walked
> plainly *in the commands and justifications of the Lord without blame*.
> Through her passion, in the depths of her mind, she received the grace of
> God. And she demonstrated this grace in her accomplishments and nour-
> ished it in her progress, because it is the salvation *of all that trust in Him*
> and from on high it urges onward, to the rewards of retribution promised
> to His own, all those placed in the lowly valleys of innocence. Freed from
> the coils of death, this grace carried her to that sole place illuminated by
> an unreachable light, by whose amazing and inscrutable brightness her
> spirit glows in the depth of heavenly splendor and flashes forth with many
> glorious miracles in the deep of this darkness. These miracles by their
> virtue bring forth an increase of love and hope to true believers; and the
> way of truth is set out for the faithless, and much is heaped up to confound
> heretics while they spin in a numbing whirlwind due to their dread of
> Margherita's miracles. While still shut in this prison of the flesh, she was
> truly *poor in spirit, meek* in mind, weeping over her sins, or rather, the
> sins of others, *thirsting after justice*, given to *mercy, clean of heart*, truly a
> *peacemaker*, suffering from *persecutors*, if the sword of persecutors had
> been there, wounded by the torment caused by the unending ulcer of her
> livid thigh, like a long suffering ewe who *would not open* her *mouth* in
> lamentation. I will now set out in writing briefly and separately some of
> her miracles. For on the next to last day of December she was released
> from the bonds of death and went to the source of heavenly joy.

Again, Stefania has altered passages that refer to Elizabeth's marriage. The passage in which Elizabeth exchanged the "yoke of obedience" to a husband for a religious habit is now clevery reworded to portray Margherita taking on a "yoke of obedience" by adopting the religious habit of "the most blessed Clare." The passage simultaneously serves to emphasize Margherita's quasi-religious status and humble obedience, even though in fact she never took the vows of a nun. In addition, descriptions of persecutions suffered by Elizabeth of Hungary are replaced by a specific account of the painful ulcer that afflicted Margherita's leg. Thus, this last physical detail can probably be taken as Stefania's attempt at a real depiction of Margherita's physical ailment.

The rest of Stefania's text is much less derivative. Six brief miracles follow as chapters 10 through 15, and chapters 16 through 18 then add three visions in which Margherita after her death appears to Stefania herself, to Brother Bartholomeo of Gallicano, and to one of Margherita's biological sisters. Chapter 19 is really just a summary praise of Margherita and Cardinal Giacomo Colonna. In chapter 20, however, Stefania offers a prayer for "the intercession of lady Margherita," which is in fact largely a repetition of a prayer attributed (in a Vatican manuscript) to Abbot Odilo of Cluny (ca. 962–1048):

Odilo of Cluny:

Domine Ihu Xpe, lux vera, qui illuminas omnem hominem venientem in hunc mundum, **illumina** quaeso **caecitatem cordis mei** per **fidem rectam, spem** certam, **caritatem** perfectam **et reliquas virtutes per quas** intelligam te **amare et timere,** et tua **praecepta** servare; et **cum mihi extrema dies advenerit, angeli pacis me sucipiant, et de potestate** diaboli **eripiant, ut merear** in **sanctorum** tuorum **consortio beata requie perfuit et ad dexteram** tuam **collocari.**

Stefania:

Oro igitur ut intercessionibus domine Margarite, **mei cordis** Dominus **illuminet cecitatem,** accendat in me ignem amoris sui, donet mihi **fidem rectam, spem** ad superna tendentem et **caritatem** non fictam, **et reliquas virtutes per quas** eum **amem et timeam,** et eius **precepta** custodiam, ut **cum mihi extrema dies** finisque vite **advenerint,** emundatam delictis omnibus, **angeli pacis me sucipiant et de potestate eripiant** tenebrarum, **ut merear sanctorum** suorum **consortio** in **beata requie perfuit, et ad** suam **dexteram collocari.**[38]

Stefania's text reads as follows:

> I pray therefore that, through the intercession of lady Margherita, the Lord may illuminate the blindness of my heart; kindle in me the fire of His love; give to me the true faith, hope aspiring to heaven and *unfeigned charity*, and all the other virtues by which I may love and fear Him; and that I may keep his commandments so that when my last day and the end of my life come to me, the angels of peace may take me up, cleansed of all sin, and pull me out of the power of darkness so that I may deserve to enjoy the company of his saints in blessed rest and be placed at his right hand.

The concluding section of Stefania's *Statement* (chs. 21–31) is in fact quite original. A story dated April 1280 may well have been told to Stefania by Giovanni or Giacomo Colonna (chap. 21), and a brief vision experienced by Margherita (chap. 22) precedes a final retelling (chaps. 23–31) of Margherita's death from Stefania's eyewitness perspective (with a posthumous miracle rather awkwardly inserted as chapter 25).

Conclusions

This essay has used a close textual demonstration of Stefania's borrowings to shed fresh light on the way she composed and compiled her *New Statement on Margherita Colonna's Perfection of the Virtues*. Identifying these borrowings shows that some seemingly specific labels, such as "president" (and "anchoresses"), are lifted directly from much earlier sources and so cannot be taken at face value here. But showing where Stefania's own original prose shines through her borrowings also helps highlight the importance of passages in which she really was making a historical claim specific to the thirteenth century. Moreover, reading this text with a better grasp of Stefania's reuse of sources explains the seemingly uneven nature of her Latin prose. Some of her flowery imagery and complex syntax results from these borrowings; but at the same time, Stefania's ability to manipulate her sources demonstrates a level of Latin competence that should dissuade us from disparaging her as merely a plagiarist. In fact, there is some danger that the present analysis could foster the mistaken impression that there is nothing new in Stefania's text. To the contrary, many of the long, involved visions experienced by Stefania or reported to her are strikingly original and certainly deserve to be closely studied by scholars interested in the "unquiet souls" of the later Middle Ages. And in the light of her substantial textual borrowings, it is worth noting that Stefania does not reuse material from Giovanni Colonna's "First Life" of Margherita. Where she treats scenes from Margherita's life that had already been written about by Giovanni, she always provides her own perspective, often adding to and not infrequently contradicting some aspect of the first vita.[39]

Whereas this essay has thus tried to present new answers to several specific textual questions, the analysis here also raises some puzzling interpretive issues that await future research. One such question might concern the textual resources at Stefania's disposal. After Margherita Colonna's followers took over San Silvestro in Capite in 1285, did they gain access to a library left behind by the departing Benedictines? The resources of such a library might explain, for instance, Stefania's heavy use of the well-known text by Cassian, and perhaps the references to (pseudo) Odo and Odilo of Cluny, and to Arnulf of Lisieux's letter.[40] To my knowledge, however, there has been no study of books owned by San Silvestro, before or after 1285.

And what of Stefania's substantial reliance on the papal bulls canonizing Francis of Assisi and Elizabeth of Hungary? Might these texts perhaps have been supplied by a churchman such as Giacomo Colonna? Beyond the exact means by which Stefania gained access to these papal bulls, there is the question of how to understand her own intentions in reusing them so audaciously. Could she have thought that this borrowing would have slipped by undetected? If so, perhaps her calculation was not unfounded, given that twentieth-century scholars (including the very learned Franciscan Oliger!) did not pick it up. But surely in the 1280s one would have had to assume that reusing long passages from the bull canonizing Francis of Assisi, the iconic saint of the thirteenth century, would not pass unnoticed. In that case, did Stefania think it was simply a cagey authorial strategy to so overtly proclaim Margherita a "new saint Elizabeth" and a "new saint Francis"? And should any significance be attached to the fact that she apparently made no use of the corresponding bull of canonization (1255) for Clare of Assisi? These questions only grow in interest if one envisions Stefania writing for an imagined papal audience in the context of an envisioned canonization hearing for Margherita. Surely, in that case, Stefania would have known that simply reusing such texts would not be acceptable to the curia. So might this interpretation in turn imply that Stefania in fact saw her texts only as "internal" reading for San Silvestro and the Colonna clan? Questions such as these remain to be investigated. In sum, though I hope to have exposed the main sources of Stefania's fascinating text, there is still a great deal to be said about its significance.

NOTES

1. Thirteenth-century female-authored texts about contemporary saintly women (that is, texts about women the author had actually known, not about martyr-saints from the deep Christian past) include the Franciscan abbess Agnes of Harcourt's *Life of Isabelle of France* (ca. 1283) and the Franciscan-inspired beguine prioress Felipa of Porcelet's *Life of Douceline of Digne* (ca. 1297). If one includes the first decade of the fourteenth century, the *Life of Beatrice of Ornacieux* by the Carthusian prioress Marguerite of Oignt and the life of Gertrude of Helfta written by a fellow Benedictine nun (after 1302) can be added. For readily accessible translations, see Sean L. Field, *The Writings of Agnes of Harcourt: The Life of Isabelle of France and the Letter on Louis IX and Longchamp* (Notre Dame: University of Notre Dame Press, 2003); Kathleen Garay and Madeleine Jeay, trans., *The Life of St. Douceline, a Beguine of Provence* (Cambridge: D. S. Brewer, 2001); Renate Blumenfeld-Kosinski, trans., *The Writings of Margaret of Oingt: Medieval Prioress and Mystic* (Newburyport, Mass.: Focus, 1990); and Alexandra Barratt, ed., *Gertrude the Great of Helfta: The Herald of God's Loving-Kindness: Books One and Two* (Kalamazoo, Mich.: Cistercian, 1991), 37–95. Gertrude's *Life* is actually inserted as book 1 of her *Legatus divinae pietatis*. For study of the vernacular texts, see Sean L. Field, "Agnes of Harcourt, Felipa of Porcelet, and Marguerite of Oingt: Women Writing about Women at the End of the Thirteenth Century," *Church History* 76 (2007): 298–329.

2. Richard Kieckhefer, *Unquiet Souls: Fourteenth-Century Saints and Their Religious Milieu* (Chicago: University of Chicago Press, 1984).

3. Livario Oliger, ed., *B. Margherita Colonna († 1280): Le due vite scritte dal fratello Giovanni Colonna senatore di Roma e da Stefania monaca di S. Silvestro in Capite* (Rome: Facultas Theologica Pontificii Athenaei Seminarii Romani, 1935). This edition has recently been reprinted, with a facing-page Italian translation, in Attilio Cadderi, O.F.M., trans., *Beata Margherita Colonna (1255–1280): Le due vite scritte dal fratello Giovanni, senatore di Roma e da Stefania, monaca di San Silvestro in Capite*, ed. Celeste Fornari and Luigi Borzi (Palestrina [s.n.], 2010). Cadderi and his team did not, however, notice the borrowings detailed in the present study.

4. The most widely cited twentieth-century study has been Giulia Barone, "Margherita Colonna e le Clarisse di S. Silvestro in Capite," in *Roma: Anno 1300; Atti della IV Settimana di Studi di storia dell'arte medievale dell'Università di Roma "La Sapienza" (19–24 maggio 1980)*, ed. Angiola Maria Romanini (Rome: L'Erma di Bretschneider, 1983), 799–805. See also Barone, "Le due vite di Margherita Colonna," in *Esperienza religiosa e scritture femminili tra medioevo ed età moderna*, ed. Marilena Modica (Acrireale: Bonnano, 1992), 25–32, and Barone, "Margherita Colonna," in *Mein Herz schmiltzt wie Eis am Feuer: Die religiöse Frauenbewegung des Mittelalters in Porträts*, ed. Johannes Thiele (Stuttgart: Kreuz Verlag, 1988), 136–45; the latter essay has now been translated by Larry F. Field as "Margherita Colonna: A Portrait," *Magistra* 21, no. 2 (2015): 81–91. Robert Brentano used Margherita as a key example in his delightful *Rome Before Avignon: A Social History of Thirteenth-Century Rome* (1974; repr., Berkeley: University of California Press, 1990), and more recent contributions include Federica Voci, "La guérison du corps malade dans les miracles post mortem de Margherita Colonna," *Arzanà: Cahiers de littérature médiévale italienne* 18 (2016), at https://arzana.revues.org/959; Bianca Lopez, "Between Court and Cloister: The Life and Lives of Margherita Colonna," *Church History* 82 (2013): 554–75; Emily E. Graham, "The Patronage of the Spiritual Franciscans: The Roles of the Orsini and Colonna Cardinals, Key Lay Patrons and Their Patronage Networks" (Ph.D. diss., University of St. Andrews, 2009); and Lezlie S. Knox, *Creating Clare of Assisi: Female Franciscan Identities in Later Medieval Italy* (Leiden: Brill, 2008), 108–13.

5. I first identified these borrowings while Larry F. Field, Lezlie S. Knox, and I were preparing English translations of Margherita Colonna's vitae and related texts, published now as *Visions of Sainthood in Medieval Rome: The Lives of Margherita Colonna by Giovanni Colonna and Stefania* (Notre Dame, Ind.: University of Notre Dame Press, 2017) (hereafter, *Visions of*

Sainthood). The notes and introduction to that translation thus point out Stefania's borrowings in general terms but without being able to detail them specifically or to fully explore their implications.

6. For starting points on the Colonna family, see Sandro Carocci, *Baroni di Roma. Dominazioni signorili e lignaggi aristocratici nel duecento e nel primo trecento* (Rome: École française de Rome, 1993), 353–69; and Andreas Rehberg, *Kirche und Macht im römischen Trecento: Die Colonna und ihre Klientel auf dem kurialen Pfründenmarkt (1278–1378)* (Tübingen: Max Niemeyer Verlag, 1999).

7. Sean L. Field, *The Rules of Isabelle of France: An English Translation with Introductory Study*, additional documents trans. Larry F. Field (St. Bonaventure, N.Y.: Franciscan Institute Publications, 2014).

8. Honorius IV, *Ascendit fumus aromatum*, September 24, 1285, edited in *Bullarium franciscanum*, vol. 3, 544–46; translated in *Visions of Sainthood*, 145–50. For overviews on San Silvestro in Capite, see Eileen Kane, *The Church of San Silvestro in Capite in Rome* (Genoa: Edizioni d'Arte Marconi, 2005); and J. S. Gaynor and I. Toesca, *S. Silvestro in Capite* (Rome: Marietti, 1963).

9. The translation of Margherita's relics is known only from the early sixteenth-century account in Mariano of Florence, *Libro delle degnità et excellentie del Ordine della seraphica madre delle povere donne Sancta Chiara da Asisi*, ed. Giovanni Boccali (Florence: Edizioni Studi Francescani, 1986), 235–37, and translated in *Visions of Sainthood*, 202–4.

10. Michael Petschenig and Gottfried Freuz, eds., *Cassiani opera, Collationes 24*, 2nd ed., CSEL 13 (Vienna: Verlag der Österreichischen Akademie der Wissenschaften, 2004), 311. English translation in John Cassian, *The Conferences*, trans. Boniface Ramsey (New York: Newman Press, 1997), 399.

11. Though it is also sometimes difficult to know whether a change such as "*luminaria*" to "*iubaria*" was deliberate or the result of scribal error.

12. One could, of course, hypothesize that Stefania was indeed serving as president and that she thus seized on this passage precisely because it included the participle *praesidens*. This interpretation, however, seems unlikely.

13. Vincenzo Federici, "Regesto del monastero di S. Silvestro de Capite," *Archivio della Società romana di storia patria* 23 (1900): 67–128, 411–47, at 418–23. For a partial list of abbesses up to 1400, see Étienne Hubert, "Économie de la propriété immobilière: Les établissements religieux et leurs patrimonies au XIVᵉ siècle," in *Rome aux XIIIᵉ et XIVᵉ siècles: Cinq études*, ed. Étienne Hubert (Rome: École française de Rome 1993), 177–229, at 188 n. 36.

14. See, for example, chap. 28 (Oliger, *Due vite*, 217–18; *Visions of Sainthood*, 186–87), where Stefania convinces Giacomo Colonna to get some rest after three days at his sister's sickbed.

15. André Salmon, ed., "De reversione beati Martini a Burgundia tractatus," in *Supplément au chroniques de Touraine* (Tours: Guilland-Verger, 1856), 14–34.

16. Salmon, "De reversione beati Martini," 16–17.

17. MS "fecunda."

18. MS "hos."

19. MS "mox."

20. MS "dento."

21. Oliger, *Due vite*, 190–91; *Visions of Sainthood*, 157–58.

22. Oliger, *Due vite*, 192; *Visions of Sainthood*, 158–59.

23. Leo Santifaller, "Zur Originalüberlieferung der Heiligsprechungsurkunde der Landgräfin Elisabeth von Thüringen vom Jahre 1235," in *Acht Jahrhunderte Deutscher Orden in Einzeldarstellungen* (Bad Godesberg: Wissenchaftliches Archiv, 1967), 79–80.

24. MS "quidam."

25. Oliger, *Due vite*, 192–93; *Visions of Sainthood*, 159–60.

26. Petschenig and Freuz, *Cassiani opera, Collationes 24*, 314–15.

27. Oliger, *Due vite*, 194; *Visions of Sainthood*, 162.

28. Oliger, *Due vite*, 196; *Visions of Sainthood*, 163.

29. *Mira circa nos* (July 19, 1228), printed in *Bullarium franciscanum*, vol. 1, 42–44. English translation in Regis J. Armstrong, J. A. Wayne Hellmann, and William J. Short, *Francis of Assisi: Early Documents* (New York: New City Press, 1999), vol. 1, 565.

30. Oliger mistakenly read "unicam."

31. Oliger, *Due vite*, 198–99; *Visions of Sainthood*, 165–66.

32. Santifaller, "Zur Originalüberlieferung der Heiligsprechungsurkunde," 80.

33. ms "eundem."

34. ms "affectum."

35. ms "obveluti."

36. ms "quedam materia."

37. Oliger, *Due vite*, 201–2; *Visions of Sainthood*, 168–69.

38. Oliger, *Due vite*, 210–11; *Visions of Sainthood*, 180.

39. On the subject of rewriting saints' lives in general, see Monique Goullet, *Écriture et réécriture hagiographiques: Essai sur les réécritures de Vies de saints dans l'Occident latin médiéval (VIIIᵉ–XIIIᵉ s.)* (Turnhout: Brepols, 2005); and Goullet and Martin Heinzelmann, *La réécriture hagiographique dans l'occident médiéval: Transformations formelles et idéologiques* (Stuttgart: Jan Thorbecke Verlag, 2003).

40. Anne Clark presented new research on the transmission history of this letter, including Stefania's use of it, in "From Anonymity to a New Identity: A Twelfth-Century Letter to a Nun and Its Hagiographic Afterlife," paper presented at the International Medieval Congress, Leeds, July 7, 2016.

Part 2 | CONFLICTS OVER THE HOLY

3

MATERIALIZING CONFLICT:
HOW PARISH COMMUNITIES REMEMBER THEIR MEDIEVAL PASTS

Kristi Woodward Bain

During the second year of my Ph.D. program, I spent a good deal of time searching for the perfect case study around which to frame my burgeoning dissertation proposal on late medieval community identity and memory. While looking through Richard's vast collection of church guidebooks, I came upon a fascinating story: in 1409, the prior of an English Benedictine monastery in Wymondham, Norfolk, petitioned the king for assistance against the parishioners with whom he and his monks shared a church.[1] He reported that a group of parishioners had attacked him, harassed his monks, and destroyed monastic property in reaction to blocked access to the parish belfry. The prior defended his act, claiming that the monastery's bells had called the parishioners to worship from "time out of mind."[2] Even so, by 1411 the parishioners emerged victorious, having received light punishment for their actions and, a few decades later, permission to build their own bell tower that was free from monastic control. Particularly fascinating is not just the medieval dispute itself, but also that it has become part of the parish community's collective memory. Moreover, the original documentary record became the touchstone for the adjudication of later and sometimes very different disagreements in the last two centuries.

Inspired by Richard's remarkable study of past and present ideologies and uses of church architecture in *Theology in Stone*, this study takes seriously an English community's memorialization of medieval parish conflict.[3] Through an archival and ethnographic examination of the church, its history, and its historians, it becomes clear that both the conflict and its documentation have been subjected to complex forces of forgetting and remembering through the Middle Ages and beyond. Its memory was particularly strong in the nineteenth century, when Wymondham's antiquarians shaped the town's medieval history and archives, forging twentieth- and twenty-first-century perspectives on the medieval conflict and present parish identity. Thus, this study examines the parish church physically and conceptually, both in its architectural transformations and in its ever-changing meanings—as a space that can adapt to new needs and can link today's parishioners with their medieval counterparts. Ultimately, this is a story of a parish community's search for a more stable corporate identity and a story that sheds light on the ambiguous and mercurial relationship between history and memory.

The Fifteenth-Century Conflict

Wymondham has a rich historiography thanks to its wealth of surviving medieval, early modern, and antiquarian records. The earliest record of Wymondham's parish church comes from documents referring to the foundation of the monastery by Lord William de Albani (d'Aubigny) in 1107. He dedicated the Benedictine priory to St. Mary and endowed it with the town's parish church, along with its tithes, revenues, land, tenants, and the right to appoint the priest.[4] Endowing a monastery with the tithes of parish churches was common practice; what was not as common was the construction of the monastery on the site of the parish church and requiring the two communities to share the new one. Although some clarification from the pope was needed in the 1240s concerning episcopal oversight of the shared church, outright conflict was not evident until the monastery began a rebuilding project that included the demolition of the Norman central tower in 1376 and the final construction in 1409 of the octagonal central tower that remains today.[5] Most invasive to the parish church was the monks' temporary transfer of the abbey bells to the parishioners' northwest tower. After moving their bells into the priory's new tower, they blocked the parishioners' access to the northwest tower and the bells therein. The churchwardens and parishioners responded by hanging three bells in a temporary tower above the north porch and then boarded up the doors that provided entry to the monks for the collection of offerings.

We also know from the prior's petitions to royal courts that several parishioners in the summer of 1409 attacked the prior and convent by stealing his cattle, cutting down trees in the churchyard, and ultimately forcing the prior into hiding in his chambers, ostensibly in reaction to blocked access to the parish church bells.[6] Twenty-four parishioners are regularly named in documents addressing the conflict. The recurrence of several names—William Growt, Thomas Boteler, and Robert Kempe—suggests sustained organization on the parishioners' part.[7] Demonstrating the significance of the conflict beyond the confines of the town was Archbishop Thomas Arundel's admonition to the parishioners in 1410, as well as the arrival of a commission comprising Norfolk nobles and the sheriff in 1411 to settle the dispute.[8] Parishioners issued a petition at some point during these proceedings: they asserted that the short stature of their tower made it difficult to hear the bells, resulting in missed services and unbaptized children.[9] After two years of litigation, the archbishop confirmed that parishioners had the right to hang bells in the northwest tower provided that their ringing did not disturb the monks.[10] Several years later, in 1445, with the support of patrons Sir John Clifton and Sir Andrew Ogard, the prior surrendered the land for the project that would produce the west tower, which continues to hold the parish church's bells today.[11] Soon after, in 1448, the priory became its own independent abbey until its dissolution during the English Reformation.[12]

The conflict at Wymondham reveals two primary catalysts for monastic-parochial disputes: access to the shared space, including for collection of tithes and offerings, and control over bells.[13] Regarding bells in particular, not only were they the primary method of calling parishioners to Mass, but they were also important signs of status for both parish and monastery. It was not unusual for villages to compete with each other over the height of their bell towers or for parishes in urban regions to fight over bell-ringing rights. More generally, monks and parishioners came into conflict over unclear delineations of space, both in terms of their obligations to that space and their use of it. Shared churches arose out of church reform movements of the eleventh and twelfth centuries when the papacy began to revoke the nobility's proprietary rights over the parish church and other sacred foundations.[14] Not only did reform popes and other clergy demand an end to what is known as "lay investiture"—when the laity granted spiritual and political power to clerics—but they also demanded that the laity rescind their rights over various religious establishments they had founded. Consequently, parish churches had become political and spiritual liabilities for the nobility, who responded by transferring most of their patronage rights to monastic institutions that then appropriated these churches, their tithes, and their land. In most cases, monasteries would oversee their appropriated parish churches from afar, but one study points out that possibly two hundred or more English parish churches were attached to the monasteries that had appropriated them, giving the prior or abbot the right to appoint the vicar of the parish church.[15] These deeds of transfer required caution because the Council of Westminster (1102) had decreed that only bishops could transfer parish churches to monasteries.[16] As wealthy laity gradually gave up rights over monastic foundations and parish churches, monasteries began to profit significantly from their control over the land and tithes that came with appropriation. Also, since monastic institutions were exempt from episcopal jurisdiction, priors and abbots had unregulated control over their appropriated parish churches, which prompted new canonical decrees by the end of the twelfth century that barred monks from serving parish churches. Gradually we see perpetual vicarages, taken on by secular clergy not associated with the governing monastery, established in these shared parish churches. This move would ensure that local parishioners' spiritual needs were regularly met and also allowed for episcopal rather than monastic oversight in parish matters.[17] But the very need for such decrees, as well as the conflicts that concern this study, reveal how fraught this relationship between monasteries and parish churches was by the late Middle Ages, whether or not they shared a physical space.

Wymondham's Antiquarians and Crafting Local History

There are many ways Wymondham's medieval disputes could be historically contextualized—within the frameworks of anticlericalism, economic and political conflicts of interest, or changes in lay responsibilities for the parish church. Wymondham's nineteenth- and twentieth-century antiquarians took none of these approaches. Instead, they recalled these disputes when they were in the midst of restoring the church building to its medieval glory, with implied and sometimes explicit goals of linking the current parish community to its medieval roots. The prolific Wymondham antiquarian E. B. Pomeroy, solicitor by profession as well as devoted churchwarden, played a key role in connecting his parish community's history to its contemporary identity. In particular, Pomeroy was a leader in planning what is known today as the church's Great Restoration, which began shortly after his death in 1902. Especially remarkable are his notes scribbled on a few scraps of paper for a lecture on the restoration of the west tower, the very tower the medieval parishioners built after their disputes with the monks. Pomeroy's story begins in the thirteenth century, which he describes as a time dominated by the monks' efforts to usurp control of the shared church while ignoring the laity's customary rights, which laid the groundwork for a "history of arrogant claims by the monks and stout resistance by the vicar and parishioners."[18] He described the fifteenth-century disputes as "open warfare" and asserted that the parishioners' victory was inevitable, not least because the archbishop supported their cause. It was especially important to Pomeroy that the parishioners desired to build a tower "worthy of the edifice"—the tower Pomeroy was pleading to restore—which not only would hold more bells but would also equal and even surpass the beauty of the monks' new octagonal tower.

Pomeroy's primary goal was not so much to educate parishioners about their past as to make it relevant to the present, to make medieval parishioners' efforts relatable and laudable in order to elicit an emotional response from the congregation. The medieval conflict over the bell tower was an enthusiastic, collective effort, he explained, one that garnered support "from all the classes of the inhabitants and their neighbors, and numerous legacies were left . . . by the religiously disposed towards the erection of . . . the bell tower."[19] This was a wistful memory of medieval collectivity, which Pomeroy longed to see in the actions of his own parish community:

> Such an undertaking could not be carried out at all, in our day, without extraordinary efforts and rare benevolence. We have no unpaid cleric to act as architect, materials nowadays are not given for nothing to the Glory of God, and workmen who find, in the sanctity of their work, a sufficient substitute for any wages beyond those necessary to a bare sub-sistence, do not exist . . . it would be sad to reflect on, if such a work of our forefathers were to be allowed to go to ruin for the sake of a little over £100.[20]

This story serves to remind the community that the church "belongs to the parish, and it is for the parish to provide the means" to preserve and restore the fifteenth-century edifice their ancestors fought so hard to build.[21]

It is clear from this lecture that Pomeroy's interest in the medieval conflicts was driven by both the urgent need to repair the late medieval tower as well as the desire to return to what he thought was ideal churchmanship. Other regional antiquarians found Wymondham's medieval conflicts important because they shed light on the church's architectural history. Keen interest in the church's archaeological, architectural, and historical record especially became prominent when the churchyard was extended in 1833 to landscape the monastic ruins and improve the view of the church from the south. Antiquar-ians undertook studies of the graves that were discovered at the site of the monastic choir, produced sketches of the monastery's layout based on their archaeological findings at the work site, and produced scrapbooks that detailed their excavations and discoveries.[22] Later antiquarians used these archaeologi-cal details to further explore the history behind the monastery's medieval architecture. For instance, Norfolk antiquarian Henry Harrod claimed that the "miserable squabbles" of the fifteenth century would "not interest anyone at all" if it were not for the influence they had on the existing architecture.[23] He used these "squabbles" to confirm the existence of at least one northwest tower prior to the conflicts and also to establish the date of the existing west tower. He further used the legal documents that arose from the conflict to correct errors about the church's history found in Francis Blomefield's well-known multivolume work on the county of Norfolk.[24] Despite a few observations that the monks were to blame for these conflicts, Harrod was more interested in how the conflict created and informed the church's fabric than in nostalgically remembering the event itself.

Ninian Comper (1864–1960), a nationally renowned architect responsible for the church's elaborate altar screen, relied on these architectural histories to inform his plans for the chancel's renovation. Writing in 1913 about his design proposal, he suggested that it would be architecturally appealing for an arch and a great window to be added to the east end, with the altar placed under the tower between the old arch and the new one.[25] However, Comper complained that these alterations were not approved because parishioners and local antiquarians protested the removal of the late medieval east wall that represented "the long history of quarrels between parish and monks," referring to the wall that was more likely erected as part of the monks' fourteenth-century construction of the central tower.[26] Comper was openly frustrated by this opposition, claiming that parishioners should emulate their medieval predecessors' enthusiasm for good architecture and remove the wall that prevented a new and more beautiful chancel. Local objections to Comper's design suggest that E. B. Pomeroy's interpretation of the medieval conflicts, especially his valorization of parishioners' actions, had become the accepted and authoritative narrative in Wymondham.[27] For example, one essay by Pomeroy insists that the east wall was constructed by parishioners to block the monks from "open infringement of their rights" over the church.[28] A later essay by his son J. B. Pomeroy, written a decade later, explains, "from the middle of the fourteenth century until 1921, that blank wall remained to remind many generations of parishioners of their ancient squabbles between monks and townspeople."[29] Particularly important to the latter Pomeroy was the gradual division of parish and monastery throughout the Middle Ages, resulting in two entirely separate churches existing underneath one roof after the fifteenth-century conflict (fig. 3.1).[30] Thus, the east wall's imagined role in the medieval conflict made it worthy of preservation, even if it was rather dull and impractical in Comper's eyes.

Nostalgia and Local Histories of Church and Conflict

Figuring prominently in these and other English antiquarian sources is an evocation of nostalgia for the medieval past in order to create a palpable link

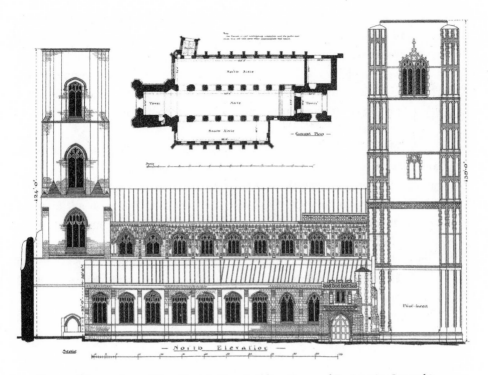

Fig. 3.1 Wymondham Abbey Church Plan. *Building News and Engineering Journal* 87
(1904): 294–97.

between the medieval and contemporary parish church. Nostalgia is a problematic topic for scholars because of its pejorative connotation as an ahistorical
or flawed understanding of the past, but scholars of medieval cultural studies
have reconsidered its role in the formation of modern *medievalism*, which
refers to an anachronistic adoption of presumed medieval ideals, values, and
practices. Linda Austin's literary analysis of nineteenth-century medievalism
concludes that the nostalgia of English antiquarianism is not merely naïve and
simplistic but a deliberate technique to elicit an affective response to the medieval past, embedding it in the primary rather than secondary memory.[31] In
other words, nineteenth-century antiquarians and novelists attempted to provoke a deep, emotional connection to medieval England by remembering the
distant past as part of their own experiences rather than indirectly. *Affect*,
therefore, is a memory strategy that "helps to make the past continuous with
the present."[32] Such a technique is certainly present in Pomeroy's lecture. His
reflection on the preservation and fundraising efforts of Wymondham's late
medieval parishioners was not a simple history lesson but brought the past
parish community into the present. It was intended to give meaning to the

fabric of the church, to ensure that this relationship between the parish community and its church was not forgotten and, even more important, that it was
kept in practice. Pomeroy and local historians and parishioners following in
his footsteps sought to create a collective memory that was also a connective
memory, one that inspired the individual to understand his or her relationship
with the history of the parish community and church and to *remember* how to
act as a member of this community.[33]

Recognizing endeavors to reconnect a religious community with its past is
Danièle Hervieu-Léger's study, *Religion as a Chain of Memory*, which claims
that while modernity rejects the notion of any real continuity between past and
present, religious communities persist in their efforts to maintain it.[34] Similarly, many narratives of Wymondham's parish history encourage parishioners to see themselves as part of a religious lineage and to maintain that link
by remembering their collective past. In particular, parish guidebooks, aptly
named because they guide visitors through the history and architecture of
the church, function as guides for remembering the traditions believed to be
the glue holding parish communities together since their inception. But to
forge a strong collective memory, certain cultural symbols must be created,
maintained, and sustained.[35] As we have seen, Wymondham's conflict is a
powerful symbol that has influenced how subsequent parishioners have understood their history.[36] Local histories written well after Pomeroy strive to
maintain links with past traditions and identities through remembering the
achievements of their medieval counterparts. Wymondham's 850th anniversary
guidebook, for instance, memorializes the late medieval conflict by ridiculing
the monks and casting the parishioners as champions of their church. The
author, who was also vicar at the time, emphasizes that the monks "did all they
could to usurp the rights of the parishioners and annoy them," especially by
erecting a new tower that blocked parishioners' "clear view through a majestic
archway."[37] Instead, they "were confronted with a mass of solid masonry, bleak
and ugly in the extreme," a reference to the east wall that Comper sought to
remove.[38]

Therefore, the fabric of the Wymondham's parish church has served not
only as a catalyst for conflict but also as an anchor for later remembrances of
the conflict.[39] Local antiquarians such as Pomeroy relied on the original medieval spaces of the parish church to elicit affective nostalgia, equating contemporary parishioners' experience of their parish church with firsthand experience
of the medieval past. An awareness of the memories and emotions that the
church building can evoke was part of a larger Victorian trend in church architecture—that churches were meant to be read and experienced and to convey
the past.[40] Proponents of this architectural ideology were inspired by the 1830s

Oxford (Tractarians) and Cambridge (Ecclesiologists) Movements, the former seeking to revive Catholic doctrine within the Church of England, and the latter advocating for a Catholic revival in architecture and liturgy.[41] Both Tractarians and Ecclesiologists wanted congregations and visitors to truly feel and experience the space of parish churches, which resulted in large-scale restorations of medieval architecture and the reinstitution of liturgical and processional practices to remind people of the medieval past they imagined. Thus, for Wymondham's nineteenth- and twentieth-century historians, not only were the physical building and its spatial layout of interest, but they were also the "hook" for drawing parishioners' and visitors' attention to the fifteenth-century parish community and its fight with the monks. Indeed, if the medieval past is not continuous in the community's actual memories, it is undeniably continuous with the fabric of the church, and nineteenth-century local historians brought this continuity to the fore. As one local historian has written recently, the "shell" of the church, despite centuries of transformations, has remained constant.[42]

With this context in mind, we can see and experience more acutely the church as nineteenth-century local historians wanted us to experience it. Upon entering the church from the north porch, one encounters an extraordinarily wide aisle, also known as the "people's aisle," which was constructed soon after the fifteenth-century conflict was resolved. Walking from north to south one sees an interesting distinction—both the parishioners' aisle and the nave are adorned with lavish hammerbeam roofs, the nave being a remarkable example of a medieval angel roof, whereas the south aisle that once would have connected the church to the monastic buildings is rather plain and was used until recently as a makeshift vestry.[43] The ruined east tower has been left in its post-Dissolution state, a monument to the monastic past rather than an integral part of today's use of the church. Meanwhile, the laity's west tower, built in the 1460s, stands tall and is well-maintained and regularly used by the parish church's bell ringers. The spatial cues are subtle but distinctive—the church today has preserved, maintained, and made most presentable the fabric in which the late medieval parishioners had invested. Only recently, as part of the church's Heritage Lottery–funded capital works and heritage interpretation activities, has there been a renewed interest in making the east tower more accessible and in providing interpretation for the ruined monastery.[44]

These physical and ideological distinctions between parish and monastic space were especially striking when I was visiting in 2011 and had the opportunity to observe tours offered to visitors. The steward began his tour in the north aisle, then moved to the nave, emphasizing the medieval parishioners' role in paying for their expansion and embellishments in the fifteenth century. He then brought visitors before the chancel, pointing not only to its magnificent Comper screen but also to the east wall that was the focus of so much scrutiny in the nineteenth century. The tour offered the same story told by the Pomeroys—the wall was the dénouement of medieval parishioners' persistent efforts to gain independence from the monks who, according to the steward, kept taking parish offerings.[45] Even though local historians today know that it is more likely that the wall was built initially as part of the fourteenth-century construction of the central tower, they still emphasize the wall's importance in the history of the parishioners' struggles for the church, carrying into the twenty-first century the antiquarian narrative that "the division between monks and people was, literally, set in stone."[46] From antiquarian essays to modern tours of the church, the medieval conflict signposts the space of the church, helping visitors and parishioners see and understand the space of the building according to the accepted narrative. Seen within this framework, a wall becomes a lasting vestige of medieval ideologies, and the scattered ruins on the south and east sides of the church recall a powerful monastery that was humbled by the parishioners who loved their church and that was then destroyed in the wake of the sixteenth-century English Reformation.

Shaping the Archives, Shaping Meaning

In addition to the ways antiquarians have shaped the history of Wymondham Abbey, it is also significant just how influential they have been in shaping the archives, through designing the space as well as cataloguing and controlling access to the church's documents. The muniment room was created in 1916 by then-vicar Martin Jones to ensure the safekeeping of the documents that had been scattered among various churchwardens or were haphazardly collected in the parish chest. It then took another eighty years for several hundred boxes of documents, which had for generations been stored by solicitors at Pomeroy and Sons, to be discovered and returned to the church.[47] Pierre Nora notes that the archive is the most common form of modern memory, and Jones's creation of the muniment room coincides with a time when, Nora argues, historians feared that history and memory were "on the verge of disappearing, coupled with anxiety about the precise significance of the present and uncertainty about the future."[48] Boxes upon boxes of antiquarian papers, which sought to reconstruct both the structure and ideology of their medieval church, corroborate Nora's argument. As Pomeroy's writings implied in the discussion above, without a documented history, the meaning, the very essence of the church, would be entirely forgotten.

The physical space through which one moves to access the muniment room is significant. Researchers enter through the north door into the "people's aisle," then climb the winding stone steps to the top of the north porch, which provides a physical and historical context for reading the documents. Moreover, the local influence on the creation of these archives, organized thematically or according to local antiquarian, subtly shapes how researchers approach and read the medieval and modern documents held in this room. In particular, most of the medieval documents for the parish are classed as conflict or legal documents, signaling the fifteenth-century dispute's historical importance. Paul Cattermole, archivist and local historian from 1992 until his death in 2009, spent the better part of a decade reorganizing the entire muniment room so that it would be more accessible to academic researchers. In a 2001 lecture to the Friends of Wymondham Abbey, Cattermole expressed a sentiment shared by many local historians in Wymondham—that to move these documents out of the church would strip them of their particular meaning. Cattermole remarked, "archivists are grumpy when they have to come here, but then when they see the Abbey, they realize it is the right place to read these documents."[49]

This sentiment was echoed during my first research visit in 2010. As I was sorting through the box of conflict records, a young curate entered the room along with a grantwriter, whom he was hoping the church would hire to raise money for the archives. His idea was to reignite interest in the church's history so that parishioners would offer donations to update the archives as well as move them downstairs where they would be more accessible. He also thought the room as it stood could seem intimidating for inexperienced researchers. However, as the archivist explained later, it would take a lot of coaxing to convince Wymondham residents to move documents out of the muniment room.[50] Like Cattermole, locals believe that the documents are safer in the church; moving them to the Norfolk Record Office would be especially detrimental because it is too far away (about ten miles) and could take several years to catalogue and make publically available. More important, the parishioners who insist on retaining their church's documents want to ensure that we read them correctly, and that we understand their history in terms of the space that produced and was produced by that history. In this context, these documents are just as much part of the church as its fabric and furnishings. In their recent Heritage Lottery Fund bid,[51] churchwardens and heritage consultants emphasized the significance of the archives for educating the community about their religious and civic past. Once funding was secured, a permanent exhibition was installed, featuring original documents as well as interpretive materials to guide visitors in how to understand and experience the church. Accordingly, the abbey itself *is* the exhibition and becomes something much more than a building—it is a place that connects people to their past.

Competing Meanings, Competing Interests

Just as space is not fixed in function or meaning, neither are the ways in which people relate to their church's history and architecture. Indeed, the varied visions of today's English parish churches stem from a combination of local nostalgia, community piety, and national heritage initiatives. This final section takes an ethnographic approach to explore how the parish church still serves as a site of memory for Wymondham's locals. As we shall see, affective nostalgia is subtler in modern perceptions of the past than in antiquarian writings. Interviews with leaders in the parish revealed a sense of duty to ensure that people remember the importance of their church building and its community. It emerged that whereas some parishioners are skeptical of the importance of the medieval disputes, others believe that they are integral to the history of their parish church building. Recall the church tour discussed above, which highlighted the fifteenth-century riots and the east wall that has been assumed to be a result of those riots. That tour was one of many that I observed and in which I participated, and particularly revealing in all of them was how the conflict has come to influence not just the interpretation of the building but also how many in the community perceive their historical and present identity. In another tour, the steward explained that Wymondham folks have always been a "stroppy lot," beginning with their bold defiance of the monks in the Middle Ages and continuing with the post-Reformation rebellion against the Crown by the Kett family. Even the recent protests at the city council over a new construction project in town were, in her mind, a continuation of medieval parishioners' recalcitrance.[52]

Conversely, Paul Cattermole expressed qualms about such emphasis on the medieval conflicts. In a 2007 collection of essays on the abbey, he wrote that the late medieval dispute had been given too much attention, arguing that "despite occasional flash-points, the monks and townsmen of Wymondham understood that mutual cooperation was beneficial since the two communities were interdependent."[53] Certainly, records reveal a reciprocal relationship, through which the parish relied on the priory's supervision and the priory depended on parishioners' offerings and services. However, Cattermole's assessment is no more confirmed by the limited medieval sources defining this relationship than those conclusions that assert the importance of the conflict. What sources we do have reveal that this interdependence was exactly what ignited the disputes in the first place. But what Cattermole was trying to temper is any implicit or explicit approval of the parishioners' violent actions, and his essays pointedly differentiate between appropriate forms of conflict and unreasonable ones.[54] Moreover, he had little reason to contextualize the church building through the medieval conflict—his motives were not to raise funds or to emphasize the parishioners' pious, albeit violent, actions on behalf of the church. He mentioned more than once in his lecture to the Friends that he was interested in social history and had little to say about the religious motivations of medieval parishioners. As for the fabric of the parish church, he saw no continuity. In the same lecture, he quipped, "Have we got a medieval roof in the Abbey? I don't know." By Cattermole's calculations, about 75 percent of the figures supporting the nave and north aisle roofs are replicas.[55] Historic preservation and social history were important to Cattermole, but not preservation or promotion of any continuity with the medieval past or religious tradition.

Parishioners not directly associated with the archives but active in preserving the church's heritage have also weighed in on the fifteenth-century conflicts. One such parishioner, who is also a museum professional, local historian, and former churchwarden, agrees with Cattermole that local historians have exaggerated the medieval conflicts. He maintains that the relationship between the medieval monastery and the parish church and town is integral to their heritage but that the conflicts were rare and have overshadowed the otherwise harmonious relations between the two communities. He is similarly concerned about the ways earlier histories of the church have emphasized the "rupture" of the Dissolution. He explains that we do not know at all how their medieval ancestors felt about the removal of the monks from their church, and the abbot at the time "not only received a very generous pension but went on to be a notable Protestant preacher."[56] Such comments are in reaction to Anglo-Catholic leanings in Wymondham's antiquarian writings as well as Anglo-Catholic clergy who have served the parish church on and off since the nineteenth century, which have in turn skewed the community's understanding of their church's and community's history.[57] Related to these concerns is the parishioner's frustration that the church is still called an abbey, which he believes obfuscates the subtle divisions between the medieval parish church and monastery. Continued reference to the church as an abbey underscores the complicated relationship today's parishioners have had with their church—defeating the monks is a source of pride, but so is their building's distinction as a former abbey church.

Especially important about the competing meanings assigned to the turbulent medieval history of Wymondham's parish church is that not all locals and parishioners, in any time or place, value their churches solely for devotional reasons. If anything, they take for granted the importance of the parish church, insisting on its centrality to national and local heritage but unable to articulate precisley why this is important. For instance, a well-known English architectural historian writing on the function of the church in England today makes a claim that has become a truism—that "the image of the country church . . . is deeply ingrained in our appreciation of the texture of Britain. Whether we use them or not, we would certainly miss them if they were not there."[58] Wymondham's archivist said much the same to me when I was researching there in May 2012. Preserving the historical documents and the very fabric of the church is not just for the sake of religion but for the sake of the community. She stressed that communities have grown up with their medieval parish church and that it has been so ingrained in their upbringing that even if some do not consider themselves to be believers, the building, along with the music and ceremonies that have taken place within it, has shaped the lives of those living nearby. The closure of a parish church would be a terrible loss, especially for the townspeople who have grown up around it, and this helps explain why so many—both believers and nonbelievers—are willing to raise money for Wymondham Abbey's restoration and continued maintenance.[59]

The 2010 National Churches Trust survey states that more than half of the members of Friends' Groups throughout the U.K. are not active in the parish church to which they donate. Indeed, over a third of the members of the Friends of Wymondham Abbey live outside of the parish.[60] This membership suggests that church buildings have an important function in the United Kingdom well beyond a religious one, specifically in terms of enriching national life, maintaining local identity, and preserving the country's historic environment.[61] Further, along with the National Churches Trust, most of England's national heritage bodies, as well as the Church of England, insist that parish church buildings are both community hubs and places of worship. This juxtaposition of the secular and religious in parish life is by no means new—the medieval parish was both a legal and religious entity, and the parish church itself was used for religious and secular activities.[62] But these dual functions do not necessarily have an easy relationship on the ground. The committee that has overseen Wymondham Abbey's £1.75 million grant from the Heritage Lottery Fund has been charged with developing and implementing a learning program that can balance religious and secular education. In order to meet funding criteria, they must offer a well-rounded education program that does not entail church history alone but also includes national science and math curricula, supported by original documents stored in the muniment room. At the same time, the committee has insisted that the religious function of the parish church should remain foremost in the minds of fundraisers, visitors, and the community at large. The heritage consultants insisted during the application stage that all historical interpretation should eventually lead visitors and the community to see that the abbey's primary function is worship.[63] If people leave without realizing this, one consultant explained, the committee has failed in its task.[64] Parishioners and consultants also debated over a proposed sculpture to memorialize the fifteenth-century conflicts. In the design, parishioners and monks wrestle a model of the abbey, held aloft across the rho of the Chi-Rho symbol dividing the two groups. On the left, the parishioners grasp their west tower, and the monks grasp their east tower on the right (fig. 3.2). The conflict is further represented in the fault line that runs through the stem of the rho. In the explanatory notes, the designers envisioned the sculpture as representing the history behind the Abbey's "unique" appearance. From the bell conflict in the fifteenth century to the "final fissure" of the Dissolution, the sculpture's depiction of the at first collaborative, then fractious, relationship between the parishioners and monks demonstrates the designers' perception that conflict is the defining feature in the history and fabric of the present church. However, the churchwardens and other parishioners on the project committee were uncomfortable with the content and the cost. When disagreement arose over this depiction of the medieval conflict, with the design concept ultimately being scrapped, it is easy to buy into the local characterization of Wymondham parishioners being a "stroppy lot."

These applications of the medieval past to present circumstances are particularly important because they reveal that nostalgia in Wymondham's local narratives has been not just *affective* but also *effective*. As demonstrated above, local historians writing in the late nineteenth or early twentieth centuries used the medieval disputes to appeal to parishioners' pious sensibilities when they sought to restore the church to its late medieval glory. Using similar affective strategies, parishioners have effectively drawn national attention to this rural church's historical value. And while today's parishioners have different motivations than their medieval counterparts for restoring their church, the medieval conflicts have nonetheless inspired interest in its history and preservation. More to the point, these conflicts have provided a usable past for Wymondham's locals who are trying to encourage the rest of the community to invest in their town and church building.

Moreover, to observe a community's creation of a usable past requires some exploration of the academic's role in complicating these narratives. Exploring a church's history among those who are highly invested in it has allowed me to observe Wymondham's parish community—their practices as well as their

Fig. 3.2   Wymondham Abbey sculpture proposal. Simon Hill / Chris Kelly; copyright 2014 © JANVS Design (www.janvs.com).

relationships to the space of the church and its history—from the vantage point of their historical documents and as a participant who is likewise keeping the historical narrative alive. Whether or not we medievalists are aware of this role, when we enter a church for the purposes of observing its medieval space, we cannot help but encounter a living, breathing, active parish church and community, one whose everyday practices and experiences influence how we understand and encounter its medieval past. Apropos is Robert Orsi's study *Between Heaven and Earth*, in which he explains that scholars of religion explore "a network of relationships between heaven and earth involving humans of all ages and many different sacred figures together."[65] In the process, we become entangled in the networks of past and present through regular interactions with parishioners and their church's history, and we inhabit this religious environment in palpable ways.[66] When working in the muniment room at the abbey, I researched to the sounds of children singing in the morning as well as the organ playing for an afternoon funeral. I once spent two hours wandering the aisles of the church with the chief steward as he narrated its history in great detail and later managed to convince the master ringer that I was up to the task of climbing the fifteenth-century west bell tower. And four years after I had first visited the abbey for research, I was invited to advise on new interpretation boards about the church's history as well as speak to the Friends of Wymondham Abbey about the medieval conflict. In researching the ways historians and parishioners have shaped Wymondham's history, I quite unintentionally became a part of that process.

Conclusion

This study began with the goal of exploring the relationship between Wymondham's parishioners today and the late medieval conflicts that have played a role in giving meaning to the space in which they congregate. Many historians of Wymondham—whether they have been antiquarians, dedicated parishioners, or enthusiastic vicars—have infused these conflicts with religious meanings, whereas some have viewed these conflicts as stories to generate interest in joining or funding their church. And although the medieval documents that record these conflicts reveal that social and economic motivations are just as responsible for these disputes as religious ones, these more prosaic causes do not disaffirm the connection that Wymondham's historians and parishioners throughout the centuries have forged with their medieval ancestors. Let me be clear: I am not arguing for a notion of a continuous, unbroken line of medieval practice in Wymondham's parish community, for to do so is untenable. But, as I hope this study has shown, it is equally untenable to argue that parishioners have no relationship with their past, imagined or concrete. Amid these negotiations of continuity and context, parishioner and outsider, academic and local historian, there exists a common ground—the space of the parish church. In this space, past and present conceptions of religious and secular practice intersect imaginatively and in reality. Religion as lived in the parish church is not fossilized in liturgy or stones but is kept in motion by parishioners who maintain and also transform the practices of their church in accordance with varying needs through the ages.

NOTES

1. The archival research and fieldwork forming the basis for this study was undertaken in 2012/13 and made possible by generous funding from the Schallek Fellowship, awarded by the Medieval Academy of America and the Richard III Society (American Branch).

2. Wymondham Parish Church, U.K. (hereafter WPC), 9/2/1.

3. Richard Kieckhefer, *Theology in Stone: Church Architecture from Byzantium to Berkeley* (Oxford: Oxford University Press, 2004).

4. Wymondham was a priory from 1107 through 1448 and then an abbey from 1448 until its dissolution in 1538 (see note 12). Although it is no longer a functioning abbey, parishioners have continued to refer to it as the Abbey.

5. WPC 9/2/1 and WPC 9/2/2. Original papal bull dated 10 Kalends July (June 22) 1249, transcribed in Martin Jones, *Wymondham and Its Abbey* (Wymondham: H. G. Stone, 1914; repr. 1946), 50; Francis Blomefield, *An Essay Towards the Topographical History of the Country of Norfolk*, vol. 1 (London: W. Bulmer, 1805).

6. WPC 9/1/5. See also The National Archives, U.K. (hereafter TNA), KB 9.82.

7. Archbishop's admonition, WPC 9/1/3; See also WPC 9/1/2, 9/1/5, TNA KB 9.82, and C1.69.146.

8. WPC 9/1/2 and 9/1/3.

9. WPC 9/1/1.

10. WPC 9/1/2; WPC 9/1/3; WPC 9/1/4; WPC 9/1/6.

11. WPC 9/1/6.

12. Henry VIII declared himself the supreme head of the Church in 1534, breaking with the pope and the Roman Catholic Church. Two years later he enacted the Dissolution of the Monasteries and sent his deputies to appropriate all monastic property and dismantle their communities and buildings. Wymondham Abbey was dissolved in 1538.

13. Specifically, the case studies of my dissertation, "From Community Conflict to Collective Memory: Lived Religion and the Late Medieval Parish Church," include four disputes with male Benedictine houses in Norfolk, Essex, Dorset, and Lincolnshire, respectively, and two with female monastic houses in Dorset and Hampshire. Many of these case studies are noted in Martin Heale's article, "Monastic-Parochial Churches in Late Medieval England," in *The Parish in Late Medieval England: Proceedings from the 2002 Harlaxton Symposium*, vol. 14, ed. Clive Burgess and Eamon Duffy (Donington: Shaun Tyas, 2006), 54–77. For case studies of parish bell conflicts, see Katherine French, "Competing for Space: Medieval Religious Conflict in the Monastic-Parochial Church at Dunster," *Journal of Medieval and Early Modern Studies* 27, no. 2 (Spring 1997): 216–44; Norman Tanner, *The Church in Late Medieval Norwich 1370–1532* (Toronto: Pontifical Institute of Medieval Studies, 1984); and Daniel Thiery, *Polluting the Sacred: Violence, Faith and the "Civilizing" of Parishioners in Late Medieval England* (Leiden: Brill, 2009), esp. 67–68. For an analysis of the importance of bells in the shift from religious to secular time, see J. Le Goff, "Merchant's Time and the Church's Time in the Middle Ages," in *Time, Word, and Culture in the Middle Ages*, trans. A. Goldhammer (Chicago: University of Chicago Press, 1980), 29–42. For a general history of bells in the medieval West, see John H. Arnold and Caroline Goodson, "Resounding Community: The History and Meaning of Medieval Church Bells," *Viator* 43, no. 1 (2012): 99–130; and for a study of the relationship between bells and community identity, see Alain Corbin, *Village Bells: Sound and Meaning in the Nineteenth-Century French Countryside*, trans. Martin Thom (New York: Columbia University Press, 1998).

14. B. R. Kemp, "Monastic Possession of Parish Churches in England in the Twelfth Century," *Journal of Ecclesiastical History* 31, no. 2 (April 1980): 133–60. See also Susan Wood, *The Proprietary Church in the Medieval West* (Oxford: Oxford University Press, 2006). G. H. Cook notes the monasteries that usually possessed parish churches were Augustinian canons and Benedictine monks and nuns, whereas Cistercians and Carthusians were usually adverse to such arrangements because of their desire to withdraw from the outside world. See *The English Mediaeval Parish Church* (London: Phoenix House, 1954). Proprietary rights were also known as the "right of advowson."

15. Heale, "Monastic-Parochial Churches," 54–77.

16. Kemp, "Monastic Possession," 137.

17. Ibid., 146–47.

18. WPC 16/4/4, 3.

19. WPC 16/4/4, 7.

20. WPC 16/4/4, 7–8.

21. WPC 16/4/4, 9.

22. Paul Cattermole, ed., *Wymondham Abbey: A History of the Monastery and Parish Church* (Wymondham, U.K.: Wymondham Abbey Book Committee, 2007), 12–16.

23. WPC 16/7/10: Henry Harrod, "Some Particulars relating to the History of the Abbey Church of Wymondham in Norfolk," presented May 6, 1869.

24. See note 5.

25. WPC 3/4/7/1: Ninian Comper, "1913: Wymondham Church."

26. WPC 3/4/1.

27. WPC 16/7/10: E. B. Pomeroy, "Wymondham Church: Notes connected with the History of the Building," in *Wymondham Parish Church Magazine*, circa late nineteenth or early twentieth century.

28. WPC 16/7/10, 5–6.

29. WPC 16/7/10.

30. WPC 16/7/10.

31. Linda M. Austin, "The Nostalgic Moment and the Sense of History," *Postmedieval: A Journal of Medieval Cultural Studies* 2 (2011): 127–40.

32. Ibid., 138.

33. These notions of collective and connective memory come from a chapter entitled "Remembering in Order to Belong: Writing, Memory, and Identity," in *Religion and Cultural Memory: Ten Studies*, ed. Jan Assmann (Stanford: Stanford University Press, 2006), 81–100.

34. Danièle Hervieu-Léger, *Religion as a Chain of Memory*, trans. Simon Lee (New Brunswick, N.J.: Rutgers University Press, 2000), 123.

35. See David Gross, *Lost Time: On Remembering and Forgetting in Late Modern Culture* (Amherst: University of Massachusetts Press, 2000).

36. See ibid. and Angelika Rauch, *The Hieroglyph of Tradition: Freud, Benjamin, Gadamer, Novalis, Kant* (London: Associated University Presses, 2000).

37. Rev. J. G. Tansley Thomas, *The Abbey Church of St. Mary and St. Thomas Canterbury: A History and Guide Published to Mark the 850th Anniversary of its Foundation in 1107 by William D'Albini, Earl of Arundel* (Wymondham, U.K.: Souvenir Guidebook, 1960), 5–6.

38. Ibid., 5–6.

39. It was, in the words of Pierre Nora, the key site in a community's *lieux de mémoire*. See *Realms of Memory: The Construction of the French Past*, ed. Lawrence D. Kritzman and trans. Arthur Goldhammer (New York: Columbia University Press, 1998).

40. William Whyte, *Unlocking the Church: The Lost Secrets of Victorian Sacred Space* (Oxford: Oxford University Press, 2017).

41. Ibid., 11. See also the book's bibliography for a comprehensive list of studies of the Oxford and Cambridge Movements.

42. John Barnes, "Furnishing and Liturgy," in *Wymondham Abbey: A History of the Monastery and Parish Church*, ed. Paul Cattermole (Wymondham, U.K.: Wymondham Abbey

Book Committee, 2007), 187. See also Kate Giles, "Seeing and Believing: Visuality and Space in Pre-Modern England," *World Archaeology* 39, no. 1 (2007): 105–21.

43. An angel roof is an open-timber roof with carved representations of angels, particularly prominent in East Anglian churches, which is usually but not exclusively in the nave.

44. Wymondham Abbey was awarded a £1.75 million grant in 2013, with new building works completed and a new heritage exhibition and activities program launched in 2015.

45. Conversation with author, November 14, 2011, Wymondham Abbey. The altar screen is also known as the Comper Screen, designed by Sir J. Ninian Comper starting in 1913, dedicated in 1921 and fully completed in 1928, as part of a redecoration project of the entire chancel. See Cattermole, *Wymondham Abbey*, 221.

46. Richard Barton-Wood, "Wymondham Abbey Norfolk—Souvenir Guide" (East Harling: Taverner Publications, 2011), 5.

47. Paul Cattermole, "A Missing Link" (lecture to the Friends of Wymondham Abbey on September 22, 2001, compact disc, WPC 16/6/15). Note that E. B. Pomeroy was a solicitor at this firm.

48. Nora, *Realms of Memory*, 8–9.

49. Cattermole, "A Missing Link."

50. Conversation with author, November 18, 2010, Wymondham Abbey.

51. See above and note 44.

52. Conversation with author, Wymondham Abbey, April 2, 2013.

53. Cattermole, *Wymondham Abbey*, 39.

54. Ibid., 55.

55. Cattermole, "Missing Link."

56. E-mail correspondence, July 18, 2012.

57. See notes 38 and 39 regarding movements relating to Anglo-Catholicism.

58. Colin Cunningham, *Stone of Witness: Church Architecture and Function* (Stroud, U.K.: Sutton, 1999), 172.

59. Conversation with author, Wymondham Abbey, May 15, 2012.

60. *National Churches Trust Survey: How the United Kingdom's Church Buildings Are Maintained, Funded and Contribute to Their Wider Communities*, conducted April–July 2010, 5; conversation with author, February 26, 2012.

61. *National Churches Trust Survey*, 18.

62. See J. G. Davies, *The Secular Use of Church Buildings* (New York: The Seabury Press, 1968).

63. In some cases, nostalgic attachment to architecture can be linked with nostalgic notions of an age of faith. See John Van Engen, "The Christian Middle Ages as an Historiographical Problem," *American Historical Review* 91, no. 3 (June 1986): 519–52.

64. "The Wymondham Abbey Experience," Activities Planning Meeting, the Vicarage, Wymondham, May 16, 2012.

65. Robert Orsi, *Between Heaven and Earth: The Religious Worlds People Make and the Scholars Who Study Them* (Princeton: Princeton University Press, 2005), 2.

66. Ibid., 166.

4

RAPE AND RAPTURE:
VIOLENCE, AMBIGUITY, AND *RAPTUS* IN MEDIEVAL THOUGHT

Elizabeth Casteen

In 1248, as he wrote the vita of the virginal nun Lutgard of Aywières (d. 1246), the hagiographer Thomas of Cantimpré was forced to contend with the fact that the same word—*raptus*—was used to describe both Lutgard's mystical rapture and her near rape and abduction before her entry into religious life. For Thomas, as for other hagiographers of the High Middle Ages who described the religious lives of women who experienced raptures, this was not a simple case of one word having two distinct meanings. Rather, *raptus* presented Thomas with a rich semantic range that encompassed both sexual violence and mystical rapture, a range he exploited as he worked to construct Lutgard's reputation for sanctity. Thomas's textual play with the multiple and overlapping meanings of *raptus* points to the violent and even erotic overtones of medieval discussions of rapture, and it raises important questions about how *raptus* was defined and understood in medieval Europe.

In examining the link between rape and rapture, scholars have generally focused on the erotic implications of rapture in hagiography or in mystical texts like Mechtild of Magdeburg's *The Flowing Light of the Godhead*. This chapter will analyze the relationship between discussions of mystical rapture in the High and late Middle Ages and contemporary treatments of rape in canon and civil law, arguing that the conceptual relationship was more complex and deeper than scholarship has previously recognized. The very ambiguity of *raptus* is suggestive of the fraught nature of the idea of rape in medieval thought and its relationship to female desire and romance, and to understandings of gender and power. Indeed, the relationship between rape as a sexual crime and rapture as a mystical state was reflexive, and legal understandings of *raptus* shaped both the characterization and the testing of rapture when it involved the body of a female saint.

Rapture, Proof, and Testing

In the middle of the thirteenth century, a Provençal beguine, Douceline of Digne (d. 1274), came before her secular lord, Charles of Anjou (d. 1285), the count of Provence and future king of Sicily, to be tested. In a painful episode to which Douceline's hagiographer, Philippine Porcellet, returns three times, Charles subjected Douceline to public torture and examination that becomes crueler with each retelling. In its first iteration, it has an element of the fairy tale, and Douceline resembles a benevolent fairy godmother. Charles's wife, Beatrice of Provence (d. 1267), was heavily pregnant, and the entire court feared for her and for her unborn child. In a dream, Beatrice saw a beguine whose prayer safely delivered Beatrice and her child. Beatrice told Charles of her dream, and the worried husband and father sought the beguine until he finally found her. Through Douceline's prayer, Beatrice was saved and gave birth to a baby girl. In gratitude, Charles and Beatrice made Douceline their daughter's godmother, essentially incorporating her into their family as a coparent. At the same time, Douceline soothed the great anger Charles felt with the Franciscan Order, restoring the friars and their houses to the count's good graces, effecting through her influence a happy ending that reconciled estranged parties.[1]

When Philippine next recounts Douceline's encounter with Charles, the story, which has a decidedly more sinister cast, plays out in the context of describing Douceline's raptures (*raubimens*). During rapture, Douceline would be "lifted above everything and transported out of herself."[2] While enraptured, she became oblivious to her surroundings, something that observers verified through testing her: "Seeing her so caught up in these raptures, they would push her and shake her forcefully and even inflict pain on her, but they would be unable to move her."[3] Philippine recounts numerous episodes in which witnesses tested Douceline, particularly when she was enrapt in church, when she often levitated. They measured the distance between Douceline's feet and the floor. Some kissed her feet in reverence. Others, not content with the testimony of their eyes, felt compelled to test her physically. Philippine stresses the cruelty of the tests, but she also frames them in her narrative as proof that Douceline's raptures were genuine: "The certainty of her true raptures has been proven in many ways; for, some people who wanted more proof would stick awls into her body and would prick her with needles, but she felt nothing and did not move."[4] Nevertheless, although Douceline felt no pain during rapture, she suffered deeply after she returned to her senses, feeling every bruise and prick and bearing their marks on her body.

Charles, like other observers, felt compelled to test Douceline, which Philippine in her second version of the story makes clear happened when she prayed for Beatrice's safe delivery:

> The first time that King Charles saw her enraptured [*raubida*], he wanted to test if the ecstasy was real. This was at the time when he was count of Provence. He tested it in the following way. He had a quantity of lead melted and had it thrown, boiling, onto her bare feet, in his presence. She felt nothing. The king held her in such affection because of this that he made her his co-mother. But afterward, when she had come back from her rapture [*raubiment*], she felt great pain in her feet and her anguish was unbearable. She was very ill from it and unable to walk.[5]

Philippine goes on to describe the increasing intensity of Douceline's raptures over time as they became ever more violent and irresistible. Whereas many hagiographers describe rapture as a state of ineffable joy, Philippine characterizes Douceline's raptures as so forceful and overwhelming that her sister beguines "feared that they might lose her in this way; for her body, which had been weakened by the long penitence that she had done, could not bear the spirit's great strength."[6] Douceline was compelled into rapture by love of God, "impelled and drawn by the force of the wonderful feeling that she had" whenever she heard of holy things.[7] Despite that wonderful feeling, Douceline is portrayed actively resisting the spirit that overpowered and enraptured her. She fled people who spoke of divine things in order to stave off rapture and the spectacle it presented to observers, often injuring herself in her flight.[8]

Curious religious folk, drawn to Douceline by her fame, found that they could force her into rapture, as did a friar who persistently spoke holy words so that he could witness her rapture. The friar's tactic bore fruit, and it exposed— both to him and to the readers of Philippine's narrative—the great and painful lengths to which Douceline went to escape rapture: "And then one could see that her hands were all torn and bluish in places, because she had pricked them with needles under her cloak, so that she would not hear what the friar was saying to her. But such was the ardour of the spirit, with a strength greater than that of the flesh, that no pain that she felt in her body could take from her the feeling that she had for God."[9]

When Philippine returns a third time to the tale of Douceline's testing by Charles, she adds further detail to the story, representing Beatrice as Douceline's tormenter and as the facilitator of her violation. Beatrice began by inviting Douceline to receive the Eucharist with her, but Douceline informed her that "she was not prepared to receive her Lord"—a formulation that in this instance refers both to the consecrated host and to the raptor whose force would draw her into rapture. Not to be deterred, Beatrice—a persistent spiritual procuress—enlisted the help of a friar who "spoke most ardently about Our Lord." The friar's ardor drove the reluctant and resisting Douceline into rapture: "At his words, the Saint was immediately moved by a fervor of spirit and fell into a state of rapture [*e illi fon raubida*], despite her efforts to do those things to herself that might keep this from happening. She had so tortured her hands during the sermon that they were covered in bruises. When the countess observed this wonder, she rejoiced greatly in Our Lord."[10]

Beatrice may have been persuaded of the veracity of Douceline's rapture, but other members of the court, "who wanted to be more convinced," apparently were not. They continued to test Douceline in ways that Philippine describes as unscrupulous, until eventually the entire court was content with the proof that Douceline's tormented body presented.[11]

What is a reader to make of Douceline's suffering? Philippine herself, even in redisplaying Douceline's ravaged body in text, emphasizes her reluctance to be made a spectacle of and portrays her, as Aviad Kleinberg has pointed out, as "at the mercy of her spectators," an apparently unwilling participant in the process by which her sanctity was apprehended by her community, who took "by force what she refused to give willingly."[12] Indeed, Douceline is said to have experienced her display as a form of violation, berating her sisters when she returned to herself after she was forced into rapture before the count of Artois: "Unfaithful sisters, why did you allow this? Why did you put me on display like that? How could you do such wickedness and betray me in this way?' After that, with bitterness of heart, she said to Our Lord, 'Lord, I beg you to confound me in the hearts of each one.' She seemed so upset that it was as if some great wrong had been done to her."[13]

Douceline's story reads as one of communal violation—indeed, as one in which Douceline is publicly abused through the collusion of God and her community. But it can also be read as a description of a judicial process by which Douceline's feudal lord—Charles—examined her, seeking the truth of her spiritual transportation in the visible proof that rapture imprinted on her body, either through levitation and immobility during rapture or through the bruises and wounds that demonstrated her resistance to the overwhelming force of her raptor.

Scholars have long recognized both the erotic dimensions of mystical literature—which describes union with the divine as, for example, piercing, penetrating, inebriating, consuming, and self-annihilating—and the violence of this eroticism, as in the narrative of Douceline's ravishment. To describe Douceline's rapture, Philippine uses the Occitan word *raubida* (infinitive *raubar*), which means "to steal or rob" but which can also, like the Old French *rober* to which it is related, mean "to rape." Her use of *raubida* situates it as an analog to the Latin *raptus*, conventionally used to denote mystical rapture in hagiographic and theological texts; indeed, Philippine's portrayal of Douceline's rapture replicates the established tropes of rapture and ecstasy in Latin hagiography of the High Middle Ages.[14]

Both Barbara Newman and Dyan Elliott have commented on the "strong and disturbing sexual overtones" of *raptus*—which could mean rape, abduction, or theft—in its application to mystical rapture, which was linguistically constructed as a form of sexual violence, particularly when applied to the relationship between "a swooning female mystic and an overpowering male deity."[15] Julie B. Miller, examining the language used by female mystics such as Mechtild of Magdeburg, Angela of Foligno, Catherine of Genoa, and Theresa of Avilà, has argued forcefully that scholars need to acknowledge that the language of *imitatio Christi* and bridal mysticism so prevalent in mystical texts of the High and late Middle Ages "was often brutally violent, replete with descriptions of assault and annihilation, agony and affliction."[16] As Miller points out, the language that medieval holy women used to describe their relationship to Christ often drew on "the explicitly sexual imagery of penetration—by arrows, darts, swords, rays of divine love" to characterize a mystical experience that was explicitly a form of divine assault and textually encoded as rape.[17] She recognizes that the semantic range of *raptus* allows for this, and she argues that mystical writers, in "coupling together two distinct understandings of the Latin term *raptus* in its construction of the love relationship between the soul and God . . . contribute to the eroticization of violence, and in particular, to an eroticization of rape."[18]

Miller's argument hinges in part on the conceptual elision of the legal understanding of *raptus* as rape and the religious understanding of it as rapture. Yet, I argue, mystical literature, like high and late medieval hagiography, quite deliberately played with the range of *raptus* and, rather than "coupling together two distinct understandings" of *raptus*, exploited its conceptual range to construct female sanctity.[19] The very ambiguity of *raptus* gave it force and hagiographic utility, in part because it could evoke multiple meanings simultaneously. Its suggestive potential and range undergird accounts of female sanctity that helped define tropes that dominated hagiography in the later Middle Ages and shaped legal and official responses to rapture that echo and reflect the contemporary handling of rape.

Scholars like Richard Kieckhefer, Gàbor Klaniczay, Nancy Caciola, and Elliott have explored the ambiguous and conceptually fraught construction of sainthood in medieval culture, which made the female saint vulnerable to charges of heresy, demonic possession, insanity, and witchcraft. As Caciola has pointed out, the ambivalent performance of divine possession by holy women could be read as demonic possession, which evinced the same signs and behaviors—for example, speaking in tongues, unkempt appearance, self-harm—and challenged any observer who sought to interpret it.[20] Kieckhefer has argued similarly that an incident that could be "counted as evidence for sanctity" in one context "under slightly different circumstances might have marked [its performer] as a sorceress," because "sainthood and witchcraft were ascribed roles and could give occasion for competing ascription, with different observers thinking of a single person as a saint or as a witch."[21] Elliott has demonstrated that female piety was constructed by and alongside the inquisitional culture that elaborated the process of both canonization trials and inquests into heresy; ultimately, the proofs and process that identified a saint in the thirteenth century could be used to unmask a heretic, particularly as clerical culture grew wary of possessed behaviors and resentful of feminine influence in the religious sphere.[22] Drawing on this research, I argue that the rapt female saint also conceptually mirrored and overlapped the victim of rape, as hagiographers and mystical writers drew on legal and literary conventions of *raptus* to describe the experience and physical manifestation of mystical rapture.

Both rapture and claims of sexual violence were often doubted, and the proving of both hinged on understandings of women's volition, physicality, and tendency to deceive and be deceived. The claims of the rape victim, like those of the putative saint, were tested and verified using similar criteria. In rape as in rapture, the woman's reputation, chastity, and behavior were scrutinized, and in both cases, *raptus* was assumed to leave decisive physical and spiritual traces on the woman's body, much as Douceline's raptures did on hers. Yet the conceptual relationship between the victim of rape and the object of rapture was less one of inversion than one of conceptual kinship, as the tropes of rapture—both in hagiographic texts and in canonization proceedings—drew on and adapted conventions of proof applied to rape in the courtroom and legal texts. Rape and rapture were both *raptus*, bound together in language, and both were imprinted on the body of the raped/ravished/rapt woman.

Definitions and Conceptual Difficulties

The meanings of the Latin noun *raptus* (verb: *rapere*, popular Latin *rapire*) are notoriously slippery. Both feminist scholars and scholars of medieval law have devoted considerable time and many pages to trying to get a firm purchase on the term, which denotes violent, hurried action—particularly that of snatching or seizing—and whose semantic range in medieval Europe extended from theft to abduction to elopement to rape to mystical rapture. *Raptus/rapere* gives us the modern English "rapture" (and its corollaries, "rapt" and "rapturous"), "rape" (along with "rapine"), "rapid" (via the Latin *rapidus*), "raptor," and—via the Old French *ravissement*—"ravishing," in both its aesthetic and its sexual or erotic sense.[23] The etymological relationship between modern terms whose meanings are quite distinct reflects the ambiguity and polysemous meanings of *raptus* in medieval culture.

Raptus found its way into medieval European legal culture through Roman law. Roman law defined *raptus* as "forcible abduction as well as forcible sexual relations."[24] *Raptus* was marked by its violence: it was an assault that could not be resisted, one that succeeded because the perpetrator—the raptor—overpowered the person he abducted. The raptor seized or raped—*rapuit*—while his object was seized, abducted, transported, or raped—*raptus est*. In Roman law, as in much subsequent medieval law, the primary victim of *raptus* was the male guardian (or, in the case of slaves, the owner) of the person abducted or assaulted, rather than that person her- or himself. Thus, as a result, the term *raptus* occluded the will and intentions of the person who was its object, complicating the task of any modern scholar who seeks to disentangle accounts of *raptus*. A woman who was violently sexually assaulted was the object of *raptus*, but so was a woman who left her family home and married without her father's permission, as was any person who was abducted, regardless of whether the abduction included sexual violation.[25] Indeed, by the late Roman Republic, when *raptus* was included among the *leges de vi*—laws that prosecuted violence—it did not necessarily "denote, at least strictly speaking, a sexual act."[26] Increasingly, however, the crime of *per vim stuprum* (sexual intercourse coerced by force) came to be absorbed into *raptus*, so that *raptus* often had a sexual dimension by the classical period, although *raptus* continued to denote nonsexual crimes as well.[27]

In early Christian law, *raptus* primarily meant the abduction or removal of a woman, who might or might not be complicit, from the protection of her male guardian for the purpose of marriage. Before the twelfth century, it did not necessarily imply sexual violence or rape in the modern sense, and even afterward, it often meant simply abduction or theft.[28] Medieval law only deepened and complicated the ambiguous range of *raptus* as it developed. For much of medieval history, *raptus* featured most prominently in secular law, which included severe penalties for the theft and forcible marriage and (or) rape of women.[29] Some Frankish rulers, like Childebert II (d. 595), followed the Roman-law precedent set by Constantine, who defined *raptus* as a public crime punishable by death.[30] Yet, whether rulers punished raptors—and complicit victims—harshly or showed lenience, they defined *raptus* primarily as a crime against social order, and their primary concerns centered on male honor and on preserving the peace.[31]

Running in parallel to early medieval legal tendencies to treat *raptus* primarily as a property crime—a form of theft—was a tendency to preserve the older Roman law tradition that associated the theft of a woman with her sexual violation. According to Isidore of Seville (d. 636), *raptus* was "illicit coitus" that corrupted the woman abducted and thus a form of fornication.[32] It was this definition of *raptus* that Gratian adopted and adapted in the *Decretum* in the twelfth century, revolutionizing canon law treatments of the crime of *raptus*. For Gratian, *raptus* encompassed both the "abduction of a girl without her parents' consent (even if she was a willing party to the abduction) [and] intercourse with her against her will."[33] He defined *raptus*, as had Roman lawyers before him, in part through its violence: *raptus* was an act of forcible theft that targeted a woman's body and her family's property. However, unlike secular law, canon law as Gratian and subsequent decretists defined it did not call for the execution of perpetrators of *raptus*, proscribing instead excommunication and, if possible, marriage as the appropriate forms of redress.[34] Thus, Gratian both contributed to the codification of *raptus* as a crime that involved sexual violence and began a process of softening its severity. Later decretists expanded the definition of *raptus* as a sex crime even further, incorporating into it degrees of force. Their definition of *raptus* came to hinge on the woman's resistance and struggle. It might be either a "grievous offence that involved violent coercion" or a "less serious offence involving moderate coercion, where the victim was induced to yield against her will, but without being physically forced to submit." *Raptus* in the sense that comes closest to the modern understanding of "rape" was distinguished by physical force and required the victim to "resist or protest in order for the incident to be regarded as rape."[35] Significantly, in canon law as in civil law, rape was adjudicated based on the evidence of how violently the woman had struggled. Rape was written on her body, and its proof lay in her behavior and in the visible traces of her struggle on her clothing and her skin—something to which I will return.

Further complicating the meanings and conceptual range of *raptus* in medieval Christian thought was the definition of *raptus* as mystical rapture—the seizing of the soul when it was rapt to heaven, which Barbara Newman describes as the "only positive meaning" of *raptus*.[36] The archetypal rapture was that of St. Paul to the third heaven, which the Vulgate characterizes as *raptus* (2 Cor. 12:1–4). Paul was unable to say whether he was rapt to heaven in spirit or in body, but his transportation was sudden and forceful, seizing him from himself and bringing him into contact with the divine. Nor was Paul's the only instance of *raptus* as divine rapture in the Vulgate: the male child of Revelation 12:5, who will rule the nations with an iron scepter, was rapt (*raptus est*) or caught up to God's throne, much as, in Latin literature, Ganymede was seized and transported to Jove.[37]

Yet, *raptus/rapere* and its derivatives carry a range of other biblical meanings. In the Gospel of Luke, the Pharisee praying in the Temple gives thanks that he is not like other men, who are thieves (*raptores*), unjust, adulterers, or even publicans (Luke 18:11).[38] In Acts 19:29, it is Paul's companions, Gaius and Aristarchus, who are the objects of *raptus* when they are seized by the people of Ephesus, while in Acts 8:39, the Spirit of the Lord seizes (*rapuit*) Phillip and carries him away. As a verb, *rapere* is used to describe raiding, as in Matthew 11:12, where Christ says that violent people have been despoiling the Kingdom of Heaven (*violenti rapiunt illud*) since the time of John the Baptist, a sense similar to that of Psalm 103:21, in which young lions roar to hunt (*ut rapiant*) their prey. In the Old Testament, *raptus* and its variants also denote theft or bereavement, as in the case of the bear robbed of her cubs in Proverbs 17:12 (*ursæ . . . raptis fœtibus*), or of the father of Wisdom 14:15, suddenly bereft of his children (*pater, cito sibi rapti filii*). Elsewhere, *raptus/rapere* carries the sense of pillaging and robbery, as in Ezekiel 18:16, where the righteous son is he who does not plunder (*rapinam non rapuerit*). In Job 20:29, the wicked are described as those who seize houses (*domum rapuit*) they did not build, while in Proverbs 1:19 the greedy are those who gain by violence (*possidentium rapiunt*). In other cases, *raptus/rapere* describes sudden, swift action: in 1 Chronicles 11:23, Benaiah kills an Egyptian after snatching a spear (*rapuit hastam*) from his hand. *Raptus* is also used to describe the disappearance of embers or dust caught up in wind (Dan. 2:25, Hosea 13:3). In Amos 4:11, too, it carries the sense of being snatched or caught up, in this case like charred sticks pulled from flames.

Biblical *raptus*, thus, carries the connotation of unexpected, violent, or forceful seizure or theft. Paul's rapture entailed being snatched or caught up to heaven, carried suddenly and forcefully away, just as wind carries off chaff or the Holy Spirit Phillip. Yet, in the Vulgate as in Roman law, *raptus/rapere* can also involve sexual violence, as in the case of Shechem, who seized (*rapuit*) and raped Dinah, overpowering her by force (Gen. 34:2). It also carries the Roman law sense of abduction for the purpose of marriage, as when the Benjamites carried off (*rapuerunt*) the women of Shiloh to be their wives (Judg. 21:23). Thus, in the spiritual realm as in the legal realm, *raptus* was ambiguous and multifaceted, allowing for the conceptual overlapping of rapture, violence, and rape.

Raptus, Rape, and Rapture in High Medieval Culture

During the twelfth and thirteenth centuries, as scholars revolutionized European law and hagiographers and theologians helped codify new understandings of mysticism, they had at their disposal the full semantic range of *raptus*. The textual genres that grappled with *raptus* bled into and informed one another, so that *raptus* in mystical texts was not truly separable from *raptus* in law. Indeed, the clerics who wrote the vitae of female saints shared in the same learned university culture that produced legal and theological scholars, and *raptus* took on enhanced meaning in law, theological treatises, and hagiography simultaneously and reflexively.

Rape law, thanks in part to Gratian's treatment of *raptus*, evolved rapidly. In England in the twelfth and thirteenth centuries, common law clearly defined *raptus* as rape. The *Tractatibus de legibus et consuetudinibus regni Angliae* (ca. 1187–89) of Ranulf de Glanvill (d. 1190), more commonly known simply as *Glanvill*, defines *raptus* as an act of violence committed against a woman by an assailant who overpowers her, a definition picked up and amplified in the following century in the *Legibus et consuetudinibus Angliae* attributed to Henry de Bracton (d. ca. 1268).[39] It was only late in the thirteenth century—in the statutes known as Westminster I and Westminster II, which do not actually use the word *raptus*—that "rape" and "abduction" began to be conflated, as English lawmakers became increasingly concerned about abduction.[40] Caroline Dunn has argued that in English law before about 1275, *raptus* usually meant sexual violation rather than abduction, although the term became increasingly ambiguous after that, reaching "its peak of ambiguity during the fourteenth century."[41] In French law of the twelfth and thirteenth centuries, *raptus* was more ambiguous, perhaps reflecting contemporary trends in canon law, which, like the chivalric literature written at the same period, "blurr[ed] . . . distinctions between forced and voluntary sex, between love and violence."[42] *Raptus* often preceded marriage, in law as in romance, which Kathryn Gravdal has suggested reflects a diminishing sense of rape's ethical seriousness.[43] Yet, in Philippe de Beaumanoir's (d. 1296) *Coutumes de Beauvaisis*, rape—called both *fame esforcier* and *rat*, a French derivative of *raptus*—is treated as a crime of equal severity to murder and treason, and thus punishable by death.[44] In Flemish law, as in the twelfth-century precepts of Philip of Alsace, *raptus* was classified as a serious crime, similar to theft; by 1191, men who seized women were subject either to death or to banishment.[45] *Raptus* and its vernacular equivalents thus encompassed, in the legal realm, abduction—often with sexual ends—and rape and referred both to violent crime and to coerced sex that initiated lawful marriage.

Legal elaboration of the crime of *raptus* unfolded in tandem with other marked cultural changes of the twelfth century. Significantly, Gravdal has argued that rape plays a central role in the romance narratives of Chrétien de Troyes, ultimately becoming constitutive of romance as a genre. She points out that "rape, attempted rape, and the punishment of a rapist . . . constitute familiar episodic units in the construction of a romance. Sexual violence is built into the premise of Arthurian romance; medieval romance is a genre that by definition must create the threat of rape."[46] Given the influence of courtly literature on high medieval mysticism—which Newman has aptly termed *la mystique courtoise*—it is perhaps no surprise that the language of rape should shape mystical texts as well, particularly given the semantic overlap of rape and rapture.[47]

Thirteenth-century religious texts incorporate the full range of *raptus*, both as it was used in Roman law and as it figured in Latin literature, including the Vulgate. Caesarius of Heisterbach (d. ca. 1240), for instance, employs *raptus/rapere* in multiple ways in the *Dialogus miraculorum*. For Caesarius, usurers are raptors who steal mercilessly, but so, too, are wolves, whom he describes violently seizing children and freedmen, and a kite that seizes a small bird canny enough to call upon Thomas Becket for aid.[48] Demons are raptors par excellence in the *Dialogus*, snatching and transporting the sinful, the doubtful, the unwitting, and occasional livestock everywhere from Jerusalem to Purgatory to the local church choir, but angels and saints can also affect *raptus* in the sense of spiritual or physical transportation. To Caesarius, demonic *raptus* could have a distinct sexual component, as in the case of a demon in the shape of a woman who punished a man by seizing him under the arm and carrying him off when he refused her sexual advances.[49] Caesarius also uses *raptus* to describe mystical rapture, as in the case of a virtuous paralytic whose spirit was separated from her body and transported to the heavenly Jerusalem and whose rapture Caesarius explicitly equates to that of Paul.[50]

Before the thirteenth century, the language used to describe mystical rapture was primarily associated with monastic contemplation and with an affective form of piety championed by Bernard of Clairvaux.[51] Cistercian monks labored for rapture, seeking to be transported out of themselves, if only momentarily, during prayer and contemplation.[52] Yet, beginning in the twelfth century, as Elliott argues, hagiography began the process of "identifying the female body as a privileged zone of receptivity to divine infusions," a pattern discernible in the visions of Hildegard of Bingen (d. 1179) and Elisabeth of Schönau (d. 1164), whose vita, composed by her brother, describes her raptures.[53] The thirteenth-century vitae of holy women—particularly beguines—construct them as both the active suitors of their heavenly bridegroom and the passive objects of sudden and transformative rapture.[54] In his vita of the Flemish beguine Marie of Oignies (d. 1213), Caesarius's direct contemporary Jacques de Vitry (d. 1240) helped shape a new understanding of feminine piety marked by long, trancelike states and prolonged experiences of rapture. Jacques described not only Marie's raptures but also those of the other women in her community, who appear in the prologue to Marie's vita as members of "colonies of women who are enraptured and literally wasting away in divine love as a result of bodily illness as well as self-mortifications."[55] He wrote during a period when medieval medical wisdom, elaborated at rapidly growing universities, identified women's bodies as "particularly suited to such rapture," both because they were conceived of as more porous—and thus more easily infiltrated—than men's and because their greater softness and humidity rendered them "more impressionable and so more imaginative."[56] As he describes a type of somatic piety constructed as uniquely feminine, Jacques characterizes Marie's raptures, among other things, as periods when she was rapt out of herself in a state of inebriation or rapt in the spirit so that her spirit and body were separated.[57] With Marie, the living female saint became the rapt saint. Indeed, rapture—like rape—was linked to physical frailty, to the tendency to be overcome, which meant that "the female body was clearly more susceptible."[58] And once rapture became an attribute of feminine spirituality, enacted on the female form, it became ever more linguistically and conceptually linked to rape.

Jacques and the Dominican Thomas of Cantimpré (d. 1272), who wrote a supplement to Jacques's vita of Marie of Oignies, along with vitae of a number of other holy women, recorded, interpreted, and codified the lives of pious women at a time when the theology of mysticism was being elaborated in the schools.[59] As Elliott notes, both Alexander of Hales (d. 1245) and Thomas Aquinas (d. 1274)—drawing on the conceptual ambiguity of *raptus*—argued that rapture "implies a certain amount of violence."[60] The Thomistic definition of rapture identifies it as an "elevation contrary to nature" that entails violence because the will is superseded or suppressed when one is alienated from one's senses.[61] For a hagiographer like Thomas of Cantimpré, who studied briefly with Aquinas and became something of a specialist in shaping and recording mystical women's textual lives, it would likely have been impossible to describe a woman's *raptus* without being aware of the full valence of the word and of the implications of such violence when enacted on the female body.

Thomas wrote during a period when *raptus* was a particular concern of both canon and civil lawyers. And as rape law was evolving, his characterization of rapture echoes contemporary legal thought about rape. Like canon law, civil law laid the burden of proof on the woman who brought charges of rape against an assailant. Precisely because rape was such a serious charge and carried such severe penalties, legists cautioned against accepting a woman's rape plea without skepticism and rigorous examination. Trevor Dean sums up the prevailing legal attitude thus: "in the scales of justice the woman's broken hymen counted for little against the rapist's life."[62] Dean argues that in England, France, and the Low Countries, "accusatory procedure persisted as the sole means of prosecution [for rape] for much longer than for other serious crimes," and convictions and punishment were relatively rare, "because of the difficulty of proof: in the absence of witnesses, it was her word against his, and her word was more easily impugned."[63]

In northern France at the period when Thomas wrote, rape prosecution proceeded by first investigating the reputation—particularly the reputed chastity—of the woman, who was then required to demonstrate that force had been used and how it had been used, as well as that she had done everything in her power to defend herself and only succumbed to her rapist out of fear for her life.[64] Philippe de Beaumanoir counseled that justice could be served only by inquiring carefully into the crime to ensure that the woman had not fabricated the charges. A judge should ask whether she had cried out and should not believe her if she had been in a settled area and no one had heard. Likewise, if she had not cried out, the judge should seek to discover whether she had failed to do so because she feared death. Finally, he should probe the details of the case—where had she been taken? how? into what town?—and should be attentive to any facet of her story that might prove false.[65]

English law at the same period required rape victims to "raise the hue and cry" and to provide physical evidence of the crime.[66] Legal scholars have examined the tropes of English rape narratives, which hewed to a set formula because of the need to shape accounts of sexual violence to fit narrow, codified legal definitions of rape.[67] As in French law as described by Phillipe de Beaumanoir, the English rape narrative should stress how and where the rape had occurred, making sure to establish that the woman had struggled but had been overpowered. According to *Glanvill*, "Rape [*raptus*] is a crime in which a woman charges a man with overpowering her by force in the peace of the lord king. A woman who suffers in this way must go, soon after the deed is done, to the nearest vill, and there show to trustworthy men the injury done to her, and any effusion of blood there may be and torn clothing."[68]

Rape, in other words, could only be certified by "trustworthy men" and was recognized as such by the visible evidence of the violence done to the woman, who had struggled enough to sustain bleeding wounds and torn clothing. Flemish rape narratives follow a similar pattern, stressing that the female victim had cried out and resisted, and that her cries had been heard.[69] *Glanvill's* insistence that the woman must show herself and the signs of her rape to the authorities appears in thirteenth-century English legal treatises as well, such as *Bracton*, *Britton*, and *Fleta*; indeed, *Britton* defines rape as "a felony committed by a man by violence on the body of a woman" and characterizes the "presumptive signs" of rape as "stains of blood . . . and tearing of clothes."[70] In France, too, by the fourteenth century, it was the practice to have reliable women examine the bodies of women who brought charges of rape in search of physical signs of sexual force, as wounds and bruises corroborated victims' accounts.[71]

The requirement that rape victims display evidence of their violation was not a recent innovation, nor was it unique to England. English law in this respect was similar to Continental law, as "secular law codes across Europe, canon law, legends and inquisition testimony, court records and *pastourelle* poetry all stress the critical importance of the victim's outcry" for determining whether a rape had been committed.[72] The eighth-century *Lex Baiuvariorum* required that victims show their disheveled hair and torn clothes, a stipulation still in force in the *Sachsenspiegel* (ca. 1220). Indeed, as Diane Wolfthal has argued, "medieval society shared a collective image of how a rape victim should look" that had its own immediately recognizable tropes and iconography.[73] The legal process that evolved between the twelfth and fifteenth centuries to deal with rape defined it, Kim Phillips has argued, as "a crime written on the body."[74] At the same time, however, rape law increasingly stressed the importance of the victim's will and consent, which was also discernible in her body. Indeed, English law ultimately ruled that pregnancy—because, reflecting contemporary medical wisdom imported from France, pregnancy could not occur if the woman had not experienced pleasure—acted as physical evidence that a rape had *not* taken place, because the woman, even if she had resisted initially, must have given in to pleasure and consented as the rape occurred.[75]

Just as medieval society shared a collective image of the rape victim, it also shared an image of the enraptured female saint, whose physical signifiers—bleeding, bruises, wounds—often reflected those expected of rape victims. As Elliott points out, "hagiographers of the Low Countries . . . frequently provid[e] a very literal translation of mystical imagery. Such literalism was at least partially driven by a kind of pragmatism: . . . the case for sanctity required concrete proofs, which meant that the apprehension of the divine presence by the spiritual senses was often registered on their corporeal counterparts, even as spiritual graces were enacted directly on the body."[76]

Thus, the interior disposition of the rapt saint was printed on her body, and her rapture marked her just as "true" rape marked a rape victim. Like women who appeared before secular authorities to press charges of rape, women who claimed—or whose supporters and hagiographers claimed on their behalf—to be recipients of *raptus* in the mystical sense had to provide somatic proof that was both displayed to and, as was the case of Douceline of Digne, probed, tested, and ratified by those in positions of power, whether secular lords who would champion their cause or the ecclesiastical judges who conducted canonization trials.

Thomas of Cantimpré's *vita* of the Flemish Cistercian nun Lutgard of Aywières demonstrates the continuities between rape and rapture in thirteenth-century religious thought. Thomas revered Lutgard as a spiritual mother, and his *vita* uses *raptus* in both its secular legal sense and its mystical sense to construct her as a saint. He transparently modeled Lutgard's life on that of the early virgin martyr Agnes.[77] She thus begins her saintly career in his text under sexual threat from an impious suitor—a hagiographic trope that also reflects the omnipresent risk of sexual violence and abduction that women who chose beguinages or convents over marriage faced.[78] For a woman of Lutgard's time, place, and social standing, *raptus* in the worldly sense was a threat that entry into religion could alleviate but not eliminate. Angry about his rejection, the suitor—a knight—determined to waylay Lutgard as she traveled to visit her sister. When the knight and a band of armed supporters attempted to seize (*rapere*) Lutgard, she struggled free from her captors' grasp and ran through the night, eluding them with the aid of an angel. Lutgard's waiting nurse had been forewarned by her fleeing servants, who denounced her would-be lover as a rapist (*ut raptorem*), and thus "suspected rape" (*suspicata raptum*) when she saw Lutgard, asking, "Did the young man attack you violently during the night?"[79]

Despite her miraculous escape, Lutgard's reputation, Thomas tells us, suffered because of the widespread suspicion that she had been raped. In an act of sacrifice that was also an act of self-display, Lutgard offered up her modesty to Christ. Reflecting the legal convention that her rape would be discernible on her body had it occurred, she unveiled her face before the eyes of the curious people who came to examine her—seeking visual evidence of her assault—an action that instilled in her a profound sense of shame but that also brought her closer to Christ by giving her a small share in His humiliation at the Crucifixion.[80] Not long afterward, her participation in the Crucifixion became even more pronounced, when she first experienced mystical rapture (*rapiebatur in spiritu*) and encountered the bloodied Christ on the Cross, who allowed her to drink from His wounded side.[81] Significantly, this second *raptus* rests on the establishment and preservation of Lutgard's reputation for chastity, because both in law and in hagiography chastity was a precondition for *raptus*. She thus evaded one form of *raptus* to become the object of another—a progression from control by an earthly raptor to a heavenly raptor that Thomas must have intended the reader to note and apprehend.

Lutgard experienced frequent raptures to heaven, receiving visions and rev-elations. Although her raptures entailed joy, they could also be quite violent. Significantly, they left visible marks that were witnessed (and recorded) as exter-nal proof of the veracity of her rapture. Thomas tells the story of a priest—per-haps himself—who learned that Lutgard remembered and shared in the Passion when she was enraptured (*rapta in spiritu*), so that it seemed as though her entire body was bathed in blood. Curious, he arranged to observe her during rapture. What he saw provided tangible proof of her *raptus*: her bare face and hands appeared to shine with recently shed blood, and her hair—that important signifier of rapine—was drenched in blood.[82] Given his earlier emphasis on the importance to Lutgard of her veil, Thomas's description suggests that she, like a rape victim, was disheveled, with disarrayed clothing, and that like a rape vic-tim she bled, even as her abstracted state revealed that her rapture was not counterfeit. Whereas Lutgard had earlier exposed her face to demonstrate that she had not been raped, here her bare face provides the evidence that was lack-ing after her first, earthly assault.

Ultimately, it was Lutgard herself who protected women from rape, main-taining the textual association between *raptus* in its mystical and sexual senses. Through her prayerful intervention, a sister nun was finally freed from the sexual predation of an incubus who had tormented her for years. Although in this instance Thomas does not use the word *raptus* to characterize the demon's assault, he is clear about the sexual nature of the attacks, which polluted the nun's body and nearly drove her to prostitution.[83] In *De bonum universale de apibus*, Thomas does discuss demonic *raptus*, and he notes that—like other forms of *raptus*—it leaves distinct physical signs, so that its victims are pallid, wan, and discolored (from bruises?), with unfixed eyes.[84] Thomas also provides more detail about the nun's demonic rape in *De apibus*, revealing that he could not understand how God could allow an innocent to suffer so until he finally forced her to confess that she had been defiled in mind before the incubus defiled her body, making her complicit in her own rape.[85] Perhaps because of her initial complicity, nothing could banish the incubus—not the consecrated host, not the sign of the cross, not holy water. When another nun attempted to bear the burden for her, she found it unbearable. Yet, Lutgard's prayers ban-ished the incubus, which fled without a trace, so that the recipient of one form of *raptus* liberated the victim of another.[86]

Raptus also figured prominently in Thomas's other hagiographic works. Christina Mirabilis (d. 1224) was the recipient of sudden, unlooked-for rapture (*subito ei inopinate rapiebatur a spiritu*) that took her out of herself, but she was also the victim of seizure by her own neighbors, who captured and bound her (*a suis requisite, inventa et rapta est*) after they found her wandering in the woods, nourished (suggestively) only by her own miraculously lactating breasts.[87] Christina's body, like Lutgard's, provided proof both of her raptures and of their violence. While in rapture, she would contort and roll about, and she "whirled around with such extreme violence" that one limb could not be distinguished from another until her body quieted, as though exhausted and weakened by the violence of her experience.[88] Margaret of Ypres (d. 1237) rushed, weeping, to show herself to her confessor when, because enrapt, she had failed to say the hours when she should, her tears and anguish providing proof, Thomas suggests, that her rapture was real.[89]

The tropes of rapture permeated later medieval hagiography, as they did mystical thought. In mystical texts, the feminine soul—whether the mystic was male or female—was rapt by a loving God. True rapture, according to the fourteenth-century English mystic Richard Rolle (d. 1349), was violent and supernatural, as opposed to the elevation of the mind to God through contemplation, which some called rapture but which could be attained by any "perfect lover" of God.[90] Rolle, like other mystics, to quote Rick McDonald, described the "soul as the forlorn sexual partner of God" as he sought language to describe the ineffable.[91] Yet, the sense that mystical rapture marked and transformed the rapt saint in discernible, verifiable ways that needed to be decoded by authoritative observers was particularly important to the construction of female mysticism. It was the female saint in particular who had to be tested and whose body was to be examined, especially by skeptical observers who approached her claims with doubt.

Walter Simons has argued that scholars, like medieval clerical observers of sanctity, can read the bodily performance of thirteenth-century beguines in texts in which "the body and bodily movement take centre stage" and in which hagiographers attempted to translate the "external signs" of a woman's rapture.[92] As scholars like Caroline Walker Bynum, Caciola, and Elliott have well established, medieval belief in women's greater embodiment compared to men and their impressionable natures—in the literal and figurative senses—made their bodies ideal texts that recorded their religious experiences. There is no need to belabor that point here. What is noteworthy, in interrogating the link between rape and rapture in medieval thought, is the suspicion of women's veracity that underpins both religious and legal examinations of *raptus*, as well as the doubt that lack of somatic proof occasioned in the minds of examiners. The contorted, bleeding body of the saint had to be examined, just as Philip of Clairvaux famously examined Elisabeth of Spalbeek (fl. 1246–1304) by seeking to jolt her from rapture and expose her as a fraud, only to be persuaded that her *raptus* was genuine by her bleeding wounds and rigid form, or as Charles of Anjou certified and participated in Douceline's sanctity by testing and then publicly authenticating her rapture.[93]

When the physical signs of rapture—like those of rape—were absent or might have been counterfeited, the appropriate clerical response was doubt and condemnation. The Swedish Dominican Peter of Dacia (d. 1289), for instance, describes the doubts of those who observed the rapt rigidity of Christina of Stommeln (d. 1312).[94] According to Peter's vita of Christina, he took a friar named Albrandinus to see her as she lay, apparently rapt, in bed. Albrandinus climbed onto Christina's bed and touched her arm. Rather than finding it immobile, as he expected that it should be during rapture, he found it pliable. Peter relates, "He turned toward me in indignation and cried out with these words—for he was a very fiery man—'Brother Peter! It is a lie that, as has been related to me, this girl is so enraptured that she is made rigid.'"[95] Peter was later vindicated and Christina's rapture proved when Albrandinus returned to test her again. This time, he went to the head of her bed and examined her. When he perceived no sign of life, he again placed his hand on her arm. Now he found her flesh extremely rigid, as though she were dead. Perhaps in punishment of his doubt, Christina somewhat returned to herself, regaining mobility as she was moved by the Spirit. As she moved, she raised the palm of her left hand, which Albrandinus very much hoped to inspect. In her palm, he observed a most beautiful cross—a physical wound, which Peter tellingly calls "the sign of the Spouse," that gave proof to Christina's rapture—and cried out, lamenting his unbelief. Even as Albrandinus contemplated Christina's marks, she reentered full rapture (*rapuit totum*), seizing his hand in her own and holding it fast in an unbreakable grasp until her rapture ended.[96]

In textually constructing Christina's reputation for sanctity, Peter thus provided evidence that she had been tested, and that the bodily evidence for her rapture had been certified by a cleric qualified to do so. The performance of Christina's rapture was the mystical equivalent of raising the hue and cry, and the immobility of her body and the marks on her hand constituted somatic evidence of the violence of her *raptus* that functions textually much as the tale of Beatrice's and Charles's torment and testing of Douceline of Digne does. Such proof was indispensable to the identification of the female mystic according to the tropes of thirteenth-century hagiography, which played freely with the understanding of the female form as the passive object of *raptus*.

As Elliott has argued, such signs were crucial to the process by which inquisitional procedure examined sanctity, even as ambivalence about such embodied, affective piety increased in the fourteenth century. In the case of Dorothea of Montau (d. 1394), a Prussian mystic who spent the last year of her life as an enclosed recluse and experienced nearly continuous rapture, the absence of clear physical signs of *raptus* occasioned anxiety during her canonization procedure. Dorothea's revelations to her hagiographer, John Marienwerder, and John's subsequent shaping of her life identified her as rapt in all senses of the word. Elliott, discussing Dorothea's marking with "wounds of love" by Christ, notes the competition and conflation between Christ as Dorothea's raptor and Spouse and Dorothea's violent husband, Adalbert: "Christ would remind Dorothea, 'I frequently raptured (*rapui*) you from your husband when . . . he thought he possessed you.' The Latin word *raptus* simultaneously signified rape and mystical rapture: so in essence, Christ is simply exchanging one kind of sexual congress for another kind. But both forms of union are forced. This concurrence points to the greater tautology underlying Dorothea's mystical marriage that behind the face of the Christ who wounds . . . violently imposing himself on his bride, looms the face of Adalbert."[97]

Dorothea's last days were spent in Marienwerder, where, enclosed her cell, "she took on a special vocation" as the local holy woman and became famous and valued for her regular raptures, which brought her revelations.[98] John describes her as aflame or inebriated with love, and his accounts of her raptures are replete with talk of tears, of ardor, of burning or sweating—which Dorothea did copiously while in rapture—and of being filled with joy that indicated that her experiences were divine in origin.[99] John's language evokes the full violent and sexual range of rapture, as when he describes Dorothea as enflamed and wounded by love and reveals that her rapturous delight—which recalls the erotic tropes of ravishment in chivalric literature and the contemporary collapsing of the categories of rape and abduction—resulted in a mystical pregnancy, itself a sign that, even if Dorothea initially resisted her rapture, she ultimately consented to it.[100]

Yet, the canonization commission that examined Dorothea's reputed sanctity harbored doubts regarding her claims to rapture that may, in part, reflect the failure of her body to evince the expected proofs. The commission questioned numerous witnesses about Dorothea's raptures. Some testified that they believed in them because of the true revelations she received.[101] Others certified that they resulted in immobility and insensibility before yielding violent weeping when Dorothea returned to herself, tropes common to accounts of rapture.[102] The most detailed and most troubling testimony came from John himself, who revealed that, for the last three years of Dorothea's life, she experienced rapture rather than sleeping at night. The examiners repeatedly asked John how he knew that Dorothea was enrapt rather than asleep—suggesting conceptual difficulty with rapture whose external signs were ambiguous and doubt about Dorothea's performance. John insisted that he firmly believed that she was rapt rather than sleeping.[103] Pressed about the physical signs of her rapture, he offered the proof that she could not walk or hear bells ringing.[104] More conventional proof of Dorothea's rapture came when John was interrogated about her marriage. He revealed that her husband beat her "so forcefully on the breast that a great abundance of blood poured from her mouth" after she became so abstracted during rapture that she failed to complete an errand on which he had sent her.[105] Thus, Dorothea's rapture did occasion violence that left physical traces on her body, although that violence was inflicted by Dorothea's earthly husband and not by her heavenly raptor. Yet, the commission—which ultimately failed to canonize Dorothea—was unconvinced.[106] John's description suggested that Dorothea's body evinced rapturous delight, but no sign of trauma: her face was serene, rosy, splendid, charming, and joyful; her eyes were modest; her gestures were chaste and restrained; her voice was happy; and her tones were pleasant, delightful, and sweet. Pressed further, John admitted that he did not dare to look on her face while she was enraptured, lest she be recalled from the heights of her rapture, which may have called his credibility into doubt.[107]

The commission's persistent questioning reveals doubt about the veracity of Dorothea's raptures. Dorothea was an aspiring saint as the tropes of sanctity were shifting and as clerical anxiety about women's raptures and revelations, particularly when they occasioned dramatic performance, was growing increasingly acute, which may help explain in part why medieval efforts to canonize Dorothea foundered.[108] Yet, it is interesting to note that her performance of rapture deviated from the older model, which more closely mirrored the proofs offered for criminal *raptus* and gave tangible evidence of rapture's violence. Even as Dorothea's description of rapture aligns with trends in late medieval mysticism, there was a disconnect between her internal experience and the external signs that constituted evidence of *raptus*, which may help explain the commission's skepticism. Rapture that lacked evidence of struggle, violence, and coercion and that appeared to inspire only joy was difficult to prove and, perhaps, difficult to conceive of as true rapture.

By the late fourteenth century, as *raptus* became increasingly ambiguous in the law and increasingly eroticized in mystical and chivalric texts, it also became less external, and the conceptual overlap that had characterized thirteenth-century hagiography faded somewhat as the semantic range of *raptus* grew wider and more slippery. The erotic implications of mystical *raptus* remained or even intensified, but the emphasis on bodily (if not spiritual) violence became less important in characterizing the raptures of female mystics. Yet, the full semantic range of *raptus* remains vital to understanding the construction of female sanctity in the later Middle Ages. Hagiographers like

Thomas of Cantimpré and Philippine Pourcellet, prompted by the polysemous meanings of *raptus*, assimilated the female object of divine *raptus* to the rape victim. Indeed, it may have been inevitable that rapture and rape would collapse onto one another when the object of *raptus* was a woman. The male contemplative might experience fleeting, rapturous union with the divine, but the rapture of women was enacted not merely on the soul but also on the body, which could be examined for evidence of the sudden, unlooked for (and sometimes unwanted) assault that hagiographers understood rapture to be when its object was a woman.[109] As a result, the testing of the rapturous saint mirrored the physical examination of the rape victim. The rapt female saint was the passive object of divine seizure, and rapture—at least as the clerics who conducted Dorothea's canonization trial seem to have understood it—was violent in ways that necessarily involved pain and left physical signs, even as, paradoxically, it was also a source of joy and spiritual fulfillment. Without physical proof—bleeding, bruises, rigidity, unkempt hair and clothing—rapture, like rape, should be doubted. Unsubstantiated claims of rapture, as of rape, could be adduced to women's innate tendency to fabricate, to deceive, or to be themselves deluded. Thus, although—as Bynum and others have argued—the embodied nature of feminine piety could be empowering by aligning the suffering female saint with the suffering, human Christ, language and law also helped construct the female saint as the victim of violence and suffering not only shared with but also imposed by her heavenly Spouse.

NOTES

1. Joseph Mathias Hyacinthe Albanès, ed. and trans., *La vie de sainte Douceline, fondatrice des beguines de Marseille, composée au treizième siècle en langue Provençale, pub. pour la première fois, avec la traduction en français et une introduction critique et historique* (Marseille: E. Camoin, 1879), 4.10–4.17. See also the English translation, Kathleen Garay and Madeleine Jeay, eds. and trans., *The "Life" of Saint Douceline, Beguine of Provence* (Cambridge: D. S. Brewer, 2001), 36–37. Although Douceline's vita is anonymous, the likely author is Phillippine de Porcellet, who was her prioress.

2. Garay and Jeay, *"Life" of Saint Douceline*, 9.4, p. 48; Albanès, *Vie de sainte Douceline*, 72.

3. Garay and Jeay, *"Life" of Saint Douceline*, 9.5, p. 48; Albanès, *Vie de sainte Douceline*, 74.

4. Garay and Jeay, *"Life" of Saint Douceline*, 9.14, p. 51; Albanès, *Vie de sainte Douceline*, 78.

5. Garay and Jeay, *"Life" of Saint Douceline*, 9.16, p. 51; Albanès, *Vie de sainte Douceline*, 78–80.

6. Garay and Jeay, *"Life" of Saint Douceline*, 9.20, p. 51; Albanès, *Vie de sainte Douceline*, 82.

7. Garay and Jeay, *"Life" of Saint Douceline*, 9.31, p. 55.

8. I am indebted to an anonymous reviewer who points out the similarity between Douceline's resistance and that of the Sibyl in book 6 of the *Aeneid*, when she is violently possessed by Apollo. Mystical rapture certainly resembles possession in many ways, but I would argue that the violence and sexual overtones are amplified by characterization of divine possession as *raptus*.

9. Garay and Jeay, *"Life" of Saint Douceline*, 9.31, p. 55.

10. Garay and Jeay, *"Life" of Saint Douceline*, 9.35, p. 56; Garay and Jeay in this instance translate *raubida* as ecstasy rather than rapture. Cf. Albanès, *Vie de sainte Douceline*, 92.

11. Garay and Jeay, *"Life" of Saint Douceline*, 9.35, p. 56; Albanès, *Vie de sainte Douceline*, 92.

12. Aviad M. Kleinberg, *Prophets in Their Own Country: Living Saints and the Making of Sainthood in the Later Middle Ages* (Chicago: University of Chicago Press, 1992), 123, 125.

13. Garay and Jeay, *"Life" of Saint Douceline*, 9.40, p. 57; Albanès, *Vie de sainte Douceline*, 96.

14. There is a substantial scholarly literature on hagiographic tropes of rapture and ecstasy. See especially Barbara Newman, "What Did It Mean to Say 'I Saw'? The Clash between Theory and Practice in Medieval Visionary Culture," *Speculum* 80, no. 1 (January 2005): 1–43; Dyan Elliott, "The Physiology of Rapture and Female Spirituality," in *Medieval Theology and the Natural Body*, ed. Peter Biller and A. J. Minnis (York: York Medieval Press, 1997), 141–74; Dyan Elliott, *"Raptus*/Rapture," in *The Cambridge Companion to Christian Mysticism*, ed. Amy Hollywood and Patricia Z. Beckman (Cambridge: Cambridge University Press, 2012), 189–99; and Julie B. Miller, "Eroticized Violence in Medieval Women's Mystical Literature: A Call for a Feminist Critique," *Journal of Feminist Studies in Religion* 15, no. 2 (Fall 1999): 25–49.

15. Newman, "What Did It Mean," 9; Elliott, "Physiology of Rapture," 160.

16. Miller, "Eroticized Violence," 27. See also Julie B. Miller, "Rapt by God: The Rhetoric of Rape in Medieval Mystical Literature," in *The Subjective Eye: Essays in Culture, Religion, and Gender in Honor of Margaret R. Miles*, ed. Richard Valantasis, with the assistance of Deborah J. Haynes, James D. Smith, and Janet F. Carlson (Eugene, Ore.: Pickwick Publications, 2006), pp. 235–53.

17. Miller, "Eroticized Violence," 32–33.

18. Miller, "Rapt by God," 235.

19. Male saints were also described as experiencing rapture, but their rapture was generally characterized as a brief moment of transcendence. See below.

20. Nancy Caciola, "Mystics, Demoniacs, and the Physiology of Spirit Possession in Medieval Europe," *Comparative Studies in Society and History* 42, no. 2 (April 2000): 268–306; Caciola, *Discerning Spirits: Divine and Demonic Possession in the Middle Ages* (Ithaca: Cornell University Press, 2003). On the performances of and audience response to possessed behaviors, see also Barbara Newman, "Possessed by the Spirit: Devout Women, Demoniacs, and the Apostolic Life in the Thirteenth Century," *Speculum* 73, no. 3 (July 1998): 733–70.

21. Richard Kieckhefer, "The Holy and the Unholy: Sainthood, Witchcraft, and Magic in Late Medieval Europe," *Journal of Medieval and Renaissance Studies* 24 (1994): 355–85, at 369, 385.

22. Dyan Elliott, *Proving Woman: Female Spirituality and Inquisitional Culture in the Later Middle Ages* (Philadelphia: University of Pennsylvania Press, 2004). On the overlapping and coincidence of heresy and sanctity, see also Barbara Newman, "The Heretic Saint: Guglielma of Bohemia, Milan, and Brunate," *Church History* 74, no. 1 (March 2005): 1–38.

23. Both medieval and modern scholars have grappled with the meanings of *raptus* extensively. In particular, see Kathryn Gravdal, *Ravishing Maidens: Writing Rape in Medieval French Literature and Law* (Philadelphia: University of Pennsylvania Press, 1991), esp. 4–6; Elliott, "Physiology of Rapture," 142; Henry Ansgar Kelly, "Meanings and Uses of Raptus in Chaucer's Time," *Studies in the Age of Chaucer* 20 (1998): 101–65; Newman, "What Did It Mean," 9; Jeremy Goldberg, *Communal Discord, Child Abduction, and Rape in the Later Middle Ages* (New York: Palgrave Macmillan, 2008), 163–67; and Caroline Dunn, *Stolen Women in Medieval England: Rape, Abduction, and Adultery, 1100–1500* (Cambridge: Cambridge University Press, 2013), esp. 38.

24. James Brundage, *Law, Sex, and Christian Society in Medieval Europe* (Chicago: University of Chicago University Press, 1987), 48.

25. Ibid.

26. Diana C. Moses, "Livy's Lucretia and the Validity of Coerced Consent in Roman Law," in *Consent and Coercion to Sex and Marriage in Ancient and Medieval Societies*, ed. Angeliki E. Laiou (Washington, D.C.: Dumbarton Oaks Research Library and Collection, 1993), 39–82, at 50.

27. Ibid., 51, 57.

28. See Gravdal, *Ravishing Maidens*, 6; cf. Pierre Payer, *Sex and the Penitentials: The Development of a Sexual Code, 550–1150* (Toronto: University of Toronto Press, 1984), 117. Henry Ansgar Kelly has argued that *raptus* in English law during Chaucer's lifetime denoted theft rather than rape in most instances, and both Caroline Dunn and Jeremy Goldberg warn of the dangers of translating *raptus* or *rapuit* as rape without clear evidence that a sexual crime is meant. See Kelly, "Meanings and Uses of *Raptus*"; Dunn, *Stolen Women in Medieval England*, 38; Goldberg, *Communal Discord*, 166.

29. Gravdal, *Ravishing Maidens*, 6. Gravdal argues that early medieval law followed Roman legal precedent in rejecting the Biblical (and common pre-Christian Germanic) argument that marriage between a raptor and his victim could serve as reparation for rape or abduction, although Roman *controversiae* did sometimes advocate this remedy. On the *controversiae* and rape, see Lauren Caldwell, *Roman Girlhood and the Fashioning of Femininity* (Cambridge: Cambridge University Press, 2015), 74–76.

30. Gravdal, *Ravishing Maidens*, 7.

31. Ibid., 8.

32. Isidore of Seville, *Etymologiae* V.26.14 [*Etymologiarum sive Originum libri xx*, ed. W. M. Lindsay (Oxford: Clarendon Press, 1911)]; cf. Gravdal, *Ravishing Maidens*, 8.

33. Brundage, *Law, Sex, and Christian Society*, 249.

34. Ibid., 249–50; cf. Gravdal, *Ravishing Maidens*, 8–9.

35. Brundage, *Law, Sex, and Christian Society*, 311.

36. Newman, "What Did It Mean," 9.

37. Vergil, *Aeneid* 5, lines 252–55: *puer . . . rapuit Iovis*.

38. In this instance, modern English translations vary in their rendering of the word *raptores*. The American-Standard and Douay-Rheims bibles, like the King James translation, translate *raptores* as "extortioners," while the New International Version translates it as "robbers" and the New American Standard as "swindlers." All of these translations are plausible, but the proximity of *raptores* to *adulteri* in the list of malefactors may also suggest a sexual dimension.

39. Christopher Cannon, "*Raptus* in the Chaumpaigne Release and a Newly Discovered Document Concerning the Life of Geoffrey Chaucer," *Speculum* 68, no. 1 (January 1993): 74–94, at 79; Kim M. Phillips, "Written on the Body: Reading Rape from the Twelfth to Fifteenth Centuries," in *Medieval Women and the Law*, ed. Noël James Menuge (Woodbridge, U.K.: The Boydell Press, 2003), 125–44, at 129.

40. Cannon, "*Raptus* in the Chaumpaigne Release," 79.

41. Dunn, *Stolen Women in Medieval England*, 50.

42. Gravdal, *Ravishing Maidens*, 11.

43. Ibid.

44. Philippe de Beaumanoir, *Coutumes de Beauvaisis: Texte critique publié avec une introduction, un glossaire et une table analytique*, ed. Amédée Salmon (Paris: A. Picard et fils, 1899–1900), item 824, p. 429, and item 926, p. 467.

45. For Philip of Alsace's precepts, see Raoul C. Van Caenaegem and Ludo Milis, "Kritische uitgave van de 'Grote Keure' van Filips van de Elzas, graaf van Vlaanderen, voor Gent en Brugge (1165–177)," *Bulletin de la Commission royale d'Histoire* (1977): 207–57, at 234, 236, 250, 253. Cf. R. C. van Caenegem, "Considerations on the Customary Law of Twelfth-Century Flanders," in *Law, History, the Low Countries and Europe*, ed. Ludo Milis, Daniel Lambrecht, Hilde de Ridder-Symoens, and Monique Vleeschouwers-van Melkebeek (London: Hambledon Press, 1994), 97–106. On the legislation of 1191, see Peter Arnade and Walter Prevenier,

Honor, Vengeance, and Social Trouble: Pardon Letters in the Burgundian Low Countries (Ithaca: Cornell University Press, 2015), 134–35.

46. Kathryn Gravdal, "Chrétien de Troyes, Gratian, and the Medieval Romance of Sexual Violence," *Signs* 17, no. 3 (Spring 1992): 558–85, at 564.

47. Barbara Newman, *From Virile Woman to WomanChrist: Studies in Medieval Religion and Literature* (Philadelphia: University of Pennsylvania Press, 1995), esp. 137–39.

48. Caesarius of Heisterbach, *Dialogus Miraculorum*, ed. Joseph Strange, 2 vols. (Cologne: Sumptibus J. M. Heberle [H. Lempertz], 1851), 1:233 (part 4, chap. 44); 2:63 (part 7, chap. 45); 2:255 (part 10, chap. 55); 2:260 (part 10, chap. 65).

49. Ibid., 1:123 (part 3, chap. 11).

50. Ibid., 2:26, 27 (part 7, chap. 20).

51. Bernard McGinn, *The Flowering of Mysticism: Men and Women in the New Mysticism (1200–1350)* (New York: Crossroads, 1998), 37–38; cf. Elliott, "*Raptus* / Rapture," 191–92.

52. Newman, "What Did It Mean," 12.

53. Elliott, "Physiology of Rapture and Female Spirituality," 161.

54. Newman, "What Did It Mean," 20–21.

55. Elliott, "Physiology of Rapture and Female Spirituality," 162.

56. Amy Hollywood, "The Mystery of Trauma, the Mystery of Joy," in *Monument and Memory: Fourth Nordic Conference in Philosophy of Religion*, ed. Jonna Bornemark, Mattias Martinson, and Jayne Svenungsson (Zürich: Lit Verlag, 2015), 85–100, at 96; cf. Elliott, "*Raptus* / Rapture," 193.

57. Jacques de Vitry, *Vita Maria Oigniacensi in Namurcensi Belgii dioecesi*, in *Acta sanctorum* (Paris: Victorem Palmé, 1865), 25:542–72; see especially para. 7 of the prologue and book 1, chap. 2, para. 25.

58. Elliott, "Physiology of Rapture and Female Spirituality," 160.

59. On Thomas of Cantimpré's role as a hagiographer of female mystics, see John Coakley, "Thomas of Cantimpré and Female Sanctity," in *History in the Comic Mode: Medieval Communities and the Matter of Person*, ed. Rachel Fulton and Bruce W. Holsinger (New York: Columbia University Press, 2007), 45–55.

60. Elliott, "Physiology of Rapture and Female Spirituality," 142.

61. Thomas Aquinas discusses rapture both in *Summa theologica* 2–2.171 and 175 and in *De veritate* 13. See Barbara Faes, "Per una storia della dottrina del *raptus* in Tommaso d'Aquino," *Bruniana and Campanelliana* 12, no. 2 (2006): 411–30, esp. 419–20, 425–26.

62. Trevor Dean, *Crime in Medieval Europe: 1200–1550* (New York: Routledge, 2014), 85.

63. Ibid., 84–85.

64. Philippe de Beaumanoir, *Coutumes de Beauvaisis*, item 829, p. 430, and item 926, p. 467.

65. Ibid., item 929, p. 469.

66. Dunn, *Stolen Women in Medieval England*, 68.

67. Shannon McSheffrey and Julia Pope, "Ravishment, Legal Narratives, and Chivalric Culture in Fifteenth-Century England," *Journal of British Studies* 48, no. 4 (October 2009): 818–36, esp. 819; Goldberg, *Communal Discord*, 165–66; Anthony Musson, "Crossing Boundaries: Attitudes to Rape in Late Medieval England," in *Boundaries of the Law: Geography, Gender and Jurisdiction in Medieval and Early Modern Europe*, ed. Anthony Musson (Aldershot: Routledge, 2005), 84–101.

68. Phillips, "Written on the Body," 129.

69. By the late fourteenth century, Flemish pardon letters revealed a set of formulaic tropes drawn on to demonstrate that a woman had resisted as she was required to. See Arnade and Prevenier, *Honor, Vengeance, and Social Trouble*, esp. the cases discussed on pp. 149, 176, 190.

70. Phillips, "Written on the Body," 131–33.

71. Walter Prevenier, "Violence Against Women in Fifteenth-Century France and the Burgundian State," in *Medieval Crime and Social Control*, ed. Barbara Hanawalt and David Wallace (Minneapolis: University of Minnesota Press, 1999), 186–203. Prevenier (190 n. 30) cites the case of Jehan de Thuisy (Archives Nationales, Paris, X 2 12, fols. 259r–260r), in which

the bailiff reported that the victim's sexual violation was confirmed by matrons who examined her and certified that physical proof of the rape existed.

72. Diane Wolfthal, "'A Hue and a Cry': Medieval Rape Imagery and Its Transformation," *Art Bulletin* 75, no. 1 (March 1993): 39–64, at 42.

73. Ibid., 44.

74. Phillips, "Written on the Body," 125.

75. Elise Bennett Histed, "Mediaeval Rape: A Conceivable Defence?," *Cambridge Law Journal* 63, no. 3 (November 2004), 743–69, esp. 749–50, 755–56. Histed suggests that English law reflects twelfth-century French debates about conception, which passed into English law via the influence of William of Conches, who left Chartres and became tutor to Henry Plantagenet ca. 1146–49 (749–50).

76. Dyan Elliott, *The Bride of Christ Goes to Hell: Metaphor and Embodiment in the Lives of Pious Women, 200–1500* (Philadelphia: University of Pennsylvania Press, 2011), 181.

77. Thomas of Cantimpré, *Vita Lutgardis Virgine in Aquiriae Brabantia*, in *Acta sanctorum* (Paris: Victorem Palmé, 1897), 24:189–210; Thomas of Cantimpré, *The Life of Lutgard of Aywières*, trans. Margot H. King (Toronto: Peregrina, 1987), 13.

78. Walter Simons, *Cities of Ladies: Beguine Communities in the Medieval Low Countries, 1200–1565* (Philadelphia: University of Pennsylvania Press, 2001), 70–72.

79. Thomas of Cantimpré, *Life of Lutgard of Aywières*, 14 (*Vita Lutgardis*, 1.1.4).

80. Ibid., 17 (*Vita Lutgardis*, 1.1.7).

81. Ibid., 21–22 (*Vita Lutgardis*, 1.1.13).

82. Ibid., 53 (*Vita Lutgardis*, 2.2.23).

83. Ibid., 42–43 (*Vita Lutgardis*, 2.1.1).

84. Thomas of Cantimpré, *De bonum universale de apibus: In quo ex mirifica apum repub. universa vita bene & Christiane instituende ratio traditur* (Duaci: ex pyp. Baltazaris Belleri, 1627), 2.57.18 (p. 550).

85. Ibid., 2.57.14 (p. 546). Cf. Elliott, *Proving Woman*, 103, 103 n. 74; Elliott, "Physiology of Rapture," 162; Elliott, *Bride of Christ*, 202–3.

86. Thomas of Cantimpré, *De apibus*, 2.57.14–15 (pp. 546–47).

87. Thomas de Cantimpré, *The Life of Christina the Astonishing: Latin Text with Facing English Translation*, trans. Margot H. King, 2nd ed. (Toronto: Peregrina, 1999), 28–29 (1.9), 58–59 (4.35). On Thomas's vita of Christina, see Claire Fanger's chapter in this volume.

88. Ibid., 58–59 (4.35).

89. Thomas of Cantimpré, *The Life of Margaret of Ypres*, ed. and trans. Margot H. King (Toronto: Peregrina, 1990), 20.

90. Richard Rolle, *Incendium Amoris*, ed. Margaret Deanesly (Manchester: Manchester University Press, 1915), 255.

91. Rick McDonald, "The Perils of Language in the Mysticism of Late Medieval England," *Mystics Quarterly* 34, nos. 3/4 (2008): 61.

92. Walter Simons, "Reading a Saint's Body: Rapture and Bodily Movement in the *Vitae* of Thirteenth-Century Beguines," in *Framing Medieval Bodies*, ed. Sarah Kay and Miri Rubin (Manchester: Manchester University Press, 1994), 13.

93. On Elisabeth, see Simons, "Reading a Saint's Body"; Elliott, *Proving Woman*, 186–89; Caciola, *Discerning Spirits*, 114–16; and Jesse Njus, "The Politics of Mysticism: Elisabeth of Spalbeek in Context," *Church History* 77, 2 (June 2008): 285–317.

94. On Peter's hagiographic treatment of Christina and Christina's reputation, see Kleinberg, *Prophets in Their Own Country*, 71–98.

95. Peter of Dacia, *Vita Christinae Stumbelensis*, ed., Johannes Paulson (Göteborg, 1897 [New York: Lang, 1985]), 34.

96. Ibid., 36.

97. Elliott, *Bride of Christ*, 225.

98. Richard Kieckhefer, *Unquiet Souls: Fourteenth-Century Saints and Their Religious Milieu* (Chicago: University of Chicago Press, 1987), 31. Kieckhefer discusses Dorothea's

career and reputation and their place within the tropes of fourteenth-century sanctity on pp. 22–33.

99. John of Marienwerder, *Liber de festis magisitri Johannis Marienwerder: Offenbarungen der Dorothea von Montau*, ed. Anneliese Triller, Ernst Borchert, and Hans Westpfahl (Cologne: Böhlau Verlag, 1992).

100. Ibid., chap. 74, p. 124.

101. Testimony of Nicholas of Hoenstein, June 26, 1404, in Richard Stachnik, ed., *Die Akten des Kanonisationsprozesses Dorotheas von Montau von 1394 bis 1521* (Cologne: Böhlau Verlag, 1978), 80.

102. Testimony of Metza Hugische, October 13, 1404, in Stachnik, *Akten des Kanonisationsprozesses*, 108. Johannes Reyman, a canon and doctor of law, testified at length about Dorothea's trances, offering the opinion that the signs of her rapture lay in her subsequent cheerfulness, her facial expression, and her illuminating speech. Testimony of Johannes Reyman, October 22, 1404, in Stachnik, *Akten des Kanonisationsprozesses*, 211.

103. Testimony of John of Marienwerder, October 27, 1404, in Stachnik, *Akten des Kanonisationsprozesses*, 257.

104. Testimony of John of Marienwerder, October 30, 1404, in Stachnik, *Akten des Kanonisationsprozesses*, 275.

105. Ibid., 280.

106. The primary reasons for the failure of Dorothea's canonization were political, linked to crises facing the Teutonic Knights and the Dominican Order in Prussia in the early fifteenth century. Yet, support for Dorothea's canonization was insufficient for a new process to succeed during the medieval period, and Dorothea would not be canonized until 1976. See Ute Stargardt, "The Political and Social Backgrounds of the Canonization of Dorothea of Montau," *Mystics Quarterly* 11 (1985): 107–22.

107. Testimony of John of Marienwerder, October 30, 1404, in Stachnik, *Akten des Kanonisationsprozesses*, 313.

108. On shifting conceptions of female piety and increasing clerical doubt about women's dramatic performances of sanctity and claims to visions and possession, see Elliott, *Proving Woman*, esp. 232–303, and Caciola, *Discerning Spirits*, esp. chap. 6, as well as Renate Blumenfeld-Kosinski, "The Strange Case of Ermine de Reims (ca. 1347–1396): A Medieval Woman Between Demons and Saints," *Speculum* 85, no. 2 (April 2010): 321–56, and Blumenfeld-Kosinski, *The Strange Case of Ermine de Reims: A Medieval Woman Between Demons and Saints* (Philadelphia: University of Pennsylvania Press, 2015).

109. By the later Middle Ages, investigations of sanctity, particularly when the putative saint was a woman, involved close examination of the deceased woman's corpse because of the understanding that sanctity marked and transformed the body. See, for example, Katharine Park's account of the examination of Clare of Montefalco's body and the discovery of physical manifestations of the divine in her heart and gall bladder (*Secrets of Women: Gender, Generation, and the Origins of Human Dissection* [New York: Zone Books, 2006], 39–76.)

5

SYNEISAKTISM:

SACRED PARTNERSHIP AND SINISTER SCANDAL

Maeve B. Callan

Syneisaktism is a cumbersome word for a controversial practice. It comes from the Greek *syneisaktoi*, referring to religious women, often vowed virgins, living in partnerships with religious men, including priests. The term began as an insult: *parthenoi syneisaktoi* in Greek became *virgines subintroductae* in Latin, meaning "virgins who have been brought in covertly," that is, to the man's dwelling. Modern scholars have reclaimed the term, some broadening it to refer to the general ideal of religious men and women working together with mutual respect and consideration, without being blinded by sexual difference.[1] My discussion focuses on a narrower definition, but the broader spirit shapes the context. Repeatedly rejected as a "new and unheard of" aberration in the Middle Ages, syneisaktism continues practices found in Christianity since its foundation. Especially after church merged with empire, however, authorities urged separation between religious men and women, deeming intimacy between them too great a threat to Christians' conscience, whether it resulted in actual sexual transgressions or merely scandalized people with the possibility. Yet what was scandalous to some was sacred to others, as is also true of Christianity's core claims that a rabble-rousing Jewish peasant whom the state killed as a criminal was actually God incarnate, saving the world through his agonizing death. Moreover, the practice's spiritual power lay partly in the suspicion and scandal it caused among others. Syneisaktoi who suffered persecution from those they scandalized could find ample scriptural assurance that such treatment confirmed that they traveled the righteous path, as well as

I thank Emily Potts and Western Michigan University's graduate history students for inviting me to serve as their spring speaker in 2016, when I delivered a version of this paper. I also thank Seth Andersen, Janet Everhart, Matt Hussey, David Collins, and my own *syneisaktoi* (the word is grammatically masculine, but gender inclusive), especially Matthew Stratton.

scriptural examples of Christ's own intimacies with women.[2] Syneisaktism continued one of Christianity's earliest and most egalitarian gender practices, but its opponents' views have dominated through the centuries, marginalizing it almost to the point of erasure. Its reintregration into the historical record can prompt a fuller understanding of the Christian past, thus better informing the present and inspiring the future.

Biblical Bases

Although I first learned about syneisaktism in graduate school while working with Richard Kieckhefer and Barbara Newman,[3] I soon realized I had been hearing of it for a long time—every time I read 1 Corinthians, in fact. Two passages are particularly relevant. In chapter nine, Paul asserts his apostolic rights, including "the right to take along a believing woman/wife, as do the other apostles and the brothers of the Lord and Cephas" (9:5). The key word, "woman" (*gynaika*), can also mean "wife." Peter (Cephas) was married, but unless syneisaktism or something similar is allowed, this seems an odd right for Paul, who celebrates his chaste celibacy, to assert. Perhaps he intended women like Phoebe the deacon, whom he commends in Romans 16.1, or Junia, whom with her partner Andronicus Paul praises as "prominent among the apostles" (Rom. 16:7). If Paul ever acted on this right, however, it has been lost to history. This is not surprising; later Christian authorities became scandalized not just by syneisaktism's mixed partnerships, but by the very idea of female leadership—so much so that tradition at times changed Junia into a man to keep her an apostle.[4]

Two chapters earlier, Paul advises, "If anyone thinks that he is not behaving properly toward his virgin/betrothed, if his passions are strong, and so it has to be, let him do as he wishes: let them marry—it is no sin. But if someone stands firm in his resolve, being under no necessity but having his own desire under control, and has determined this in his heart, to keep her as his virgin, he will do well. So then he who marries his virgin does well, and he who refrains from marriage will do even better" (1 Cor. 7:36–38).

As with 9.5, we have a word that specifically means "virgin" (parthenon) translated as "betrothed" or "engaged daughter." In part this is because it sounds odd to say, "If anyone thinks that he is not behaving properly toward his virgin"—why would someone have a virgin? The context applied to the situation is most commonly one of two, both shaped by early Christian apocalypticism, as the world's anticipated imminent end rendered marriage somewhat moot. Paul is interpreted as responding either to a father wondering whether he should marry off his daughter or have her remain a virgin or to the virgin's fiancé, who is debating the wisdom of their plans to marry. Yet it could refer to a syneisaktic couple struggling with sexual desire, prompting them to consider marriage.[5] Paul responds in customary fashion: if the man cannot control his lust, they should marry, but if they can persevere in purity, it would be preferable for him "to keep her as his virgin"—that is, as his syneisaktic partner. Such an interpretation stretches back at least to Ephrem the Syrian in the fourth century.[6]

A third Pauline passage expresses a similar ideal to syneisaktism, that men and women can transcend gender differences and be partners in their mutual love of Christ. In Galatians 3.28, thought to be based on a baptismal formula, Paul declares that Christians have transcended ethnic distinctions and social class as well as gender: "There is no longer Jew or Greek, there is no longer slave or free, there is no longer male and female, for all are one in Christ Jesus." According to Jo Ann McNamara, syneisaktism, "the most deeply radical social concept that Christianity produced," builds upon Christ's deliberate inclusion of women; it was part of Christianity's initial appeal to women, as early followers mirrored Christ's attitude, seeing beyond gender to a truly inclusive community where all were one in Christ Jesus.[7] Their intense spirituality and apocalypticism broke down conventional barriers, allowing people to attempt previously unthinkable options. A profound and pervasive sense of God's grace made all things possible, including men and women living together intimately without sexual desire to divide them.[8] Christianity itself began as a scandal to pagans, "notorious for close association with women," condemned by the same suspicions later directed at syneisaktism.[9]

Two additional passages further illuminate the practice. In reference to sexual sin, Proverbs 6:27 rhetorically asks, "Can fire be carried in the bosom without burning one's clothes?" with the intended answer a resounding no, so one should not subject oneself to temptation. In the New Testament, however, James implies that this burning may be a blessing: "Blessed is anyone who endures temptation. Such a one has stood the test and will receive the crown of life that the Lord has promised to those who love him" (James 1:12). Later expressions of syneisaktism that allow us to glimpse practitioners' perspectives suggest that some engaged in the experiment precisely because it thrust them into the fire of temptation over which they might prevail. As Pierre Payer notes, dominant medieval Christian perspectives proclaimed lust as "integral to the present state of human nature, bred in the bones if you will. . . . It is the permanent and pervasive tendency of the sensual desire to pursue its own animal ends in disregard of the dictates of natural reason. While it can be controlled, channelled, and bridled, it can be neither eliminated nor escaped."[10] Some individuals discussed below apparently immersed themselves in this struggle precisely because it was the most demanding test they could undergo to expiate their sins, discipline their bodies, and demonstrate their devotion to the divine. And, according to certain sources, at least some *could* embrace fire without getting burned, both figuratively and literally.

Church Fathers and Councils

As with much in the Bible, these passages are ambiguous. The relevant passages in 1 Corinthians suggest that syneisaktism was an admirable practice, but the precise nature of the relationships to which Paul refers remains uncertain. Church Fathers, however, spoke more plainly about the subject—and more negatively, although not universally. For example, Tertullian advocated syneisaktism as the holier alternative to second marriage, provided the woman be "beautiful only in spirit."[11] John Chrysostom addressed it at greatest length, and with such hostility that the resentment he aroused among clerical practitioners helped prompt his exile from Constantinople in 404.[12] Yet Chrysostom deeply valued his own friendships with women, especially the deaconess Olympias, to whom seventeen of his letters survive. She built her own women's community beside his episcopal palace and followed him into exile. Curiously, or perhaps tellingly, given his closeness with Olympias, he was convinced that only sexual desire would bind a man to a woman, declaring, "Why else would a man put up with the faults of a woman? He would find her despicable."[13] He maintained that Christianity enabled certain women to transcend their sex's inferiority and even become men's spiritual superiors.[14] Syneisaktism perverted this relative equality, however; a man who attempted the practice would soon become like a lion with a sheared mane, reduced to ridiculousness, made easy prey for the devil just as Adam was made by Eve. He insists that syneisaktoi "take all their corrupting feminine customs and stamp them into the souls of these men,"[15] while the women simultaneously become domineering instead of submissive, overturning the divinely ordained gender hierarchy.[16] This unnatural relationship made men more like women and women more like men, to the detriment of us all.

Chrysostom recognized their shared culpability and wrote two treatises against syneisaktism, one directed at each sex. He allows us to hear an echo of what the practice's proponents might have said, as he systematically sets them up to knock them down. The men apparently contended that they protected the women, helping wealthy ones with their finances and providing for those who were poor. Chrysostom retorted that the religious should not have worldly concerns, and that any good they might offer these women could cost them their salvation. To the men's claims that they were practicing charity by caring for the needy, Chrysostom pointed to the abundance of old and sick of both sexes who could benefit from such kindness—rather than these sweet, young syneisaktoi. To male insistence that they needed a woman to provide for their domestic needs, Chrysostom shot back that men can cook and clean too. He also imagined a woman saying she needed someone to run errands for her, but, he replied, she should have a servant or an older woman do so. His bottom line, beyond an emphasis on self-reliance with help only from one's same sex, is that those dedicated to God should not care about worldly things. We cannot have it all ways, living like religious virgins and married partners, too, and still keep our salvation.[17]

Chrysostom believed syneisaktism caused constant sexual arousal, since the desire was never satisfied (unlike marriage, when, he claimed, the ability to have sex would soon make you stop wanting it).[18] He insisted it could end only in failure, although he granted that people could prevail over lust—but not without scandal. And *this* was the ultimate problem—not the passion, but the scandal, to weaker Christians and to outsiders who could only assume the worst. He applied Paul's teachings about food offered to idols in 1 Corinthians 8 to syneisaktism. Paul recognizes that such food in itself is harmless since the idols are empty and powerless, yet he also understands that not everyone has firm enough faith to realize this. Weaker members are scandalized when their fellow Christians eat such food, causing them to stumble. "When you sin against members of your family, and wound their conscience when it is weak, you sin against Christ" (1 Cor. 8:12). Thus the righteous should abstain from such foods so they do not harm those less developed in their understanding. This teaching equally pertains to syneisaktism, according to Chrysostom. The people practicing these partnerships might be pure, but the thoughts they inspired in others would not be, and so they must be stopped.

In his constructed conversations with syneisaktics, Chrysostom allows that each might make a rather obvious defense. "We are not responsible for the ignorance of others," protests the imagined man, and when the woman castigates those who see scandal when they behold chaste purity, "Their blame falls on their own head."[19] Chrysostom, however, sees syneisaktism as inherently scandalous, and thus a scandal to God. He adds that scandals can be allowed if a greater good results, but in syneisaktism, "nothing results save that the weak are cast down[;] even if they suffered this a thousand times over from their own irrationality, we should spare them."[20] Yet Chrysostom's words condemn his own behavior. He insists that men burn with desire for women, subscribing to the view of lust described by Payer above. Thus virtually any interaction between the sexes becomes suspect—including whatever contact a bishop like himself might have with his female faithful, and especially including his intimate associations with women such as Olympias.[21] For those who believe that lust consumes humanity, that it is the primary lens through which the sexes behold each other, any interaction between them, outside of family and marriage, is prone to scandal. Even total separation offers no escape. No matter how far ascetics fled into the desert, their sexual demons followed, tormenting them with desires that they had tried to renounce but that now ravaged their minds.

Chrysostom's contemporary Jerome was one such ascetic. He described his ordeal in a letter to Eustochium, the adolescent daughter of his closest female companion, Paula.

> Oh, how often, when I was living in the desert, in that lonely waste, scorched by the burning sun, which affords to hermits a savage dwelling-place, how often did I fancy myself surrounded by the pleasures of Rome! . . . But though in my fear of hell I had condemned myself to this prison-house, where my only companions were scorpions and wild beasts, I often found myself surrounded by bands of dancing girls. My face was pale with fasting; but though my limbs were cold as ice my mind was burning with desire, and the fires of lust kept bubbling up before me when my flesh was as good as dead.[22]

In this same letter, filled with such misogyny that it has been called "the greatest slander of women since Juvenal's sixth satire,"[23] he fulminated against syneisaktism specifically, denouncing the women as "this plague of female beloveds [*agapetarum pestis*] . . . these unwed wives by another name, this new kind of concubines [*nouum concubinarum genus*], . . . whores each for their own man [*meretrices univirae*]. They are bound to the same house, one room, and often one bed, but they call us suspicious if we consider anything improper. . . . These women do not wish to be virgins, but rather to seem as if they are."[24]

Yet to Ascella, another female friend, he lamented being the target of such suspicion, given his own intimate association with women: "A crowd of virgins often surrounded me, and I often contemplated the sacred books with some of them, as best I could. Study led to constant attention, constant attention to intimacy, and intimacy to trust. Let [my critics] say if they have detected anything in my behavior not befitting a Christian! . . . Nothing is brought against me except my sex, and even for this I am not condemned except when Paula comes to Jerusalem."[25]

According to Jerome, a crucial difference exculpated him and condemned syneisaktics: they lived together while he never even dined with his female intimates. Unlike Chrysostom, Jerome refused to believe that syneisaktics could remain chaste, perhaps because of the force with which fantasy dancing girls hounded him in the desert.

Although Jerome believed the worst of others, he resented that others suspected him and his companions. Over seven centuries later, Peter Abelard shared a similar struggle. He referred to Jerome's letter to Ascella in his *Historia calamitatum* while lamenting the criticism he endured for his involvement with the nuns of the Paraclete and especially Heloise, his former wife and before that his student. After he learned of their affair, Heloise's uncle had Abelard castrated, and the now-married lovers entered religious orders, at Abelard's insistence. Abelard understandably saw a connection with the third-century Origen, whose alleged self-castration was supposedly done "to end false suspicion putting a stop to his instruction of women."[26] Castration was an extreme response, however; Jerome claimed abstinence alone could eliminate sex differences, with reference to Galatians 3:28.[27] Yet such purgation was never complete this side of paradise. Confident in his own purity and that of his female companions, Jerome reviled others, particularly women, who attempted syneisaktism on a more intimate level.

Condemnation preceded and continued long after Chrysostom and Jerome. In the middle of the third century, Cyprian of Carthage spoke against syneisaktism, claiming it corrupted virgins. The Council of Antioch disciplined Paul of Samosata, bishop of Antioch, for living with two "young and pretty" women[28] and officially condemned the practice. Over the next five centuries, it was denounced in over twenty councils and synods held in North Africa,[29] the Middle East,[30] Byzantium,[31] Gaul,[32] and especially Spain.[33] Ecclesiastical efforts were further supported by emperors, like Honorius and Theodosius in 420. The Church that emerged out of the ashes of the martyrs and then the Roman Empire increasingly insisted that sanctity required strict separation between the sexes, and these decrees furthered that agenda. Yet the repeated condemnations reveal the practice's pervasiveness and the impotence of protestations against it—as does its continuation for centuries more, including in Ireland.

Ireland

As often happens, Ireland offers alternative and underappreciated perspectives. The first area in western Europe outside of the Roman Empire to convert to Christendom, the form of the faith that developed there allowed for a diversity of approaches to the religious life that included partnerships between the sexes and their strict separation. The seventh-century *Liber Angeli* ("Book of the angel") suggests syneisaktism shaped Armagh, considered to be St. Patrick's original episcopal see and thus a font of Irish Christianity: "In this city of Armagh Christians of both sexes are seen to live together in religion from the coming of the faith to the present day almost inseparably."[34] This could refer to intimate partnerships or simply to mixed-sex communities, which are often mentioned in passing in Irish saints' vitae, praised as places "where a multitude of holy men and nuns have served God faithfully from antiquity."[35] The *Catalogus sanctorum Hiberniae* (Catalogue of the saints of Ireland) celebrates companionship between religious men and women as the holiest lifestyle and suggests that sex segregation is a sign of how the holy have fallen. It outlines successive stages of Irish Christianity in terms of its male saints: "The first order was the holiest, the second beneath them in holiness, but above the third. The first blazes like the sun, enflamed with the fervor of love, the second glows like the moon, and the third shines like the dawn."[36] Heterosexual interaction serves as one of two indications of exceptional holiness, the other being uniformity. Members of the first order were all bishops who followed Patrick, celebrated one Easter, and wore one tonsure. Mass services were identical throughout Ireland, and what was excommunicated by one church was excommunicated by all. This idyllic community of saints "did not refuse women's assistance [*administrationem*], and they did not refuse their companionship, because, founded upon the rock which is Christ, they did not fear the wind of temptation."[37]

Without Patrick's central authority, diversity entered with the second order, which had various rites of mass and rules of life but celebrated the same Easter and wore the same tonsure. They, however, "fled the companionship and services of women, and they shut women out from their monasteries."[38] Though the first order outnumbered the second (350 to 300), the most celebrated male saints, apart from Patrick, belong to the second order. The list could serve as a roster for Ireland's most respected school, that of Finnén of Clonard, including the teacher and his most renowned supposed students—Colmcille, Brénainn (Brendan), Ciarán, Enda, and Coémghen (Kevin), among others—yet their own vitae show several of them living with women or including women in their communities, and Clonard itself was "co-educational." The third order makes no reference to women. These were Ireland's great hermits, who "despised all earthly things"[39] but otherwise lacked unity, with different tonsures, Easters, rules, and celebrations of mass. This third order is often interpreted to refer to Ireland's *céli Dé* movement, but rather than shunning women, their communities included both sexes and married people as well as celibates.[40]

According to this possibly ninth-century pseudohistorical sketch of the fifth through mid-seventh century, women begin as partners, become shunned as Other, then disappear in silence, depending on the virtues or deficiencies of their male compatriots. Yet, "all through the early history of the Church, and long after the close of the three periods referred to, frequent mention occurs of the so-called sisters of saints living with [male saints], and assisting in their work."[41] Uniform gender arrangements, whether close collaboration or strict separation, seem to have been a pious fiction, no matter the age. Clearly a work of Patrician propaganda, the *Catalogus* nevertheless raises a tantalizing question: Why is women's companionship found among the holiest order, while isolation from women marks the middle? The text itself does not answer the question. Does it celebrate the sexual equality of an almost forgotten past as the highest path of virtue, which has lamentably fallen away? Or does it suggest that this was a trial that only the holiest men could pass, and the lesser saints wisely recognized that to engage in such intimate association with women would cause their downfall? Were the holiest saints impervious to temptation, or was such temptation part of their asceticism? Scholars generally agree that the *Catalogus* refers to syneisaktism for the first order,[42] but it could be extolling a more general ideal of gender relations in which men and women respected each other as Christian colleagues without being blinded by sexual difference, embodying the example espoused in Galatians 3:28.

The Irish regarded syneisaktism as a trial to be endured for heavenly reward and a form of realized eschatology, a glimpse of what awaits the saved in heaven and an echo of Eden's innocence.[43] The sixth- or seventh-century "Second Synod of St. Patrick" permitted the practice if "the love and desire of sin have ceased, since a dead body does not harm another's dead body; if this is not the case they shall be separated."[44] As Chrysostom indicated, this heterosexual union could serve practical purposes, the woman assisting the man with his domestic needs or, if her partner were a priest, in his performance of the mass, and receiving in turn protection by the man from natural and human dangers.[45] In his *Confessio*, Patrick testifies to the hardships faced by his female converts, cast out by their families and often suffering persecution and threats, and thus in need of protection.[46] Apart from gender roles and sexual tension, such ascetics offered each other mutually rewarding friendship. They encouraged one another in the quest for sanctification not only through mortification of their fallen flesh but through a profound love born in Christ and for each other that looked beyond the lustful temptation of the gendered body.

However free from lust participants may have been, few outsiders believed purity to be possible in such circumstances. According to his Tripartite Life, "At a certain time Patrick was told, through the error of the rabble, that bishop Mél had sinned with his [sister], for they used to be in one habitation a-praying to the Lord." Patrick investigated and "knew that no sin was between them," since the woman could carry fire in her chasuble without any injury to herself or her cloak, a miraculous "yes" to Proverbs 6:27's implicitly rhetorical question whether such a feat was possible, attesting to her virtue. Yet Patrick advised the two to separate anyway, to avoid scandal.[47] The same criticisms leveled at syneisaktism were made against mixed-sex communities. For example, Daig founded a monastery for women and served as their teacher. Áengus, abbot of Clonmacnoise, sent some monks to rebuke Daig for their living arrangements. The men, however, were won over by the women's chastity and holiness, particularly since, like Mél's partner, they carried fire without damaging themselves or their clothes. "The guests, seeing this, did penance. Blessed Daig led the nuns northwards, however, and he built different monasteries in varied places, in which they might serve God with other virgins apart (from men), just as was proper for them."[48] As with Mél's partnership, the supposed sin in their cohabitation was not sex but the scandal it arose among "the rabble." Whatever fear of a scandal the monks felt disappeared when they met the women in question, however; Daig's response stands at odds with the rest of the text. Though the hagiographer deems this segregation the proper course, he describes Daig's subsequent syneisaktism with one of the virgins, Cunne, as well as his visit to a monastery wherein lived the sons of Flescaig with the holy virgin Riceilla, without condemnation.

A tale told in the martyrology *Félire Óengusso* confronts critics as it emphasizes syneisaktism's spiritual gains. St. Scothín slept between two virgins "that the battle with the Devil might be the greater for him. And it was proposed to accuse him on that account." St. Brénainn came to investigate, but ended up being the one tested when he took Scothín's place that night:

> So when [it] reached the hour of resting the girls came into the house wherein was Brénainn, with their lapfuls of glowing embers in their chasubles; and the fire burnt them not, and they spill the embers in front of Brénainn, and go into the bed to him. "What is this?" asks Brénainn. "Thus it is that we do every night," say the girls. They lie down with Brénainn, and nowise could he sleep with longing. "That is imperfect, O cleric," say the girls: "he who is here every night feels nothing at all. Why goest thou not, O cleric, into the tub (of cold water) if it be easier for thee? 'Tis often that the cleric, even Scothín visits it." "Well," says Brénainn, "it is wrong for us to make this test, for he is better than we are."[49]

The guardians of conventional Christianity as represented by Brénainn regarded syneisaktism with suspicion and distrust, yet they also recognized that some practitioners possessed sufficient virtue to maintain the relationship, even in bed. Scothín's feat could be read as propaganda proclaiming his power over the lust that burns most of humanity so deeply, but varied references attest that it was more than a select saint's miraculous accomplishment. Syneisaktism may not have been for everyone, as it was not for Brénainn, but it remained a possibility at least until the twelfth century for those who had the strength to endure not only sexual temptation but also the persecution arising from the scandal the arrangement brought to others.

Regrettably, the women in these syneisaktic situations are often unnamed, as are Scothín's companions and Mél's partner. The women prove their virtue, not only by not indulging their lust, but perhaps by not even feeling it, as suggested by their ability to embrace fire without getting burned,[50] but their names remain unrecorded. Yet one text may have been written at least in part by a woman and focused especially on the female partner's perspective, the famed *Comrac Líadaine ocus Cuirithir*, "the Meeting of Líadain and Cuirithir."[51] This text, written between the seventh and ninth centuries, recounts two poets' tragic love affair and may preserve their own words, although it has been embellished and edited by anonymous others. The two met during Líadain's professional tour of Ireland. Cuirithir fell in love with her and proposed marriage, but she refused, lest it interfere with her career. Instead she advised him to come to her home after she had finished her circuit of Ireland. When he arrived, he was devastated to learn that she had become a nun. Mutually consumed with love, they appealed to Cuimíne Fota, a celebrated seventh-century saint who wrote one of Ireland's great penitentials. Cuimíne gave the lovers the choice of hearing or seeing each other; they chose voice over visage, deepening their torment. Cuimíne next suggested syneisaktism, insisting that a "little scholar" sleep between them. Apparently the lovers failed the test; both Cuimíne and Cuirithir threatened to kill the student, the former if he concealed anything that occurred between the lovers, the latter if he confessed, and Cuirithir was soon banished to another monastery. He then went on pilgrimage elsewhere in Ireland, but Líadain followed him and lamented her decision; whether to become a nun or not to give into desire during their one night together is unclear:

'Twas madness
Not to do his pleasure,
Were there not the fear of the King of Heaven.

To him the way he has wished
Was great gain,
To go past the pains of Hell into Paradise.[52]

Cuirithir could endure the agony no longer and took his pilgrimage across the sea, whereupon his heartbroken lover sat on the stone on which he used to pray until she died and went to heaven.

Like the twelfth-century Heloise to whom the seventh-century Líadain is often compared, Líadain resisted marriage owing to its career complications. Heloise, however, was concerned with her lover Abelard's career, Líadain with her own. Her decision to become a nun, one of the tale's many unexplained aspects, may have been another career move, as Heloise understood Abelard's progression as a philosopher to depend on his position in the church. Significantly, Líadain does not seem to have had a vocation, as her love is directed entirely to Cuirithir; for "the King of Heaven" she expresses only fear, which she resents for keeping her from living out her love with Cuirithir. What transpired during their night together remains their and the "little scholar's" secret. Yet that night radically turned the tables; she followed him when he fled from her into monastic life and pilgrimage. He still bemoaned their separation, with each moment without her an agonizing eternity, yet he chose a religious life over one with her, whereas, according to her lament's last strophe, her love dissolved her heart to the point of death. This could imply a critique of syneisaktism, but it reads as a critique of choosing the religious life over marriage when truly in love. Líadain's story implicitly criticizes the Christianity represented by the penitentialist Cuimíne, who saw sex as a grave sin requiring rigorous penance. Though she regretted not committing the act and choosing to be a nun rather than a wife, her tale ends with her exoneration, if such she needed, given her entrance into heaven.

Twelfth-Century Examples

The twelfth century stands among the most momentous in European history. Its military campaigns still reverberate today, including Ireland's invasion by the Anglo-Norman rulers of England and the crusades called by Western Christians, ostensibly to reclaim the Holy Land for Christ. Cities took shape, universities emerged out of monastic schools, and trade increased, giving rise to what would become the middle class and greater disposable movable wealth. Vernacular literature, already found in Ireland and Wales for half a millennium or more, spread across the Continent, broadening access to ideas and expression, although still largely confined to the elite. The Gregorian Reform that began in the eleventh century transformed the church, intensifying papal power, entrenching an elaborate hierarchy, and achieving unprecedented success in its insistence on clerical celibacy. Various councils had issued similar decrees before, but they were less binding before the Gregorian Reform. Across Europe clerical marriages were severed or disguised, the priests' wives denounced as the devil's whores, and the priests themselves, or at least those who passed as pure by not openly having wives, were increasingly proclaimed to be in Christ's own image. A shadow of the *Catalogus*'s second age loomed over Western Christendom. Though Christianity has ever included a range of gender perspectives, those insistent on the sexes' strict separation and women's submission to male authority dominated the discussion, declaring everyone's eternal salvation dependent on their views. As McNamara has argued, "the carefully nurtured fear of women [stood] at the base of the clerical reform. By the thirteenth century, the forces of separation had successfully equated syneisactism with heresy."[53] Yet, as authoritative voices vehemently avowed the official line, many sought a more personal and immediate expression of Christianity and challenged dominant gender conventions. Enthusiasm for the *vita apostolica*, living like Christ and his apostles, intensified, including the yearning for mixed gender partnerships; those who felt it often cited 1 Corinthians 9:5 in justification.[54] Consequently, the twelfth century offers some of syneisaktism's strongest examples, and its most scathing denunciations.

The vita of the Anglo-Saxon Christina of Markyate, written by a monk of St. Albans Abbey while she was still alive, provides the most complete portrait of a *syneisaktos*. She had three partners, the first two resulting from her determination to honor her religious vocation and escape a forced marriage. Her family strove to return her to her husband, so she hid with an anchoress before moving to share the cell of an elderly hermit, Roger. He resolved never to look at nor speak with her directly, but this resolution did not survive their first day. Roger stepped over her as she lay prostrate in his chapel, averting his eyes. Yet each wished to observe the other's holiness: he looked back, she looked up, and it was spiritual love at first sight.

> And so they saw each other, not by design and yet not by chance, but, as afterwards became clear, by the divine will. For if they had not a glimpse of each other, neither would have presumed to live with each other in the confined space of that cell: they would not have dwelt together: they would not have been stimulated by such heavenly desire, nor would they have attained such a lofty place in heaven. The fire, namely, which had been kindled by the spirit of God and burned in each one of them cast its sparks into their hearts by the grace of that mutual glance; and so made one in heart and soul in chastity and charity in Christ, they were not afraid to dwell together under the same roof.

Furthermore, through their dwelling together and encouraging each other to strive after higher things their holy affection grew day by day, like a large flame springing from two brands joined together. The more fervently they yearned to contemplate the beauty of the creator, the more happily they reign with Him in supreme glory. And so their great progress induced them to dwell together. Yet they acted with circumspection in not letting this become known, for they feared scandal to their inferiors.

Christina's biographer's description of that first irresistible connection combines the sacred and the scandalous, as also applies to Christina's living conditions for the next four years. A log barricaded her foot-wide part of their cell, rendering her virtually immobile and totally dependent on Roger to leave her "prison," causing her intense bodily suffering.[55]

After Roger's death, Christina moved to another syneisaktic relationship, this time with a well-respected cleric. Soon the lust that never interfered with Roger overwhelmed them both, the man most spectacularly. Wild with desire, the cleric attempted to win her over with his naked body, among more despicable deeds that the author refused to recount. When she did not succumb, he tried to manipulate her pity, to no avail. Christina felt the burning passion herself—so much so that she thought her clothes would catch fire from her skin's heat—but faith and discipline fortified her, as did the fact that her passion abated in his presence.[56] Chrysostom's gender-bending fears here came to fruition, as Christina's cleric said she was more like the man, and he the woman,[57] but this—and the entire situation—is used not to condemn Christina but to confirm her sanctity. God eventually cured her lust through an experience of mystical motherhood with the Christ-child. "And with immeasurable delight she held Him at one moment to her virginal breast, at another she felt His presence within her even through the barrier of her flesh. Who shall describe the abounding sweetness with which the servant was filled by this condescension of her creator? From that moment the fire of lust was so completely extinguished that never afterwards could it be revived."[58] This purifying passion prepared her for her most meaningful mortal relationship, with Geoffrey, the Norman abbot of St. Albans.

The bishop of Lincoln, whom Christina's family had bribed to oppose her vocation, died about the time she triumphed over her lust for the cleric. As she no longer had to hide in others' homes, she claimed her inheritance of Roger's cell at Markyate, which Geoffrey helped her grow into a community. Geoffrey was Christina's truest partner; the vita portrays him as her disciple, obeying her wishes, but their mutual love balanced and anchored their relationship, while also causing her consternation. God himself helped her keep Geoffrey by her side, as shown most vividly in a vision she had of Geoffrey, "whom she loved above all others, encircled with her arms and held closely to her breast," but she feared that he would escape her embrace; Christ placed his hands over hers, preventing that possibility.[59] Trying to understand her love for Geoffrey in the context of her relationship with God, Christina once prayed even longer than usual and received incomprehensible bliss. Then God asked her if she would want Geoffrey to die for him; she wholeheartedly affirmed that not only would she, she would do it with her own hands. She likened herself to Abraham and Geoffrey to Isaac, but she differentiated between Abraham's carnal love for his son and her spiritual love for Geoffrey, which God alone could understand. She then received a vision that set the proper positions in the love triangle. Christ stood at the altar, facing Christina at his right and Geoffrey at his left. Apprehensive about Geoffrey's less auspicious placement, she tried to switch, but God helped her understand that "there was only one thing in which a person should not place another before self, God's love."[60]

Though her relationship with Geoffrey is the only one of the three without cohabitation, it caused the greatest criticism. Christina's biographer attributes this to the envy and malice some felt at being excluded from their intimate association. He referred to 1 Corinthians 9:5 to defend their integrity and to denigrate her detractors; he also invoked Jerome and Paula as positive precedent for their relationship. He ascribed this slander to the devil, who "wanted the cause of their extraordinary progress to be considered as the cause of their failure."[61] Yet God would not allow his handmaid to be persecuted for long, and her critics admitted their error. Perhaps this acceptance was in part because Christina of Markyate was not the only twelfth-century English syneisaktos. Eve of Wilton left England for western France in 1080 and eventually entered into syneisaktism with a man named Hervé, a follower of Robert of Arbrissel. Their relationship so moved Hilary of Orléans, Abelard's former student, that he wrote a poem praising them shortly after Eve passed around 1125, declaring, "Eve lived there a long time with her companion Herveus. I feel that you are troubled, you who hear such talk. Brother, avoid all suspicious thought; let this not be the cause. Such love was not in the world but in Christ."[62] Whether they practiced Scothín's advanced form of syneisaktism of sharing the same bed is unknown, but Hervé's former religious leader did—or at least so claimed his critics.

Robert of Arbrissel is best known as the founder of Fontevraud, a double monastery that became one of the most prestigious and influential in France. He insisted that the abbess lead the community and the men serve the women. This could be seen as a more elaborate, institutionalized form of syneisaktism, but Fontevraud itself was not the problem—at least then he settled his community down and housed them in separate dormitories. Earlier, according to

Marbode of Rennes, when Robert lived in the forests with his followers, he had the sexes sleep side by side, with himself in the middle: "You deem women worthy not only to share a common table by day but also a common bed at night—or so it is reported—and your whole flock of disciples does likewise, so that lying in the middle amongst them, you fashion the law of wakefulness and sleep for both sexes. . . . How dangerous is this practice the wailing of babies has betrayed."[63] Interestingly, Marbode believes that Robert himself does not indulge his lust, but he thinks him guilty of a worse sin, pride, immersing himself in the very sin he seeks to avoid and deeming himself better than David or Solomon, who committed sexual sin. Soon after Marbode wrote this letter, Robert and his supporters started building Fontevraud, but Robert's sleeping arrangements continued to cause concern.

This time the critic was Geoffrey of Vendôme, Hervé's former abbot. In 1102, Geoffrey wrote to Hervé and Eve and acknowledged their syneisaktism with implicit approbation.[64] Robert did not fare as well with one of Geoffrey's letters five years later, although Geoffrey was more respectful than Marbode had been. Geoffrey expressed his shock over rumors that not only did Robert often speak privately with women in his order, but also, "you do not blush to frequently lie in bed between these women at night. Hence you seem to yourself, as you assert, to worthily carry the cross of our Lord Savior, since you try to abolish the badly inflamed passion of the flesh. If you do this now, or have done so at any time, you have contrived a new and unheard of but barren type of martyrdom."[65] Robert's aspirations to this innovative martyrdom may have resulted from his conversion to the Gregorian Reform. A priest's son from Brittany, he probably was married himself before he went to Paris and became immersed in reform. "Only after the age of thirty did the Breton priest learn that he was a sinner, guilty of something he never suspected wrong, in which he was fixed, and in which, worse yet, he had been conceived."[66] This fueled his call to repentance, not only for himself, but for all his followers, including priests' wives now denounced as whores. Instead of adding to the scorn heaped upon them, he saw them as agents of redemption, both for himself and the other men of Fontevraud who humbly served those their society cast as lowest.[67] As Fiona Griffiths has observed, "Care for women allowed these men not simply to obey what they understood to be Christ's injunction from the cross [to John to care for the Virgin Mary, and thus women more broadly speaking] but daily to embrace the self-crucifixion involved in maintaining their chastity in the midst of close encounters with women."[68] What Robert and his followers saw as a steep path to salvation Geoffrey of Vendôme declared a novel scandal. "New and unheard of" was a common medieval insult; six centuries earlier, in these same parts of western France, the bishops of Angers and Rennes similarly denounced syneisaktism as "a new and unheard of superstition." Apparently, Breton priests let their female partners serve as liturgical ministers, prompting these bishops' objections.[69]

Even without such female priestly participation, syneistaktism signified heresy, according to Bernard of Clairvaux. The men were sly foxes, feigning virtue and claiming biblical justification, but, Bernard sneered, "To be always with a woman and not to know her carnally, is not this more than to raise the dead? The lesser of these you cannot do, so why shall I believe that you are capable of the greater?" He described a life of constant contact similar to the one Jerome derided to Eustochium and expressed the same disbelief: "You wish to be thought continent? Perhaps you are, but I doubt it. To me you are a scandal." He continued that anyone who scandalized one member transgressed against the entire church and, if not corrected, fell from sin into heresy.[70] What constituted this sin/heresy was not chastity or lack thereof, but the scandal inherent in intimacy between unrelated men and women. As with Chrysostom and Jerome, however, Bernard enjoyed his own relationships with women, like Countess Ermengarde of Brittany, who previously had been influenced by Robert of Arbrissel and who eventually moved to Burgundy to be closer to Bernard, becoming a nun under his direction.[71]

Bernard insisted that "the Gospel plainly forbids the causing of scandal," yet in Matthew 5:10–11, Christ declares, "Blessed are those who are persecuted for righteousness' sake, for theirs is the kingdom of heaven. Blessed are you when people revile you and persecute you and utter all kinds of evil against you falsely on my account. Rejoice and be glad, for your reward is great in heaven, for in the same way they persecuted the prophets who were before you." In John, Christ assures his disciples, "If the world hates you, be aware that it hated me before it hated you. If you belonged to the world, the world would love you as its own. Because you do not belong to the world, but I have chosen you out of the world—therefore, the world hates you" (15.18–19). Such examples, easily multiplied, have fortified Christians throughout the centuries—including Christina of Markyate, who comforted herself in her prayers, "The more someone is despised by others, the more precious she is to you [Lord]."[72] That faith and shared experience of rejection and persecution merited her being renamed Christina after Christ, instead of her given name, Theodora.[73] The scandal that critics felt condemned syneisaktics could be interpreted as another trial that ascetics bear for their love of God in a fallen world and hence as leading to greater virtue. Giraldus Cambrensis opposed syneisaktism for lesser mortals, but he recognized that St. Aldhelm engaged in Scothín's intensive form "so that he might be defamed by men, but his continence rewarded the more copiously in the future by God, who understood his conscience."[74]

Conclusion

Syneisaktism extends beyond intimate partnerships between religious men and women to concerns regarding more general mixed-sex interactions. Men like Jerome and John Chrysostom saw virtually all interaction between unrelated men and women as inherently scandalous and insisted on separation; not coincidentally, however, they excused their own relationships, engaging in practices they condemned in others—a standard definition of hypocrisy. Scandal is in the eye of the beholder, but hypocrisy blinds people to their own faults, causing them to see only others' failings; as Christ declares in Matthew, hypocrites see only the speck in others' eyes, oblivious to the log in their own (7:3–5). Vituperations against syneisaktism included worse offenses than hypocrisy, however—consider, for example, Jerome's sexually explicit letter to the adolescent Eustochium that further sought to corrupt her mind with venemous misogyny. Jerome and John, two among Christian patriarchy's many architects, insisted on female inferiority and objected to syneisaktism in part because it threatened male superiority and female subordination. Such architects further sought to indoctrinate females into this cult of oppressive and distorted gender relations so that they, too, believed themselves inherently inferior and condemned themselves as sexual temptresses, even in the case of their own rapes.[75]

To state the obvious that can too easily get ignored, all of the authors whom we hear speaking about syneisaktism, from the first century to the twelfth (with the possible exception of Líadain), are male. Male dominance is so pervasive in Christian history, especially after church merged with empire in the fourth century, that it can seem simply the norm instead of a sinister perversion of the inclusivity preached and practiced by Christ, warped by the sexism that also sought to eradicate syneisaktism. The holy partnerships of the *Catalogus*'s first order were replaced by shunning women in the second order, then their erasure in the third. This dynamic has not only separated religious men and women; it has created a stained-glass ceiling that bars women from positions of authority in certain denominations to this day. Tradition often gets cited as justification for keeping women in their "place," yet tradition is inherently selective, simplifying the past and ignoring complexities such as syneisaktism, which may have begun with Christianity itself and continued for over a millennium. It flourished especially among the Irish, who recognized that at least some men and women could partner in ways that rivaled Eden's innocence and prefigured heaven's perfection. Examples from the twelfth century like Christina of Markyate confute critics of earlier centuries, but the strict segregation championed by men like Bernard of Clairvaux won the day, forcing women's retreat into the cloister.

So, was syneisaktism a sacred practice or a sinister scandal? The answer depends on whom you ask, but the range of responses reminds me of Sheela-na-gigs, especially since what matters to critics is less what the partners actually do than what others see when they look at them. Sheela-na-gigs are carvings of female figures that emphasize their genitalia. They are found throughout the British Isles on high and late medieval buildings, generally above windows or doors. Medieval sources do not tell us what they mean, or really anything about them. An initial dominant theory was that they symbolized the evils of women and especially their sexuality, female genitalia being a gateway to hell. This view has been increasingly challenged, with scholars seeing them more as positive celebrations of fertility. Surviving Sheela-na-gigs reflect the varied responses—some have had their genitalia hacked off, as if too offensive to see; others have been rubbed in devotion so often they have lost some of their features.

Similarly, some see prehistoric pieces called Venus figurines—like the Venus of Willendorf, from ca. 27,000 BCE—as an example of "prehistoric porn," as headlines blared when another statuette was discovered in 2009. Paul Mellars, a University of Cambridge archaeologist, put it particularly bluntly, "you can't avoid being struck by its very sexually explicit depiction of a woman. The breasts really jump out at you. . . . I assume it was a guy who carved it, perhaps representing his girlfriend, [perhaps as a kind of] Paleolithic Playboy."[76] Other archaeologists, like Marija Gimbutas, have challenged such views, arguing that these statuettes are less about sexually stimulating males than about venerating the Goddess and her fertility, upon which all life was thought to depend.[77] We cannot know for sure: Are these statuettes prehistoric porn or veneration of divine fertility? Do Sheela-na-gigs signify fear and loathing of women as a gateway to hell, or do they honor women's roles as the gateway to life?

The cultures themselves can no longer explain their meaning; instead, what we see often reveals ourselves. Historical evidence provides a partial window onto the past but also functions as a mirror of our own projections. Some thought syneisaktism a scandal, others thought it sacred; those who subscribed to the former view often undercut their argument by engaging in their own intimate associations, for which they stood condemned by others but found themselves blameless. Given human nature, some probably did fall short of their ideals, or even deliberately deceived others so they could indulge their lusts. But friendships between the sexes can be among the most profound and meaningful; some people are quite capable of seeing beyond gender differences as well as celebrating those differences as assets, without lust defining their relationship. Chrysostom's imaginary syneisaktos had an incontrovertible point: you cannot control what others think of you, only your own behavior; God alone knows your conscience and ultimately only God's judgment matters. Some men may see a woman only in sexual terms, but that does not define her, nor does it dictate how she sees men, including her potential partners in Christ. Syneisaktism points to the possibility that men and women could regard each other as equal partners in their efforts to imitate Christ. In a history dominated by patriarchy and sexism, with deep suspicion of any interaction between the sexes, such partnerships may seem inherently scandalous to some. But Christianity itself began as a scandal to many, in part because it embraced greater gender equality and intimacy than was the norm. In syneisaktism, men and women followed an advanced sacred path, following after Christ and the apostles, despite and perhaps in part because of the scandal it brought to others. Their efforts to experience the egalitarian relations of a redeemed humanity can inspire those who continue to combat sexism and oppression, more sinister and pervasive scandals than syneisaktism's sacred partnerships might be.

NOTES

1. E.g., Jo Ann Kay McNamara, *Sisters in Arms: Catholic Nuns Through Two Millennia* (Cambridge: Harvard University Press, 1996); Felice Lifshitz, *Religious Women in Early Carolingian Francia: A Study of Manuscript Transmission and Monastic Culture* (New York: Fordham University Press, 2014).

2. E.g., Matt. 5:10–12; 28:1–10; Mark 14:3–9; 16:9; Luke 7:36–50; 8:1–3; 21:12–19; and John 4, 12:1–8, and 15:18–25.

3. During my first semester at Northwestern, I learned of twelfth-century examples of syneisaktism in a class with Barbara and then encountered Irish evidence of the practice in my research with Richard. This essay integrates both, and I gratefully offer it to honor Richard and his sacred partnership with Barbara.

4. Eldon Jay Epp, *Junia: The First Woman Apostle* (Minneapolis: Fortress Press, 2005).

5. Hans Achelis, *Virgines Subintroductae: Ein Beitrag zum VII. Kapitel des I. Korintherbriefs* (Leipzig: J. C. Hinrichs, 1902), 21–26; Elizabeth A. Clark, "John Chrysostom and the Subintroductae," *Church History* 46 (1977): 174.

6. Greg Peters, *The Story of Monasticism: Retrieving an Ancient Tradition for Contemporary Spirituality* (Grand Rapids: Baker Academic, 2015), 27–29.

7. McNamara, *Sisters in Arms*, 12.

8. Achelis, *Virgines Subintroductae*, 74; Rosemary Rader, *Breaking Boundaries: Male/Female Friendship in Early Christian Communities* (New York: Paulist Press, 1983), 65. The primary sources discussing syneisaktism largely assume an all-pervasive heteronormativity, hence my discussion does the same.

9. Peter Brown, *The Body and Society* (New York: Columbia University Press, 1988), 140.

10. Pierre J. Payer, *The Bridling of Desire: Views of Sex in the Later Middle Ages* (Toronto: University of Toronto Press, 1993), 181.

11. Quoted in McNamara, "Chaste Marriage and Clerical Celibacy," in *Sexual Practices and the Medieval Church*, ed. Vern L. Bullough and James A. Brundage (Buffalo: Prometheus Books, 1982), 26.

12. Rader, *Breaking Boundaries*, 67.

13. Quoted in Clark, "John Chrysostom," 177; see also Clark, *Jerome, Chrysostom, and Friends: Essays and Translations*, Studies in Women and Religion 1 (New York: The Edward Mellen Press, 1979), 178–79.

14. Rader, *Breaking Boundaries*, 89.

15. John Chrysostom, *Instruction and Refutation Directed Against Those Men Cohabiting with Virgins* 11, in Clark, *Jerome*, 197.

16. John Chrysostom, *On the Necessity of Guarding Virginity* 7, in Clark, *Jerome*, 231.

17. Clark, "John Chrysostom," 179–80.

18. John Chrysostom, *Instruction and Refutation Directed Against Those Men Cohabiting with Virgins* 1 and 3, in Clark, *Jerome*, 166 and 171; Clark, "John Chrysostom," 176–77.

19. John Chrysostom, *Instruction and Refutation* 3, and *On the Necessity of Guarding Virginity* 4, in Clark, *Jerome*, 171 and 221.

20. John Chrysostom, *On the Necessity of Guarding Virginity* 6, in Clark, *Jerome*, 226.

21. Chrysostom himself would later be accused of trying to kill a lover, who also bore him a child; see Timothy Husband, *The Wild Man: Medieval Myth and Symbolism* (New York: The Metropolitan Museum of Art, 1980), 102, 107–9.

22. Jerome, "Letter to Eustochium," in *Select Letters of Jerome*, trans. F. A. Wright (London: William Heinemann, 1933), 67, 69 (Latin 66, 68).

23. David Wiesen, *St. Jerome as a Satirist: A Study in Christian Latin Thought and Letters* (Ithaca: Cornell University Press, 1964), 119.

24. Jerome, *Ad Eustochium* ("Letter to Eustochium"), in Corpus Scriptorum Ecclesiasticorum Latinorum (CSEL) 54 (Leipzig: G. Freytag, 1910), 22.14, pp. 161–62, my translation.

25. Jerome, *Ad Asellum* ("Letter to Ascella"), in CSEL 54, 45.2, p. 324, my translation.

26. Betty Radice, trans., *The Letters of Abelard and Heloise* (Harmondsworth: Penguin, 1974), 98 (Jerome), 182 (Origen).

27. Jerome, *Ad Theodoram* ("Letter to Theodora"), in CSEL 55, 75.2, p. 31.

28. Eusebius, *The History of the Church from Christ to Constantine* (New York: Dorset Press, 1965), 7.30, pp. 317–18.

29. Carthage in 348, 397, and ca. 400, and Hippo in 393.

30. After Antioch in 267–68, the Synod of Persia in 410 and the Synod of Acacius in 486, both held at Seleucia-Ctesiphon; Synod of Sabaryeshu in 596; and the Synod of 605.

31. Ancyra in 314 and Nicaea in 325 and 787.

32. Arles in 443, Agde in 506, Orléans in 538, and Tours in 567.

33. Elvira in 300; Girone 517; Lérida 524; Toledo 531, 581, and 633; Séville 590; and Braga 675. For the complete list, see Pierre de Labriolle, "Le 'mariage spirituel' dans l'antiquité chrétienne," *Revue historique* 137 (1921): 222 n. 1.

34. Ludwig Bieler, *The Patrician Texts in the Book of Armagh*, Scriptores latini hiberniae 10 (Dublin: School of Celtic Studies Dublin Institute for Advanced Studies, 2004), 187.

35. Charles Plummer, ed., *Vitae sanctorum Hiberniae* (Oxford: Clarendon Press, 1910), 2:268, my translation.

36. W. W. Heist, ed., *Vitae sanctorum Hiberniae*, Subsidia Hagiographica 28 (Brussels: Société des Bollandistes, 1965), 83. All translations from Heist are my own. The first age, according to the document, dates roughly 432–43, the second, 544–99, the third, 600–64.

37. Ibid., 81.

38. Ibid., using the same word in the plural (*administrationes*); it could also mean "ministry."

39. Ibid., 82.

40. E.g., E. J. Gwynn and W. J. Purton, eds. and trans., "The Monastery of Tallaght," *Proceedings of the Royal Irish Academy* 29C (1911): 130, 134–37, 140, 143, 145–46, 166; Colmán Etchingham, *Church Organisation in Ireland A.D. 650 to 1000*, repr. ed. (Maynooth: Laigin Publications, 2002), 349–50, 352.

41. T. Olden, "On the *Consortia* of the First Order of Irish Saints," *Proceedings of the Royal Irish Academy* 3 (1894): 418.

42. E.g., Achelis, *Virgines subintroductae*, 57–58; Olden, "On the *Consortia*"; Roger Reynolds, "*Virgines subintroductae* in Celic Christianity," *Harvard Theological Review* 61 (1968): 549, 554; Lisa Bitel, *Land of Women: Tales of Sex and Gender from Early Ireland* (Ithaca:

Cornell University Press, 1990), 167–68; Mary Condren, *The Serpent and the Goddess: Women, Religion, and Power in Celtic Ireland* (San Francisco: Harper, 1989), 95–96; Ludwig Bieler, *Ireland: Harbinger of the Middle Ages* (London: Oxford University Press, 1963), 25; Louis Gougaud, "*Mulierum Consortia*: Étude sur le Syneisaktisme chez les Ascètes Celtiques," *Ériu* 9 (1923): 151–52; James F. Kenney, *The Sources for the Early History of Ireland: An Introduction and Guide*, repr. ed. (Dublin: Four Courts Press, 1997), 479 n. 339.

43. Reynolds, "*Virgines subintroductae* in Celic Christianity," 564.

44. Ludwig Bieler, ed., *The Irish Penitentials* (Dublin: The Dublin Institute for Advanced Studies, 1975), 188–89.

45. Reynolds, "*Virgines subintroductae* in Celic Christianity," 551, 556.

46. Patrick, *Confessio* 42, in Ludwig Bieler, ed., *Libri Epistolarum Sancti Patricii Episcopi* (Dublin: Royal Irish Academy, 1993), 81–82.

47. *The Tripartite Life of Patrick* (London: Eyre and Spottiswoode, 1887), 89–91; Olden, "On the *Consortia*," 419.

48. Heist, *Vitae sanctorum Hiberniae*, 392–93.

49. Whitley Stokes, ed., *Félire Óengusso Céli Dé: The Martyrology of Oengus the Culdee*, Henry Bradshaw Society 39, repr. ed. (Dublin: Dublin Institute for Advanced Studies, 1984), 41.

50. Embodying the message of Prov. 6:27 and James 1:12.

51. My discussion of Líadain closely follows my analysis in "Líadain's Lament, Darerca's Life, and Íte's *Ísucán*: Evidence for Nuns' Literacies in Early Ireland, " in *Nuns' Literacies in Medieval Europe: The Kansas City Dialogue*, ed. Virginia Blanton, Veronica O'Mara, and Patricia Stoop, Medieval Women: Texts and Contexts 27 (Turnhout: Brepols Press, 2015), 213–17.

52. Kuno Meyer, ed. and trans., *Liadain and Curithir: An Irish Love Story of the Ninth Century* (London: Nutt, 1902), Irish on pp. 22 and 24, English translation pp. 23 and 25.

53. McNamara, *Sisters in Arms*, 236.

54. Herbert Grundmann, *Religious Movements in the Middle Ages: The Historical Links Between Heresy, the Mendicant Orders, and the Women's Religious Movement in the Twelfth and Thirteenth Century, with the Historical Foundations of German Mysticism*, trans. Steven Rowan (Notre Dame: University of Notre Dame Press, 1995), 16–17.

55. C. H. Talbot, ed. and trans., *Life of Christina of Markyate* (Oxford: Clarendon Press, 1959), 102–3.

56. Ibid., 116–17.

57. Ibid., 114–15. Dyan Elliott, "Alternative Intimacies: Men, Women and Spiritual Direction in the Twelfth Century," in *Christina of Markyate: A Twelfth-Century Holy Woman*, ed. Samuel Famous and Henrietta Leyser (London: Routledge, Taylor and Francis Group, 2005), 169.

58. Talbot, *Life of Christina of Markyate*, 118–19. See also C. Stephen Jaeger, "The Loves of Christina of Markyate," in Famous and Leyser, *Christina of Markyate*, 99–115.

59. Talbot, *Life of Christina of Markyate*, 168–69.

60. Ibid., 180–83.

61. Ibid., 175.

62. Lines 101–4; Nikolaus M. Häring, ed., "Die Gedichte und Mysterienspiele des Hilarius von Orléans," *Studi Medievali* 17 (1976): 928; Jean Leclerq's translation, "Solitude and Solidarity," in *Peaceweavers*, vol. 1 of *Medieval Religious Women*, ed. Lillian Thomas Shank and John A. Nichols, Cistercian Studies Series, no. 72 (Kalamazoo, Mich.: Cistercian Publications, 1987), 72.

63. Translated and quoted in Bruce L. Venarde, "Robert of Arbrissel and Women's *Vita Religiosa*," in *Female* vita religiosa *between Late Antiquity and the High Middle Ages: Structures, Developments and Spatial Contexts*, ed. Gert Melville and Anne Müller (Berlin: Lit Verlag, 2011), 334. See also *Robert of Arbrissel: A Medieval Religious Life*, trans. Bruce L. Venarde (Washington, D.C.: The Catholic University of America Press, 2003), 93.

64. Geoffrey of Vendôme, "Epistola 48," in *Patrologiae cursus completus*, Series Latina, ed. Jean-Paul Migne (Paris, 1854), 157:184.

65. Geoffrey of Vendôme, "Epistola 47," in Migne, *Patrologiae cursus completus*, 157:182, my translation. See also Venarde, *Robert of Arbrissel*, 104.

66. Jacques Dalarun, *Robert of Arbrissel: Sex, Sin, and Salvation in the Middle Ages*, trans. Bruce L. Venarde (Washington, D.C.: The Catholic University of America Press, 2006), 17.

67. Ibid., 126.

68. Fiona J. Griffiths, "The Cross and the *Cura monialium*: Robert of Arbrissel, John the Evangelist, and the Pastoral Care of Women in the Age of Reform," *Speculum* 83 (2008): 327.

69. Ralph W. Mathisen, *People, Personal Expression, and Social Relations in Late Antiquity*, 2 vols. (Ann Arbor: The University of Michigan Press, 2003), 1:215, 2:172.

70. Sermon 65 in Walter Wakefield and Austin Evans, eds. and trans., *Heresies of the High Middle Ages* (New York: Columbia University Press, 1969), 132–38.

71. Shawn Madison Kramer, "Interpreting the Letters of Bernard of Clairvaux to Ermengarde, Countess of Brittany: The Twelfth-Century Context and the Language of Friendship," *Cistercian Studies Quaterly* 27 (1992): 217–50.

72. Talbot, *Life of Christina of Markyate*, 56, my translation.

73. Ibid., 56–57.

74. Quoted in Reynolds, "*Virgines subintroductae* in Celic Christianity," 563.

75. E.g., Barbara Newman, *From Virile Woman to WomanChrist: Studies in Medieval Religion and Literature* (Philadelphia: University of Pennsylvania Press, 1995), 25, 61–62.

76. Jennifer Viegas, "She's Still a Pin-up After 35,000 Years," *NCBNews.com*, May 13, 2009, http://www.nbcnews.com/id/30727293/ns/technology_and_science-science/t/shes-still-pin-up-after-years/.

77. E.g., Marija Gimbutas, *The Civilization of the Goddess*, ed. Joan Marler (San Francisco: HarperSanFrancisco, 1991).

Part 3 | IDENTIFYING AND GRAPPLING WITH THE UNHOLY

6

WAS MAGIC A RELIGIOUS MOVEMENT?

Michael D. Bailey

Few works of historical analysis manage to exert a fundamental influence over an entire field of study. Fewer still continue to do so for the better part of a century. Such, however, is the case with Herbert Grundmann's *Religious Movements in the Middle Ages* and its pathbreaking identification of the issues framed by its long subtitle—*The Historical Links Between Heresy, the Mendicant Orders, and the Women's Religious Movement in the Twelfth and Thirteenth Century, with the Historical Foundations of German Mysticism.*[1] In a seminal historiographical article in 1986, John Van Engen declared *Religiöse Bewegungen* to be "the foundation for the historical study of [all] medieval religious life," and in the introduction to the English translation in 1995, Robert Lerner mustered a long list of eminent scholars who placed Grundmann at the very center of their respective fields of study within the history of medieval religion.[2] In 2015, a series of panels that were organized to examine "Grundmann's legacy" at the International Congress on Medieval Studies at the University of Leeds revealed much nuancing and some outright rejection of portions of his arguments, but also much continued utility and vitality.[3]

Among the many topics he covered, Grundmann did not address magic or magicians at any point in *Religious Movements*, nor might they immediately appear to fit into his model of religious history shaped by official ecclesiastical orders and defined heretical sects. The only magical sects that existed in the Middle Ages, after all, were the entirely imaginary ones that supposedly gathered at witches' sabbaths, and these first appeared only in the fifteenth century, outside the period of Grundmann's main investigations. Scholars of late medieval magic and witchcraft rarely refer to Grundmann, although Richard Kieckhefer has noted the influence of Grundmann's important article "Ketzerverhöre des Spätmittelalters" on his now-classic study *European Witch Trials*, and Kathrin Utz Tremp has drawn on Grundmann's "Der Typus des Ketzers" to frame the analysis of "real" and "imaginary" sects in her monumental *Von der Häresie zur Hexerei*.[4] Neither, however, engages directly with Grundmann's broader arguments about the nature of medieval religion.

Nevertheless, magic clearly could be included in the project that Grundmann advanced in *Religious Movements* in the sense that he endeavored to write an encompassing cultural history of medieval religion, conceived, after the manner of his mentor Walter Goetz, as "total history with an emphasis on intellectual history."[5] His omission of magic might then be seen as an example of Grundmann's lack of attention to "mundane religious practices," as some later critics have noted, and his preference for focusing instead on highly motivated religious elites, whether they ultimately were categorized as orthodox or heretical.[6] Of course, there were practitioners of magic among educated elites in the Middle Ages, but they never coalesced into a full-blown movement, in Grundmann's sense of the word, nor did contemporary critics ever cast them as such. Looking especially at the recent historiography of medieval magic, however, it is clear that many scholars have been engaging in a very Grundmannesque endeavor—namely, to explain how practices that have frequently been categorized as aberrant or even oppositional in fact fit coherently into the dominant cultural, intellectual, and religious systems of their time.[7]

In this essay, I first consider how the history of magic reflects some of the larger historical dynamics of the medieval period. I then discuss the vexing issue of whether our limited and often clearly biased sources reveal actual magical practices that medieval people really performed, or whether they more often present us only with a magical *imaginaire* constructed by their authors, a point on which Grundmann can offer insight and guidance. Finally, I suggest how the actual religious movement identified by Grundmann, grounded in the *vita apostolica* and, in his analysis, instrumental in the formation of group identities but ultimately driven by individual and personal perceptions of what constituted true religiosity, informs the history of magic and in particular the dilemmas church authorities faced as they tried to differentiate magical practices from religious rites. Such efforts at discernment became especially intense in the late Middle Ages, after the period of Grundmann's main analysis, but they adhere to patterns that he would have recognized.

Magic and the Dynamics of Medieval History

Magic is an expansive subject, so much so that some scholars argue it should not be treated as a single, coherent category at all. In particular, the range of practices that could be classified as common, traditional, or everyday magic is extremely broad.[8] Experts cannot even agree on basic terminology or general demarcations.[9] More coherent categories exist for various elite forms of magic, with details of their operations and intellectual framework laid out in texts written by proponents and practitioners, as well as by persecuting authorities. Here too, however, there is some debate about what range of practices should be grouped together. Should quasi sciences such as alchemy and astrology, for example, be kept apart from necromantic conjurations? While critical medieval authorities typically lumped these practices together in their condemnations of magic arts, since they suspected that demonic entanglements lay hidden within them all, careful research into codicological traditions has shown how texts containing *naturalia* frequently circulated separately from those dealing with ritual magic and spirit conjuring.[10]

Because of this diversity, I cannot possibly replicate Grundmann's elegance and identify a single dynamic that fundamentally shaped the entire history of medieval magic. Nevertheless, as Richard Kieckhefer has insisted, magic does have a history, and that means it has been shaped by other historical developments.[11] In the early Middle Ages, magic as it had been known and practiced in the late ancient world was reshaped by the forces of Christianization and subsequent, long-enduring concerns about residual paganism in European society. The history of magic was then dramatically affected by the intellectual revival of the twelfth and thirteenth centuries. Finally, although concerns about magic had always existed within Christianity, they increased considerably in the fourteenth and fifteenth centuries, driven in part by dynamics of reform that dominate so much of late medieval religious history.

From the earliest days of the church, Christian authorities linked magic to pagan practices. The church fathers declared that pagan deities were in fact Christian demons, and so in their analysis all pagan rites became inherently superstitious and magical. For many centuries, critical clergymen continued to frame magical practices as the residue of paganism not yet fully eradicated from the Christian world. Perhaps the most famous early medieval text dealing with magic, the canon *Episcopi*, encoded into ecclesiastical law around the beginning of the tenth century but believed by medieval authorities to date to the early fourth, described "wicked women, who have given themselves back to Satan and been seduced by the illusions and phantasms of demons, [who] believe and profess that, in the hours of the night, they ride upon certain beasts with Diana, the goddess of the pagans." Because of this, they "wander from the right faith and return to the error of the pagans."[12] Equally explicit is the mid-eighth-century Carolingian *Indiculus superstitionum et paganiarum*, which, as one expert states, "stands at the core of any discussion of magic in the early medieval West."[13] This simple list includes among its (presumably proscribed) points "sacred rites of Mercury and Jupiter," "the observance of the pagans on the hearth or in the inception of any business," and "wooden feet or hands in a pagan rite." These are intermingled with points mentioning "amulets," "incantations," "auguries," and "diviners and sorcerers," and the belief that certain woman "command the moon, and that they may be able to take away the hearts of men, according to the pagans."[14]

It is important to note that the identification of magic with paganism, which initially stemmed from an age of real pagan-Christian competition, did not simply linger on as a trope in clerical writings as Northern Europe became more thoroughly Christianized. Rather, such connections were strongly reaffirmed from the late seventh and early eighth centuries onward, most likely owing to the greater emphasis on correct and uncorrupted forms of Christian piety advocated by Anglo-Saxon missionaries to the Continent and then by the powerful Carolingian reform movement within the Frankish church. These dynamics, and not simply a perduring Christian assertion that pagan rites were magical and magical rites were pagan, shaped characterizations of medieval magic down to the end of the first millennium.[15] By the eleventh century, however, paganism no longer resonated as a threatening "other" against which Latin Christianity constructed itself, and it began to fade from conceptualizations and condemnations of magic. Some discourse about magic as pagan persisted through the later medieval period and even into the early modern, but this was increasingly an empty rhetoric, kept in place for the sake of tradition but not reflecting ongoing historical developments.

Of course, how much paganism really characterized magical rites as they may actually have been practiced in early medieval Europe is a subject of much debate. Yitzhak Hen has argued that church opposition had effectively eliminated most real pagan practices as early as the sixth century.[16] Others maintain that to dismiss completely the myriad descriptions of at least a strong residue of pagan practices surviving into later centuries is to be "too pessimistic" about the possible veracity of our sources.[17] Nor should we dismiss the possibility that clerical rhetoric could shape real practices. From the far better documented period of the Reformation, for example, we know that Protestant fulminations against certain Catholic practices such as supplication of Mary or the saints, or conversely reformers' valorization of biblical texts and "the word" itself, caused ordinary parishioners either to expunge or emphasize certain elements of common magic to create distinctly Protestant magical rites.[18]

Returning to the Middle Ages, and moving into the twelfth and thirteenth centuries, scholars have long recognized how the general intellectual revival within Western Christendom during this period altered conceptions of magic, particularly among educated elites.[19] Magical texts of considerable sophistication flowed into Europe from the Byzantine east and especially from the Muslim world, and scholars began to debate the nature of the occult forces that lay behind astrology, alchemy, astral image magic, the crafting of amulets and talismans, and the invocation of demons. Whereas earlier critics had lambasted magical practices as empty superstition or mere demonic trickery, able to ensnare only the feebleminded (a characteristic line from the canon *Episcopi* asked "who is so stupid and foolish as to think that all these things which are only done in spirit happen in the body"[20]), opponents now saw magic as a very serious threat indeed. A clerical underworld of magic emerged in schools and later universities, and a magical demimonde developed at aristocratic courts as well.[21]

In addition to new attitudes, new practices also emerged in this period. Both chiromancy (divination by reading lines in the palm) and spatulamancy (divination using animals' shoulder blades) appeared in Western Europe in the twelfth century, imported via Arabic texts.[22] Likewise the first alchemical treatise in the medieval West appears to have been an 1144 translation of an Arabic source.[23] Clearly some bright young minds rushed to experiment with rites found in these alluring texts. Critics recognized new kinds of practice, as well, although they continued to assert that almost all magic ultimately relied on demonic power. Already in the mid-eleventh century, the Italian rhetorician Anselm of Besate described how his own cousin possessed a book of demonic invocations, and also that he learned some of his dark arts from a Saracen doctor.[24] In the twelfth century, the English clergyman John of Salisbury discussed magic in a work criticizing the "follies of courtiers." In particular he described how he himself had been made to take part in magical rites as a young boy by the priest who taught him Latin.[25]

As always with texts written to criticize and condemn magical practices, we can question how accurately such writings depicted real practices. Led by Richard Kieckhefer, however, scholars have increasingly turned to magical texts themselves, exploring their authorship, content, and circulation, in order to understand how magic was actually conceptualized and employed, at least among elite practitioners.[26] I will discuss these learned magicians' goals and motivations in the next section of this essay, but here we should briefly consider whether these men comprised a kind of movement. Again, better evidence comes from a later period, so let us jump forward a few centuries and work our way back.

Scholars often associate the emergence of a distinct form of "Renaissance" magic with Marsilio Ficino's *De vita libri tres*, written in the 1480s. Thereafter, a diverse but still coherent intellectual tradition of magic grounded in Neoplatonism, Kabbalah, and Hermeticism proliferated among humanist scholars:

men such as Giovanni Pico della Mirandola, Cornelius Agrippa von Net-
tesheim, Paracelsus, John Dee, and Giordano Bruno, who were as much philosophers, physicians, and protoscientists as they were magicians. They knew
each other's works and can certainly be seen as representing a distinct intellectual movement, and a spiritual one as well.[27] Frank Klaassen has stressed
basic continuities between elite medieval and Renaissance forms of magic, as
has Richard Kieckhefer, although he notes that Renaissance mages took a more
philosophical approach to their art.[28] This is a weighty point, given that much
of the coherence of Renaissance magic as a movement resides in its philosophical bent.[29] In addition, Renaissance magicians enjoyed the benefits of the
printing press when they sought to circulate their ideas. Still, given that the
prodigious manuscript production and circulation patterns of the late medieval period are only beginning to be studied, it is tempting to postulate at least
a nascent movement among practitioners of learned magic in this era, albeit
less sophisticated than what subsequently developed. Frank Klaassen has
noted, in fact, that ritual magic texts circulated in ways quite similar to those
of one well-studied religious movement in this period, that of heretical Lol-
lards.[30] Moreover, as I will suggest in the next section of this essay, the movement of late medieval magic could easily have grown more sophisticated itself
if only the church in the fourteenth and fifteenth centuries had not opposed it
so vigorously, which was perhaps not as much of a foregone conclusion as
might be assumed.

Before coming to that point, however, I want here to turn to those final
medieval centuries and consider the vexing question of why concerns about
magic darkened so dramatically, culminating in the construction of diabolical
witchcraft as an accusation directed mainly against ordinary Christians engaging in magic rites but affecting elite practitioners as well. Scholars of witchcraft
and magic have been trying to explain this phenomenon for a long time. The
rise of inquisitorial procedure and standing inquisitorial courts provided a
mechanism. Refinements in Scholastic theology and what some have identified
as the first serious demonology in Latin Christendom since late antiquity
offered an intellectual framework.[31] The broadest dynamic, however, and the
one most easily defined as a religious movement, was the drive for religious
reform that flourished in the fourteenth and fifteenth centuries. I have written
extensively elsewhere about the connections between reform and rising concerns about sorcery and superstition, so here I will offer only a sketch.[32]

The reform movements that began in several religious orders in the late
medieval period were not inherently concerned about magical practices. Many
ecclesiastical reformers, however, also sought to promote a more general religious renewal across Christian society, and in this capacity a number of them

targeted what they considered to be dangerous superstitions and magical practices among the laity. Of course, not all religious reformers were concerned about magic, and not all critics of magic were otherwise involved in reform, but the overlap between these two areas is notable.

In Vienna, Nicholas of Dinkelsbühl, although not a monk himself, penned *Reformationis methodus*, which, because of support from the Austrian duke Albrecht, became a foundational text for Benedictine reform, particularly as it emerged from the major reforming center at Melk. Nicholas also wrote an influential treatise on the Decalogue, which targeted diabolical magic and superstition as an affront against the first commandment.[33] The Dominican order had among its reformist leaders Johannes Nider, who was also the author of a major early work about diabolical witchcraft, *Formicarius*.[34] A generation later, Nicolas Jacquier, author of *Flagellum haereticorum fascinariorum*, was closely associated with the reformist Dominican Congregation of Holland.[35] The Franciscan order's first reformist saint, Bernardino of Siena, was a fierce opponent of witchcraft as well as other moral failings among the laity, castigating spells and superstitions in fiery sermons that inspired at least a few early witch trials in Italy.[36] The Carthusian order produced Jacob of Paradise and Denys the Carthusian, important reformers who also wrote extensively against magic and superstition. And the reformist councils of Constance and especially Basel appear to have served as clearinghouses for information about early conceptions of diabolical witchcraft.[37]

When reformers preached or penned treatises against superstitious and magical practices, they typically stressed their utterly corrupt and corrupting nature, rooted in the inevitable involvement of demons as the main actors in such rites. Undoubtedly many reformers believed their own message, but it also provided them with a powerful rhetoric through which they could, essentially, frighten laypeople into more rigorous adherence to approved devotional practices. Johannes Nider, for example, explicitly argued that people should rely on prayer, the sign of the cross, and the power of holy relics rather than magical rites when they faced hardships or crises in their lives. Even if they regarded themselves as having been bewitched, they should never turn to further witchcraft to effect a cure, for this would jeopardize their souls.[38] Bernardino of Siena was even more aggressive. In a famous sermon against magic and witchcraft delivered in his hometown in 1427, he warned the Sienese that the common "spells and divinations" on which they were accustomed to rely—including such practices as palm reading, wearing protective talismans, casting lots, and various healing rites—were all demonic abominations, and if they did not abandon them, God's vengeance would rain down and wreck their beloved city.[39]

It is certainly not the case that reformists' concerns alone drove churchmen to develop the conceptions of diabolical witchcraft that took root in the fifteenth century. But the natural tendency of reformers to see, or to project, corruption and demonic threat at every turn made them more liable to accept and propagate darker imaginings about the practice of magic than had troubled even zealous opponents of magic and superstition in previous centuries. My point here, again, is not to postulate a single, Grundmannesque unifying cause behind multifarious developments, but to show how the history of medieval magic interweaves with other aspects of medieval religious history.

Real and Imagined Magic

The critique could be raised, at this point, that much of what I have described so far pertains not to how actual magical practices were shaped by or reflected broader currents of medieval history, but rather how clerical authorities' perceptions of such practices were reshaped over time. This is true, and it is an inevitable problem that scholars of medieval magic must confront. Most of the surviving sources that discuss medieval magical practices are hostile ones: condemnatory accounts by theologians, jurists, moralists, and preachers, along with some scattered trials records, mainly from the late medieval period.[40] The descriptions of magic that these sources present, from the supposedly pagan-inflected rites of early medieval discourse to the horrific *imaginaire* of the witches' sabbath that emerged only in the fifteenth century, can be extremely formulaic. Of course, the history of medieval heresy raises the same problems, and in some ways so, too, does the history of religious orders. Certainly the hagiographies of their leading figures, through which the orders often constructed much of their own identities, are replete with stock formulas of sanctity. Some orders may even have recrafted their own early history in light of later developments and to justify later practices and organizational structures.[41]

Grundmann confronted this problem when he engaged with the history of heresy, and he certainly knew that clerical condemnations of heretical depravities could not be taken at face value. More deeply, he recognized a formulaic "Typus des Ketzers" that informed clerical accounts and even clerical perceptions of supposed heretical groups.[42] Although he never discussed a "Typus des Magiers," he recognized the applicability of his insights about heretics to later stereotypes concerning supposedly diabolical witches.[43] Moreover, in *Religious Movements* Grundmann suggested that what ecclesiastical authorities constructed as the late medieval heresy of the Free Spirit never comprised a coherent sect, as Robert Lerner later conclusively proved.[44] Grundmann's skepticism did not run so deep with other heretical movements, such as the Cathars, but some scholars now suggest that even the great high medieval heresies existed more as figments of clerical imagination than in reality.[45] Other scholars continue to see more substance to heresy's existence, and I do not intend to venture too deeply into these debates here.[46] I merely want to point out that, as the lines between "real" and "imagined" heresies become increasingly fluid, the reasons to bracket off the imagined sect of witches categorically from other heretical sects encompassed in Grundmann's religious movement become less substantial as well.

In the history of witchcraft, one of Richard Kieckhefer's early contributions was to show that elements of diabolism in witchcraft accusations emerged only at the very end of the medieval period, mainly in the fifteenth century, and then to demonstrate how those elements were, for the most part, grafted by clerical authorities onto more basic accusations of simple *maleficium* in the course of early trials.[47] His conclusions in this regard have been generally confirmed by subsequent studies of late medieval witch trials.[48] Although witch trials typically were driven by multiple causal factors, Kathrin Utz Tremp has demonstrated how some of the earliest major outbreaks of witch-hunting in Western Europe arose when, for various reasons, inquisitorial authorities shifted their concerns from more "real" heresies to these new, "imagined" sects.[49]

There have, of course, been many attempts to discover an actual movement of some kind underlying the elaborate stereotypes of diabolical witchcraft and the witches' sabbath. Though the famous but ill-founded arguments of Margaret Murray have been repeatedly debunked,[50] Carlo Ginzburg's discovery of the Friulian *benandanti* has gained more sustained traction, and other scholars have confirmed how shamanistic or other kinds of visionary experience helped support the idea of diabolical witches gathering at sabbaths.[51] For the most part, however, such structures of belief appear to have survived in relatively diffuse ways within certain cultures or subcultures. Particular people claimed or were recognized to have such abilities, but these individuals did not become members of coherent, organized movements. In a different vein, Michael Tavuzzi has suggested that a "very loose, informal movement" of laypeople resistant to church authority, and perhaps anti-Eucharistic in focus, may have existed in certain Alpine regions in the fifteenth century, and this movement could have provided the genesis of inquisitors' ideas about witches' sabbaths.[52] Such speculation, however, has never been supported by any close studies of Alpine trials. The most "real" element of medieval witchcraft, by general agreement, has always been the practice of harmful magic, or at least the very real fear felt by the laity and clerical elites alike that harmful magic was being practiced widely within Christian society.

Rather than continue to search for elements of a movement, shamanistic or otherwise, that may have underlain stereotypes of diabolical witchcraft in the late medieval period, I want to follow Kieckhefer's insight that we often gain useful perspective by pulling back from witchcraft and studying magic as a whole.[53] I will begin by observing that diabolical witchcraft was not the only "imagined" form of medieval magic. In some respects, almost all of them were. Obviously, in many cases practices that came to be labeled as magical were quite real. For various kinds of elite ritual magic, manuals were composed and then used by actual practitioners.[54] Yet, as Frank Klaassen has observed, such magic could be both a real practice and still an imagined construct.[55] Meanwhile, across all levels of medieval society, people could access a host of common healing, divinatory, or protective rites, such as are described in a wide range of sources, albeit perhaps not always with complete fidelity to the real nature of actual practices.[56] Some of these people may have thought of themselves as performing magic or even identified themselves as magicians, but more typically those appellations emerged only when such practices came to be condemned. Moreover, even if practitioners conceived of what they did as magic, they almost always understood it differently from the authors of condemnatory accounts.

For most ecclesiastical authorities throughout the medieval period, magic was an inherently illicit activity. This conclusion rested on the influential early declarations by Augustine and other church fathers that magic always entailed demonic agency.[57] Just like many people accused of more "real" heresies, however, most people who performed what authorities came to identify as demonic magical rites probably thought of themselves as good Christians engaged in entirely permissible and even laudable acts. The simple spells and charms that proliferated across Europe in the medieval era almost always incorporated explicitly Christian ritual, often drawing directly from the liturgy or otherwise including patently religious elements. People might erect crosses in fields to protect crops from hailstorms, for example, or invoke the wounds of Christ to achieve the same end. Invocations of Christ's wounds were also used to cure injuries, and gospel verses could be copied out and placed on the sick to reduce fever or avert other ailments. Herbs and roots were used to similar effect, but people often fortified their power by reciting certain prayers while gathering these medicinal plants. They also took holy water from churches to wash wounds, for it was believed to stave off infection, and it could supposedly cure toothaches and other ills.[58]

Among elite magicians, too, even avowed necromancers thought of themselves as commanding demons in Christ's name, not supplicating and worshiping them as their opponents insisted. Hence authorities writing throughout the thirteenth, fourteenth, and fifteenth centuries felt the need to assert again and again far narrower limits to legitimate exorcism, usually drawing on Thomas Aquinas's influential arguments in this regard.[59] Moreover, much elite ritual magic in the Middle Ages was actually not demonic, but scientific (natural magic) or theurgic in nature, and scholars have recently begun to pay more attention to this reality. Such magic provided a means to explore the wonders of the divinely created universe, but also a mechanism by which to obtain visionary experience, the desire for which was becoming increasingly widespread in the later medieval period. Sophie Page has demonstrated how monks at St. Augustine's monastery, Canterbury, incorporated magical texts into their religious vocation, and Claire Fanger has shown how a French monk relied first on the *ars notoria* and then developed his own rites to achieve visions of the Virgin Mary.[60]

Men such as these clearly did not believe themselves to be magicians in the sense that opponents meant when they deployed that term. Comparing the distinctions drawn between different kinds of magical practices by both opponents and proponents (when we are able), it soon becomes clear that both sides usually agreed on the basic conditions that rendered practices licit or illicit. Subservience to demons was to be avoided at all costs, but demons were profoundly deceitful creatures bent on deluding otherwise faithful Christians into sin. Thus the most basic charge leveled by opponents of magic, who always spoke with a louder voice, was that proponents seriously misunderstood the rites in which they engaged. So profound were the dangers of demonic deception, and ultimately so pronounced became the allegations of critics, that no category of permissible theurgic magic ever gained broad legitimacy in the Middle Ages. But one can imagine that it might have. And if so, then those who engaged in such practices might well have come to comprise a movement in the sense meant by Grundmann.

To clarify this speculation, let us return for a moment to the history of heresy. There, too, we find those accused of a terrible crime proclaiming their innocence, with the rank and file often declaring that they did not realize what they believed or had been taught was wrong, whereas others, frequently more educated elites, professed that their beliefs and practices were not what their opponents made them out to be but instead represented a pure and laudable form of Christianity. In Grundmann's analysis, the church itself recognized some truth to these claims. He identified the "decisive turning point" in the history of the overall medieval religious movement as occurring during the papacy of Innocent III, who codified certain aspects of that moment into approved religious orders even as he harshly condemned other groups that he deemed to be heretical.[61] I would suggest a comparable turning point in the history of medieval magic, but one that was not so evenly balanced.

In the early fourteenth century, Pope John XXII, fearful of magical practices rife within Christian society, and above all of magical assaults on his own person, convened a panel of legal and theological experts to determine precisely what sins these practices entailed, and then promoted the condemnation of almost all such magic as demonic and heretical through a series of papal pronouncements.[62] Certainly much Scholastic theology was already moving in this direction. Thomas Aquinas had subverted the possibility of any major categories of nondemonic magic in the mid-thirteenth century, and the majority of theologians followed suit, progressively eliminating intellectually respectable space for most kinds of natural magic by the early fifteenth century.[63] But it was John who added the weight of papal censure and paved the way for inquisitorial action against a host of magical practices by declaring that all magic involving demons automatically entailed heresy.[64] Later authorities drew on notions of tacit demonic pacts to declare that those accused of practicing magic should be considered heretics even if they performed their rites without any nefarious intent or even any awareness that they might covertly be invoking demons. Magic conceived in this way conforms remarkably well to Grundmann's description of earlier religious movements that the church had proclaimed to be heretical, even though they lacked "a particular heretical doctrine defining the nature of the heresy."[65]

If, however, John XXII had been less suspicious, or less driven, the story might have been different. If the monks of St. Augustine's and others had been allowed or indeed encouraged to pursue their experiments with magical rites for intellectual and devotional purposes openly and free from any significant threat of censure or reprobation, then we might have seen a split develop in medieval magic very much like the fundamental division that Grundmann saw in other religious movements: certain groups condemned in strident terms as demonic heretics, but others, upholding similar ideals and engaging in similar practices, exalted as exemplars of religious virtue. In fact, as I have already noted in the previous section, a kind of movement promoting intellectually and even morally respectable magic was soon to reappear in Europe, grounded in "Renaissance" Neo-Platonism, Hermeticism, and Kabbalah.[66] The church never comfortably accommodated itself to these new systems either, and for the most part Thomistic thought continued to shape mainstream theology and demonology deep into the early modern period. If the church had taken a different stance in the later Middle Ages, however, all this might have been different, too. Rather than a clerical underworld, an explicitly magical religious movement might have emerged as a recognized manifestation of Christian piety.

Of course, this proposition is counterfactual. Nevertheless, the very real problems that inquisitors, magistrates, and theologians faced when trying to separate what they held to be demonic magical rites from legitimate devotional practices illustrate how illusory that boundary was. By the late Middle Ages, defining magic more stringently and punishing its manifestations, real or perceived, more severely had come to be an important part of the church's effort to control increasingly personal, individual religiosity. Here too, we will find magic fitting into the framework of Grundmann's movement.

Magic and Personal Religion

As Grundmann notes in *Religious Movements*, after Innocent III bestowed papal approval on certain apostolic movements in the form of new religious orders in the early thirteenth century, many of his bishops had trouble differentiating these new religious from heretics that the pope had ordered them to eradicate.[67] In particular, some of the first Franciscans to venture north out of Italy were taken by church authorities in the Rhineland as Waldensians, "since there was in fact no basic or visible difference between them."[68] Likewise there might be no readily discernable difference between a pious blessing and a magical spell. According to one fifteenth-century demonologist, a man living in the diocese of Constance had been injured through witchcraft and sought to cure himself by means of other magical rites. These all failed, until finally he turned to a pious women he knew who murmured the Lord's Prayer and Creed and also made the sign of the cross over his injury. Feeling immediate relief, the man demanded to know what "spells" (*carmina*) she had used to heal him, and she berated him profusely for not recognizing legitimate prayer when he saw it.[69] In fact, however, many educated clerics had the same problem. In 1405, a clergyman from Landau, Werner of Friedberg, stood before a panel of theologians from the University of Heidelberg, accused, among other counts, of using a superstitious healing spell. Fifty years later, however, another cleric, the Zurich canon Felix Hemmerli, wrote a tract defending the rite Werner had used, calling it an entirely laudable Christian blessing.[70]

Another murky issue that clerical authorities had to debate was whether some kinds of magical practices were better than others. Established doctrine proclaimed that all demonic magic was heresy, no matter how it was used. Yet inquisitors seeking to enforce this position also faced a long legal tradition that concerned itself only with magic used to cause harm.[71] Magistrates who tried to pursue a stricter line could face considerable resistance. Even the most infamous inquisitorial witch-hunter of the fifteenth century found himself reluctantly countenancing, or at least less vociferously condemning, forms of magic used for positive purposes, especially to defend against diabolical witchcraft.

Like other demonologists before him, Heinrich Kramer admitted that witch-craft could be used to heal as well as to harm, although faithful Christians should never seek to benefit from such inherently corrupt and diabolical prac-tices.[72] He then muddied the waters, however, by asserting that, so long as one did not turn to an actual witch, to be healed by "witch-like rites" (*maleficiales ritus*) was at least somewhat less condemnable.[73] He also gave equally marginal approval to various other magical rites intended to provide protection against the diabolical witchcraft that was the main target of his fulminations.[74]

For all that the medieval church propounded a putatively clear line between illicit magic and tolerable or even laudable rites, that line was in fact a shim-mering abstraction laid over far more complex realities. Some scholars have seen a certain hypocrisy, or at least an easy opportunism, in the occasionally facile means by which early medieval missionaries converted pagan rites into Christian religion. Richard Kieckhefer gives an example of a Germanic charm intended to heal a horse's leg that invoked Odin, who was said to have once healed his horse when it came up lame while he rode it through some woods. Later Christianized versions simply replaced the figure of Odin with that of Christ riding into Jerusalem.[75] Yet according to the categories those missionar-ies understood, this alteration was not mere window dressing but instead fun-damentally changed the nature of the act from one that called on demonic power (since pagan deities were all demons in disguise) to a pious supplication of Christ's mercy.[76]

In the later medieval period, clergymen no longer worried about explicitly pagan rites but rather about objectively Christian ones that could become cor-rupted through misuse or even unintentional misunderstanding. As Christian religiosity as a whole came to emphasize more personal and internalized forms of devotion, so, too, the line separating illicit magic from proper prayer or blessing became more a matter of the interior condition of the practitioner. Thus Heinrich Kramer could argue that a "witch-like rite" was at least some-what less execrable when performed by someone other than an actual witch, that is (in his understanding), a committed servant of the devil.

Again we confront the conundrum of real versus imagined magic, but as I have shown already, that distinction is not always a meaningful one. Of course, by suggesting that magical practices were enmeshed in the late medieval drive toward more personal and internalized religion, I do not mean that there were actual groups of diabolical witches motivated by a deeply felt allegiance to Satan. Neither do I mean that ordinary Christians were driven by any profound internal piety when they performed some rite that they hoped would heal a sick loved one or protect their crops from storms. They probably did think of many such acts as drawing, at least in part, on divine power, however, and thus in a loose way as an expression of their basic faith. It is clear that the monks and other elite practitioners who saw magic as a means for expressing personal devotion or attaining visionary experience participated in a general religious culture in which desire for such experience was becoming increasingly pronounced.[77] To speculate again, one might wonder whether, if that form of magic had become the basis for a religious movement in its own right, it would have come to inform the devotional practices of the laity as well.[78] Clearly, however, magic was most fully implicated in the flowering of more personal religion when it became part of the church's drive to impose systems of control on those forms of religiosity.

Grundmann argued that, in the wake of the Gregorian Reform, Christian religion in Western Europe came to be perceived as a "way of life immediately binding upon every individual."[79] The increasingly individual and internal nature of religiosity created a dilemma for ecclesiastical authorities, however. How could purely internal states be monitored or regulated effectively? The faithful were instructed through sermons and other mechanisms of pastoral care, and then asked to monitor themselves through the process of yearly confession, but this was soon deemed to be insufficient. The close connection between the dynamics of personal confession, imposed as an obligation on all Christians by the Fourth Lateran Council, and the growing apparatus of inquisition in the thirteenth and fourteenth centuries has often been noted.[80] Still, accurately perceiving the internal state of individual souls remained a daunting task. One fundamental response was to rely on structures: quasi-clear categorizations of religious orders and heretical sects, and then other groupings, such as beguines or mystics, that fell either in between or just outside of these categories. These were the manifold offspring of Grundmann's singular religious movement.

Magic, at least as church authorities conceived of it, was also caught up in this dynamic. Once demonic magic was declared to entail heresy, magical practices of all sorts became another prism through which authorities tried to discern the practitioner's soul. The practices themselves, however, or at least their observable elements, were often ambiguous. As Denys the Carthusian wrote in a treatise castigating magic and superstition and composed around the middle of the fifteenth century, "however much the aforesaid blessings and adjurations may not be superstitious or illicit in themselves . . . they must nevertheless be shunned and forbidden due to attendant dangers, because often some superstitions get mingled into them."[81] Driven by such ambiguities, authorities began to fashion more or less clear categories of demonic magic and ultimately of diabolical witchcraft that would serve to inform and guide their processes of discernment. Especially around the category of witchcraft, they clustered all the stereotypes that had long been directed against supposed heretics, and many more besides. This represented more than just their inclination to ascribe set "types" of characteristics to their targets. It was also an extension of one of the basic dynamics that Grundmann saw underlying the development of medieval religious movements—namely, the church's need to try to clarify loose and often dangerously uncertain sets of behaviors by ascribing them to different groups, real or imagined. These groups could then be sharply distinguished from and ideally set in opposition to one another.

Scholars have long recognized how stereotypes of diabolical witchcraft represent an inversion of multiple proper orderings of Christian society.[82] The image of the witch gave authorities a perfect target against which they could judge a range of more ambiguous practices. So did the idea of learned necromancers who explicitly worshiped the demons they invoked, "inasmuch as they sacrifice to them, adore them, offer up horrible prayers to them . . . burn candles or incense or aromatic spices, [and] sacrifice animals and birds."[83] Although learned magicians undoubtedly tried to conjure demons in the Middle Ages, that they did so in such a patently worshipful manner may have been as much an imagined construct as any witches' sabbath.[84]

Medieval authorities never depicted necromancers operating as part of an organized group, as they did with witches at a sabbath, but that does not undercut this analysis. Grundmann did not argue that the imperative to parse sets of practices into distinct groups was so powerful that it utterly blinded church officials to the more nuanced realities they regularly encountered, and neither would I. These stark dichotomies were tools through which they sought to resolve the sometimes very complicated problems of discernment that their reality presented, although once established they could take on a terrible force of their own. That force helped shape medieval understandings of magic, which authorities from the later medieval period onward often approached as if it were a kind of dark and oppositional religious movement.

NOTES

1. Herbert Grundmann, *Religiöse Bewegungen im Mittelalter: Untersuchungen über die geschichtlichen Zusammenhänge zwischen der Ketzerei, den Bettelorden und der religiösen Frauenbewegung im 12. und 13. Jahrhundert und über die geschichtlichen Grundlagen der deutschen Mystik* (Berlin: E. Ebering, 1935); all citations here are to *Religious Movements in the Middle Ages*, trans. Steven Rowan, intro. Robert E. Lerner (Notre Dame: University of Notre Dame Press, 1995), hereafter cited as *RM*.

2. John Van Engen, "The Christian Middle Ages as an Historiographical Problem," *American Historical Review* 91 (1986): 519–52, at 523; *RM*, xxii–xxiii.

3. See Jennifer Kolpacoff Deane and Anne E. Lester, eds., *Between Orders and Heresy: Rethinking Medieval Religious Movements* (Toronto: University of Toronto Press, forthcoming).

4. Richard Kieckhefer, *European Witch Trials: Their Foundations in Popular and Learned Culture, 1300–1500* (Berkeley: University of California Press, 1976), 91; Kathrin Utz Tremp, *Von der Häresie zur Hexerei: "Wirkliche" und imaginäre Sekten im Spätmittelalter* (Hannover: Hansche Buchhandlung, 2008), 28–34.

5. *RM*, xvi.

6. Ibid., xxv.

7. See Richard Kieckhefer, *Forbidden Rites: A Necromancer's Manual of the Fifteenth Century* (University Park: Pennsylvania State University Pres, 1997); Frank Klaassen, *The Transformations of Magic: Illicit Learned Magic in the Later Middle Ages and Renaissance* (University Park: Pennsylvania State University Press, 2013); Sophie Page, *Magic in the Cloister: Pious Motives, Illicit Interests, and Occult Approaches to the Medieval Universe* (University Park: Pennsylvania State University Press, 2013); Claire Fanger, *Rewriting Magic: An Exegesis of the Visionary Autobiography of a Fourteenth-Century French Monk* (University Park: Pennsylvania State University Press, 2015).

8. Richard Kieckhefer, *Magic in the Middle Ages* (Cambridge: Cambridge University Press, 1989), 56–94; Karen Jolly, "Medieval Magic: Definitions, Beliefs, Practices," in *Witchcraft and Magic in Europe: The Middle Ages*, ed. Bengt Ankarloo and Stuart Clark (Philadelphia: Univeristy of Pennsylvania Press, 2002), 1–71, esp. 27–58.

9. Kathryn A. Edwards, "Introduction: What Makes Magic Everyday Magic?" in *Everyday Magic in Early Modern Europe*, ed. Kathryn A. Edwards (Burlington, Vt.: Ashgate, 2015), 1–10.

10. Esp. Klaassen, *Transformations of Magic*.

11. Kieckhefer, foreword to the Canto edition of *Magic in the Middle Ages* (Cambridge: Cambridge University Press, 2000), ix–x.

12. Joseph Hansen, ed., *Quellen und Untersuchungen zur Geschichte des Hexenwahns und der Hexenverfolgung im Mittelalter* (1901; repr., Hildesheim: Georg Olms, 1963), 38–39; translation from Alan Charles Kors and Edward Peters, eds., *Witchcraft in Europe 400–1700: A Documentary History*, 2nd ed. (Philadelphia: University of Pennsylvania Press, 2001), 62.

13. Yitzhak Hen, "The Early Medieval West," in *The Cambridge History of Magic and Witchcraft in the West: From Antiquity to the Present*, ed. David J. Collins (Cambridge: Cambridge University Press, 2015), 183.

14. Ibid., 183–84.

15. See ibid.

16. Hen, *Religion and Culture in Merovingian Gaul A.D. 481–751* (Leiden: Brill, 1995), 154–206.

17. Bernadette Filotas, *Pagan Survivals, Superstitions and Popular Cultures in Early Medieval Pastoral Literature* (Toronto: Pontifical Institute of Medieval Studies, 2005), 46, 56.

18. R. W. Scribner, "The Reformation, Popular Magic, and the 'Disenchantment of the World,'" *Journal of Interdisciplinary History* 23 (1992–93): 475–94; R. W. Scribner, "Magic and the Formation of Protestant Popular Culture in Germany," in Scribner, *Religion and Culture in Germany (1400–1800)*, ed. Lyndal Roper (Leiden: Brill, 2001), 323–45. See also the classic account of Keith Thomas, *Religion and the Decline of Magic* (New York: Scribner's, 1971).

19. Kieckhefer, *Magic in the Middle Ages*, 116–50.

20. Kors and Peters, *Witchcraft in Europe*, 62.

21. Kieckhefer, *Magic in the Middle Ages*, 151–75; Edward Peters, *The Magician, the Witch, and the Law* (Philadelphia: University of Pennsylvania Press, 1978), 110–35.

22. Charles Burnett, "The Earliest Chiromancy in the West," *Journal of the Warburg and Courtauld Institutes* 50 (1987): 189–95; Burnett, "An Islamic Divinatory Technique in Medieval Spain," in *The Arab Influence in Medieval Europe*, ed. Dionisius A. Agius and Richard Hitchcock (Reading, U.K.: Ithaca Press, 1994), 100–135.

23. Lawrence M. Principe, *The Secrets of Alchemy* (Chicago: University of Chicago Press, 2013), 51.

24. Karl Mantius, "Magie und Rhetorik bei Anselm von Besate," *Deutsches Archiv für Erforschung des Mittelalters* 12 (1956): 52–75; Peters, *Magician*, 21–28.

25. John of Salisbury, *Policraticus 1–4*, ed. K. S. B. Keats-Rohan, Corpus Christianorum Continuatio Mediaevalis 118 (Turnhout: Brepols, 1993), 167–68.

26. See Kieckhefer, *Forbidden Rites*; Klaassen, *Transformations of Magic*; Page, *Magic in the Cloister*; Fanger, *Rewriting Magic*; and also Benedek Láng, *Unlocked Books: Manuscripts of Learned Magic in the Medieval Libraries of Central Europe* (University Park: Pennsylvania State University Press, 2008).

27. On magic as an intellectual movement within Western history, see Brian P. Copenhaver, *Magic in Western Culture: From Antiquity to the Enlightenment* (Cambridge: Cambridge University Press, 2015).

28. Klaassen, "Medieval Ritual Magic in the Renaissance," *Aries* 3 (2003): 166–99; Klaassen, *Transformations of Magic*, 161–218; and Kieckhefer, "Did Magic Have a Renaissance? An Historiographic Question Revisited," in *Magic and the Classical Tradition*, ed. Charles Burnett and W. F. Ryan (London: Warburg Institute, 2006), 199–212.

29. Copenhaver, *Magic in Western Culture*, 38.

30. Frank Klaassen, "The Middleness of Ritual Magic," in *The Unorthodox Imagination in Late Medieval Britain*, ed. Sophie Page (Manchester: Manchester University Press, 2010), 138.

31. Alain Boureau, *Satan the Heretic: The Birth of Demonology in the Medieval West*, trans. Teresa Lavender Fagan (Chicago: University of Chicago Press, 2006).

32. Much of what follows summarizes my "Reformers on Sorcery and Superstition," in *A Companion to Observant Reform in the Late Middle Ages and Beyond*, ed. James D. Mixson and Bert Roest (Leiden: Brill, 2015), 230–54.

33. Michael D. Bailey, *Fearful Spirits, Reasoned Follies: The Boundaries of Superstition in Late Medieval Europe* (Ithaca: Cornell University Press, 2013), 155–56.

34. Bailey, "Reformers on Sorcery and Superstition," 249–53; more fully Michael D. Bailey, *Battling Demons: Witchcraft, Heresy, and Reform in the Late Middle Ages* (University Park: Pennsylvania State University Press, 2003).

35. On Jacquier's demonology, see Martine Ostorero, *Le diable au sabbat: Littérature démonologique et sorcellerie (1440–1460)* (Florence: SISMEL, 2011).

36. Franco Mormando, *The Preacher's Demons: Bernardino of Siena and the Social Underworld of Early Renaissance Italy* (Chicago: University of Chicago Press, 1999); Bailey, "Reformers on Superstition and Sorcery," 243–49.

37. Michael D. Bailey and Edward Peters, "A Sabbat of Demonologists: Basel, 1431–1440," *Historian* 65 (2003): 1375–95.

38. Johannes Nider, *Formicarius* 5.3, 5.4, 5.6, ed. G. Colvener (Douai, 1602), pp. 352, 357, 371; for *Formicarius* 5.3 and 5.4, see also Martine Ostorero, Agostino Paravicini Bagliani, and Kathrin Utz Tremp, eds., with Catherine Chène, *L'imaginaire du sabbat: Edition critique des textes les plus anciens (1430 c.–1440 c.)* (Lausanne: Université de Lausanne, 1999), 158, 176.

39. Bernardino, *Prediche volgari sul Campo di Siena, 1427*, ed. Carlo Delcorno, 2 vols. (Milan: Rusconi, 1989), 2:1003–4.

40. On the rising number of trials in the fourteenth and fifteenth centuries, see Kieckhefer, *European Witch Trials*, esp. 10–26, 106–47.

41. Constance Berman, *The Cistercian Evolution: The Invention of a Religious Order in Twelfth-Century Europe* (Philadelphia: University of Pennsylvania Press, 2010).

42. Herbert Grundmann, "Der Typus des Ketzers in mittelalterlicher Anschauung," in *Kultur- und Universalgeschichte: Walter Goetz zu seinem 60. Geburtstage* (Leipzig: Teubner, 1927), 91–107; reprinted in Grundmann, *Ausgewählte Aufsätze*, 3 vols. (Stuttgart: Hiersemann, 1976), 1:313–27.

43. Grundmann, "Typus," 326. I know of no scholarship that employs the concept of a "Typus des Magiers," but the phrase "Typus der Hexen" appears at least as early as Ludwig Meyer, "Die Beziehungen der Geisteskranken zu den Besessenen und Hexen," *Westermanns Monatshefte* 10 (1861): 258–64, at 258; referenced in the 1880 edition of Wilhelm Soldan,

Geschichte der Hexenprozesse, ed. Heinrich Heppe, 2 vols. (Stuttgart: Cotta, 1880), 2:378 (a section added by Heppe).

44. *RM*, 153–86; Robert E. Lerner, *The Heresy of the Free Spirit in the Later Middle Ages*, rev. ed. (Notre Dame: University of Notre Dame Press, 1991).

45. Mark Gregory Pegg, *The Corruption of Angels: The Great Inquisition of 1245–1246* (Princeton: Princeton University Press, 2001); R. I. Moore, *The War on Heresy* (Cambridge, Mass.: Belknap Press, 2012).

46. See Antonio Sennis, ed., *Cathars in Question* (York: York Medieval Press, 2016).

47. Kieckhefer, *European Witch Trials*, drawing on methodology advanced in Herbert Grundmann, "Ketzerverhöre des Spätmittelalters als quellenkritisches Problem," *Deutsches Archiv für Erforschung des Mittelalters* 21 (1965): 519–75.

48. See Kathrin Utz Tremp, "Witches' Brooms and Magic Ointments: Twenty Years of Witchcraft Research at the University of Lausanne (1989–2009)," *Magic, Ritual, and Witchcraft* 5 (2010): 173–87.

49. Utz Tremp, *Von der Häresie zur Hexerei*.

50. See Elliot Rose, *A Razor for a Goat: A Discussion of Certain Problems in the History of Witchcraft and Diabolism* (Toronto: University of Toronto Press, 1962); reprinted with a new foreword by Richard Kieckhefer in 2003.

51. Ginzburg, *The Night Battles: Witchcraft and Agrarian Cults in the Sixteenth and Seventeenth Centuries*, trans. John and Anne Tedeschi (Baltimore: Johns Hopkins University Press, 1983); for subsequent work, see the special forum section "Shamanism, Witchcraft, Magic," *Magic, Ritual, and Witchcraft* 1 (2006): 207–41.

52. Michael Tavuzzi, *Renaissance Inquisitors: Dominican Inquisitors and Inquisitorial Districts in Northern Italy, 1474–1527* (Leiden: Brill, 2007), 205–8.

53. Kieckhefer, *Magic in the Middle Ages*, ix.

54. Kieckhefer, *Forbidden Rites*; Julien Véronèse, *L'Ars notoria au Moyen Âge: Introduction et édition critique* (Florence: SISMEL, 2007); John of Morigny, *Liber florum celestis doctrine / The Flowers of Heavenly Teaching*, ed. Claire Fanger and Nicholas Watson (Toronto: Pontifical Institute of Medieval Studies, 2015).

55. Klaassen, "Middleness of Ritual Magic," 132.

56. See n. 8 above.

57. Richard Kieckhefer, "The Specific Rationality of Medieval Magic," *American Historical Review* 99 (1994): 813–36.

58. Bailey, *Fearful Spirits*, 148, 171–72, 177–78, 217.

59. Thomas Aquinas, *Summa theologica* 2–2.90.2, 2–2.92.2; Nicolau Eimeric, *Contra demonum invocatores*, MS Paris, Bibliothèque nationale de France, Lat. 1464, fol. 114v; Jean Gerson, *De erroribus circa artem magicam*, in Jean Gerson, *Oeuvres complètes*, ed. P. Glorieux, 10 vols. (Paris: Desclée, 1960–73), 10:84–85; Johannes Nider, *Preceptorium divine legis* 1.11.29 (Milan, 1489).

60. Page, *Magic in the Cloister*; Fanger, *Rewriting Magic*.

61. *RM*, 31.

62. Boureau, *Satan the Heretic*, 8–42; Isabel Iribarren, "From Black Magic to Heresy: A Doctrinal Leap in the Pontificate of John XXII," *Church History* 76 (2007): 32–60.

63. E.g., Béatrice Delaurenti, *La puissance des mots—"Virtus verborum": Débats doctrinaux sur le pouvoir des incantations au Moyen Âge* (Paris: Cerf, 2007).

64. Hansen, *Quellen und Untersuchungen*, 5–6.

65. *RM*, 22. On various ways magic could be considered heretical, see Richard Kieckhefer, "Witchcraft, Necromancy, and Sorcery as Heresy," in *Chasses aux sorcières et démonologie: Entre discours et pratiques (XIVᵉ–XVIIᵉ siècles)*, ed. Martine Ostorero, Georg Modestin, and Kathrin Utz Tremp (Florence: SISMEL, 2010), 133–53.

66. See n. 27 above.

67. *RM*, 49.

68. *RM*, 66.

69. Nider, *Formicarius* 5.4, *L'imaginaire du sabbat*, 174–76.

70. Robert E. Lerner, "Werner di Friedberg intrappolato dalla legge," in *La parola all'accusato*, ed. Jean-Claude Maire Vigueur and Agostino Paravicini Bagliani (Palermo: Sellerio, 1991), 268–81; Felix Hemmerli, *Varie oblectationis opuscula et tractatus* (Strasbourg, 1487 or after), fols. 106r-110v.

71. Kieckhefer, *Magic in the Middle Ages*, 176.

72. Kramer, *Malleus maleficarum* 2.2, ed. and trans. Christopher Mackay, 2 vols. (Cambridge: Cambridge University Press, 2006), 1:496; an earlier example is Nider, *Formicarius* 5.3, *L'imaginaire du sabbat*, 158.

73. Kramer, *Malleus* 5.4, p. 496.

74. Bailey, *Fearful Spirits*, 213–19.

75. Kieckhefer, *Magic in the Middle Ages*, 45.

76. See Kieckhefer, "Specific Rationality," responding to Valerie I. J. Flint, *The Rise of Magic in Early Medieval Europe* (Princeton: Princeton University Press, 1991).

77. Page, *Magic in the Cloister*, 126.

78. Jeffrey Hamburger notes how monastic "aspirations" could be "inherited by the laity." See Hamburger, "The Visual and the Visionary: The Image in Late Medieval Monastic Devotions," *Viator* 20 (1989): 182.

79. *RM*, 8.

80. Dyan Elliott, *Proving Woman: Female Spirituality and Inquisitional Culture in the Later Middle Ages* (Princeton: Princeton University Press, 2004), 9–43; Christine Caldwell Ames, *Righteous Persecution: Inquisition, Dominicans, and Christianity in the Middle Ages* (Philadelphia: University of Pennsylvania Press, 2009), 137–81.

81. Denys the Carthusian, *Contra vicia superstitionum* (Cologne, 1533), 607.

82. Stuart Clark, "Inversion, Misrule, and the Meaning of Witchcraft," *Past and Present* 87 (1980): 98–127; Clark, *Thinking with Demons: The Idea of Witchcraft in Early Modern Europe* (Oxford: Oxford University Press, 1997).

83. Nicolau Eimeric, *Directorium inquisitorum* 2.43.2, ed. F. Peña (Rome, 1587), p. 338; translation from Kors and Peters, *Witchcraft in Europe*, 123.

84. Klaassen, "Middleness of Ritual Magic," 136.

7

THE JURISDICTION OF MEDIEVAL INQUISITORS OVER JEWS AND MUSLIMS: NICHOLAS EYMERIC'S *CONTRA INFIDELES DEMONES INVOCANTES*

Katelyn Mesler

Of Nicholas Eymeric's (before 1320–1399) more than forty works on subjects ranging from theology and philosophy to magic and eschatology, and from exegesis and the papal schism to astrology and the thought of Raymond Lull, very few can be dated to his first period as inquisitor of the Crown of Aragon, which began in 1357 and culminated in his exile to Avignon in 1376.[1] In addition to two collections of sermons written during this period, Eymeric produced three inquisitorial treatises that all addressed issues of jurisdiction and the prosecution of sorcery.[2] The first of these, *De iurisdictione inquisitorum in et contra christianos demones invocantes* (1359), was written shortly after his appointment as inquisitor and defends the notion that Christians who invoke demons are heretics and thereby subject to inquisitorial prosecution. At the other end of this period is his influential guide for inquisitors, the *Directorium inquisitorum* (1376), completed in Avignon at the beginning of his exile.

Less well known, even among specialists, is Eymeric's extended argument for inquisitorial jurisdiction over non-Christians, *De iurisdictione ecclesie et inquisitorum contra infideles demones invocantes vel alias fidem catholicam agitantes* (ca. 1370),[3] which not only expands the argument of his previous

In my first lesson as Richard Kieckhefer's student, he placed before me a copy of Nicholas Eymeric's treatise on Christians invoking demons and asked me to read it. I knew no paleography, but he guided me patiently as I picked up the skill. Over the years, Richard has generously devoted countless hours of his time to poring over manuscripts with me and other students. To show my appreciation for all he has done, and to commemorate where it all began, I have prepared in Richard's honor this partial edition of Eymeric's work on infidels invoking demons.

I would like to express my gratitude to Claudia Heimann, the Fundación Bartolomé March, Carolina Tur Serra, Christine Morerod-Fattebert, and Nicolas Weill-Parot for support at various stages of my work with this manuscript.

treatise but also offers a window into the development of material that would later appear in the *Directorium*. This work was thought lost until a single copy was discovered in the library of the Fundación Bartolomé March (Palma de Mallorca) and announced in 1979.[4] In the nearly forty years that have passed since its recovery, this work has only once been the subject of analysis.[5] It is my hope that this partial edition, which preserves the full structure of the text and reproduces Eymeric's key points while omitting most of his prooftexts and extended discussions, will generate new interest and will make the content of this overlooked treatise more accessible. I hope this text will eventually receive the full annotated edition that it deserves.

Contra infideles consists of an introduction, five articles of unequal length, and then a series of ten objections and responses. The main issue in question is under what circumstances inquisitors, rather than secular judges or ordinary bishops, have jurisdiction over non-Christians. Eymeric begins by asserting that all are under the authority of Christ, and therefore of his vicar the pope, who delegates some matters to inquisitors. After establishing in article 1 that non-Christians can, in fact, commit faults against laws (Eymeric's preferred term throughout is *delinquere*), article 2 establishes some of Eymeric's key distinctions.[6] There are two types of "faith," one that is a moral virtue and is based on fulfilling any promise or pact, and another that is a theological virtue and refers specifically to Christian faith as instilled in baptism. Whereas non-Christians don't possess this second form of faith, they do possess the first type, especially in their commitment to abide by the laws of their respective sects. For Jews, he argues, this is established in circumcision, which he presents as a parallel to baptism. Non-Christians can thus violate *in fide* only with respect to their own faith, whereas they are capable of violating *apud, circa, et contra* Christian faith, whether through their general disbelief, only by actively insulting Christianity, or by going so far as to lead Christians into heresy. Article 3 then asks in what senses Jews can be considered heretics.[7] In short, he argues, they can be considered heretics *directly* inasmuch as they violate the laws of the Old Testament. However, they are *indirectly* heretics with respect to Christian faith when they reject articles of faith held in common with Christians (such as the unity of God).

Articles 4 and 5 turn to the main question of jurisdiction. In article 4, Eymeric establishes the primacy of inquisitors over both secular judges and ordinary bishops in matters of heresy. With all of his premises now in place, Eymeric proceeds in article 5 to the question of jurisdiction over non-Christians. He argues that Jews are subject to inquisitorial rather than secular jurisdiction (1) when they actively transgress *in* or *contra* Christian faith, as established in article 2, and (2) when they can be considered indirectly heretical toward Christianity, as established in article 3. These two conclusions are evidently built on two legal precedents from the thirteenth century: The first is the bull *Turbato corde*, issued by Clement IV in 1267, which granted inquisitors jurisdiction over Jews who aided or encouraged anyone who was baptized to (re)turn to Judaism.[8] For Eymeric, there is no significant difference in a Jew encouraging a Christian to Judaize, to invoke demons (and thus commit idolatry, as Eymeric argues here and elsewhere), or to commit any other act that would be deemed heretical for Christians. The second precedent is from Innocent IV's *Apparatus* to the *Decretals*, which was written sometime between 1244 and 1254. In defense of Talmud burnings, Innocent wrote, "Indeed, we believe that the pope, who is the vicar of Jesus Christ, has authority not only over Christians but also over all infidels, since Christ had authority over all. . . . Therefore, the pope can judge the Jews if they violate the Law (*contra legem faciant*) in moral matters and their own prelates do not check them, and also if they invent heresies against their own Law (*hereses contra suam legem inveniant*)."[9]

Eymeric thus argues that if Jews themselves invoke demons, they violate the shared theological law of God's unity and thus fall under the jurisdiction of the pope and his delegates. If they hold to beliefs of the Talmud, they are heretics against their law (i.e., Mosaic Law) and thus fall under ecclesiastical jurisdiction. If they blaspheme or otherwise offend *apud/contra/circa* Christian faith, they are thereby encouraging Christians to disbelieve and thus are subject to the judgment of inquisitors.

Although Eymeric constantly refers to "Jews, Saracens, and other infidels" and occasionally to "Tartars" as well, it is clear that much of the argument is directed toward Jews and hinges on the scripture and beliefs they share with Christians. Only a few sections consider Muslims in greater detail. As Claudia Heimann has argued, this is surely a reflection of the practical reality of the inquisitors' activities.[10] But the subject announced in the title is puzzling in other ways, too. There are very few mentions of invoking demons, especially compared to the lists of crimes against Christians. If the treatise was indeed occasioned by the case of Astruc da Piera, then Eymeric may have had reason to highlight this particular implication of his argument, even though the argument itself applies to a much wider range of issues. It is also unclear exactly what is meant by the end of the title, ". . . and otherwise *agitantes* the catholic faith." Given the context here and elsewhere in the text, the term must mean something like "assailing,"[11] and this is confirmed by a parallel use of *impugnantes* (5.Concl.19). The term appears in the same way in the title of Eymeric's later *Tractatus brevis . . . contra infideles fidem catholicam agitantes*, and yet it does not appear anywhere else in that text.

The partial edition presented here, as noted above, lacks most of the proof-texts underlying Eymeric's argument, not because they are unimportant but, on the contrary, because there is not enough space here to do them justice. In addition to biblical references, Eymeric relies heavily on Thomas Aquinas and occasionally on authorities such as Augustine, Jerome, Bede, Isidore of Seville, Hrabanus Maurus, Papias the Lombard, and Huguccio of Pisa. Citations from Roman civil law help support procedural issues, and discussions on heresy, inquisitors, and the status of non-Christians come often from the standard compilations of canon law from Gratian through the *Extravagantes*. Eymeric also draws on several commentators on canon law, including Bartholomew of Brescia, Bernard of Parma, Raymond of Penyafort, Geoffrey (Godfrey) of Trani, Henry of Segusio, Innocent IV, Johannes Andreae, Paulus de Liazariis, and Jesselin de Cassagnes. Several of the prooftexts adduced here are discussed in the *Directorium*, although not always in the same context. However, question 46 in the second part of the *Directorium* is assembled almost verbatim from the present treatise. Question 46 is divided into 17 subsections, which correlate to *Contra infideles* as follows:

DI pt. 2, q. 46.1–4	3.Concl.10
DI pt. 2, q. 46.5	5.Cons.5.4.6
DI pt. 2, q. 46.6	5.Cons.5.4.6–7
DI pt. 2, q. 46.7	N/A
DI pt. 2, q. 46.8	Responsiones–Can.1.Arg.
DI pt. 2, q. 46.9	Can.1.Resp.–Can.2.Arg.
DI pt. 2, q. 46.10	Can.2.Resp.–Can.2.Resp.2.
DI pt. 2, q. 46.11	Can.2.Resp.3.–Can.3.Arg.
DI pt. 2, q. 46.12	Can.3.Resp.–Can.4.Resp.
DI pt. 2, q. 46.13	Can.4.Resp.
DI pt. 2, q. 46.14	Can.4.Resp.–Can.5.Arg.
DI pt. 2, q. 46.15	Can.5.Resp.–Leg.5.Resp.
DI pt. 2, q. 46.16	after Leg.5.Resp.
DI pt. 2, q. 46.17	N/A

The only subsections that are not found here are 46.7, which is an additional discussion concerning Thomas Aquinas, and 46.17, on Astruc da Piera, whose trial concluded in 1372. More textual work on the *Directorium* will be necessary before we can determine to what extent the few differences represent edits to the text or are merely the result of copyists' errors. In the edition that follows, I have signaled a few of the more notable differences.

Edition

Manuscript

Palma de Mallorca, Biblioteca de la Fundación Bartolomé March, MS 104-II-7 (*olim* 15-III-6), fols. 227r–245v.

This manuscript, which belonged to the convent of Saint Dominic in Gerona, was produced sometime between 1385 and Eymeric's death in 1399. It is annotated in several different hands, which include Eymeric's own autograph corrections.[12]

Ratio editionis

It is unfortunate that the *Contra infideles* has been recovered in only one manuscript, for this copy presents numerous textual difficulties. The initial copying of the text was full of errors and omissions, which the indispensable corrections from Eymeric and other hands have reduced. Nevertheless, difficulties remain, and I have employed an interventionist approach in clarifying some of the more problematic passages. Since this is not a complete and definitive edition, I present the text as it stands *post correctionem*, except where I have intervened.

The future editor of the full treatise will face challenging decisions concerning the scribe's creative orthography. I have opted to preserve the orthography of this unicum as closely as possible, intervening only when particularly unusual spellings may hinder the reader. However, the scribe shows no consistency in writing *c* and *t*. Any solution is necessarily artificial, and I have chosen to retain *t* everywhere it is expected in classical spelling. I have tried to keep punctuation as light as possible while facilitating reading of the text.

I have imposed a numbering system that usually follows Eymeric's own numbering of divisions and subdivisions. Where Eymeric's key arguments are further subdivided into self-contained units, I have often followed suit, although in some cases more subdivisions are possible than what I include here. After the prologue and incipit, the text contains five articles consisting of *consideranda* (Cons.) and *conclusiones* (Concl.), and it ends with a series of objections and responses, five rooted in canon law (Can.) and five in civil law (Leg.).

Sigla

<—>	editorial insertions; markers of the text's general structure
[—]	illegible or conjectural text
|227r|	folio numbers
Bold	rubricated text

Abbreviations

Note the following abbreviations used in citations:

Apparatus	Innocent IV, *Commentaria Innocentii quarti pont. maximi super libros quinque Decretalium* (Frankfurt am Main, 1570)
Auth. coll.	Numbering by *collatio* of the *Authenticum*. See below, s.v. "Nov."
Clem.	Clement V, *Constitutiones clementinae*, in Emil Friedberg, ed., *Corpus iuris canonici*, 2nd ed. (Graz: Akademische Druck, 1959), 2:1125–1200
Cod.	Paul Krueger, ed., *Codex Iustinianus*, vol. 2 of *Corpus iuris civilis*. (Berlin: Wiedmann, 1892)
DI	Nicholas Eymeric, *Directorium inquisitorum* (Venice, 1607)
Extrav. comm.	*Extravagantes communes*, in Friedberg, *Corpus iuris canonici*, 2:1287–1312
Nov.	Gustav Heimbach, ed., *Authenticum: Novellarum constitutionum Iustiniani versio vulgata*, 2 vols. (Leipzig: I. A. Barth, 1851)
VI	Boniface VIII, *Liber sextus Decretalium*, in Friedberg, *Corpus iuris canonici*, 2:929–1124
X	Gregory IX, *Decretales (Liber extra)*, in Friedberg, *Corpus iuris canonici*, 2:1–928

|227r| **Incipit prologus in librum de iuridicione ecclesie et inquisitorum contra infideles demones invocantes vel alias fidem catholicam agitantes, editum a fratre Nicholao Eymerici ordinis predicatorum sacre theologie magistro et inquisitore heretice pravitatis.**

Alias oves habeo que non sunt de hoc ovili, et illas oportet me adducere, Iohannis decimo.[1] Premissum Christi verbum ad presens nostrum propositum potest congrue tripliciter adaptari. . . .

---

1. John 10:16.

1. Primo dico quod potest esse verbum humani generis redemptoris, hoc est domini nostri Ihesu Christi. . . . In verbo proposito dominus Ihesus dicit, *Alias oves habeo*, id est iudeos et infideles ceteros in mea potestate teneo, *que non sunt ex hoc ovili*, scilicet ecclesie sancte dei nec numero nec merito, *et illas oportet me adducere* ad ovile videlicet fidei et ecclesie sancte dei.

2. Secundo potest esse verbum dominici gregis pastoris, hoc est domini nostri pape. . . . Dominus noster Ihesus Christus non solum est et fuit dominus fidelium sed et iudeorum et omni generaliter infidelium ceterorum. . . . |227v| . . . Ideo dominus noster papa vicarius est generaliter omni homini de iure quicquid sit de facto domini nostri Ihesu Christi. . . . Ideo congrue potest dicere dominus noster papa verbum preassumptum quod *alias oves habeo in meo*, scilicet dominio de iure licet non de facto, *que non sunt ex hoc ovili*, collatione videlicet fidei, *et illas oportet me adducere* ad ovile scilicet ecclesie quod quandoque *fiet*, quia quandoque erit *unus pastor et unum ovile*.

3. Tertio dico quod potest esse verbum pestis heresis inquisitoris, cum autem inquisitor sit delegatus domini nostri pape ad extirpandam hereticam pravitatem et ad reducendas et reducendos oberrantes in fide et contra fidem ad sancte ecclesie unitatem. Christiani hereticando nonnunquam errant in fide; iudei autem et saraceni christianos ad eorum ritum execrabilem pertrahendo errant contra fidem, et tales etiam infideles ydola colentes demonibus sacrificantes deum fore unum negantes, que sunt de lege nature, deum non esse creatorem <asserentes> et filium negantes, que sunt de eorum scripta lege quam fideiusserunt et promisserunt, in quibus tamen nobiscum conveniunt nec ut sic iudei vel saraceni sunt, in et contra legem et fidem nostram et suam faciant et committant.[2] . . . In lege et contra legem in fide ac contra fidem nostram delinquentes punitionibus compescendo et persuasionibus pertrahendo, ut inquisitor domini nostri pape delegatus merito possit dicere verbum preassumptum, *Alias oves habeo que non sunt ex hoc ovili*, christianos scilicet hereticantes et infideles contra legem Christi agendo, christianos ad eorum ritum execrabilem pertrahentes, ac contra legem nature ac scripture in quibus nobiscum conveniunt et quam promiserunt asserentes, quas oves *me aducere oportet*. Explicit prologus.

Incipit tractatus

Quia vero nonnulli adversarii veritatis et contrarii sancte ecclesiastice potestati nisi sunt publice deffendere et nituntur cognitionem et punitionem infidelium

---

2. Cf. "contra legem faciant" in *Apparatus* to X 3.34.8, §5.

de et pro predictis non pertinere ad ecclesiasticos iudices sed potius |228r| ad dominos temporales, hinc est quod ego frater Nicholaus Eymerici, in sacra theologia magister indignus inquisitor Aragonie heretice pravitatis ordinis predicatorum, pro sancta fidei defensione et predicte sancte iuridicionis ecclesiastice causa huiusmodi quamplurimum agitatus et amplus pro ea pati paratus, presentem brevem tractatum inepte et rude compaginatum edidi, quem[3] submitto totaliter et ex toto correcioni domini nostri pape et ecclesie sancte dei. In quo tractatu taliter procedetur:

Nam primo videbitur iudei et infideles ceteri si et quibus modis possint delinquere. Secundo si et quibus modis possint in fide delinquere. Tertio si in fide delinquendo possint vere dici hereticare. Quarto in fide delinquentes et hereticantes quis habet iudicare. Quinto videtur propositum clare quis scilicet iudeos et infideles ceteros in fide et contra fidem delinquentes habeat sententiare.

1. **Primus articulus principalis**. Primus articulus est iudei et infideles ceteri si et quibus modis possint delinquere, ubi consideranda sunt duo:

<Consideranda>

1.Cons.1. Primum est quod . . . hii vero qui in mortali corpore degunt mereri et demereri possunt quamdiu in illo existunt, et per consequens procedere et etiam deviare et per bona opera tendere et per mala etiam delinquere. Et hac de causa isti ab Apostolo ubi prius notantur peregrini, *scientes quod quamdiu sumus in hoc corpore peregrinamur.*[4] Peregrini autem sunt viatores; viatores autem contingit oberrare deviare et delinquere atque cadere multipliciter. . . .

1.Cons.2. Secundum quod considerari oportet est quod quia viatores et peregrini a domino sunt quicunque in corpore mortali persistunt, ideo deus contulit eis in omni statu legem aliquam per quam se dirigant ne delinquant sed incedant. Et hec lex fuit triplex secundum triplicem mundi statum. Prima lex dei dicitur lex nature. . . . Et hec lex omnes homines generaliter obligat atque ligat tam fideles quam etiam infideles. . . . Secunda lex dei dicitur lex iustitie. . . . Et hanc legem quantum ad decem precepta decalogi scripsit deus in tabulis lapideis. . . . Hec decem precepta seu leges sunt non solum de lege scripta et iustitie ymo de lege nature, et ideo omnes generaliter obligant atque ligant. Huic legi scripte simul et nature subiunxit deus per Moisem alias leges et pre-

---

3. MS "quam."
4. 2 Cor. 5:6.

cepta quia iudicalia per que Moyses et ceteri maiores populum iudicarent, et etiam cerimonialia per que domino deservirent et que ventura erant de Christo figurarent. Et he[5] leges iudiciales et cerimoniales populum iudaicum cui soli date fuerant et explicate ligabant et obligabant. |228v| Tertia lex dei dicitur lex gratie et hec fuit lex Christi. . . . Hec lex generaliter omnes obligat tam fideles quam infideles ad suscipiendum quia omnibus generaliter data est. . . .

<Conclusiones>

1.Concl.1. Prima conclusio est quod iudei et infideles ceteri delinquere possunt. . . .

1.Concl.2. Secunda conclusio est quod iudei et infideles ceteri delinquere possunt in lege nature. . . .

1.Concl.3. Tertia conclusio<est> quod iudei in lege mosayca et saraceni in secta macumetica,[6] quantum ad contenta in eis que sunt de lege nature, delinquere possunt non pro eo quia in lege Moisi vel secta Macumeti scripta sunt sed quia de lege nature sunt. . . .

1.Concl.4. |229r| Quarta conclusio est quod iudei in lege mosayca et saraceni in secta Macumeti, quantum ad contenta in eis que non sunt de lege nature, si non observant non delinqunt. . . . Ponitur quod iudei non peccant si traditiones eorum patrum non observant.

1.Concl.5. Quinta co<n>clusio est quod iudei saraceni et infideles ceteri omnes in legem Christi vel circa vel contra eam delinqunt et delinquere possunt. Hec patet, nam ad fidem et legem Christi a deo vocati sunt et venire renuerunt atque delinquunt. . . .

2. **Secundus articulus principalis**.[7] Secundus articulus est iudei et infideles ceteri si et quibus modis possunt in fide delinquere, ubi primo videndum est an sit verum quod iudei fidem veram habeant. Secundo ex hoc videbitur si et quibus modis in fide delinquere valeant. Circa primum consideranda sunt tria:

<Consideranda>

---

5. MS "hec."
6. MS *fort.* "matumintica"; *marg.* "alias mahometica."
7. On this article, see Claudia Heimann, "*Quis proprie hereticus est*," 607–12.

2.Cons.1. Primum est quod fides potest sumi dupliciter: Uno modo generaliter pro cuiuslibet promissionis vel pactionis observantia alteri facta. . . . Alio modo potest sumi fides specialiter pro singulari pactionis et promissionis observantia Christo. . . . Prima fides est virtus moralis et consequens adquisita; secunda fides est virtus theologalis et per consequens a deo infusa. . . . |229v| Qui igitur fidem prestat homini legi se ligat humane, ut faciunt faudatarii; qui autem fidem exibet deo legi se obligat divine, ut olim fecerunt iudei; qui autem fidem promittit ipso legi se obligat christiane, ut faciunt in baptismo omnes christiani.

2.Cons.2.

2.Cons.2.1. Secundum considerandum est quod lex nature est vera et bona quia cordi humano a deo insita est. . . . Ideo quilibet homo naturali obligatione et fide ad serviendum deo et uniendum secundum illam obligatus et ligatus est. . . .

2.Cons.2.2. Lex autem Moysi et vera et bona fuit quia a deo per Moysem data fuit . . . non omni populo sed tantum israelico seu iudaico. . . . Ideo quilibet de populo iudeorum adobligatus extitit, sed quia terminum tali legi deus legis conditor affixit, ideo usque ad illum terminum hec lex et non amplius obligavit. . . .

2.Cons.2.3. Lex vero evangelica vera sancta et bona est quia a Christo et de ipso est. Et quia semper bona erit ideo semper obligabit, et quia generaliter omnibus gentibus data est . . . ideo omnes gentes ad recipiendum obligantur. Sed quia non omnes receperunt legem evangelii . . . ideo non se obligaverunt omnes ad credendum nec ad servandum sed solum christiani qui in baptismo spoponderunt et fidem receperunt. . . .

2.Cons.3. Tertium considerandum est quod philosophi et alii primi patres, qui secundum legem nature tantum vixerunt, veram fidem que est virtus theologica non habuerunt quia non ea que non viderunt crediderunt. . . . Sancti autem patres qui ultra legem nature a deo revelationem de dei filio incarnando[8] vel implicite habuerunt . . . vel explicite . . . omnes isti fidem veram que est virtus theologica habuerunt. . . . Et nos omnes christiani, qui preter legem nature et legem mosaicam legem Christi seu evangelicam receperunt, omnes isti fidem veram que est virtus theologica a deo eis infusam in baptismo

---

8. MS "incarnendo."

habuerunt. . . . Et iudei qui nunc sunt veram fidem que est virtus theologica non habent nec habuerunt, quia a vera credentia eorum sanctorum patrum et prophetarum discesserunt non credentes nec implicite nec explicite que eorum sancti patres crediderunt implicite et nos christiani credimus explicite. . . . |230r| . . . Ideo sunt et dicuntur merito infideles a Christi vera fide et catholica deviantes, fidem veram que est virtus theologica a deo infusa veraciter non habentes.

2.Cons.3.1. Nec valet si dicatur quod iudei eorum que sunt christiane fidei et legis evangelice aliqua credunt, ut ea que sunt deitatis, scilicet deum esse visibilium et invisibilium creatorem, non esse tantum nisi unum deum, et similia, et aliqua non credunt, ut ea que sunt Christi humanitatis. . . . Et ideo quod saltem aliquorum, licet non omnium, habent et retinent veram fidem. Nam verum non existit quod credant omnes articulos deitatis quia non credunt articulum trinitatis. . . . Ita recte est in proposito quod iudei credant istis verbis divinis et non illis; hoc non est proprie credere sed potius opinari. . . .

2.Cons.3.2. Nec valet si dicatur quod iudei illa que sunt deitatis credunt et non que sunt humanitatis, quia in lege Moysi illa et non ista legunt. . . . Nam iudei sicut illa que sunt deitatis audierunt et legerunt, sic et illa que sunt Christi humanitatis audierunt et legerunt vel legere potuerunt et possunt si voluerunt. . . . |230v| . . . Ut sint inexcusabiles qui legere nolunt.

2.Cons.3.3. Nec prodest quicquam si dicatur quod lex Moysi apparuit per deum multis signis et portentis confirmata et non lex Christi. Nam grandiora et evidentia signa fecit deus ad confirmandum legem Christi quam legem Moisi. . . .

<Conclusiones>

2.Concl.1. Prima conclusio est quod iudei moderni et qui fidem post divulgationem[9] legis euvangelii delinquerunt et delinqunt deviarunt et deviant a fide eorum sanctorum patrum, et preteriti et presentes. Hec patet: iudei non crediderunt de deo et Christo ut eorum patres sancti. . . .

2.Concl.2. |231r| Secunda conclusio est quod iudei predicti presentes et preteriti delinquunt et delinquere possunt apud, circa, et contra fidem Christi et christianorum. Hec patet: iudei in Christum non credunt, Christum blafemant, contra Christum locuntur scribunt et invenunt, ad ritus eorum christianos

9. MS "divilgationem."

pertrahunt, frequenter christianos circuncidunt, a credentia Christi christianos pro posse abducunt, neophitos et non neophitos ad abnegandum Christum
perducunt, hereticare christianos faciunt, et similia hiis committunt. . . .

2.Concl.3. Tertia conclusio est quod predicti iudei nec delinquunt proprie, nec
existentes iudei delinquere possunt in fide eorum sanctorum patrum, nec in
fide Christi seu christianorum. Hec patet, nam nec fidem sanctorum patrum
nec fidem christianorum habent nec habuerunt. . . .

2.Concl.4. Quarta conclusio est quod predicti iudei delinquere possunt in fide,
hoc est fideiussione pactione et promissione[10] legis seu secte sue. Hec patet:
legem enim mosaycam longe ante finitam[11] tacite vel expresse in circu<n>cisione
vel alias credere et tenere pacti sunt et promiserunt, et a tali pactione declinare
aut discedere possunt. Ergo in fide huiusmodi seu legalitate delinquere pos-
sunt. . . . |231v| . . .

2.Concl.5. Quinta conclusio est quod saraceni et tartari et infideles omnes
ceteri possunt in genere a fide, in fide, circa et contra fidem, attentis in ipsorum
sectis contentis, delinquere proportionabiliter ut iudei. . . .

Ex predictis quinque conclusionibus et aliis in hoc secundo articulo antelatis
eliciuntur iste subconclusiones.

<Subconclusiones>

2.Sub.1. Prima subconclusio est quod iudei moderni saraceni et infideles ceteri
non credendo esse vera ea que sunt de lege nature non delinqunt[12] directe in
fide sed in ratione. . . . Non credere hiis que sunt de lege nature est indirecte
non credere legi divine et per consequens delinquere in fide pactione naturali
et obligatione. . . .

2.Sub.2. Secunda subconclusio est quod moderni iudei saraceni et infideles
ceteri non credendo esse vera ea que sunt de lege moysayca et aliorum primo-
rum sanctorum patrum . . . non delinqunt in fide sed deviant a fide. Hec patet,
nam predicti infideles fidem sanctorum patrum non habent nec habuerunt. . . .

10. MS "pronissione."
11. MS "finatam."
12. MS "dilinqunt."

2.Sub.3. Tertia subconclusio est quod moderni saraceni et infideles ceteri non credendo ea fore vera que sunt de lege Christi non delinqunt in fide, sed circa et contra fidem. Hec patet, nam predicti infideles fidem Christi non receperunt nec habent nec habuerunt. Sed contra: se gesserunt ipsam blafemando, hereses vanas contra eam inducendo, et christianos pro posse ab ea abducendo. . . .

2.Sub.4. Quarta subconclusio est quod moderni iudei saraceni et infideles ceteri non credendo ea que sunt de eorum lege seu potius secta non delinquerunt in fide que est virtus theologica. Hec patet, nam fidem talem non habent nec habuerunt. . . .

2.Sub.5. |232r| Quinta subconclusio est quod moderni iudei saraceni et infideles ceteri non credendo esse vera ea que sunt de eorum lege vel secta delinquerunt in fide que est virtus moralis et observantia promissionis et pactionis. . . .

3. **Tertius articulus principalis.**[13] Tertius articulus. Iudei et infideles ceteri si delinquendo in fide, circa, vel contra fidem possunt dici vere heretici? Ubi primo videndum est heresis quid proprie est. Secundo heresis quot modis sumi potest. Tertio ex hoc videbitur si et quibus modis in iudeis et infidelibus ceteris heresis cadere potest.

<Consideranda>

3.Cons.1. Circa primum considerandum est quod hoc nomine heresis ethimologizatur seu exponitur tripliciter . . . scilicet electionem adhesionem et divisionem. Ex hiis omnibus statim dictis patent tria:

3.Cons.1.1. Primum est heresis quid est proprie: quia falsa et repudiata sententia seu doctrina, quam sibi quis tanquam veram elegit et ei firmiter adheret, per quam ab aliis quibus per veram doctrinam illi oppositam ante coniungebatur nunc dividitur et separatur.

3.Cons.1.2. Secundum est hereticus quis proprie est: quia ille qui falsam atque perversam doctrinam seu sententiam tanquam veram eligit, illique doctrine sic electe firmiter et pertinaciter adheret et se iungit, et ab illis quibus antea per doctrinam illi electe oppositam erat unitus seipsum separat et dividit. Non enim proprie quis potest dici divisus nisi qui ante fuit unitus. . . .

---

13. On this article, see Heimann, *"Quis proprie hereticus est,"* 612–16.

3.Cons.1.3. Tertium est hereticare quid proprie est: quia falsam et perversam doctrinam sibi tanquam veram et sanam eligere, sic electe firmiter et pertinaciter adherere, et ab eis quibus ante erat unitus per veram doctrinam illi sic electe oppositam se dividere.

3.Cons.2. Circa secundum considerandum est quod heresis potest sumi dupliciter, uno modo secundum vocabuli propriam significationem . . . alio modo secundum iuris communem locutionem. . . .

3.Cons.2.1. Primo modo heresis dicitur quamcunque falsam doctrinam sibi eligere, sic electe firmiter adherere, et per consequens ab eis quibus uniebatur in sana doctrina illi sic electe contraria se dividere. Et hoc modo heresis cadit vel cadere potest in quacunque arte lege scientia seu doctrina humana etiam et divina. . . . |232v| . . .

3.Cons.2.2. Secundo modo heresis dicitur falsam sententiam seu doctrinam, non in quacunque scientia in generali sed in sacra theologia et scientia divina in speciali, sibi eligere eique firmiter et pertinaciter adherere, et per consequens a veris theologis quibus ante uniebatur in sacra doctrina sic illi electe contraria se dividere. . . . In hac autem sacra theologia et divina sapientia sunt in genere tres partes: prima est testamentum antiquum quod precessit, secunda est testamentum novum, tertia quatuor conscilia[14] et quecunque alia ab ecclesia determinata ut fide tenenda. . . . |233r| . . .

<Conclusiones>

3.Concl.1. Prima conclusio est quod iudei moderni delinquendo et deviando a fide eorum sanctorum patrum non[15] hereticant accipiendo heresim secundum heresis nominis significationem. Hec probatur: cetui sanctorum patrum moderni iudei fide que est pactio uniti nunquam fuerunt, ergo dividi ab eis eadem fide non potuerunt nec possunt. . . .

3.Concl.2. Secunda conclusio est quod iudei moderni delinquendo et deviando a fide eorum |233v| sanctorum patrum non hereticant accipiendo heresim secundum iuris communem de heresi locutionem. Hec probatur: congregationi sanctorum patrum iudei moderni in fide que est virtus et theologus habi-

---

14. I.e., Nicaea I (325), Constantinople I (381), Ephesus (431), and Chalcedon (451).
15. MS "vere." This emendation is suggested by the sense of the passage and by the parallel wording of 3.Concl.2.

tus nunquam fuerunt uniti, ergo dividi ab eis fide non possunt nec potuerunt, et per consequens hereticare non possunt. . . .

3.Concl.3. Tertia conclusio est quod iudei moderni delinquendo circa et contra fidem Christi et christianorum neutro predictorum modorum directe hereticant. Hec probatur: nec fide que est pactio nec fide que est virtus et habitus theologus infusus a deo iudei moderni christianis uniti sunt nec fuerunt. . . .

3.Concl.4. Quarta conclusio est quod iudei moderni delinquendo circa et contra fidem Christi et christianorum sumendo heresim primo modo secundum nominis scilicet significationem indirecte delinqunt et consequenter hereticant. Hec probatur: iudei moderni fideiubendo et promittendo credere que sunt veteris testamenti, etiam secundum rabinorum perversam traditionem et expositionem, fideiubent et promittunt se credere quedam que sunt realiter etiam testamenti novi et fidei Christi. Igitur si hereticant in testamento veteri directe, hereticant et in novo quo ad contenta in utroque indirecte. . . . Si iudei fideiusserunt prout fecerunt in circuncisione et alias tacite vel expresse credere . . . non solum a ceteris modernis iudeis per talem abnegationem dividerentur directe quibus ante pactionem et fide tali uniebantur, ymo et a sanctis patribus et a nobis christianis fidelibus de novo dividerentur. . . .

3.Concl.5. Quinta conclusio est quod iudei moderni delinquendo circa et contra fidem Christi et christianorum, etsi non possunt in illa directe hereticare, sunt tamen hereticorum fautores receptatores deffensores et celatores vel frequentius possunt esse. Hec patet: iudei christianos transire ad eorum perfidiam frequenter procurant, et ad talem perfidiam translatos receptant deffensant occultant atque celant. . . . Consequentia patent quia tales christiani taliter agentes heretici sunt. . . . Patent etiam ex processibus inquisitorum predictorum in quibus clare invenitur quod iudei moderni . . . non solum conversos ad Christi fidem ad perfidiam iudeorum inducere satagunt et inducunt, ut fidem Christi abnegent, sacrum baptismum profanant, et ad vomitum revertantur, verum etiam natura et genere christianos parvulos violenter circuncidunt[16] ad distantia loca transmittunt et nutriri et erudiri a iudeis et inter iudeos in eorum perfidia faciunt et procurant. Ymo quod scelestius[17] est et gravius christianos adultos in fide corrunpentes pretio plus quam prece ad eorum ritum execrabilem sollicitant pertrahunt et perducunt, faciendo eos fidem Christi adnegare sacrum baptismum prophanare circuncisionem recipere et

16. MS "circundunt."
17. MS "zelestius."

more iudaico conversari vivere atque mori. Et non solum hec faciunt, ymo hereses contra Christi fidem inveniunt scribunt divulgant et promulgant et christianos hiis deformant, demones invocare eis sacrificare adorare venerari et colere christianos docent, verbo facto pariter et exemplo ad ritum paganorum et hereticorum eos taliter pertrahendo. In omnibus enim predictis iudei faciunt christia|234r|anos hereticare. . . .

3.Concl.6. Sexta conclusio est quod iudei moderni delinquendo in fide seu fideiussione, quam deo fecerunt vel promisserunt in circunsisione vel legis eorum acceptatione, non credendo omnibus vel aliquibus que sunt in veteri testamento . . . vere et proprie secundum heresis nominis significationem hereticant, utpote si credant deum non creatorem fore vel dei filium incarnatum esse et similia, que sunt contra anticum testamentum secundum perversum sensum rabinorum expositum. . . . Si ergo aliquis de iudeis modernis firmiter assereret dei filium incarnatum de virgine natum et similia, in lege seu secta sua atque fide predicta hereticus verus foret.

3.Concl.7. Septima conclusio est quod iudei moderni delinquendo in fide, hoc est fidei promissione, non credendo omnibus vel aliquibus que sunt in veteri testamento . . . vere et proprie secundum communem iuris locutionem hereticant. . . .

3.Concl.8. Octava conclusio est quod iudei moderni delinquendo, ut predicitur in fide seu fideiussione, non credendo hiis que sunt de veteri testamento ab eis accepto, ut predicitur, non solum hereticant predictis duobus modis, verum etiam a iudeis ceteris secundum communem eorum extimationem et eorum doctorum declarationem heretici sunt. . . . Hec patet, nam si predicti conversi ad eorum perfidiam revertantur ut penitentes heretici ab eis in sinagoga recipiuntur et reconciliantur. . . .

3.Concl.9. Nona conclusio est quod iudei moderni delinquendo in fide modo predicto secundum promissam a deo fidelitatem, secundum eorum theologia<m> seu legem et secundum iudeorum et doctorum extimationem semper hereticent; tamen secundum rei veritatem et Christi legem non semper hereticant. . . . Hec patet: predicti ad fidem Christi conversi . . . in rei veritate a Christi fide non sunt heretici, licet sint a iudeorum perfidia divisi et in tali perfidia heretici. . . .

3.Concl.10. Decima et ultima conclusio est quod iudei moderni delinquendo quoquomodo in eorum fide seu potius fideiussione non credendo hiis que sunt eorum perfidie, licet semper a communi eorum perfidia hereticent, tamen semper non debent a christianis vexari ut heretici sed potius in quibusdam casibus nutriri etiam et deffendi. Ad cuius conclusionis evidentiam est animadvertendum:[18]

<DI pt. 2, q. 46.1, 352bD–E>

quod in veteri testamento tenentur multiplicia a iudeis vera esse extimata, que se dicunt credere et eis credendo inniti auctoritati divine ut infallibili veritati. . . .

<DI pt. 2, q. 46.2, 352bE–353aA>

Et si iudei in hiis discredant[19] a priori eorum credentia, licet heretici sint in |234v| eorum perfidia, non tamen in fide christiana. . . .

<DI pt. 2, q. 46.3, 353aA>[20]

Quedam alia sunt nobis christianis et iudeis communia, per que a nobis christianis non distinguntur nec iudei sunt nec habentur. Et si iudei in hiis vel eorum priori credentia discredant[21] et ea abnegent esse vera, heretici . . . communi iudeorum extimatione sunt et habentur.

<DI pt. 2, q. 46.4, 353aA–D>

Et quia[22] in hiis nobiscum conveniunt et talia negare est legem Christi directe agitare, ideo a christianis et fidei Christi iudicibus episcopis et inquisitoribus artandi sunt ea credere et fidem quam deo de hiis credendo promiserunt firmiter observare. Si ergo inveniantur iudei in hiis que a nobis christianis et eis sunt communia delinquere verbo vel facto ea abnegando, ut si assererent verbo deum unum non esse, vel facto demonibus sacrificando quod est facto asserere demonem esse deum et similia perpetrare, presertim in presentia christianorum, debent ut heretici in eorum lege et ut fautores hereticorum contra legem Christi et inductores artari et puniri per episcopos et inquisitores iudices fidei. Si enim infantes iudeorum vel adulti per minas vel per rerum suarum ablationem vel verbera vel similem coactionem vel etiam metu mortis coacti baptizati fuerint[23] et receperint fidem Christi, sunt cogendi quod promiserunt observare. . . .

4. **Quartus articulus principalis.** Quartus articulus est in fide delinquentes et hereticantes quis habeat iudicare, ubi primo considerandum est quod crimina

---

18. MS "animadvertandum."

19. *DI* "discendant."

20. This section is shorter than the parallel in the *DI*.

21. *DI* "discedant."

22. MS "q3" (-que; *sic* for q2); *DI* "quia." I find it more plausible that the scribe misrepresented the abbreviation for *quia* than that he mistook *que* for an enclitic.

23. MS "fuerunt."

sunt in triplici differentia.[24] Quedam namque sunt mere civilia, ut homicidia furta adulteria et similia, et de hiis habet iudicare dominus temporalis. . . . Quedam sunt mere ecclesiastica, ut symonia apostasia sacrilegia[25] periuria et similia, et de hiis habet iudicare et cognoscere dominus ecclesiasticus. . . . Quedam sunt indistincta, ut blafemia sortilegia simplicia et similia . . . et de hiis habet iudicare et cognoscere uterque, non simul sed qui prevenit. . . . Hiis premissis ponuntur conclusiones iste satis note in iure:

<Conclusiones>

4.Concl.1. Prima conclusio est quod heresis crimen mere ecclesiasticum est. . . .

4.Concl.2. Secunda conclusio est quod domini temporales de crimine[26] heresis nec cognocere nec iudicare possunt. . . .

4.Concl.3. Tertia conclusio est quod domini temporales si de crimine heresis iudicent, cognoscant, captos pro huiusmodi crimine absque licentia episcopi vel inquisitoris a carcere liberent, executionem eis iniunctam per episcopum et inquisitorem prompte prout spectat ad eorum officium retardant, |235r| vel processum iudicium seu sententiam inquisitoris directe vel indirecte impediverunt,[27] vel se opposuerunt, quod omnes tales sunt ipso facto excommunicati. . . .

4.Concl.4. Quarta conclusio est quod predicti domini temporales si aliquorum istorum predictorum casuum fuerint[28] ipso iure excommunicati, et steterint in predicta excommunicatione per annum animo pertinaci, extunc sunt ut heretici condampnandi. . . .

4.Concl.5. Quinta conclusio est quod predicti domini temporales cum fuerint pro heresi dampnandi, dominio quod habebant privantur et omnes subditi et vassalli a fidelitatis debito absolvuntur. . . .

4.Concl.6. Sexta conclusio est quod predicti domini temporales si requisiti ab ecclesia terram suam pro posse purgare contempserit ab heretica pravitate sunt

24. MS "differantia."
25. MS "sacrolegia."
26. MS "crimen."
27. MS "impeduerunt."
28. MS "fuerunt."

excommunicandi in quam. Si per annum steterint animo pertinaci extunc ut heretici, condampnantur et terra sua privantur et eorum subditi a fidelitatis homagio absolvuntur. . . .

4.Concl.7. Septima conclusio est quod predicti domini temporales cum fuerint[29] ab ecclesia requisiti, tenentur iurare quod bona fide iuxta[30] officium et posse suum ecclesiam contra hereticos et eorum complices ad<i>uvabunt, quod nisi fecerint honore et dominio privantur et excommunicati terris propriis spoliantur. . . .

4.Concl.8. Octava conclusio est quod officiales predictorum dominorum temporalium si inquisitoris officium eius iudicium sententiam vel processum directe vel indirecte impediverint, vel se opposuerint, vel capttos pro eodem crimine absque episcoporum et inquisitorum mandato liberaverint, excecutionem eis iniunctam per episcopum vel inquisitorem non exercuerint, vel ad hec dederint auxilium consilium vel favorem, vel iurare coram episcopo et inquisitore requisitus recusaverit, pro quolibet istorum excommunicati sunt ipso iure. Et si per annum steterint animo pertinaci, extunc sunt ut heretici condampnandi et aliis penis feriendi[31] ut dictum est de dominis eorundem. . . .

4.Concl.9. Nona conclusio est quod consiliarii predictorum dominorum temporalium si ad predicta aliqua vel aliquod predictorum ut fiant predictis dominis temporalibus vel eorum officialibus dederint conscilium, sunt ipso iure excommunicati. Et si per annum sustinuerint animo pertinaci, extunc sunt ut heretici condampnandi et predictis statim penis et aliis feriendi. . . .

4.Concl.10. Decima conclusio est quod quicunque alii predictis dominis vel eorum officialibus quatenus faciant aliquod predictorum dederi<n>t auxilium vel favorem, excommunicati sunt, et omnibus illis penis quibus dictum est de dominis temporalibus eorum officialibus et consiliariis sunt etiam feriendi. . . .

4.Concl.11. Undecima conclusio est quod dominus noster papa principaliter habet de fide et heresi iudicare. . . .

29. MS "fuerunt."
30. MS "uxta."
31. MS "fervendi."

4.Concl.12. Duodecima conclusio est quod episcopi habent de heresis crimine cognoscere et iudicare. . . .

4.Concl.13. Tertia decima conclusio est quod episcopi habent de heresis crimine iudicare, interdum auctoritate ordinaria interdum auctoritate auctoritate delegata. . . .

4.Concl.14. Quarta decima conclusio est quod inquisitores habent de heresis crimine iudicare non ordinaria sed delegata potestate, et ideo in tali iudicio vicem obtinent domini nostri pape sicut vicarii episcopi in tali iudicio vicem optinent |235v| episcopi. . . .

4.Concl.15. Quinta decima conclusio est quod episcopi in modo procedendi contra hereticos fautores et ceteros in hoc crimine debent semper se inquisitoribus conformare. . . .

4.Concl.16. Decima sexta conclusio est quod inquisitor est maior episcopo ordinario in inquisitionis officio. Hec patet, nam inquisitor est domini nostri pape delegatus, episcopus autem est ordinarius. Delegatus autem domini pape maior est in officio suo quam aliquis ordinarius in eodem officio. . . .

4.Concl.17. Decima septima conclusio est quod episcopus non potest inquisitoris processum aliquatenus impedire. Hec patet, nam par in parem non habet imperium nec iuridicionem, multo minus inferior in maiorem. . . .

4.Concl.18. Decima octava conclusio est quod si episcopus et inquisitor pro eadem hora vel instanti aliquem scirent divisim quatenus compareat coram eis, cum non possit coram utroque in diversis locis existentibus comparere, debet citatus coram inquisitore dimisso episcopo comparere. Hec patet, nam ut dictum est inquisitor est maior in officio suo episcopo; potius autem est obediendum potestati maiori quam minori. . . .

4.Concl.19. Decima nona conclusio est quod si episcopus citaverit aliquem prius quam inquisitor et inquisitor citet eum postea, deserto episcopi iudicio debet coram inquisitore comparere. . . .

4.Concl.20. Vicesima[32] conclusio est quod episcopi et inquisitores non solum habent de heresis crimine cognoscere et iudicare, verum etiam de criminibus

32. MS "vucesima."

contravenientibus[33] et heresim inducentibus directe, ut sunt a fide apostasya, in fide s<c>isma, blafemia, ydolatria, et in fide sacrilegia, et similia. Et inde est quod episcopi et inquisitores non solum habent cognoscere et iudicare de hereticis, de heresi suspectis, de heresi diffamatis, de hereticorum fautoribus defensatoribus receptatoribus celatoribus occultatoribus, et inquisitionis officium impetitoribus; verum etiam possunt cognoscere et iudicare de a fide apostaticis, de in fide scismaticis, de in fide blafemiis, de contra fidem sortilegis, de ydolatris, de in fide sacrilegis, et criminibus similibus aliis. Hec patet dupliciter:

4.Concl.20.1. Primo nam inquisitores seu inquisitionis officium est et dicitur in iure fidei negotium. . . .

4.Concl.20.2. Secundo patet hec eadem conclusio, nam inquisitores seu inquisitionis officium est et dicitur in iure heretice pravitatis negotium. . . . Pravitas autem heretica est a fide apostatare . . . nam apostatare est ab omnibus que sunt christiane fidei principalibus deviare. . . . Hereticare autem est non ab omnibus expresse sed ab uno etiam articulo christiane fidei deviare. . . . Pravitas[34] etiam heretica est in fide scisma facere, quod est ab unitate ecclesie se dividere et caput ecclesie non recipere. . . . |236r| . . . Pravitas etiam heretica est in fide blafemare. . . . Pravitas etiam heretica est aliquando sacramenta prophanare. . . . Hii enim sunt actus sapientes hereticam pravitatem et ideo iudices pravitatis heretice quales sunt episcopi et inquisitores habent de huiusmodi cognoscere et iudicare.

4.Concl.21. Vicesima[35] prima est quod ad simplicem requisitionem episcoporum vel inquisitorum, tenentur domini temporales hereticos credentes fautores receptatores deffensatores inquirere et investigare. . . .

4.Concl.22. Vicesima[36] secunda conclusio est quod ad requisitionem predictorum episcoporum vel inquisitorum, tenentur predicti domini temporales hereticos et alios statim dictos sic ut predicitur investigatos capere. . . .

4.Concl.23. Vicesima tertia conclusio est quod ad predictam requisitionem predictorum episcoporum vel inquisitorum, tenentur predicti domini temporales hereticos et alios statim dictos captos cum diligenti custodia tenere. . . .

---

33. MS "contraventibus."
34. MS "pravitatas."
35. MS "vicecima."
36. MS "vicecima."

4.Concl.24. Vicesima quarta conclusio est quod ad requisitionem predictorum episcoporum vel inquisitorum, predicti domini temporales hereticos et alios supradictos captos detentes tenentur ducere vel duci facere sina mora infra eorum districtum ad carcerem episcoporum vel inquisitorum, vel ad illum locum de quo ipsi episcopi vel inquisitores eis mandaverunt. . . .

4.Concl.25. Vicesima quinta conclusio est quod cum predicti episcopi et inquisitores hereticos et alios supradictos tradiderint brachio seculari, predicti domini temporales sic eis relictos tenentur recipere indilate et animadversione debita punire. . . .

5. **Quintus articulus principalis**. Quintus articulus principalis est iudeos et alios infideles in fide vel contra vel circa fidem delinquentes quis an dominus temporalis vel ecclesiasticus habeat iudicare, ubi prius videndum est ecclesia si et qualem in iudeos et in infideles ceteros potestatem habeat; secundo ex hoc videbitur si eos delinquentes in fide iudicare valeat. Circa primum consideranda sunt septem:

<Consideranda>

5.Cons.1. Primum est quod duplex est iuridicio et potestas que ponitur communiter a theologis et iuristis quarum una dicitur temporalis alia spiritualis. Prima exercetur in animam seu spiritum, secunda in corpus nostrum. Hanc duplicem iuridicionem et potestatem ponunt theologi canoniste et legiste. . . . |236v| . . .

5.Cons.2. Secundum considerandum est quod dominus Ihesus Christus utramque iuridicionem et potestatem habet et habuit supradictam spiritualem pariter et temporalem. . . .

5.Cons.3. Tertium considerandum est quod dominus Ihesus Christus utramque predictarum habet et habuit potestatem et iuridicionem super omnes homines generalem tam super in eum credentes quam super in eum non credentes, et per consequens tam super fideles quam etiam super infideles. . . . |237r| . . . Et ideo erit iudex omni generalis.

5.Cons.4. Quartum considerandum est quod dominus Ihesus Christus a nobis assumpturus et ad celos ascensurus beatum Petrum apostolum vicarium suum in terris instituit, predictam ei duplicem potestatem et iuridicionem et contulit, et eum omni humane creature tam scilicet fidelibus quam infidelibus prefecit generaliter in pastorem. . . . |237v| Quod autem beatus Petrus iuridicionem predictam in omnibus tam fidelibus quam infidelibus habuerit generalem patet specialiter ex tribus: primo per illud quod habetur Mathei XVI.[37] . . . Secundo patet hoc idem per illud quod habetur Iohannis ultimo.[38] . . . Tertio patet idem per Innocentium.[39] . . . Patet igitur ex predictis quod beatum Petrum Christus vicarium suum instituit, iuridicionem spiritualem et temporalem ei tribuit, et sup<er> omnes homines generaliter ei potestatem contulit, que omnia simul expressius antedictis declarat Bonifatius papa octavus.[40] . . . |238r| . . .

5.Cons.5. Quintum considerandum est quod dominus noster papa sive romanus quilibet pontifex Petri successor, cum domini Ihesu Christi vicarius immediatus sit, habet prout beatus Petrus predictam duplicem iuridicionem in omnes tam fideles quam infideles generalem. Hec patet multipliciter:

5.Cons.5.1. Primo sic: super omnes homines tam fideles quam infideles habuit iuridicionem beatus Petrus, ergo pari modo et pontifex romanus. . . .

5.Cons.5.2. Secundo patet sic: pontifex romanus non solum circa christianos ymo etiam directe pro circa et contra iudeos saracenos et infideles ceteros multa et varia iudicat iuste et legitime et statuit, ergo iuridicionem in omnes habet et habuit. Consequentia tenet quia nisi in infideles iuridicionem haberet legitime statuta condere contra et pro eis legitime non valeret. . . . |238v| . . .

5.Cons.5.3. Tertio sic: pontifex romanus inquisitores heretice pravitatis ad puniendum et castigandum iudeos delegavit, ergo in iudeos et pari modo in infideles alios iuridicionem habet et habuit. Consequentia plana est quia delegare non valet qui iuridicionem non habet nec potest iudicem contra et super alium assignare; qui per se non valet iudicare, delegatus enim vicem persone illius optinet a quo delegatur. . . .

5.Cons.5.4. Quarto et ultimo . . . quod romanus pontifex habet iuridicionem non tamen super fideles sed etiam super infideles, et per consequens potest[41] de

---

37. Matt. 16:19.
38. John 21:17 and several verses from John 10.
39. *Apparatus* to X 3.34.8, §§3–4.
40. *Extrav. comm.* 1.8.1.
41. MS "p̄t" (*sic* for p̄t).

omnibus iudicare. Huic veritati concordant Bartholomeus glosator *Decretorum*, Bernardus glossator *Decretalium*, Raymundus, Goffredus, Innocentius, Hostiensis, et beatus Thomas.

5.Cons.5.4.1. Bartholomeus.[42] ... |239r| ...

5.Cons.5.4.2. Bernardus.[43] ...

5.Cons.5.4.3. Raymundus.[44] ...

5.Cons.5.4.4. Gaufridus.[45] ... |239v| ...

5.Cons.5.4.5. Hostiensis.[46] ...

5.Cons.5.4.6. <*DI pt. 2, q. 46.5–6, 353aE–bD*>[47]
Innocentius.[48] ...

5.Cons.5.4.6.1. <*DI pt. 2, q. 46.6, 353bD–354aA*>[49]
Idem Iohannes Andree.[50] ...

5.Cons.5.4.6.2. <*DI pt. 2, q. 46.6, 354aA*>
Idem Paulus[51] et Gessillinus.[52] ...

5.Cons.5.4.7. <*DI pt. 2, q. 46.6, 354aB*>
Beatus Thomas.[53] ...

5.Cons.6. |240r| Sextum considerandum est quod omnia iudicia ac statuta que fecit ecclesia sive dominus noster papa pro et contra iudeos et infideles ceteros

---

42. Bartholomew of Brescia.
43. Bernard of Parma.
44. Raymond of Penyafort.
45. Geoffrey (Godfrey) of Trani.
46. Henry of Segusio.
47. This section lacks part of the text from *DI*, p. 353aE and 353bD.
48. *Apparatus* to X 3.34.8, §§3–6.
49. This section is shorter than the parallel in the *DI*.
50. Johannes Andreae.
51. Paulus de Liazariis.
52. Jesselin (Gencellinus) de Cassagnes.
53. Thomas Aquinas.

in favorem fidei catholice et non alias omnia ipse fecit. . . . Omnia statuta per ecclesiam facta pro et contra iudeos et infideles ceteros facta sunt ut fides honoretur et prosperetur et ut fides non vituperetur corumpatur vel alias subvertatur. . . .

5.Cons.7. Septimum considerandum est quod dominus noster papa potest de peccato quolibet et hominis cuiuslibet tam fidelis quam etiam infidelis, et presertim de heresi et de hiis que fiunt contra fidem, cognoscere et iudicare, et per consequens quilibet homo nullo excepto contrahit forum ecclesie ratione peccati. . . . Huic veritati concordat Raymundus et Hostiensis et Gotfridus. . . .

5.Cons.7.1. Raymundus. . . .

5.Cons.7.2. Hostiensis. . . . |240v| . . .

5.Cons.7.3. Gotfridus. . . .

<Conclusiones>

5.Concl.1. Prima conclusio <est> quod iudei pro eo quia delinqunt et deviant a fide sanctorum patrum non sunt de iure per papam seu per ecclesiam fatigandi. . . .

5.Concl.2. Secunda conclusio est quod iudei pro eo quia delinqunt et deviant a fide sanctorum patrum de iure non sunt per papam seu ecclesiam ad fidem predictorum sanctorum patrum cohercendi. . . .

5.Concl.3. Tertia conclusio est quod iudei pro eo quia deviant a fide Christi seu christianorum non sunt de iure per papam seu ecclesiam molestandi. . . .

5.Concl.4. Quarta conclusio est quod iudei pro eo quia deviant a fide Christi, non credendo omnia et singula que sunt de lege christiana, non sunt de iure quatenus Christi fidem recipiant cohercendi licet persuadendi. . . .

5.Concl.5. Quinta conclusio est quod iudei si delinquant in fide seu fidei iussione quam deo fecerunt seu promiserunt in circunsisione vel legis eorum acceptat<i>one, non credendo esse vera ea per que sunt iudei et dicuntur et a nobis christianis distinguntur, non sunt de iure per papam seu ecclesiam fatigandi, licet in lege sua sint heretici habendi. . . .

5.Concl.6. Sexta conclusio est quod iudei si delinquant in fide seu promissione quam deo fecerunt in circuncisione vel legis eorum acceptatione, non credendo ea fore vera per que iudei nec dicuntur nec sunt sed nobiscum conveniunt, quatenus ad priorem credentiam revertantur et teneant quod deo promiserunt, sunt per papam seu ecclesiam cohercendi ut heretici in lege eorum directe et in lege nostra indirecte et consequenter. Hec conclusio patet multipliciter:

5.Concl.6.1. Primo sic: in malis promissis fides est recindenda. . . . Hec iudeorum violatio supradicta legis mosaice est consequenter violatio fidei christiane, cuius est iudex dominus papa seu ecclesia. . . .

5.Concl.6.2. Secundo patet sic: licet enim iudei non credendo esse vera ea per que a nobis christianis distinguntur non delinquant in rei veritate, licet delinquant in promissa eorum quo ad hec secta vel lege. Tamen si non credant esse vera ea in quibus conveniunt nobiscum delinquunt non solum in eorum lege et fide, hoc est pactione, ymo delinquunt et peccant gravissime in rei veritate, quilibet autem trahitur ad forum ecclesie et domini nostri pape ratione peccati et maxime in hiis que sunt fidei. . . .

5.Concl.6.3. Tertio patet sic: iudei adulti si, per minas et comminationem vel rerum suarum ablationem verberationem consimilem coactionem vel etiam metu mortis coacti, vel eorum parvuli |241r| Christo per baptismum se offerunt et fidem Christo promitunt et fidem recipiunt, cogendi sunt per ecclesiam fidem retinere et quod promiserunt observare. . . . Ergo pari et fortiori modo iudei qui non coacti sed voluntarii deo fidem dederunt et promiserunt de credendo supradictis que sunt in lege Moysi, in quibus a veritate non deviant nec a Christi lege, et promiserunt quo ad hec licite, si resiliant discredendo credere sunt cogendi ab ecclesia. . . .

5.Concl.6.4. Quarta . . . arguitur quod si quis prius iudeus post christianus effectus tenetur fidem uxori infideli quam sibi promisit observare, ubi velit cum ea absque creatoris contumelia habitare, nec potest in illo casu aliam ducere sed primam retinere ab ecclesia est arcendus. Ergo in illo casu fortius fidem quam deo iudei dederunt de credendo predictis si eam irritam fecerint, redire ad priorem credentiam ab ecclesia sunt arcendi.

5.Concl.6.5. Quinto sic: iudei christianos blaphemantes vel in eos sevientes sunt penis graviter feriendi. . . . Ergo quanto magis deum blaphemantes, et asserentes deum non fore creatorem, et similia que promiserunt credere nobis et eis communia sunt puniendi ab ecclesia. . . .

5.Concl.6.6. Sexto sic: iudei transgredientes leges et statuta domini nostri pape ipsos constringentes[54] puniuntur. . . . Quanto ergo magis si legibus divinis de credendo communia iudeis et christianis se iudei obligarent, ubi violant discredendo debent puniri a domino nostro papa dei in terris vicario utique. Huic veritati assentit expresse Innocentius.[55] . . . Si delinquant contra fidem Christi indirecte puniuntur per ecclesiam . . . quanto magis si directe agant perversum dogma inveniendo vel docendo.

5.Concl.6.7. Septimo sic: sacerdotium divinis ministrat sed imperium humanis presidet . . . et pontifex in spiritualibus antecellit. . . . Ergo ad pontificem pertinet cognoscere et iudicare de fide que est res divina et spiritualis si aliquis ipsam pervertat et expugnet perversa doctrina.

5.Concl.6.8. Octavo sic: in crimine ecclesiastico iudex ecclesiasticus per se cognoscit et discernit, nec habet ibi communicare iudex civilis. . . . Ergo de talibus non habent cognoscere iudices seculares.

5.Concl.6.9. |241v| Nono <sic>: imperator Iustinianus infideles qui loquuntur contra articulos fidei, quamvis manifesta et indubitata sint[56] que moventur, defert ad notitiam pape et requirit suam voluntatem et suum expectat iudicium.[57] . . .

5.Concl.6.10. Decimo sic: predicti iudei sic contra fidem suam et nostram graviter et hereticaliter delinquentes et in suam hereticantes directe et in nostram indirecte, in et pro tali et tanto delicto aut iudicabuntur et punientur aut in sua heresi delinquere amplius dimittentur. Non est dicendum quod sint dimittendi in suo facinore quia esset materia et occasio heresibus contra Christi fidem et erroribus ministrandi et novas hereses inveniendi et fidem nostram corrumpendi; non etiam videtur intentio ecclesie quod tantum crimen heresis

---

54. MS "contringentes."
55. *Apparatus* to X 3.34.8, §5.
56. MS "siͨ" (sicut; *sic* for sīt).
57. Citing Cod. 1.1.8.10–13.

in iudeis remaneat impunitum. Ergo est puniendum: vel ergo per iudicem christianum vel per iudicem iudeum. Non per iudicem iudeum quia ablatum est eis <s>ceptrum atque iudicium, secundum prophete vaticinium *non aufer-etur*, etc.[58] Item secundum legem eorum tales debent mori. . . . Iudeis autem non licet interficere quemquam iuxta illud Iohannis XIX.[59] . . . Item in causa iudei christianus potest accusare et testificari; non licet autem secundum canones iudeum cogere christianum ad testificandum vel fidelem coram infi-deli iudice litigare, prohibente Apostolo,[60] ergo habent tales puniri per iudicem christianum, non per secularem quia per sententiam excommunicationis mandatur ei quod nec de fide nec heresi *cum sit mere ecclesiastica quoquomodo cognoscat vel iudicet.*[61] . . .

5.Concl.6.11. Hostiensis. . . .

5.Concl.7. Septima conclusio est quod si iudei inducant verbis vel factis aliquem christianum ad eorum ritum, quod sunt de iure per ecclesiam ut fautores hereticorum puniendi. . . .

5.Concl.8. Octava conclusio est quod si iudei persuadeant vel verbis vel factis inducant[62] aliquem christianum ad credendum aliquam generaliter heresim vel errorem, quod sunt de iure per ecclesiam ut fautores hereticorum puniendi. . . .

5.Concl.9. Nona conclusio est quod si iudei aliquem hereticum, vel de heresi suspectum vel de heresi diffamatum, verbis vel factis deffensant receptant occultant celent fugere procurent, hac de causa ne haberi possit |242r| et iudi-cari, per episcopum vel inquisitorem heretice pravitatis quod sunt ut heretico-rum fautores per ecclesiam puniendi. . . .

5.Concl.10. Decima conclusio est quod si iudei verbis vel factis directe vel indi-recte impediverunt[63] inquisitores seu inquisitoris processum, sententiam iudi-cium, seu alias eius officium impediendi animo quovis modo, quod sunt ut fautores hereticorum per ecclesiam puniendi. . . . .

---

58. Gen. 49:10.
59. Actually, John 18:31.
60. See 1 Cor. 6:1.
61. VI 5.2.18.
62. MS "indicant."
63. MS *fort.* "impedirerunt."

5.Concl.11. Undecima conclusio est quod si iudei delinquant contra fidem Christi antiquas hereses seu errores contra fidem Christi, quibus sunt iudei et a nobis christianis distincti, in synagogis suis predicando se invicem informando docendo sive scribendo, quod non sunt per ecclesiam puniendi stantibus canonibus quibus per ecclesiam in suis ritibus tolerantur. . . .

5.Concl.12. Duodecima conclusio est quod si iudei delinquant contra fidem Christi novas hereses seu errores contra fidem Christi et ea, quibus a nobis christianis non sunt distincti, in sinagogis suis predicando se adinvicem informando docendo vel scribendo, quod sunt ab ecclesia puniendi. . . .

5.Concl.13. Tertia decima conclusio est quod si iudei delinquant contra fidem Christi quascunque novas hereses seu errores generaliter contra Christi fidem inveniendo in sinagogis suis predicando se invicem informando, quod sunt ab ecclesia arcendi et puniendi. Hec patet per dominum Innocentium et per Iohannem Andree . . . que recitant quomodo *papa Gregorius nonus et Innocentius quartus mandaverant comburi librum Talimuth et alios, in quibus multe hereses nove erant inserte, et mandaverint puniri illas hereses invenientes docentes etiam et sectantes.*[64] Idem papa Benedictus II[I].[65]

5.Concl.14. Quarta decima conclusio est quod si iudei delinquant[66] contra fidem Christi quascunque hereses seu errores novas vel antiquas contra Christi fidem inter christianos dogmatizando[67] docendo informando seu alias promulgando, quod sunt per ecclesiam cohercendi et puniendi. Hec patet, quia hoc est christianos a Christi fide abducere et ad eorum perfidiam trahere, que quidem facere proprie hereticis est favere. . . .

5.Concl.15. Quinta decima conclusio est quod si iudei disputant de fide Christi contra eam et pro eorum perfidia loquendo cum christianis laicis publice vel secrete, quod christiani sunt per ecclesiam excommunicandi et iudei per

---

64. Citing *Apparatus* to X 3.34.8, §5.

65. MS "XII⁹I," added in a different hand. It may refer to Jacques Fournier (later Benedict XII), who was ordered to burn the Talmud in 1320. See Shlomo Simonsohn, *The Apostolic See and the Jews*, 8 vols. (Toronto: Pontifical Institute of Mediaeval Studies, 1988–1991), doc. 309, 1:321–23. Otherwise, Benedict XIII ordered the Talmud burned in 1415. See ibid., no. 538, 2:593–602. Perarnau, "Tres nous tractats," 85 n. 8, reads "XIII."

66. MS "derelinquant."

67. MS "dogmatirando."

eandem ecclesiam arcendi et puniendi. . . . De iudeis etiam patet, quia hoc est christianos in fide corumpere et hereticis per consequens favere. . . .

5.Concl.16. Decima[68] sexta conclusio est quod si iudei disputant cum clericis christianis publice vel secrete de Christi fide contra eam et pro eorum perfidia loquendo, non sunt per ecclesiam puniendi, debitis autem circunstanciis adhibitis, utpote quod disputent reverenter et cum viris in Christi fide peritis, et non in presentia laicorum et presertim simplicium, et cum licentia ecclesie si fiat disputatio publice, et pro fidei augmentatione et temporis fidei agitatione. Alias non est permittendum de fide quis publice disputare propter periculum quod potest Christi fidelibus et presertim simplicibus inminere. . . .

5.Concl.17. Decima[69] septima conclusio est quod si iudei inter christianos dominum Ihesum Christum vel Christi fidem verbis vel factis blaphemant, contra Christi sanctitatem vel eius divinitatem vel beate Marie eius matris integritatem vel fidei veritatem viliter vel contemptibiliter loquendo, vel alias fidem Christi offendendo |242v| iniuriando vel exprobando, utpote in Christi crucem spuendo crucifixi ymagines frangendo et similia faciendo in oppro-brium et contumeliam fidei christiane, quod possunt et debent per ecclesiam cohercere etiam et puniri. . . .

5.Concl.18. Decima octava conclusio est quod saraceni tartari et infideles ceteri delinquentes in, circa, et contra Christi fidem vel eorum sectam possunt et debent, si facultas adsit, iudicari et puniri per ecclesiam, attentis in ipsorum sectis contentis in omnibus et singulis casibus antedictis proportionabiliter ut iudei. . . .

5.Concl.19. Decima nona conclusio est quod asserere dominum nostrum papam seu dei ecclesiam non habere potestatem cognoscendi decernendi[70] et iudicandi de infidelibus perversa doctrina fidem christianam corrunpentibus, vel christianos ad heresim protrahentibus,[71] vel ad eorum ritum execrabilem eos verbis vel factis inducentibus, vel hereticis faventibus, vel alias Christi fidem impugnantibus, quod est hereticum plane, et asserens pertinaciter est hereticus iudicandus. . . . |243r| . . .

68. MS "secima."
69. MS "secima."
70. MS "decernandi."
71. MS "protrahantibus."

5.Concl.20. Vicesima conclusio est quod episcopi et inquisitores heretice pravitatis habent de predictis infidelibus et quibuscunque generaliter sicut predicitur fidem Christi pervertentibus cognoscere et iudicare, episcopi auctoritate
ordinaria et inquisitores delegata. . . .

Responsiones ad adversariorum rationes

<DI pt. 2, q. 46.8, 354aD>
Nonnulli autem adversarii veritatis predictam veritatem nituntur multipliciter
impugnare, volentes probare quod cognitio et punitio iudeorum et sarraceno-
rum in vel contra fidem delinquentium pertineat non ad episcopum et inquisitorem sed tantum ad dominos temporales. Et primo probatur per canones;
secundo per leges:

<Per canones>

<DI pt. 2, q. 46.8, 354aD>
Per canones impugnatur multipliciter:

Can.1.Arg. *<DI pt. 2, q. 46.8, 354aD–E>*
Et primo probatur sic: iudeus contra fidem delinquens vel est de iuridicione
episcopi vel non. Si sic, punit eum episcopus.[72] . . . Si non, punit eum dominus
temporalis, ut patet per capitulum allegatum. Ergo non omnes iudeos contra
fidem agentes potest punire episcopus, et per consequens minus ipse inquisitor, cum ille sit ordinarius et non iste.

Can.1.Resp. *<DI pt. 2, q. 46.9, 354aE–bB>*
Respondetur quod capitulum allegatum non loquitur de heresi vel de fide. . . .
Sed loquitur de excessu de quo conceditur in iudeo per ecclesiam domino
temporali quod possint cognoscere et punire. . . .

Can.2.Arg. *<DI pt. 2, q. 46.9, 354bB>*
|243v| Secundo sic arguitur: si in contumelia creatoris prorumpant iudei puni-
untur per principes temporalis.[73] . . . Sed fidem Christi perverso dogmate impugnare vel alias in et contra fidem agere est in contumelia creatoris prorumpere.

---

72. Citing X 5.6.14.
73. Citing X 5.6.15 (*In nonnullis*).

Igitur si iudei sic agitant fidem[74] non per episcopum et inquisitores debent puniri sed per principes temporales.

Can.2.Resp. *<DI pt. 2, q. 46.10, 354bC>*
Respondetur multipliciter:

Can.2.Resp.1. *<DI pt. 2, q. 46.10, 354bC–D>*
Primo quod duplex est blafemia in deum et contumelia, quedam que est mere talis, quedam que est hereticalis. Prima non agitat fidei articulum sed secunda.
. . .

Can.2.Resp.2. *<DI pt. 2, q. 46.10, 354bD–355aB>*
Secundo respondetur quod cum in dicto capitulo *In nonnullis* precipitur quod per principes seculares presumptores huiusmodi animadversione debita puniantur. . . . In foro autem ecclesiastico tales pena peccuniaria vel temporali alia citra effusionem sanguinis puniuntur. In foro autem seculari pena capitis plectuntur, quod notatur in hoc quod dicitur animadversione debita puniuntur . . . id est animam a corpore vertere. . . .

Can.2.Resp.3. *<DI pt. 2, q. 46.11, 355aB–C>*
Tertio respondetur quod in crimine heresis et iudicis ecclesiastici est cognoscere et iudicare, sed iudicis secularis est exequi et punire. . . .

Can.3.Arg. *<DI pt. 2, q. 46.11, 355aC>*
Tertio arguitur sic: rex Scicilie commisit episcopis ut punirent iudeos et[75] sarac[enos] qui mulieribus christianis et pueris parvulis abutebantur.[76] . . . Igitur rex eis commisit, ergo saracenorum punitio directe pertinet ad principes seculares.

Can.3.Resp.

Can.3.Resp.1. *<DI pt. 2, q. 46.12, 355aC–D>*
Respondetur quod dominus papa ibi commissionem episcopis factam per regem super saracenos narrat, sed eos procedere ex tali commissione non approbat, nec processerunt ex illa sed propria potestate ordinaria. . . .

---

74. *DI* "contra fidem."
75. "iudeos et" is omitted in *DI.*
76. Citing X 5.17.4. The source mentions Muslims but not Jews.

Can.3.Resp.2. *<DI pt. 2, q. 46.12, 355aD–E>*
Potest etiam et aliter responderi . . . quod[77] procedebant in casu et de excessu[78] quia de nece[79] et dampnato concubitu in quo et de quo potest cognoscere et punire dominus temporalis, secus autem est de fide et de crimine heretice pravitatis. . . .

Can.4.Arg. *<DI pt. 2, q. 46.12, 355aE–bA>*
Quarto arguitur sic: alta voce et publice in terris christianorum perfidum Macumetum et sacrilegum invocare, peregrinationes ad saracenum deffunctum aliquem[80] ut ad sanctum, palam et publice in eisdem terris facere et tolerare cedit in offensam et in opprobrium fidei christiane. Sed saracenos talia exercentes mandat dominus papa castigari |244r| per principes christianos et dominos temporales.[81] . . .

Can.4.Resp.
<DI pt. 2, q. 46.12, 355bA–D>
Respondetur quod iudei et saraceni, ut dictum est prius, aliqua habent nobis et eis communia . . . et in talibus assentire ab ecclesia non reprobantur ymo tacite approbantur. Et si post disentiant[82] in lege seu potius secta sua hereticant directe et in nostra indirecte . . . ideo de huiusmodi habet iudex ecclesiasticus cognoscere et iudicare. Nec capitulum *Cedit* allegatum ut patet ex eius serie loquitur de iudeis[83] taliter delinquentibus contra fidem. Habent etiam iudei[84] aliqua que nobis christianis et eis non sunt communia sed distincta . . . et in hiis ecclesia eos non approbat ymo reprobat, sed licet reprobet tamen tolerat et ne eos quisque ad profitendum fidem catholicam cogat prohibet atque vetat. . . .
<DI pt. 2, q. 46.13, 355bD–356aB>
Hii autem ritus plurimum distinguuntur, nam ritus iudeorum interdum fuerunt liciti, nunc vero illiciti,[85] sed semper habuerunt et habent significative et reputative[86] aliquid veritatis. . . . Et ideo ritus iudeorum ab ecclesia tolerantur, quia

---

77. *DI* "quia."
78. MS "excusu"; *DI* "excessu." The reading of the *DI* is supported by the source text in question.
79. *DI* "venereo."
80. MS "aliquam."
81. Citing Clem. 5.2.1 (*Cedit*).
82. MS "disensiant."
83. *DI* "sarracenis."
84. *DI* "iudaei et sarraceni."
85. "nunc . . . illiciti" is omitted in *DI*.
86. *DI* "repraesentative."

in illis habemus testimonium fidei christiane ab hostibus et ab hiis que foris sunt. . . . Ritus autem saracenorum . . . nunquam fuerunt nec sunt liciti, quia non continent veritatem nec aliquam aducunt utilitatem. Ideo ab ecclesia iure vel constitutione nec approbantur nec licentiantur nec etiam tolerantur, licet in mesquitis suis vel eorum domibus inter se quadam taciturnitate ab ecclesia videantur tolerari, quia sic fieri non prohibentur. . . .

<DI pt. 2, q. 46.14, 356aB–D>

Si autem fiant per modum per quem fieri prohibentur . . . |244v| . . . dominus noster papa committit et remittit eos, et[87] punitionem et ultionem in eos exequantur ad principes temporales. . . .

Can.5.Arg. <DI pt. 2, q. 46.14, 356aD>

Quinto arguitur sic: iudei proprie non possunt esse heretici nec per consequens de heresi suspecti, nam fidem christianam nunquam iudei moderni receperunt et per consequens perdere eam non possunt. Episcopi autem et inquisitores non sunt simul iudices nisi in materia heresis, ergo de hiis qualitercunque delinquentibus cognoscere non possunt.

Can.5.Resp. <DI pt. 2, q. 46.15, 356aD–bB>

Responsum est supra prolixe quod iudei hereticorum fautores receptatores et deffensores possunt esse clare, et ideo possunt puniri per episcopos et inquisitores plane. Heretici autem in lege nostra directe et proprie esse non possunt nec suspecti quia fidem Christi in re non receperunt, et sic ut tales puniri non possunt. Heretici autem in lege sua directe et in nostra indirecte esse possunt. . . . Si deviant arcendi sunt tenere quod fideiusserunt. . . . Possunt etiam contra christianam fidem agere. . . . De quibus non iudex secularis, cum sit prohibitus, sed ecclesiasticus habet de iure cognoscere et diffinire. . . .

<Per leges civiles>

<DI pt. 2, q. 46.15, 356bB>

Per leges etiam veritas supradicta multipliciter quia quintupliciter impugnatur:

Leg.1.Arg. <DI pt. 2, q. 46.15, 356bB>

Et primo sic: iudei romanis legibus iudicantur . . . quod pertinet ad principes seculares.[88]

---

87. DI "ut."
88. Citing Cod. 1.9.8.

Leg.1.Resp. <*DI pt. 2, q. 46.15, 356bB–C*>
Dicendum est quod imperator ex lege predicta nichil aliud intendit nisi quod iudei qui vivunt iure et statutis romanorum iudicentur romanis legibus in civilibus. . . .

Leg.2.Arg. <*DI pt. 2, q. 46.15, 356bC–D*>
Secundo arguitur sic: rectores provinciarum debent prohibere iudeos si faciunt aliqua in contemptum fidei christiane.[89] . . .

Leg.2.Resp. <*DI pt. 2, q. 46.15, 356bD–E*>
Dicendum est quod ex ista lege nichil aliud habetur nisi quod rectores provinciarum prohibeant iudeos ne faciant talia contra fidem, nec per hoc iudei fidem pervertebant sed contempnebant. . . . Nec per hoc excluditur ecclesia. . . . |245r| . . .

Leg.3.Arg. <*DI pt. 2, q. 46.15, 356bE*>
Tertio arguitur sic: princeps secularis iudicat pena sanguinis iudeos qui expugnant fidem Christi perversa doctrina.[90] . . .

Leg.3.Resp. <*DI pt. 2, q. 46.15, 357aA–B*>
Dicendum est quod ex ista lege nichil aliud habetur nisi quod princeps secularis iudeos expugnantes fidem punit pena sanguinis. Hec autem pena est secundum iudicium seculare, nec ex hoc excluditur iudicium ecclesie. . . .

Leg.4.Arg. <*DI pt. 2, q. 46.15, 357aC*>
Quarto arguitur sic: occasione questionis heresum nullus debet[91] provinciam commovere sed preses per se debet providere.[92] . . .

Leg.4.Resp. <*DI pt. 2, q. 46.15, 357aC–D*>
Dicendum est quod ex lege illa nichil aliud habetur nisi quod iudex ecclesiasticus non debet se intromittere de questione civili occasione heresum vel religionum, sed preses debet providere super decisione questionis civilis. Nec lex intendit quin iudex ecclesiasticus de heresi habeat[93] iudicare. . . .

89. Citing Cod. 1.9.11.
90. Citing Cod. 1.9.18.3.
91. *DI* "habet."
92. Citing Auth. coll. 3.4.11 = Nov. 17.11.
93. *DI* "debeat."

Leg.5.Arg. *<DI pt. 2, q. 46.15, 357aD>*

Quinto arguitur sic: in crimine canonice preses cum metropolitano habet discernere et non metropolitanus[94] per se.[95] . . . Ergo de illo discernere pertinet non solum ad ecclesiam ymo etiam ad presidem non disiunctive[96] sed copulative.

Leg.5.Resp. *<DI pt. 2, q. 46.15, 357aD–bB>*

Dicendum quod prout patet per verba legis sequentia illa questio non erat pure canonica sed habebat aliquid de civili. . . . |245v| . . .

<DI pt. 2, q. 46.16, 357bB–C>

Non obstantibus igitur canonum et legum allegationibus et impugnationibus antedictis, patet clare quod iudeorum et aliorum infidelium fidem christianam pravis dogmatibus impugnantium seu alias modis predictis contra fidem Christi delinquentium et agentium cognitio iudicium et punitio pertinet de iure ad iudices ecclesiasticos, quia ad episcopos et inquisitores heretice pravitatis et non ad principes seu dominos temporales, licet executio pertineat ad ipsos iudices seculares quando punitio transit in vindictam sanguinis, ut sic delinquentes debeant animadversione debita, hoc est ultimo supplicio castigari, prout in hereticis de iure et consuetudine est fiendum.

<Explicit>

Explicit tractatus contra iudeos et infideles ceteros circa vel contra fidem catholicam delinquentes, compilatus per fratrem Nicholaum Eymerici ordinis fratrum predicatorum inquisitorem heretice pravitatis.

NOTES

1. For the details of Eymeric's life, I rely on Claudia Heimann, *Nicolaus Eymerich (vor 1320–1399)—praedicator veridicus, inquisitor intrepidus, doctor egregius: Leben und Werk eines Inquisitors* (Münster: Aschendorff, 2001).

2. On Eymeric's literary output, see Heimann, *Nicolaus Eymerich*, 171–82.

3. Eymeric does not include any reference to the relevant case of Astruc da Piera (ca. 1370–72), setting 1372 as the *terminus ante quem* (see *Directorium inquisitorum* [Venice, 1607], pt. 2, q. 46.16). Josep Perarnau i Espelt, "El *Tractatus brevis super iurisdictione inquisitorum contra infideles fidem catholicam agitantes* de Nicolau Eimeric: Edició i estudi del text," *Arxiu de Textos Catalans Antics* 1 (1982): 79–126, at 83, suggests plausibly that Astruc's case provided

94. *DI* "metropolitano."
95. Citing Auth. coll. 3.4.11 = Nov. 17.11.
96. ms "distiunctive."

the occasion for this treatise, which would place it ca. 1370–71. Eymeric later returned to these questions in his *Tractatus brevis* (ca. 1383–1387).

4. Josep Perarnau, "Tres nous tractats de Nicolau Eimeric en un volum de les seves opera omnia manuscrites procedent de Sant Domènec de Girona," *Revista Catalana de Teologia* 4 (1979): 79–100, at 87–88, 92–93.

5. Claudia Heimann, "*Quis proprie hereticus est*? Nicolaus Eymerichs Häresiebegriff und dessen Anwendung auf die Juden," in *Praedicatores, inquisitores,* vol. 1, *The Dominicans and the Mediaeval Inquisition,* ed. Wolfram Hoyer (Rome: Istituto Storico Domenicano, 2004), 595–624, esp. 605–18.

6. On article 2, see ibid., 607–12.

7. On article 3, see ibid., 612–18.

8. See esp. Solomon Grayzel, "Popes, Jews, and Inquisition from 'Sicut' to 'Turbato,'" in *Essays on the Occasion of the Seventieth Anniversary of the Dropsie University,* ed. Abraham Katsh and Leon Nemoy (Philadelphia: Dropsie University, 1979), 173–88.

9. *Apparatus* to X 3.34.8, §§3, 5. Translated in Jeremy Cohen, *The Friars and the Jews: The Evolution of Medieval Anti-Judaism* (Ithaca: Cornell University Press, 1982), 97, but I have corrected his version against the text established in Benjamin Z. Kedar, "Canon Law and the Burning of the Talmud," *Bulletin of Medieval Canon Law,* new ser., 9 (1979): 80.

10. Heimann, "*Quis proprie hereticus est,*" 606–7.

11. And as much with actions as with words, in contrast to the *Oxford Latin Dictionary,* s.v. "agito" 10, which is concerned only with words. See also the usage in 3.Concl.10, Can.2.Arg., and Can.2.Resp.1. The same verb is used in the standard sense of "move to action" in the incipit and 5.Concl.16.

12. For a detailed description of the manuscript, see Perarnau, "Tres nous tractats," esp. 81–86.

8

MAGICKING MADNESS:
SECRET WORKINGS AND PUBLIC NARRATIVES OF DISORDERED
MINDS IN LATE MEDIEVAL GERMANY

Anne M. Koenig

By the late fifteenth century, Nuremberg city councilmen were no strangers to madness.[1] After years of interactions, they knew how to deal with the mad who posed problems within the city's thick walls, and they wielded absolute authority to do so. With a population of approximately twenty thousand, late medieval Nuremberg was one of the largest cities in the German-speaking world and an important center of both trade and production.[2] It was also a powerful imperial city with no ruling prince (the rights and properties of the burgrave had been systematically dismantled over the fourteenth and early fifteenth centuries), no local bishop (Nuremberg fell within the diocese of Bamberg, so its bishop was sixty kilometers away), and no powerful guilds (the elites had crushed an attempted uprising in 1348).[3] Instead, Nuremberg was ruled in every detail by the small Inner Council, the control of which was firmly in the hands of the city's patrician elites.[4] The members of this council came from only the best and oldest families in the city. These men often served on the council for years and oversaw all major (and arguably all minor) decisions and regulations that touched on civic welfare.

Members of the council had been handling problems regarding the mad within their city multiple times each year in some form or another since the fourteenth century. By the late 1470s, the council had developed a diverse range of responses with which it dealt with mad men and women who came to its attention.[5] Most of the men serving on the council by the end of the 1470s had been doing so for at least several years, and many had even ruled on the mad before, just as they would continue to do so for years to come. For instance, during a tenure as a member of the Inner Council lasting more than twenty years, the distinguished Gabriel Nutzel (mostly known today for being one of the three patricians who commissioned the *Erdapfel*, Martin Behaim's 1492 terrestrial globe) oversaw decisions in fourteen cases involving madness in the city. The earliest recorded interactions involving Nutzel include one in 1471 regarding a brassworker's mad wife and a second in 1474 regarding a mad beggar woman.[6] One of his last would be in 1493 and concerned what was by then a two-year-long struggle between the council and the family and friends of a mad peddler regarding who would take responsibility for the man and the cost of his care.[7]

Yet even to the seasoned group of ruling patricians who made up the council, 1477 must have seemed like a particularly mad-filled year. On May 24, the day before Pentecost, the council, led by Gabriel Nutzel, asked the hospital warden "to be patient with the woman who had been mad but had now come back to herself."[8] The council then specifically requested that the warden allow the woman to remain in the hospital for a bit more time, at least until warmer days arrived. By the end of the fifteenth century, Nuremberg's Heilig-Geist Spital was municipally run and was the civic institution most called upon by the council to help confine and care for mad persons whose family or friends were unable to do so. This need was so common that just a decade prior, the council had ordered a small room to be built for the mad on the hospital bridge; it was likely this space that the again-sane woman occupied.[9] This accommodation, however, apparently created a slight housing problem the following week, for on May 31 the council (still led by Nutzel) instructed that a mirror craftsman (*Spiegler*) who had gone mad was to be placed in a room in the city stables, presumably because the mad room in the hospital was still occupied.[10] Immediately following this ruling, the council, reacting to this small-scale housing crisis for the mad, called in the city's master builder and tasked him with finding a location and building a place to house those who were "robbed of their senses" for a time.[11] Three weeks later, on June 21, the council, now under the guidance of a different councilman, checked in with the master builder, whose project was apparently completed for the council, then decreed that the mad mirror craftsman was to be placed in the newly built space and that the cost of his care would be overseen by the hospital.[12] After a lull in mad activity during July, on August 9, the council, now led by Ulrich Grunther, who like Nutzel had been dealing with cases of madness at least since 1471, ruled that a local prostitute who had gone mad was to be permitted to beg for alms in front of a church so that the money she collected could be used for her care. Three days later, the council then negotiated for a transfer of care for the mad woman from the brothel to the hospital.[13] As both were municipal institutions, the move was not one of transferred responsibility so much as one apparently designed to manage better municipal resources.[14]

It was in October, however, that one of these cases developed an unusual twist. On Monday, October 6, the council asked another one of its members, Nicolas Grolant, to look into the case of the mad mirror craftsman and to "question the woman named in the case."[15] Just what this "case" involved becomes a little clearer a few days later in the records. The council minutes for Thursday, October 9, report that the mad craftsman's mother had accused a woman called Else Geistlerin of bewitching her son (with *lupperei*),[16] and the council, in response, determined that the woman and a Jewish merchant (*Veiten den gekauftner Juden*) who supposedly provided the curse should be brought in for questioning. Although there does not seem to have been an official trial, the entry has the weight of a judicial ruling, ending with a final "Schopfen," signaling the use of conciliar investigators, which was customary in cases regarding criminal matters.[17] Yet it seems to have taken the council another month to act, for it was not until November 6 that Nicolas Grolant was ordered to place the accused woman, now identified as a poor servant, in jail.[18] No further mention is made of the woman, however, nor of her accused Jewish supplier. The case has not left a trial record, and the council did not even order that the women be "put to the question," a fairly typically decree by the 1470s in criminal cases, including sorcery.[19] With the disappearance of the case in the city records, it appears that whereas the council took the mother's accusation seriously enough to investigate, it found little merit in the case early on and dropped its pursuit.

This year's collection of interactions between civic authorities and the mad offer a glimpse at the many public narratives of madness that unfolded in late medieval Nuremberg thanks to the intervention of the city council. Over the course of the year, the ruling elites of the city enacted a wide range of solutions to deal with the problems that madness and its effects brought to Nuremberg. They showed generosity to a woman who had returned to her senses but apparently had no place to go after her time spent in one of the city's "madrooms." They similarly approached the needs of a mad prostitute with a kind of liberal benevolence. They invested in the formation of more civic spaces for housing the mad, and perhaps most characteristically, they maintained a steady use of the hospital as the frontline institution caring for the mad. Each of these responses was typical for the council, enacted in various iterations and to differing degrees throughout the later Middle Ages. Taken as a whole, they depict a body of civic authorities who approached the mad not with fear, confusion, or cruelty, but with measured responses that were practical and relatively generous, and that reflected a belief that caring for the mad was in some way the council's responsibility.

But amid the more typical interactions between the council and the mad, the terse records from 1477 also contain that tantalizingly brief narrative of bewitchment, which led the council to consider, however briefly, not just the care for a mad person, but also the cause of madness itself. This consideration itself is a rarity. Municipal records overwhelmingly label, rather than describe or explain, the intellectually impaired with terms whose meanings signify madness, deficient reasoning, or the loss of mental faculties: *unsinnigen, toroten, torechten, unvernünftigen, von Vernunfft / Sinne kommen, vernunfft gebrechlich, synnlosen.* The Inner Council only very occasionally took steps to verify that a person suspected of madness was, indeed, insane.[20] Even rarer is evidence that the council expended any thought for the reason behind a mad person's condition. In general, then, civic leaders knew madness when they saw it and did not trouble themselves with explaining how it arose. But in 1477, a distraught mother's search to understand her own son's mental break managed to get the council's attention and convinced the authorities that her explanation for her son's malady had merit. Existing at this critical juncture of the world of magic and the world of madness, this public negotiation of madness—which involved the mentally compromised craftsman, his mother, another woman of low social status, a Jewish merchant, and town authorities—raises key questions in the history of madness that cross current historical methodologies: Was magic understood as a common cause for madness? How was magic even understood to have worked on the mind? How was magic related to other assumed causes and prognoses of madness? And finally, what did it mean for medieval suffers of madness and those around them to see magic as an agent in their misfortune?

This essay explores each of these questions by looking carefully at wide-ranging sources from a single cultural context, namely, late medieval southeastern Germany, in order to unveil the significance of narratives of magic in the layered world of madness. How magic was understood to work on the mind and the cultural significance of using magic to explain madness are addressed in more depth below; however, the question of whether or not magic was understood as a common cause for madness can be answered fairly simply and in the negative: magic was not referenced frequently enough by late medieval German sources to suggest that it was understood as a *common* cause for madness. Though magic was widely understood as a possible cause for madness, evidence from municipal records and miracle stories suggest that it only rarely was actually offered as an element in a person's account of madness. In fact, the 1477 case of the mad craftsman in Nuremberg is the only such example in almost 250 entries about the mad that were recorded in the city's financial and administrative logs between 1377 and 1493, indicating that observers of the urban mad almost never had magic in mind. This relative dearth was not due to any hesitance on the part of the Nuremberg council to entertain ideas about magic. As has been well-documented by scholars of magic and witch trials, Nuremberg was not only no stranger to madness but was also increasingly interested in magic and witchcraft in the later Middle Ages. Indeed, the city of Nuremberg holds a rather trailblazing role in the history of the development of the witch craze, from the city's connections to early writers on the topic to Nuremberg's own cases of witchcraft and the measured restraint the council showed to the accused, rarely executing even those found guilty.[21] Johannes Nider, author of the *Formicarius*, was prior of the Dominican convent in Nuremberg from 1427–31, and Heinrich Kramer sent advice pulled from his *Malleus maleficarum* to the Nuremberg council in 1491.[22] Between 1430 and 1520, moreover, the criminal court, overseen by members of the Inner Council, conducted thirty-one trials involving cases of accused magic.[23] In fact, over the course of the 1470s alone the municipal court handled three cases of accused sorcery and magic, finding the accused guilty in two of those cases.[24] Thus, the very Nuremberg councilmen involved in the 1477 case of the mad craftsman were members of a ruling body that consistently showed both a willingness to give credence to accusations of magic and witchcraft, at the very least treating them as serious breaches in public order, even while it responded to accused witches and sorcerers with restrained punishments like the pillory or banishment rather than execution. And yet aside from this case, there is very little evidence that the civic authorities of the town reached for magical explanations to understand the mad persons that routinely came to their attention.

The uncommonness of magic in the city's narratives of madness may be surprising, for medieval madness and magic seem to fit together. Indeed, modern scholars have been consistently confronted with the need to explain aspects or manifestations of medieval and early modern madness that touched on the spiritual, the occult, or the supernatural.[25] Literary scholars have long noted the moral and spiritual elements of madness, particularly the idea that madness was a punishment sent by God for sinful transgressions.[26] Historians have focused attention on connections between demons and madness; the two have a particularly intricate history and a problem-ridden historiography. Early histories of psychiatry and mental illness, as well as non–madness scholarship, particularly that related to miracles, tended to link demonic possession and madness (conflating them or equating them as conditions), basing this association on the assumptions that medieval observers did not know how to explain madness in "rational" terms and therefore relied on explanations of divine and demonic causation, or that medieval observers made no real distinction between madness and possession, or that they were unable to distinguish between them even according to their own (deficient) criteria.[27] As scholars have delved deeper into medieval frameworks of madness, demonology, and witchcraft, however, the relationships between demonic activity, spiritual (dis)favor, and mad behaviors have come into clearer focus. Exceptional work has been done on aspects of the murky boundaries between states of divine and demonic possession, and such discussions often touch on the problem posed by the similarity of such states to states of madness.[28] Recent works on madness and on possession have also consistently argued that there was a clear distinction between demonic possession and madness, even if some of the symptoms of the two overlapped.[29] And most recently, Catherine Rider has brilliantly explored the way that medieval medicine incorporated demons into its understanding of mental disorder, both as a cause and symptom (in the form of hallucinations) of various mental afflictions.[30]

Historians of magic and witchcraft have also been attuned to certain connections between magic and madness. The most consistent of these connections is the narrative—present in late medieval literature on the discernment of spirits and used as an argument in the literature of detraction against the prosecution of witchcraft in the early modern period—that those accused of witchcraft or claiming visionary experiences were in fact suffering from delusions, mental illness, or simplemindedness.[31] This is, however, only one facet of the relationship between madness and magic. As will be discussed more below, long before the witch trials began in Europe, magic (both demonic and natural) had a consistent role to play in the cause and cure of madness.

Indeed, while the Nuremberg council may have only rarely entertained the idea of a magical etiology for madness, such explanations in late medieval Germany were not unimportant, nor were they aberrations or exceptions to more typical narratives. As the Nuremberg case illustrates, accusations of magicked madness reveal the problems caused by a family member's mental break and the deep anxiety that madness produced, for magic appears in narratives when no other cause was clear and a reason was desperately desired. The loss of a craftsman's working potential was a heavy blow. In cases of impaired ability, or "weak-mindedness," the council could step in and help make arrangements with local craftsguilds to ensure a kind of career placement, but the raving mad could get no such accommodation.[32] To make matters more tense, by the second half of the fifteenth century, the Nuremberg council was increasing its scrutiny of a family's responsibility to care for its own mad. Though it was willing to accept the cost for the care of truly indigent mad persons, the council preferred to get family and friends to accept custodial and financial responsibility for the mad. In 1471, the council threatened to throw a brassworker in the city dungeon if he failed to take care of his mad wife.[33] In 1475 it decided to talk to the friends of a weak-minded man to see if they could assume the cost of his care and take responsibility for making sure he caused no harm.[34] And in 1479, it promulgated a new set of city laws (published in 1483) that specifically ordered sons to care for their mad fathers and fathers to care for their mad sons. Using a surprisingly positive analogy for the mad, the legal code even likened the mad family member to Christ and any defaulting caregiver to a heretic.[35]

It was in this environment that the mirror craftsman's mother brought forth her accusation of bewitchment in the case of her son's madness, an accusation that deflected attention away from her failure to care for her son (a task the council had already overtaken) and that possibly offered the chance at some financial or curative restitution. It also began a process of her own social rehabilitation while simultaneously calling into question that of the woman she accused. In addition to whatever unrecorded interpersonal politics may have been at play between the two women, the mother's accusation also drew on concerns that were simultaneously old and current—namely, Jewish perfidy and sorcery—and brought these concerns to bear on her case in the cultural climate of madness in the city.[36] She drew on the only cause that could tempt the council to consider *why* a person was mad, not just whether he was mad and what to do about it: deliberate sorcery. Magical causation, unique among accepted causes of madness, deflected the focus of the misfortune, placing blame squarely on another person, and perhaps granting the mad person and his family greater leverage in the fraught political and social economy of the city that not only judged social responsibility but also controlled municipal resources.

The connection between madness and magic, however, offers more than just the chance to see how such associations reveal the anxieties around specific cases of madness. Though not *commonly* used to explain specific cases of madness, the belief that magic could cause madness was widely held and seems to have been gaining cultural traction in the fifteenth century. Though rare and always far outnumbered by explanations that looked to transparent, natural causes for madness, magical etiologies helped define the boundaries of the explanatory world of madness and reveal the interconnectedness of the multiple intellectual frameworks that operated within that world. The conceptual world of madness was crafted by the many intellectual discourses of the later Middle Ages: medical, philosophic, theological, moral, literary. Each individual narrative of madness, by drawing on the frameworks for understanding madness that these discourses offered, thus maps out a particular point in this world. The collective result, while multivocal, is far from a cacophonous mess of contradictory understandings. There are common threads in these narratives: defining behaviors, etiological patterns, persistent social concerns, and a great level of anxiety. By looking across genres and into the various ways that different sources articulated a connection between madness and magic, we find not that magic offered a competing theory of causation and therapy to other more common explanations, but rather that it offered one that generally tapped into the same prevailing rationales that late medieval German society had developed in order to explain and manage madness. Magicked madness was not a different kind of madness from madness(es) with medical, physical, emotional, or accidental etiologies. It was, rather, a madness whose story reached past these more obvious explanations and drew on hidden aspects of the natural and supernatural world. Occult explanations offered a deeper layer of meaning for understanding and explaining madness, akin in many ways to the metaphorical layers of meaning offered by literary discourse. By drawing on the theological, philosophical, and medical rationales, cultural narratives of madness could use magic to skew that narrative toward an understanding of irrational states that served social needs. By looking more closely at how magic and madness intersected in medieval minds, or more specifically, were connected in a variety of different texts, we are thus able to explore not only how magic was perceived to work on the mind but also how beliefs about magic helped construct a way to come to terms with a similarly obscure world of meaning in the Middle Ages: the one related to madness and the mad themselves.

The general belief in the later Middle Ages that magic could cause madness had a long history, borne out in a range of sources. One of the first and most widely influential texts to link magic and madness was Isidore of Seville's seventh-century compendium, *The Etymologies*. Isidore's conspectus became an essential resource of knowledge in the learned medieval world, both forming and reflecting not only the content of an educated mind, but also widespread cultural assumptions about a complex universe with many dimensions—ranging from the linguistic to the physical to the moral and spiritual—all governed by God. Indeed, the work has been acknowledged by modern scholars as "arguably the most influential book, after the Bible, in the learned world of the Latin West for nearly a thousand years."[37] Not all elements of Isidore's text were equally influential, but they served at important starting points of knowledge for almost any subject of interest—particularly pertaining to the physical world—in the Middle Ages.

Isidore's text discussed both madness and magic. His explicit discussion of the former is in book 4, on medicine, but it proved less influential in the long-term than other sections of his work, no doubt owing to the lack of sophistication of his medical explanation of madness. Isidore presented mania, melancholy, and epilepsy (which he associated with lunacy) as a triad of mental illnesses, each affecting one part of the brain and its corresponding function: epilepsy impaired the imagination, melancholy impaired the reason, and mania impaired the memory.[38] This tripartite description was unusual; later medical texts would generally include frenzy and/or lethargy as other brain diseases paired with mania and melancholy, not epilepsy. Isidore's description, moreover, also misplaced mania in brain anatomy. By the early Middle Ages the Aristotelian intellectual functions of the soul, or faculties of the mind, were associated with the ventricles of the brain as defined by Galenic theory.[39] The resulting medieval psychological theory held that the brain was multicelled, with cells located front to back and corresponding to key brain functions. The front cell of the brain housed common sense and the imagination; intellect, cognition, and understanding resided in the middle cell; and the rear cell was the province of memory. Sense and thought thus moved logically through the brain from front to back, as sensory information came in, was cognitively processed, and then committed to memory.[40] Isidore had labeled the deprivation caused by mania as one of memory, thus placing mania in the posterior cell of the brain, but anatomical understandings of psychology by the twelfth century would agree that mania affected the anterior part of the brain and thus disrupted the imaginative function.[41] As medieval medical theory developed in the twelfth and thirteenth centuries, it quickly left Isidore behind and even the popular encyclopedias, like that of Thomas of Cantimpré, Konrad of Megenberg (who penned a German-language version of Thomas's text), and Bartholomaeus Anglicus, largely ignored his writings on madness.

Isidore's entries on magic, found in book 8 on the church and sects, however, had a more lasting influence. His focus on divination, in particular, ensured that it would maintain a hold on the laity and moralists alike even as learned medicine diversified its interests in the later Middle Ages.[42] Isidore is even cited in the fifteenth-century treatise *Das buch aller verbotenen künst*, written by Munich physician Johannes Hartlieb, who, though not following Isidore's categories entirely, was similarly concerned with the various divinatory arts.[43] It was Isidore who helped ensure that madness would remain a part of the discussion of the powers of magicians: "There are magicians who are commonly called 'evildoers' (*maleficus*) by the crowd because of the magnitude of their crimes. They agitate the elements, disturb the minds of people, and slay without any drinking of poison, using the violence of spells alone."[44] Then, citing Lucan, he explains that "a mind infected by no swallowed poison, is destroyed by incantation."[45] According to Isidore's text, these magicians seem to be the most nefarious of practitioners, concerned not with divination or foretelling, as were the kinds of magicians that the section goes on to describe in more detail, but rather with the "summoning of demons" and "evil arts." We thus find in *Etymologies* a trio of nefarious acts performed by truly dark sorcerers through the use of demons: manipulation of nature, manipulations of a person's mind, and death.

Following Isidore's lead, proscriptive witchcraft literature from much later in the medieval period reinforced the idea that magic could cause delusions, mental and emotional disorder, and outright raving madness. In his 1437 *Formicarius*, for instance, Johannes Nider explicitly listed "depriving a man of the use of his reason" as one of the kinds of evils that a sorcerer could inflict.[46] Heinrich Kramer, who knew Nider's text and was the inquisitor at the famous Innsbruck trial (see below), then included similarly brief but unambiguous statements about the magically induced in his *Malleus maleficarum*, a text that would be a kind of handbook for the witch hunts of the succeeding centuries. Perhaps most notably, the *Malleus* provided a version of what Isidore had said with a clarifying clause: "Isidore says 'They are called evil-doers because of the enormity of their misdeeds, that is, by bringing about evils that surpass those of other evil-doers.' then he adds, 'They stir up the elements,' that is, through the working of demons, 'in order to stir up hail and rain storms.' He also says: 'They throw the minds of humans into confusion' (understand: resulting in madness and irregular hatred and love)."[47]

The *Malleus*'s parenthetical commentary made explicit a fifteenth-century understanding of Isidore's vague comment on mental disturbance, interpreting it as two-fold: by throwing minds into confusion, the power of magic over the mind had two primary results-outright madness or magically induced passions. Both conditions were essentially disordered mental states, caused by magic's ability to violate normal imaginative and cognitive processes. The massive work did not linger in any way on the connections between magic and what we might term the common, prosaic iterations of madness that families, doctors, and authorities routinely confronted, but it did discuss related issues: reporting that powerful witches could cause horses to go mad, discussing more fully the turning of men's minds to inordinate love or hatred, and repeatedly addressing the ability of demons to affect both the external and internal senses, particularly the imagination.[48] Both of these texts, considered authoritative on the subject of sorcery and witchcraft, thus agreed that magic could induce madness, but neither fully focused on what that meant or how it happened. Rather like the Nuremberg councilmen, learned opinion on sorcery accepted that magic could cause madness without being too bothered to deal with it in detail.

Late medieval sources from other genres (religious, literary, medical) suggest that other intellectual and even popular opinions were very much in step with that of the authorities on magic, even though magic did not monopolize madness narratives in any of these genres. For instance, over one hundred late medieval accounts of miraculously healed madness recorded in informal registers kept at four major Bavarian shrines describe a panoply of causes for madness: accident or bodily injury, childbirth, prior illness, strong emotion, shock, and magic.[49] In most cases, the descent into madness seems to have been foreseeable or at least explainable. Ancient and medieval doctors alike reported that madness could arise out of prolonged illness, and in miracle stories the onset of madness in the course of other physical suffering needed no further explanation.[50] Likewise, the sudden onset of madness could be easily attributed to accidents or emotional triggers, like being struck by lightning or experiencing sudden fear.[51] But in some cases, the onset of madness seemed so random as to exclude obvious natural explanation. St. Simpert's fifteenth-century miracles possess two cases of extreme mental anguish (which stopped short of total madness) that were explained with reference to sorcery. In one account, a woman was nearly driven mad by the pain in her arm. The monk who recorded her story inserted himself here in the tale, an unusual narrative device in the text, in order to suggest that her condition was caused by a magical curse (*maleficiis*).[52] The monk was likely referring to the pain in the arm as the result of the curse (though it is not entirely clear), but his personal reflection was offered only after explaining the mental effect that the pain was having on the woman. Entirely natural causes for her pain and its mental ramifications were difficult for him to imagine, leaving human intervention through some form of sorcery as the logical explanation. Sorcery was not a lazy or irrational explanation, however. By the fifteenth century, pain was widely understood as a cause of madness, and magic, both demonic and natural, had a long reputation for causing bodily pain and illness.[53] The monk's suggested pathology of magic-causes-pain-causes-madness was thus entirely logical, showing one process by which magic could actually work to incite madness. In the second miracle, a man suffering from extreme anxiety for fourteen weeks could himself think of no obvious cause for his mental state and thus suspected that he was bewitched (*fascinatum*).[54] In this case, his extreme anxiety constituted a kind of mental disorder, one that was deeply unsettling and whose onset was unexplained. In the absence of a clear trigger, magic, again, was suspected.

Shrine registers thus recorded brief details that hint at a kind of general cultural facility for using magic to understand why and how madness arose, but the social functions of a link between magic and madness are revealed even more clearly in popular literary genres. Caesarius of Heisterbach's *Dialogue on Miracles*—a popular collection of moralizing tales written in Latin by a German monk in the thirteenth century and translated into German in the fifteenth century by a Munich doctor, Johannes Hartlieb (who also penned a German-language tract about magic)—reflects the popularly held layered etiologies of madness, from moral failing and demonic interference to illness, injury, and magic.[55] Caesarius's exempla offer narratives of madness that are more spiritually inflected than even those contained in miracle registers, including several miracles in which demonic temptation or moral turpitude resulted in madness.[56] But he also offers two stories in which magic and human agency seem to be in play. One tale tells of a nun who was "driven mad by the magical arts of a wretched lay-brother" and who then suffered such temptations and such deep melancholy that she drowned herself in a well.[57] Caesarius also tells a story of a laywoman of Soest, scorned in love, who pretended that the object of her desire, a clerk, had made her mad through some bewitchment. According to Caesarius's tale, the town authorities, believing the ruse, burned the youth at the stake as a "vile magician."[58] The type of magic in each case (real or feigned) remains unspecified. There is no mention of demonic involvement, though neither is it precluded.

More important, however, is the function of the accusation of madness in each story. In both cases, magic exonerated the woman at the heart of the story from public shame. In the case of the nun who was actually driven mad, the woman committed suicide, an act for which Caesarius rarely shows much sympathy. As Alexander Murray's work has explored, madness did not necessarily erase the stain of suicide, but it was generally perceived to mitigate the guilt of a suicide.[59] Indeed, the legal culpability, or lack thereof, of a mad person for his violent actions is one of the more consistent provisions regarding the mad in German law codes.[60] But Caesarius himself granted the melancholic suicide only a limited measure of compassion, in part, it seems, owing to his own uncertainty about how "mad" a person suffering from melancholia actually was. Caesarius occasionally conflated melancholy with the sin of acedia, whereas at other moments he appeared willing to see melancholy as a mental disease (as ancient and medieval medical theory held).[61] This ambiguity translates into a rather confused position on mad suicides. Suicides who acted out of sadness and despair were assuredly damned, but frenzy and mental alienation exempted suicides from moral damnation. Moreover, God never allowed the mad to suffer the ignoble end of suicide—thereby undermining all claims of a "madness defense" in cases of suicide.[62] In a story that precedes that of the nun, Caesarius tells of another nun who attempted to drown herself after she was so troubled by the "vice of melancholy" that she fell into despair.[63] Melancholy in this tale reads both as a mental illness and as a sin that led to a state that Caesarius saw unambiguously as a sin: despair. Yet with his confused position on melancholy, Caesarius remains unable to commit fully either to condemning the woman's actions or to exonerating her.

But for Caesarius, melancholy that was magically induced (rather than that which was perhaps willfully indulged) mitigated suicidal guilt even further. The nun who drowned herself in the well, whom Caesarius both calls demented [*dementata*] and describes as suffering from melancholy, was not mentally compromised because of any failure of diligence on her part. She did not willfully give in to despair, nor to ordinary temptations of demonic origin; she was bewitched by a human agent, "driven mad by the magical arts of a wretched lay-brother," and only in madness was despair allowed the foothold that led to suicide. As a result, and even despite the sexual overtones of the lay-brother's intentions and the placement of the story within a moralizing section on temptation, Caesarius studiously avoids casting judgment on the nun's mental anguish and suicide. The magical cause of her madness, and thus her suicide, seems to have made her merely a deeply unfortunate example of the human condition and a victim of a particularly pernicious lay-brother, who, as Caesarius informs us, went on to corrupt (though perhaps not enchant) another nun. A magical etiology thus seems to have helped protect the nun's reputation and her soul, even in the somewhat unwilling eyes of Caesarius himself.

Magicked madness possesses a similar social power in the story of the woman of Soest, though in all other particulars the tale is quite different. Caesarius tells us that the laywoman, when scorned in love by a cleric, accused the man of assaulting her. As a result, he was imprisoned, awaiting death. According to Caesarius, in order to try one last time at seducing the then-jailed youth (but we might also suspect in order to sell her tale), the woman then feigned a kind of love madness, which caused the judges to label the young clerk a magician and to send him immediately to the stake.[64] For Caesarius, the tale is one of dangerous female lust, but the particular insertion of the feigned love madness, especially given its apparent lack of necessity since the youth was already imprisoned and awaiting death, suggests that magicked madness had a purpose beyond Caesarius's moralizing. Indeed, the narrative actually makes a compelling case for the way in which madness and bewitchment could deflect attention from personal guilt. The woman's feigned love madness, which in no way resembled the lovesickness that doctors recognized as a medical problem stemming from real desire on the part of the sufferer, recast the woman's victimhood.[65] As mere victim of sexual assault, the accusing woman would suffer from the public *fama* and shame attached to rape; accusations of rape rarely resulted in the conviction of the rapists, and scholars have found that formal accusations often served other purposes, including the strategy of forcing the marriage of the two parties.[66] Unsuccessful in her attempts to "win" the young cleric and presumably suffering social consequences, it seems that the woman saw an opportunity to bring the situation to a speedier conclusion and to remove any lingering doubts about her own culpability. Her stunning performance of magicked madness removed the problem, casting her as a more sympathetic kind of victim in her town (though not in Caesarius's narrative) and allowing her to retain her position and status within her community.

The suspicions of magical involvement recorded in miracle narratives and the accusations of magicked madness in Casesarius's tales had real-world consequences by the fifteenth century. Magically induced madness appears with greater frequency—and not only in Germany—through the course of the fifteenth century, thanks in part to the international scandal of King Charles VI's madness and in part to the growing frequency of sorcery and witchcraft trials. The episodic madness of Charles VI (d. 1422) had both led the French court to attempt magical healings and had incited accusations of bewitchments regarding the royal person.[67] As Aleksandra Pfau has found, following this highly publicized royal madness, claims of magically induced madness begin to appear with greater frequency in French remission letters.[68] Though evidence is spotty, the same trend seems to appear in German areas, both in trials and in more proscriptive literature. In the famous 1485 series of trials in Innsbruck, for instance, magicked madness appeared as an accusation in the second week of a five-week period of witness testimony. According to the report, one sorceress was alleged to have sent another woman a magical pouch that caused the second woman to go "stupid in the head" and then be fully insane for a period of six months.[69]

Just what exactly these bewitchments were believed to have entailed, however, is less clear. Conceptions of magic in the Middle Ages were never stable and could involve a wide range of activities, from the use of herbs and charms to incantations and the conjuring of demons.[70] For instance, in Hartmann von Aue's *Iwein*, a German version of Chrétien de Troyes's *Yvain*, madness is situated at the murky intersection of moral turpitude, emotional suffering, magical intervention, and natural healing. Iwein's madness was brought on by the knight's extreme guilt at breaking a promise to his wife, but it was cured by a magic fairy salve, whose ingredients and properties are unknown but whose instructions for application—it was meant to be rubbed on the head—connected it to the ordinary medical treatments for madness discussed below.[71] Accusations of magically induced madness also tend not to give explanations for how the magic was believed to have worked, and scattered cases suggest that although magic's ability to induce madness was widespread, the methods by which it did so were by no means uniform. If a monk could posit a two-step process by which magic could in some way cause physical pain that could drive a person to the brink of madness, most narratives offer more direct pathways. The magical pouch in Innsbruck seems to imply a kind of natural magic using a collection of natural substances and acting much like a charm. Reaching across the Alps, a case from Perugia describes a woman who wanted to put her husband into a stupor in order to be able to continue an amorous affair and who attempted multiple techniques, finally succeeding through the use of a plant she mixed in his meals.[72] Another case from the same region suggests that magic could also accidentally cause madness, as happened when a love spell went wrong and the targeted woman who was supposed to begin hating her husband and loving the man who sought the spell instead went mad.[73] Such a deflected result is perhaps not unsurprising, given that the aim and the result were two sides of the "mental turmoil" coin as envisioned by the *Malleus*. Charmed pouches, magical salves, occult virtues in plants, and backfiring spells (perhaps including a demonic invocation): one begins to sense the basic variety of the ways that magic worked on the mind, but such accounts offer little clear theory behind how magic was perceived to actually work. By turning to magical texts and treatises written about magic, however, we can get a clearer picture both of the pervasive perception that magic offered a direct conduit to the mind and of the ways that magic enabled a practitioner of magic to affect the fragile but guarded recesses of the brain that housed the mental faculties, from the ability to reason to the storehouse of the memory.

Curses and cures for madness appear frequently in magical texts and involve all kinds of magical activities, from benign charms found in mainstream medical texts to demonic incantations in more learned treatises on sorcery. On the more licit, or at least positive, side of magical practice, numerous charms, amulets, and prayers were promoted as cures for madness or, even more frequently, as methods for enhancing mental abilities by well-meaning scholars. The two goals were intimately related, for they shared a conception of mental health and the belief that the mental faculties could be affected by a wide range of objects and practices, from *materia medica* and everyday behaviors (including sex) to prayers, charms, and demonic intervention.[74] Indeed, encyclopedias, regimens of health, herbals, and recipe collections attested to a variety of substances that had the ability to strengthen the brain or mind, from chamomile and cowslip to roses and cinnamon, many of which also appeared in late medieval therapies for madness.[75] All manner of substances had the ability to augment or protect the mental faculties, but stones and aromatics played a particularly large role. Scent was an ancient form of medical therapy, for aromatic particles had the ability to affect directly the animal spirits that filled the cavities of the brain and oversaw all sensory and rational functions, and the botanical and medical literature of the later Middle Ages consistently recorded the ability of certain fragrances to strengthen the mind in particular.[76] Efforts to strengthen the mind and its faculties not only drew on the same reservoirs of knowledge and practice that cures for madness did, they also reveal the same cultural anxieties over the fragility of mental abilities, which could be altered for good or for ill by a host of everyday items, events, and behaviors. It is no wonder that in this cultural morass of medieval psychology, medicine and magic alike offered methods for mental enhancement with an almost aggressive optimism for their efficacy.

Perhaps the most famous text devoted to the magical augmentation of mental abilities was the *Ars notoria*, a favorite work among university students after its appearance in the thirteenth century.[77] At first blush, the *Ars notoria* promised a clear intellectual good—the acquisition of knowledge and the strengthening of a scholar's tools of memory, understanding, and eloquence—through prayers and rituals that called on the powers of the angels and the Holy Spirit. An oration for obtaining a good memory, for instance, begins thus: "I Beseech thee, O my Lord, to Illuminate the Light of my Conscience with the Splendor of the Light: Illustrate and confirm my Understanding, with the sweet odour of thy Spirit. Adorn my Soul, that hearing I may hear, and what I hear, I may retain in my Memory."[78] (Given the ready use of fragrance to open, comfort, and heal the mind, the reference to odor in this invocation, which is repeated in other invocations designed to augment the memory, can be read as more than mere rhetorical flourish.)[79] But the book moves quickly into a murkier realm of invocation that taps into the knowledge and powers of the angels, whose names are repeatedly invoked in the works many orations.[80] As further evidence of the awesome power of the invocations contained in the book, the text warns that, if improperly done, the prayers and incantations in the book could produce the reverse effect. The text tells of a servant of Solomon who had presumed to read the book and was stricken dumb, blind, and lame and had his memory taken from him. For the rest of his life, four angels daily afflicted him, each one responsible for blocking one of the four faculties.[81] We should thus understand the invitation to angelic spirits to grant knowledge and memory as a powerful bypass into the mental and sensory faculties. Reflecting the interests of scholar monks, the *Ars notoria* was an instruction manual for a spiritual scholar who, in the interest of academic and material gain, invited the workings of supernatural forces into his mental faculties. The *Ars notoria* instructed the user in an inward-focused ritual "cursing" that voluntarily opened up the normally inviolate zone of the human intellect to interference (even if beneficial) from outside spirits.

Perhaps not surprisingly, then, the *Ars notoria* proved popular but controversial. Thomas Aquinas was particularly concerned with the ritualized method of trying to attain knowledge and found the unknown words and use of figures in the text uncomfortably close to demonic magic.[82] John of Morigny, a fourteenth-century French Benedictine monk, was so intrigued and yet troubled by the text of the *Ars notoria* that he crafted a less dangerous ritual text.[83] John had originally studied the *Ars notoria* as an antidote to an even more insidious (unnamed) necromancy text then making the rounds in his monastery. Believing there was no harm in the book's incantations, he had tried a couple, including one for memory, but found himself besieged by demonic visions. In response, John wrote what he deemed to be a purer text (a "holy" text rather than a magical text) for accomplishing mental excellence and the acquisition of knowledge. The result was the *Book of Visions of the Blessed and Undefiled Virgin Mary* (*Liber visionum*), a text that like the *Ars notoria* was known in late medieval Germany.[84] John's text mixed angelic ritual magic with Marian visions and included several prayers meant to strengthen the mental faculties.[85] Prayer 16, for instance, prays for the renovation of the senses and the mental faculties, including memory and reason, and though it focuses on God, John's text as a whole invokes angels, as well as Mary and the saints, in its search for mental acuity. Even this more "orthodox" book of rituals thus retained the key elements at the heart of invocations for mental alteration. These were elements that need not be exclusive to angelic interference, for what an angel could enter to strengthen, a demon could enter to weaken or obfuscate. (One might have expected John to have learned this lesson when, the night after saying the *Ars notoria*'s invocation for memory, he found a malign spirit lying next to him in bed.)[86] Invocations for mental strength were merely the positive side of a magical rationale that saw the human mind as a playground for spiritual forces.

The intellectual elites of Europe did not entertain ideas about outside spirits and mental states only in the context of their own desire for educational shortcuts. Some also possessed an interest in the utility of magic in more pragmatic fields. Most notably, some practitioners of medicine embraced certain forms of healing magic, including charms meant to cure madness.[87] A marginal notation by the entry on mania in a fourteenth-century text of Gilbertus Anglicus's *Compendium medicinae*, very likely produced in Bavaria, describes the practice of binding two lines of the Lord's Prayer to the right arm as a form of treatment for the disease.[88] This kind of written, verbal charm based on prayer was seen at least by most (though not by all) doctors and pastoral writers alike as broadly licit and compatible with more somatic cures.[89] Though remedies frequently made use of nondemonic ritualized language or charms and amulets that drew on natural occult powers, medical magic was not, in fact, limited to the realm of natural magic but also ventured toward that of demonic magic. John of Gaddesden's popular compendium, the "Rose of medicine" (*Rosa medicinae*), for instance, contains two charms for madness, both of which refer to demons.[90]

The presence of magical cures for madness within the realm of medicine, even those that drew on questionable spirits, shows some support among medical practitioners for including magic and demonic interference in their learned understanding of mental pathologies. Indeed, such charms had a kind of rational underpinning in key medical texts, including the magisterial medical writings of Avicenna. In his lengthy discussion of melancholy in his *Canon of Medicine*, Avicenna reported that some doctors believed melancholy was produced by demons. Avicenna himself then explained that in his opinion, it did not matter if demons were the original cause since demons worked by converting the patient's complexion toward black bile and the true cause of the melancholy (and that which should be treated) was the humoral imbalance and not the demon.[91] But Avicenna's dismissal of the importance of whether demons were a part of madness's etiology was not always the takeaway for western doctors, who found greater resonance in Avicenna's belief that demons were a part of the physical world and had physical effects on the body. In fact, Catherine Rider has shown that although medieval medicine did not see demons as a primary explanation for mental disorder, late medieval doctors were increasingly interested in the connection between demons and mental states.[92] In the light of the minority trend within medicine to entertain ideas of demonic causation for mad states, medicine's other minority trend—to experiment with magical cures that also involved demons—appears as a natural development within the logic of the medical system.

If medieval medicine occasionally incorporated demons into its logic for madness, medieval magic based much of its rationale for how cures and curses worked on the mind on the logic and vast body of knowledge of the natural and medical sciences. Many medieval writers, particularly from the thirteenth century onward, perceived occult powers and processes as occurring within the natural order.[93] Magical texts therefore offered a range of magical devices and recipes designed to help or hurt mental health, whose completion was difficult to secure but whose logic was deeply rooted in the natural world. Magical amulets described in the ancient text *The Kyranides*, a fourth-century Greek text that was translated into Latin as early as the twelfth century, included instructions for healing madness with an amulet made out of a scorpion's sting, a basil flower, and a hummingbird's heart, placed in buckskin.[94] Even in the ancient world this would have been a difficult spell; in medieval Germany only the basil and buckskin were truly attainable. The Arabic book of magic known as the *Picatrix*, which was introduced to the West in the thirteenth century and was familiar to fifteenth-century German intellectuals, also offered magical cures for madness, though their main ingredient was even more problematic than the hummingbird's heart.[95] According to the text, "human brains will heal those who have lost their memory if eaten," and "soup made from a human head drunk mixed with brains heals those who have lost their minds."[96] A like-minded recipe from a fifteenth-century manuscript recommends that pumpkin seeds buried in a human skull and smeared with human brains will produce pumpkins whose flesh will promote the "infinite development of mental faculties," especially resulting in a perfect memory.[97] Although arguably not difficult to find, and while certain human products were not unknown in magical and medicinal texts (menstrual blood being the most common), human brains had no place in medicine, nor would any benevolent scientific text support such cannibalism. The *Book of Secrets*, attributed in the Middle Ages to Albertus Magnus, offered therapies that were less complicated or taboo, including one that claimed that placing the tooth of a mare on a madman's head would deliver him from his madness and another that stated that if you wrap the chelidonius stone—a mineral deposit found inside a swallow whose healing properties for madness were discussed in medical and natural philosophic texts alike—in linen or calf skin and wear it in your left arm pit, it would cure madness.[98]

These magical prescriptions, even the more extreme examples, were deeply logical. Most of these remedies, though not explicit about the working properties or virtues of ingredients or concoctions, drew on, or at least were deeply reminiscent of, more mainstream therapies for madness found in medical texts, herbals, and encyclopedias. Therapies placed on the head were classic—the chelidonius stone appeared in Thomas of Cantimpré's popular encyclopedia as a cure of madness—and basil was discussed by Pliny the Elder, who warned that ingesting it would cause madness but who also found the scent helpful for fainting fits and lethargy.[99] These magical therapies thus tapped into natural forces that were well known in natural philosophy. Indeed, madness therapies, which routinely used substances that were well-known *materia medica* as well as substances that were well-known for their occult properties, serve as reminders of the difficulty of separating occult virtues and medicinal properties in natural substances, especially in such texts that made no effort to explain the Aristotelian properties of a substance (hot, cold, wet, dry) but also referred to few clear occult powers (ritualistic, animistic, or symbolic features).

Whereas magical cures for madness tended to be somewhat straightforward, if not always simple, magic curses or invocations meant to *cause* madness were generally more complex. The *Picatrix*, for instance, contained the following recipe to make a person lose his senses:

> Take the head of a man, freshly cut off, and put it in a large pot; and put his spleen, heart, and liver with it. Then in the same pot put the heads of

the following animals, that is, of a cat, a fox, an ape, a chicken, a hoopoe, a crow, a kite, a bat, a goose, a swallow, a tortoise, and an owl. Cover them all with oil, and seal the mouth of the jar well with luting; put it on a gentle fire, and let it remain there for three days and as many nights. Then take it off the fire, and let it cool. Strain the foregoing with your face covered, and set aside the oil. Then take the bones of the aforementioned heads, and burn them in a different oil until they are reduced to powder. Mix the powder with black henbane seeds and scialte nuts, and keep this with you for use. When you wish to work with the foregoing, give some of the powder to whomever you wish, in food or drink, and light three lamps with the oil; you will see it affect him. To make your body appear wondrous, take some of the aforesaid oil and anoint your face with it. You will begin to illuminate the house by its light, and will appear to stand out as though you were something monstrous.[100]

This formula, with its gruesome ingredients, would have been nearly impossible to replicate. But though purposefully difficult, the spell, like those previously discussed, was also quite rational in its details, which fell in step with medical and natural philosophic logic. For instance, the final set of instructions, intended to make the practitioner's body glow and appear monstrous apparently in order to frighten the victim, was connected to the widespread belief that shocking sights—like that of a demon or even just a bright light—could cause a person to lose his mind.[101] This popular belief was backed by contemporary vision theories, which supported the belief that sight involved an actual material connection between the seen object and the eye and, through the eye and the process of sight, the intellectual faculties.[102] But even more common are the kinds of ingredients used in this recipe. Henbane, for instance, was long understood throughout the Western herbal tradition as a dangerous plant that possessed some therapeutic uses but more famously caused madness.[103] The use of animal brains in the spell, moreover, acknowledged the physical location of sense, thought, and memory and displayed a belief in the sympathetic affinity of animal and human body parts. Such beliefs were widespread, but the therapeutic benefits (and dangers) of this association are perhaps most thoroughly articulated in Albertus Magnus's *De animalia*, written by the Dominican master in the 1260s as a commentary and supplement to Aristotle's treatises on animals. The last five books of Albertus's text offer a detailed dictionary of animals, drawn in part from the work of Albertus's former student, Thomas of Cantimpré, but greatly expanded.[104] It is here that we find such wisdom as that a man who eats goat testicles will produce a son (though if he eats only one testicle, the son will have only one testicle), ashes of hedgehog spines will cause hair to grow back over scars, and that a hare's tooth placed in the mouth with remove the pain of a toothache.[105] More tellingly for our purposes, we also find that a lion, a beast whose nobility makes it a particularly useful foil for man, offers a number of health benefits, but if a person ingests a lion's brain, it causes madness.[106] No matter how noble the lion may be, his brain offers only danger to man's uniquely human, rational mental workings.

The logic of the *Picatrix*'s offerings on madness is thus the same logic that undergirds medieval natural science: by ingesting animal brains or heads, a person lost his human rationality. A second recipe offered by the *Picatrix* drives home this point. It states that the smoke made by burning a putrefying mixture of hawk brains, mouse brains, and cat brains, mixed with sulfur, myrrh, and crane feces, will cause the person who inhales it to be possessed by a demon and lose his senses and memory.[107] Again we find medical logic (that fumes, vapors, and smells have a particularly direct impact on the animal spirits that oversee all mental processes) coupled with natural philosophic understandings of the dangers of animal brains to human rationality. The *Picatrix*, and magical texts like it, thus make use of well-known and deeply logical natural substances in their causes for madness. With this deeply rational world of natural and occult powers in mind, the use of human brains discussed above comes into even sharper focus. Clearly knowing that his ingredients draw on illicit occult powers, the author of the *Picatrix* offers a defense of human ingredients and lists their uses, revealing the same sympathetic virtues found in the natural philosophic writings of Albertus Magnus. Noting that many marvels are made from the human body, the author explains, for instance, that burnt human hair warms the head and that the tongue of a woman helps those who wish to tell lies.[108] It is no surprise, then, that if ingesting animal brains caused a person to go mad, ingesting human brains would make a mad person regain his human mental faculties. It was a simple, if cannibalistic, logic.

Not all magical causes of madness were based in natural magic, however. Some magical curses for madness were explicit in their use of demonic powers. Perhaps the most illustrative example for how this kind of demonic magic worked can be found in a fifteenth-century German necromancer's manual, whose collection of spells begins with a magical process for causing a person to go mad. According to the spell, the process should begin on a Saturday when the moon is waning. The conjurer, in the presence of the targeted victim, commands a demon called Mirael to enter the person. He does so by cursing the target: "May [the demon] Mirael enter into your brain and weaken and obliterate all wisdom, perception, discretion and reasoning." Then, using a sliver of wood cut from the lintel of the target's door as a pen, the conjurer writes a demonic invocation in cat's blood on a piece of linen cloth, ordering "O Mirael, Remover of wisdom, knowledge, cognition, and skill, appear in the senses of so-and-so and cause a mad spirit in his mind." Then he draws a circle with the names of ten other demons, and invokes all of them to encircle the target and "so afflict his senses that he is made unknowing, raving, foolish, and out of his mind." Returning to the victim's house, the conjurer continues the ritual by urinating "in the manner of a camel" and burying the linen in the ground. Returning home once more, the conjurer lights and then extinguishes a candle while again invoking the demons he has bound to do his bidding. After repeating the candle ritual for seven days, the conjurer can expect his target to go mad.[109]

As Richard Kieckhefer has noted, there are multiple elements in this curse that harness different kinds of forces. The use of light and lunar timing hints at astral magic and rituals associated with liturgies (most notable Pascal rites and Candlemas celebrations). The befouling of the environment is a kind of negating action to the positive environmental therapies that medical texts generally prescribed for the mad.[110] Instead of sweet smells and pleasant music prescribed for the mad in medical and scientific texts, this curse uses cat's blood and human urine.[111] And of course, there are demons. But these conjured demons are not meant to work on a person's will, nor tempt them in any way. They are meant to wage a two-front assault on the physiological structure of his mental faculties. Medical texts taught that corrupt humors and vapors could penetrate the physical reaches of the brain and affect any or all mental functions; according to this necromancer's spell, so, too, could demons. The primary demon, Mirael, takes up residence in the brain, where not only is information considered and then stored, but also where the animal spirit, the motive force of all rational and sensory perception, resides. The demon in this enchantment has no volition of its own but acts as a weapon thrown into the brain. It requires no acquiescence on the part of the victim, nor any prior weakness to gain a foothold. The other demons, meanwhile, work on the external senses, which are even more susceptible to demonic interference.

The ability of demons to affect the external senses was well-known and accepted by writers on magic, natural philosophy, and theology alike.[112] Indeed, as even nonspecialist writers like Hildegard of Bingen and Vincent of Beauvais attested, demons could alter a person's perceptions by using images and fantasies to cause a person to fall into madness.[113] The depiction of a demon sent by a sorcerer into the reaches of a person's mind, however, was a far cry from the behavior of demons and demonic possession as understood by most theologians, who held firmly to the idea that the higher faculties of the soul (including the intellect) were inviolable.[114] Such writers focused on demons as the instigating agent rather than as the weapon wielded by a practitioner of magic. There existed a long tradition of moralizing tales and commentary in which demons, on their own volition, occasionally attacked people's minds or wills, particularly if a person was weakened by grief, anxiety, or some moral failing.[115] Johannes Hartlieb took just such a stance in his *Buch aller verbotenen kunst*, in which he was careful to assert that the devil has no ability to get into the mind or reason of a pious man truly made in the image of God.[116] But like the Nuremberg council, most late medieval Germans seemed more interested in practical, not moral, approaches to madness and exhibited a basic resistance to placing blame on the victim of madness. As a result, stories of demonic harassment were actually rare in late medieval Germany, more rare, in fact, than accusations of magic. We find that the logic of magical curses, both in their natural and demonic elements, actually fit more clearly with the agenda of late medieval observers of madness than did the narratives offered by moralizing tales. Claiming that demons on their own volition made a person mad placed agency with a demon but also suggested that the person targeted by the demon was weak or partially complicit in his or her descent toward madness. This narrative worked nicely with the agendas of those like Caesarius of Heisterbach or Johannes Hartlieb. Speaking in the abstract to a noble patron, Hartlieb was more concerned with reassurances for a moral audience than in explaining actual situations of compromised mental faculties. (Indeed, Hartlieb seems to have little interest in actual madness, never discussing it in his text.) Sources closer to real cases of madness, however, were far less willing to blame the victim. Instead, claiming that a person had been bewitched into madness—that a substance or demon had been sent into the inner reaches of her mind through no fault of her own—introduced a complex hierarchy of agency and responsibility that made the problem a concern of the whole community rather than the concern only of the mad person and her confessor.

In conclusion, whereas significantly more work remains to be done on the many intersections between magic and madness in medieval thought and practice, there are two primary impressions that this essay has tried to tease out from disparate sources that were produced by or influenced late medieval German culture. The first is that for southeastern Germany, at least, late medieval narratives that linked cases of madness with magic were rare, but increasing. Miracle accounts and trial records alike suggest that magical explanations of madness were on the rise in the fifteenth century, just as debates about magic itself were gaining greater purchase in the culture.[117] This increase, however, should not be overstated: in 1500 the average person was still far more likely to see a mad person as struck by a physical ailment with a natural explanation than as bewitched. The rarity of the direct attribution of madness to a magical curse, however, does not mean that such narratives are culturally insignificant. General associations of madness and magic were present in a variety of genres in late medieval Germany, ranging from moralists' warnings or approbations to practitioners' handbooks. Although the general association of magic and madness in magical literature remained vague—madness never became a centerpiece of magical intent like impotence, wealth acquisition, or love spells—it also remained fairly constant.[118] Narratives of madness that involved magical etiologies, moreover, could perform a kind of cultural work that "ordinary" narratives of madness could not: they deflected residual ideas of sin or guilt from the sufferer, they offered another path toward communal negotiation of a situation that often blurred the lines between private/familial and public/municipal responsibility, and they offset the anxiety caused by madness by introducing a completely different kind of anxiety, one centered on magic and one that was increasingly topical.

The second impression gathered from the range of examples of magically induced madness is that magical causation expands our understanding of the medieval conceptual framework for madness; it does not represent a true counternarrative to more prosaic conceptions of the onset of madness. A close examination of narratives of magically inflected madness reveals that such narratives did not exist separately from ordinary naturalistic explanations of madness but rather existed on the same continuum with them, acting within the framework of natural science and the workings of the body, including that of psychology, medical theories about madness, and physiological understandings of demonic interference. Magical etiologies did not compete with naturalistic or medical ones; they complemented them, making use of the same logic, same forces, and even sometimes the same ingredients as their more "scientific" counterparts.

NOTES

1. For excellent defenses of the appropriateness and usefulness of the term "madness" for addressing premodern states that resemble modern mental illnesses (and even certain intellectual disabilities), see H. C. Erik Midelfort, *A History of Madness in Sixteenth-Century Germany* (Stanford: Stanford University Press, 1999), 11, and Mary Lindemann, *Medicine and Society in Early Modern Europe* (Cambridge: Cambridge University Press, 1999), 28–30.

2. Karl von Hegel, "Über Nürnbergs Bevölkerungszahl und Handwerkerverhältnisse im 14. und 15. Jahrhundert," in *Chroniken der deutschen Städte, Nürnberg* (Leipzig: S. Hirzel, 1864), 2:502; Gerald Strauss, *Nuremberg in the Sixteenth Century: City Politics and Life Between Middle Ages and Modern Times*, rev. ed. (Bloomington: Indiana University Press, 1976), 35–38; and Laura Stokes, *Demons of Urban Reform: Early European Witch Trials and Criminal Justice, 1430–1530* (Basingstoke, U.K.: Palgrave Macmillan, 2011), 50–51.

3. Strauss, *Nuremberg*, 50; 154–58.

4. Gerald Strauss, "Protestant Dogma and City Government: The Case of Nuremberg," *Past and Present* 36 (April 1967): 38–58; Ernst Mummenhoff, *Altnürnberg: Schilderungen aus der älteren reichständischen Zeit bis zum Jahre 1350* (Bamberg: Buchnersche Verlagsbuchhandlung, 1890), 19–20; Irene Stahl, introduction to *Die Nürnberger Ratsverlässe: Heft 1 1449–1450*, ed. Irene Stahl (Neustadt an der Aisch: Verlag Degner, 1983), iii–viii; and Strauss, *Nuremberg*, 78–81.

5. Anne M. Koenig, "Robbed of Their Minds: Madness, Medicine and Society in Southeastern Germany from 1350 to 1500" (Ph.D. diss., Northwestern University, 2013); Theodor Kirchhoff, *Grundriss einer Geschichte der deutschen Irrenpflege* (Berlin: August Hirschwald, 1890); Ernst Mummenhoff, "Die öffentliche Gesundheits- und Krankenpflege im alten Nürnberg," in *Festschrift zur Eröffnung des neuen Krankenhauses der Stadt Nürnberg* (Nürnberg: Selbstverlag des Stadtmagistrates, 1898), 73–77.

6. Staatsarchiv, Nuremberg (hereafter StA N), Rep. 60a, Ratsverlässe (Ratsv.) from years 1471–1493. Cited examples are in Martin Schieber, ed., *Die Nürnberger Ratsverlässe Heft 2: 1452–1471.* (Neustadt: Verlag Degener, 1995), 232; and StA N Rep. 60a, Ratsv. 38, fol. 9v.

7. StA N, Rep. 60a, Ratsv. 290 (1493), fol. 3v.

8. ". . . ein gedult zu haben mit der frawen die unvernufftig gewesen und wider zu ir selbs komen ist. . . ." StA N, Rep. 60a, Ratsv. 77 (1477), fol. 12v.

9. Ulrich Knefelkamp, *Das Heilig-Geist-Spital in Nürnberg vom 14.-17. Jahrhundert* (Nuremberg: Edelmann, 1989) 204–5.

10. StA N, Rep. 60a, Ratsv. 77 (1477), fol. 17r.

11. "Ihenen die ye zu zeiten Irer synne beraubt wird. . . ." StA N, Rep. 60a, Ratsv. 77 (1477), fol. 17r.

12. StA N, Rep. 60a, Ratsv. 78 (1477), fol. 9r.

13. StA N, Rep. 60a, Ratsv. 80 (1477), fol. 6v, 9r.

14. Peter Schuster, *Das Frauenhaus: Städtische Bordelle in Deutschland (1350–1600)* (Paderborn: Ferdinand Schöningh, 1992), esp. 36–41.

15. "Item N[iclas] Grolant sol sich erkundigen des Spieglershalb der von seinen synnen komen ist. und die frawen in den handel angezeigt zu vernemen." StA N, Rep. 60a, Ratsv. 82 (1477), fol. 7v.

16. This term for sorcery or bewitchment is unusual, but not unique in the Nuremberg records. In 1481 the council decreed that a woman in the prison for "lupperei oder zauberei" was to be questioned. StA N, Rep. 60a, Ratsv. 126 (1481), fol. 7r. (*Item die frawen Im loch die lupperei oder zauberei halb einkomen ist zu red halten Schopfen.*) Similar phrasing appears in 1501, when Barbara Schlitzin was held for "zauberei und lupperei." Hartmut Kunstmann, *Zauberwahn und Hexenprozess in der Reichstadt Nürnberg* (Nuremberg: Stadtarchiv Nürnberg, 1970), 34.

17. Laura Stokes, "Experiments in Pain: Reason and the Development of Judicial Torture," in *Ideas and Cultural Margins in Early Modern Germany: Essays in Honor of H. C. Erik Midelfort*, ed. Marjorie Elizabeth Plummer and Robin B. Barnes (Surrey, U.K.: Ashgate, 2009), 241.

18. StA N, Rep. 60a, Ratsv. 83 (1477), fol. 7v.

19. Stokes, "Experiments in Pain," 240–46; Laura Stokes, *Demons of Urban Reform: Early European Witch Trials and Criminal Justice, 1430–1530* (Basingstoke, U.K.: Palgrave Macmillan, 2011), 90–99.

20. A rare case of questioned sanity: *Item der diebin halb in loch ligende mer erfarung ze haben, ob sie synnig sei oder nit. Schopfen.* StA N, Rep. 60a, Ratsv. 64 (1476), fol. 15r.

21. Kunstmann, *Zauberwahn und Hexenprozess*; and Stokes, *Demons of Urban Reform*, 50–61.

22. Stokes, *Demons of Urban Reform*, 53.

23. Ibid., 51–52.

24. Richard Kieckhefer, *European Witch Trials: Their Foundations in Popular and Learned Culture, 1300–1500* (Berkeley: University of California Press, 1976), 137–38.

25. See H. C. Erik Midelfort, *A History of Madness in Sixteenth-Century Germany* (Stanford: Stanford University Press, 1999); H. C. Erik Midelfort, "Sin, Melancholy, Obsession: Insanity and Culture in 16th Century Germany," in *Understanding Popular Culture: Europe from the Middle Ages to the Nineteenth Century*, ed. Steven L. Kaplan (Berlin: Walter de Gruyter, 1984), 113–46; and David Lederer, *Madness, Religion and the State in Early Modern Europe: A Bavarian Beacon* (Cambridge: Cambridge University Press, 2006).

26. See Penelope Doob, *Nebuchadnezzar's Children* (New Haven: Yale University Press, 1974); Sabina Flanagan, "Heresy, Madness and Possession in the High Middle Ages," in *Heresy in Transition: Transforming Ideas of Heresy in Medieval and Early Modern Europe*, ed. J. C. Laursen, C. J. Nederman, and Ian Hunter (Burlington, Vt.: Ashgate, 2005), 29–41.

27. See Gregory Zilboorg, *A History of Medical Psychology* (New York: W. W. Norton, 1941), 127–39; Ronald C. Finucane, *Miracles and Pilgrims: Popular Beliefs in Medieval England* (Totowa, N.J.: Rowman and Littlefield, 1977), 107–9; Finucane, *The Rescue of the Innocents: Endangered Children in Medieval Miracles* (New York: St. Martin's Press, 2000), 72–78; Pierre-André Sigal, *L'homme et le miracle dans la France médiévale (XIᵉ-XIIᵉ siècle)* (Paris: Les Éditions du Cerf, 1985), 236–39; Michael Goodich, *Violence and Miracle in the Fourteenth Century* (Chicago: University of Chicago Press, 1995), 74–85; Dieter Harmening, "Fränkische Mirakelbücher," *Würzburger Diözesangeschichtsblätter* 28 (1966): 72–74.

28. Nancy Caciola, *Discerning Spirits: Divine and Demonic Possession in the Middle Ages* (Ithaca, N.Y.: Cornell University Press, 2003), esp. 36–54; Barbara Newman, "Possessed by the Spirit: Devout Women, Demoniacs, and the Apostolic Life in the Thirteenth Century," *Speculum* 73 (1998): 733–70, esp. 763–68; Renate Blumenfeld-Kosinski, *The Strange Case of Ermine de Reims: A Medieval Woman Between Demons and Saints* (Philadelphia: University of Pennsylvania Press, 2015); Dyan Elliott, "Seeing Double: John Gerson, the Discernment of Spirits, and Joan of Arc," *American Historical Review* 107, no. 1 (February 2002): 26–54; Dyan Elliott, *Proving Women: Female Spirituality and Inquisitional Culture in the Later Middle Ages* (Princeton: Princeton University Press, 2004).

29. See, for example, Jerome Kroll, "A Reappraisal of Psychiatry in the Middle Ages," *Archives of General Psychiatry* 29 (August 1973): 276–83; Richard Neugebauer, "Medieval and Early Modern Theories of Mental Illness," *Archives of General Psychiatry* 36 (April 1979): 447–83; David Roffe and Christine Roffe, "Madness and Care in the Community: A Medieval Perspective," *British Medical Journal* 311 (December 1995): 1708–12; Laura Jose, "Madness and Gender in Late-Medieval English Literature" (Ph.D. diss., Durham University, 2010), 27, 115–49; and Brian Levack, *The Devil Within: Possession and Exorcism in the Christian West* (New Haven: Yale University Press, 2013), 113–38.

30. Catherine Rider, "Demons and Mental Disorder in Late Medieval Medicine," in *Mental (Dis)order in Later Medieval Europe*, ed. Sari Katajala-Peltomaa and Susanna Niiranen (Leiden: Brill, 2014), 47–69.

31. See, for instance, H. C. Erik Midelfort, "Johann Weyer and the Transformation of the Insanity Defense," in *The German People and the Reformation*, ed. R. Po-Chia Hsia (Ithaca: Cornell University Press, 1988), 234–61; and Sophie Houdard, "Mystics or Visionaries? Discernment of Spirits in the First Part of the Seventeenth Century in France," in *Communication with the Spirits*, ed. Gábor Klaniczay and Éva Pócs (Budapest: Central European University Press, 2005), 71–83, esp. 80–82.

32. StA N, Rep. 60a, Ratsv. 121 (1480), fol. 7v.

33. Schieber, *Die Nürnberger Ratsverlässe Heft 2*, 184.

34. StA N, Rep. 60a, Ratsv. 51 (1475), fol. 12r.

35. Nürnberger Reformation of 1479, 15.2, 15.3. Published in Gerhard Köbler, ed., *Reformation der Stadt Nürnberg* (Gießen: Arbeiten zu Rechts- und Sprachwissenschaft Verlag, 1984), 228–29.

36. For Nuremberg's turbulent relationship with its Jewish population (finally expelled in 1499), see Arnd Müller, *Die Geschichte der Juden in Nürnberg, 1146–945*, Beiträge zur Geschichte und Kultur der Stadt Nürnberg (Nürnberg: Selbstverlag der Stadtbibliothek

Nürnberg, 1968), and Winfried Frey, "The Intimate Other: Hans Folz's Dialogue Between 'Christian and Jew,'" in *Meeting the Foreign in the Middle Ages*, ed. Albrecht Classen (London: Routledge, 2002), 249–67.

37. Isidore of Seville, *The Etymologies of Isidore of Seville*, trans. and intro. Stephen A. Barney, W. J. Lewis, J. A. Beach, and Oliver Berghof (Cambridge: Cambridge University Press, 2006), 3.

38. Isidore, *Etymologies* 4.7.9, p. 111. The Latin critical edition of Isidore's text is W. M. Lindsay, ed., *Isidori Hispalensis Episcopi, Etymologiarum sive originum, Libri XX*, 2 vols. (Oxford: Oxford University Press, 1911).

39. Simon Kemp, *Medieval Psychology* (New York: Greenwood Press, 1990), 53–76; Simon Kemp and Garth J. O. Fletcher, "The Medieval Theory of the Inner Senses," *American Journal of Psychology* 106, no. 4 (Winter 1993): 559–76; Irina Metzler, *Fools and Idiots: Intellectual Disability in the Middle Ages* (Manchester: Manchester University Press, 2016), 53–68.

40. As encyclopedist Bartholomaeus Anglicus explained, "The apprehended likeness of a thing is collected in the fantasy or imagination. Then it is sent to the middle cell and considered by rational judgment and finally sent to the posterior cell and committed to memory" (my translation). Bartholomaeus Anglicus, *De proprietatibus rerum* (Frankfurt, 1601; repr. Frankfurt am Main: Minerva, 1964), book 5.3, pp. 123–27.

41. See, for instance, the description of brain diseases in an anonymous twelfth-century treatise on mental disorders: *Mania est infectio anterioris partis cerebri cum imaginationis privatione . . . Melancholia est infectio medie partis cerebri cum privatione rationis. . . . [F]renesi est apostema in anteriori parte cerebri . . . [L]itargia est apostuma in puppi cerebri. . . .* London, British Library, Harley 5228, fols. 58v–60r.

42. Kieckhefer, *Magic in the Middle Ages* (Cambridge: Cambridge University Press, 1989), 85.

43. Richard Kieckhefer, "Magic and Its Hazards in the Late Medieval West," in *The Oxford Handbook of Witchcraft in Early Modern Europe and Colonial America*, ed. Brian Levack (Oxford: Oxford University Press, 2013), 13–31 at 26. For Hartlieb's tract on magic, *Das buch aller verboten kunst* (1456), see Johann Hartlieb, *Das Buch aller verbotenen Künste, des Aberglaubens und der Zauberei*, ed. and trans. Falk Eisermann und Eckhard Graf (Ahlerstedt: Param Verlag, 1989).

44. Isidore, *Etymologies* 8.9.9, p. 182.

45. My translation.

46. "Usu rationis aliquem privant." Johannes Nider, *Formicarius* 5.3.

47. *Malleus maleficarum*, part 1, q. 2. English translation in Christopher Mackay, ed. and trans., *Malleus maleficarum*, vol. 2 (Cambridge: Cambridge University Press, 2006), 61.

48. *Malleus maleficarum*, part 2, q. 1, chap. 2; part 1, qq. 7, 10.

49. St. Leonard: Munich, Bayerische Staatsbibliothek, Clm 7685, *Eberhardus professus in Fürstenfeld de miraculis S. Leonardi in Inchenhofen usque ad a. 1435*; Munich, Bayerische Staatsbibliothek, Clm 27332, *Miracula sancti Leonardi in Inchenhofen facta 1258–1447*; and "Mirakelbuch von St. Leonhard in Inchenhofen," Munich, Bayerische Staatsbibliothek, Cgm 1772. St. Simpert: *Liber miraculorum S. Simperti (1465–1471)* and *Libri miraculorum S. Simperti Pars 1 (1488–95), Pars 2 (1487–1495), and Pars 3 (1488–1495)*, in *Acta sanctorum*, October 6 (Tongerloo: Abbey of Tongerloo, 1794), 251–68 (hereafter St. Simpert, AASS). St. Richildis: Munich, Bayerische Staatsbibliothek, Cgm 1777, *Mirakelbuch von Hohenwart*. St. Mary of Altötting: Robert Bauer, "Das Älteste gedruckte Mirakelbüchlein von Altötting," *Ostbairische Grenzmarken* (1961): 144–51; and Robert Bauer, "Das Büchlein der Zuflucht zu Maria: Altöttinger Mirakelberichte von Jacobus Issickemer," *Ostbairische Grenzmarken* (1964/65): 206–36.

50. See, for example, Galen, *On the Causes of Symptoms* 2, in Galen, *On Diseases and Symptoms*, ed. and intro. Ian Johnston (Cambridge: Cambridge University Press, 2006), 263, and Ortolf of Baierland (Bavaria), *Arzneibuch* (Nuremberg, 1477), 17v.

51. For accidents as causing madness, see Ortolf, *Arzneibuch*, fols. 38v, 40v, and St. Leonard, Clm 27332, fols. 61r–v, 88v. For emotions as causing madness, see Bartholomaeus Anglicus,

De proprietatibus rerum (Frankfurt, 1601), 7.5, and St. Richildis, Cgm 177, fol. 101v. See also Aleksandra Pfau, "Crimes of Passion: Emotions and Madness in French Remission Letters," in *Madness in Medieval Law and Custom*, ed. Wendy Turner (Leiden: Brill, 2010), 97–122.

52. "Ego porro ex clara ejus narratione maleficiis eam adactam fuisse existimo." St. Simpert, AASS, 266.

53. See Karen Jolly, "The Practice of Magic: Popular and Courtly Traditions," in *Witchcraft and Magic in Europe: The Middle Ages*, ed. Bengt Ankarloo and Stuart Clark (Philadelphia: University of Pennsylvania Press, 2002), 27–71.

54. "Unde haud ab re seu ratione suspicabatur se fascinatum, praecipue cum causam tantarum nesciret anxietatum." St. Simpert, AASS, 263.

55. Karl Drescher, ed., *Johann Hartliebs Übersetzung des Dialogus Miraculorum von Caesarius von Heisterbach. Aus der einzigen Londoner Handschrift*, Deutsche Texte des Mittelalters 33 (Berlin: Weidmannsche Buchhandlung, 1929.)

56. See Caesarius of Heisterbach, *Dialogus miraculorum* (hereafter *DM*), 1.14, 3.11, 5.28, 7.26, and 9.50. Printed in Caesarius of Heisterbach, *Dialogus miraculorum*, ed. Josephus Strange, 2 vols. (Cologne: Sumptibus J. M. Heberle [H. Lempertz], 1851), vol. 1:20–21, 123–24, 311–12; vol. 2:35–36, 205.

57. Caesarius of Heisterbach, *DM*, book 4, chap. 42; Strange, *DM*, 1:211.

58. Caesarius of Heisterbach, *DM*, book 4, chap. 99; Strange, *DM*, 1:270.

59. Alexander Murray, *Suicide in the Middle Ages*, vol. 2, *The Curse on Self-Murder* (Oxford: Oxford University Press, 2000), 448.

60. See, for instance, Sachsenspiegel 3.3: *Uber toren unde uber sinnelosen man ensal man ouch nicht richten; weme si aber schaden, ir vormunde sal das gelden.* Translation in Maria Dobozy, trans., *The Saxon Mirror: A "Sachsenspiegel" of the Fourteenth Century* (Philadelphia: Univeristy of Pennsylvania Press, 1999), 112. See also Schwabenspiegel, 257: *Uber ain rechten toren und uber ain synnlosen man sol nyemant richten. wenn aber sy schaden tund das sol ir vormund puessen ob sy gut habent.* Printed in Karl August Eckhardt, ed., *Schwabenspiegel: Kurzform*, MGH, Fontes Iuris Germanici Antiqui Nova Series Tomi 4, Pars 1 et 2 (Hannover: Hahnsche Buchhandluch, 1974), 345.

61. Caesarius of Heisterbach, *DM*, book 4, chap. 38; Strange, *DM*, 1:206.

62. Caesarius of Heisterbach, *DM*, book 4, chap. 44; Strange, *DM*, 1:212.

63. Caesarius of Heisterbach, *DM*, book 4, chap. 40; Strange, *DM*, 1:209–10.

64. Caesarius of Heisterbach, *DM*, book 4 ,chap. 99; Strange, *DM*, 1:270.

65. Mary Wack, *Lovesickness in the Middle Ages: The Viaticum and Its Commentaries* (Philadelphia: University of Pennsylvania Press, 1990).

66. Edna Ruth Yahil, "A Rape Trial in Saint Eloi: Sex, Seduction and Justice in the Seigneurial Courts of Medieval Paris," in *Voices from the Bench: the Narratives of Lesser Folk in Medieval Trials*, ed. Michael Goodich (New York: Palgrave, 2006), 251–71; Caroline Dunn, "The Language of Ravishment in Medieval England," *Speculum* 86 (2011): 79–116.

67. See Edward Peters, "The Medieval Church and State on Superstition, Magic and Witchcraft: From Augustine to the Sixteenth Century," in *Witchcraft and Magic in Europe*, vol. 3, *The Middle Ages*, ed. Karen Jolly (London: The Athlone Press, 2002), 221.

68. Aleksandra Pfau, "Madness in the Realm: Narratives of Mental Illness in Late Medieval France" (Ph.D. diss., University of Michigan, 2008), 188, 193–95.

69. Kieckhefer, *Witch Trials*, 53; Hartmann Ammann, "Der Innsbrucker Hexenprozess von 1485," *Zeitschrift des Ferdinandeums für Tirol und Vorarlberg* 34 (1890): 16.

70. Michael D. Bailey, "The Meanings of Magic," *Magic, Ritual, and Witchcraft* 1 (Summer 2006): 1.

71. Hartmann von Aue, *Iwein*, lines 3419–30, ed. G. F. Benecke and K. Lachmann, 7th ed. (Zurich: Manesse Verlag), 108.

72. Kieckhefer, "Magic and Its Hazards," 24. Original records published in Ugolino Nicolini, "La stregoneria a Perugia e in Umbria nel Medioevo: Con i testi di sette processi Perugia e uno a Bologna," *Bollettino della Deputazione di storia patria per l'Umbria* 84 (1987): 5–87.

73. Kieckhefer, "Magic and Its Hazards," 24.

74. For magic and medical substances more generally, see Jerry Stannard, "Greco-Roman *Materia medica* in Medieval Germany," *Bulletin of the History of Medicine* 46, no. 5 (1972): 455–68; Jerry Stannard, "Magiferous Plants and Magic in Medieval Medical Botany," in *Herbs and Herbalism in the Middle Ages and Renaissance*, ed. Katherine Stannard and Richard Kay (Aldershot: Ashgate, 1999), 33–46.

75. Konrad von Megenberg, *Buch der Natur* 5.16, printed in Franz Pfeiffer, ed., *Das Buch der Natur von Konrad von Megenberg* (Stuttgart: Karl Aue Verlag, 1861), 388; Johannes Hartlieb, *Das Kräuterbuch des Johannes Hartlieb: Eine deutsche Bilderhandschrift aus der Mitte des 15. Jahrhunderts*, ed. Franz Speta (Graz: Akademische Druck u. Verlagsanstalt, 1980); Thomas Cantimpratensis, *Liber de natura rerum: Editio princeps secundum codices manuscriptos*, ed. H. Boese, part 1, *Text.* (Berlin: Walter de Gruyter, 1973), 325–26; chap. 33; Bartholomaeus Anglicus, *De proprietatibus rerum* 17.26.

76. E. Ruth Harvey, *The Inward Wits: Psychological Theory in the Middle Ages and the Renaissance* (London: Warburg Institute, University of London, 1975), 27. See also James J. Bono, "Medical Spirits and the Medieval Language of Life," *Traditio* 40 (1984): 91–130; Simon Kemp and Garth J. O. Fletcher, "The Medieval Theory of the Inner Senses," *American Journal of Psychology* 106, no. 4 (Winter 1993): 559–76; and Simon Kemp, *Medieval Psychology* (New York: Greenwood Press, 1990).

77. Frank Klaassen, *The Transformations of Magic: Illicit Learned Magic in the Later Middle Ages and Renaissance* (University Park: Pennsylvania State University Press, 2013), esp. 89–113.

78. Julien Véronèse, ed., *L'Ars notoria au Moyen Age: Introduction et édition critique* (Florence: SISMEL, 2007), 42. English translation from Robert Turner, *Ars Notoria: The Notary Art of Solomon* (London, 1657), 11.

79. Véronèse, *L'Ars notoria*, 46.

80. Ibid., 44.

81. Ibid., 52.

82. Claire Fanger, "Plundering the Egyptian Treasure: John the Monk's *Book of Visions* and Its Relation to the Ars Notoria of Solomon," in *Conjuring Spirits: Texts and Traditions of Medieval Ritual Magic*, ed. Claire Fanger (University Park: Pennsylvania State University Press, 1998), 222–23.

83. See Claire Fanger, "Sacred and Secular Knowledge Systems in the 'Ars Notoria' and the 'Flowers of Heavenly Teaching' of John of Morigny," in *Die Enzyklopädik der Esoterik: Allwissenheitsmythen und universalwissenschaftliche Modelle in der Esoterik der Neuzeit*, ed. A. Kilcher and P. Theisohn (Munich: Wilhelm Fink, 2010) 157–75.

84. Claire Fanger and Nicholas Watson, introduction to John of Morigny, "The Prologue to John of Morigny's *Liber Visionum*: Text and Translation," ed. and trans. Claire Fanger and Nicholas Watson, *Esoterica* 3 (2001): 116–17.

85. Nicholas Watson, "John the Monk's *Book of Visions of the Blessed and Undefiled Virgin Mary, Mother of God*: Two Versions of a Newly Discovered Ritual Magic Text," in *Conjuring Spirits: Texts and Traditions of Medieval Ritual Magic*, ed. Claire Fanger (University Park: Pennsylvania State University Press, 1998), 195.

86. Fanger and Watson, introduction, 184.

87. Lea T. Olsan, "Charms and Prayers in Medieval Medical Theory and Practice," *Social History of Medicine* 16, no. 3 (2003): 343–66.

88. "Empericus in hiis egritudinibus est ut accipiantur isti duo versus et ligentur dextro brachio cum oratione dominica" [following line is expunged]. Munich, Bayerische Staatsbibliothek, Clm 28187, fol. 57v.

89. Catherine Rider, "Medical Magic and the Church in Thirteenth-Century England," *Social History of Medicine* 24, no. 1 (2011): 92–107; Michael D. Bailey, *Fearful Spirits, Reasoned Follies: The Boundaries of Superstition in Late Medieval Europe* (Ithaca: Cornell University Press, 2013), 148–94.

90. Olsan, "Charms and Prayers," 365–66.

91. "Et quibusdam medicorum visum est quod melancholia contingat a demonio Sed nos non curamus cum physicam docemus: si illud contigat a demonio aut non contingat: postquam dicimus quam si contingat a demonio sufficit nobis ut convertat complexionem ad coleram nigram et sit causa eius propinque colera nigra deinde fit causa illius colere nigre demonium aut non demonium." Avicenna, *Liber Canonis*, liber 3, fen 1, tractatus 5, chap. 19 (1522), 150r.

92. Rider, "Demons and Mental Disorder," 66–69.

93. Richard Kieckhefer, "The Specific Rationality of Medieval Magic," *American Historical Review* 99, no. 3 (June 1994): 813–36.

94. Claude Lecouteux, *The High Magic of Talismans and Amulets: Tradition and Craft* (Rochester, Vt.: Inner Traditions, 2014), 141. Originally published 2005 in French.

95. Hellmut Ritter and Martin Plessner, eds., *Picatrix: Das Ziel des Weisen von Pseudo-Magriti* (London: Warburg Institute, University of London, 1962), xx.

96. *Picatrix* 3.11. Latin text in David Pingree, ed., *Picatrix: The Latin Version of the "Ghayat Al-Hakim"* (London: Warburg Institute, 1986), 161. English translation is from John Michael Greer and Christopher Warnock, eds., *The Complete Picatrix: The Occult Classic of Astrological Magic Liber Atratus Edition* (Iowa City: Adocentyn Press, 2010), 210–11.

97. Claude Lecouteux, *The Book of Grimoires: The Secret Grammar of Magic* (Rochester, Vt.: Inner Traditions, 2013), 162. Originally published as *Le Livre des Grimoires* (Paris: Éditions Imago, 2002).

98. (Pseudo-)Albertus Magnus, *The Book of Secrets* 94, 37–38. See also Cantimpratensis, *Liber de natura rerum*, book 13, chap. 17, pp. 259–60, and Lynn Thorndike, *A History of Magic and Experimental Science*, vol. 1 (New York: Columbia University Press, 1923), 755.

99. Hildegard of Bingen recommends binding therapies to the head (*Causes and Cures*, book 3, "De amentia" and *Physica*, book 1.209). Thomas writes, "Rufus quidem cum reperitur, lunaticos sedat et insanos et languores diuturnos" (Cantimpratensis, *Liber de natura rerum*, book 13, chap. 17, pp. 259–60). Pliny, *Naturalis historia* 20.40.

100. *Picatrix* 3.11 (Latin text, 161; English translation in Greer and Warnock, *Complete Picatrix*, 209–10).

101. Caesarius of Heisterbach, *DM*, book 5, chaps. 28 and 32; Strange, *DM*, 1:311–12, 316.

102. For medieval theories of vision, see David C. Lindberg, *Theories of Vision from Al-Kindi to Kepler* (Chicago: University of Chicago Press, 1976).

103. Pliny, *Naturalis historia* 20.51, 20.81, 25.17; Konrad of Megenberg, *Buch der Natur* 5.44; Hartlieb, *Kräuterbuch des Johannes Hartlieb*, chap. 35, p. 83.

104. Kenneth F. Kitchell Jr. and Irven Michael Resnick, trans. and eds., *Albertus Magnus, "On Animals": A Medieval Summa Zoologica*, 2 vols. (Baltimore: Johns Hopkins University Press, 1999), 40.

105. Albertus Magnus, *On Animals* 22.20, 22.43, 22.60. English translation in Kitchell and Resnick, *Albertus Magnus*, 1466–67, 1507, 1516.

106. Albertus Magnus, *On Animals*, 22.58. English translation in Kitchell and Resnick, *Albertus Magnus*, 1514.

107. *Picatrix* 3.11. (Latin text, 161; English translation in Greer and Warnock, *Complete Picatrix*, 210).

108. Ibid.

109. Richard Kieckhefer, *Forbidden Rites: A Necromancer's Manual of the Fifteenth Century* (University Park: Pennsylvania State University Press, 1997), 196–99; 74–75.

110. Ibid., 75.

111. For environmental therapies and fragrant treatments, see, for instance, Gilbertus Anglicus, *Compendium medicinae* (Lugdunum, 1510), fols. 102v–106r, and Bartholomaeus Anglicus, *De proprietatibus rerum* (Frankfurt, 1601; repr. 1964), 7.5.

112. Caciola, *Discerning Spirits*, 157–58, 189.

113. Hildegard of Bingen, *Physica*, book 1.47 (Fern). Latin text in Hildegard of Bingen, *Physica: Liber subtilitatum diversarum naturarum creaturarum*, ed. Reiner Hildebrandt and

Thomas Gloning, 2 vols. (Berlin: de Gruyter, 2010), 1:83–84. English translation in Priscilla Throop, ed., *Hildegard von Bingen's "Physica": The Complete English Translation of Her Classic Work on Health and Healing* (Rochester, Vt.: Healing Arts Press, 1998), 29–30.

114. Nancy Caciola, "Mystics, Demoniacs, and the Physiology of Spirit Possession in Medieval Europe," *Comparative Studies in Society and History* 42, no. 2 (April 2000): 268–306; Caciola, *Discerning Spirits*, 2003.

115. Guibert of Nogent, *On His Life (De vita sua)*, book 1, chap. 13. English translation in Paul J. Archambault, *A Monk's Confession: The Memoirs of Guibert of Nogent* (University Park: Pennsylvania State University Press, 1996), 40; Latin edition in Guibert of Nogent, *Autobiographie*, ed. Edmond-René Labande (Paris: Belles Lettres, 1981), 90.

116. "Am ersten zuhalten das der tiuffel in kains menschen gemüt sol noch vernunft kain ding genöten noch pringen müg wann der mensch ist so edel und hoch geformiert von got und nach seiner pildung und form geschaffen." J. Hartlieb, *Buch aller verbotenen kunst*, Heidelberg Universitätbibliothek, CPG 478, fol. 3v. A modern German translation exists in Johannes Hartlieb, *Das Buch aller verbotenen Künste, des Aberglaubens und der Zauberei*, ed. and trans. Falk Eisermann and Eckhard Graf (Ahlerstedt: Param Verlag, 1989).

117. Bailey, *Fearful Spirits*, 148–94.

118. Catherine Rider, *Magic and Impotence in the Middle Ages* (Oxford: Oxford University Press, 2006).

Part 4 | MAGIC AND THE COSMOS

9

A LATE MEDIEVAL DEMONIC INVASION OF THE HEAVENS

Sophie Page

The starting point of this chapter is a particular moment in medieval intellectual history: the adaptation by late medieval Christian thinkers of the Aristotelian cosmological model and its implications for thinking about demons. I
will suggest that an increased feeling of human helplessness in the face of the
cosmological pressures outlined in the Aristotelian model led some writers
to suggest that demons worked with celestial influences to cause evil and suffering. My focus on this topic is part of a wider attempt to recover some of the
numerous cosmologies, both written and unwritten, that are likely to have been
conceived during the Middle Ages—since most, perhaps all, people have views
of some sort about the structure and operations of the universe.[1] My discussion
is also intended to contribute to ongoing historiographical debates about the
fifteenth-century coalescence of witchcraft mythologies and the textual strategies that led to some types of ritual magic having a positive reception at the end
of the Middle Ages.

As the Aristotelian model began to dominate medieval cosmological thought
and to be adapted to essential theological principles, the physical location of
demons seemed relatively unproblematic. At the center of this cosmological
model was Earth, enclosed first within the spheres of the four elements, then
the spheres of the seven planets, a crystalline sphere, and the empyrean heaven.[2]
The transparent celestial spheres, closely nested within one another like the
layers of an onion (a popular analogy of the time), moved with continuous
circular motions and exerted a powerful influence on the physical world. In the
outermost sphere was the most sacred part of this cosmos, the empyrean
heaven: the dwelling place of the highest group of angels, the saints, and Christ.
It had also once been the habitation of the fallen angels, before they had rebelled
against God and lost the war in heaven.[3] In the Aristotelian cosmological
model, the demons fell through the spheres, alighting deep in the earth's core

at the furthest point from God's natural location in the highest heaven (fig. 9.1). But as Aristotle's cosmology made a strong distinction between a perfect, unchanging celestial realm and the imperfect and corruptible region beneath the sphere of the moon, it was easy to imagine some demons, perhaps those who were less evil, swarming in a higher airy realm from which they converged on the physical world of men to tempt and torment them.[4]

The emphasis on general celestial influences on the earth in Aristotle's cosmological model enabled the art of astrology to find a large degree of acceptance in intellectual circles.[5] Astrology was the study of the movements and relative positions of celestial bodies in order to make predictions about human personalities, dispositions, and public and personal events. It included the belief that the planets could incline men to good or evil and negatively influence the course of events.[6] This had implications for medieval discussions of the origins of evil and human suffering because it raised the question of whether and how demons could provoke, manipulate, or make use of celestial influences. This chapter examines how three different kinds of medieval authors responded to this question and the different approaches to the medieval universe they subsequently proposed: theologians explaining the structure and operations of the cosmos, authors of literary and popular scientific texts exploring the origins of evil in the world, and writers of texts on astrology and magic identifying networks of power in the cosmos that could be manipulated by humans.

Theologians, Malign Planets, and Fallen Angels

In the medieval understanding of the cosmos, the planets, including the sun and moon, were thought to be moved by "intelligences," a subgroup of the angels, and to exert influence on the physical world in ways that were determined by the planets' nature and motion.[7] The term "intelligence" (*intelligentia*) applied to an angel associated with a celestial orb was an adaptation to the Aristotelian cosmos that followed the Arabic philosopher Avicenna. To preserve the key Scholastic notions of a good, omnipotent God and a perfect, incorruptible celestial region in this cosmological model, it was necessary to argue that demons could not move the planets or inhabit their spheres and that planets were natural celestial bodies that were not evil by nature or the direct cause of evil on earth. The need to clarify the relationship between planets and demons was made more pressing by theologians' awareness of the history of pagan worship of planetary deities and the contemporary circulation of both astrological texts that described malign planetary properties and magic texts

Fig. 9.1   Fall of the demons. London, British
Library, MS Egerton 2781, Neville of Hornby Hours
(1325–1350). Photo: British Library, London, UK /
Bridgeman Images.

that located morally ambiguous spirits, including demons, within the planetary spheres.[8]

The earliest medieval author to examine the relationship between celestial
influences and manifestations of evil in the physical world in detail was William
of Auvergne, bishop of Paris from 1228 to 1249 and an important theorist of
magic. William's views were based on his knowledge and condemnation of
ritual magic texts that assigned spirits to different parts of the heavens and
explained when and how to invoke them. In William's interpretation these
spirits are identified as demons who in the past had taken the names of the
planets in order to be thought to be celestial gods and in at least one case had
even been permitted by God to transform into a celestial body to trick men into
idolatry.[9] At the time he was writing, William thought demons tried to deceive
magical practitioners into believing that they had descended from heaven
when in fact they had no association with the celestial realm.[10] In contrast to

most of his contemporaries, William denied the existence of celestial intelligences, whether good or evil. Planets were natural bodies under the direction of a good Creator, and William vehemently criticized those who attributed evils (vices and sins) on earth to the planets and fixed stars.[11] His criticism focused particularly on the infamous planets Mars and Saturn, noted for their malign influences in medieval cosmological and astrological texts. This kind of criticism was compatible with the defense of astrology. William's comments were cited approvingly by the French theologian, cardinal, and author of astrological texts Pierre d'Ailly. His 1410 treatise *De legibus et sectis contra superstitiosos astronomos* argued that it was blasphemous against God to say that the planets were evil or to attribute evils like murder, thefts, fighting, and fraud to the influences of the planets.[12]

Most medieval thinkers accepted the idea of the natural celestial influence of the planets under the guidance of a good Creator. However, this idea raised two further questions: could demons manipulate the astral influxes descending from the heavens, and could they move the planets to influence events on earth? Several theologians, including Albertus Magnus and Thomas Aquinas, accepted that the first was possible. In his commentary on the *Sentences* of Peter Lombard, the theologian and natural philosopher Albertus Magnus considered the first question and argued that demons could manipulate celestial influences or take on the appearances of the planets in order to do three things: perfect the magical operation of a necromancer (*necromanticus*), make a magician (*magus vel Chaldaeus*) less fearful of them, and tempt practitioners into worshipping the planetary bodies.[13] Like William of Auvergne, Albertus's assessment of the relationship between demons and celestial influences was influenced by his reading of image magic texts (*libri imaginum*). He denied the assertion in such texts that spirits (in Albertus's interpretation, evil demons) inhabited the constellations and planets, but he thought that they worked with particular constellations and signs, presumably from a sublunary location. Albertus also uses surprisingly positive language when explaining this relationship, asserting, for example, that the superior bodies help demons (*superiora iuvant daemones*).

The art of astrology and the category of angelic movers provided new opportunities to explain the malign activities of demons. In his *Summa theologica*, Thomas Aquinas accepted the demons' use of the phases of the moon to work out when human brains were most moist and therefore susceptible to confusion (he suggests that they also do this in order to defame God's creature, i.e., the moon).[14] But he explicitly denied that demons could move the planets in order to influence events on earth in his important treatise *On Evil (De malo)*, probably published in 1272 toward the end of his life.[15] Aquinas argued that this was not possible because of their inferior spiritual nature and their culpable damnation.[16] The angelic movers did, however, provide a useful analogy for Aquinas's argument that demons had the ability to move material substances in the physical world: "as higher spiritual substances move higher heavenly bodies, so also lower spiritual substances such as devils can cause the locomotion of material substances."[17] In the fifteenth century the same analogy was used much more ambiguously by the Spanish theologian Alonso Tostado (ca. 1400–1455) to support the reality of the witches' flight to the sabbath. Tostado argued that demons could carry witches through the air to many places, by day as well as by night, on the basis that they are "equal in those natural parts to good angels," and whoever can move the heavens will also be able to move many people very quickly through the air.[18] By the early fifteenth century, then, the climate of increasing belief in witchcraft had magnified the threat of demonic power: a demon with the power to move a planet no longer seemed so incredible.

Idiosyncratic Cosmologies in Literature and Popular Science

The mainstream medieval cosmological model was formulated, circulated, and debated by university-trained scholars. Despite the tensions between some of Aristotle's ideas and medieval theology, and the dominance of the scholarly *quaestio* that privileged specific questions and debate over synthesis, the Aristotelian cosmos was a remarkably persuasive, popular, and long-lasting model. Cosmology was never an independent academic discipline, and academic syntheses of the mainstream model were rare, partly because the approaches of theologians and astronomers to the cosmos were not particularly compatible (astronomical data did not support an earth-centered cosmos). Instead, cosmological ideas and discussions flourished in diverse places, especially in works of natural philosophy, theology, astronomy, and medicine. Idiosyncratic cosmologies can also be found in these genres, as well as in visionary literature and poetic works, in heresy trials, in works of popular science, and in magic texts.

The need to make sense of the relationship between planetary influences and evil in the physical world was particularly pertinent to vernacular texts disseminating astrological ideas to general readers who were unlikely to be familiar with the theological explanations discussed above. Two creative, but nonetheless sophisticated, responses to the challenge of explaining the origins of evil and suffering are found in Chaucer's *Knight's Tale* (1380s) and the *Middle English Wise Book of Philosophy and Astronomy* (ca. 1400). In different ways both texts try to explain the relationship between planetary influences and demonic malice and activity in the context of a world overseen by an all-powerful and good Creator.

Chaucer's *Knight's Tale* is set in a mythological past in which the pagan deities Saturn, Venus, and Mars are divine actors worshipped by humans who seek their aid in various trials. Toward the end of the narrative, Saturn intervenes to resolve the apparently irreconcilable promises of Venus and Mars to help their respective human followers Palamon and Arcite, who are in love with the same woman. Arcite wins the tournament that will determine which knight will marry Emily, the idealized object of both knights' desire, but at the moment of his victory a "furie infernal" sent by Pluto erupts out of the ground and startles Arcite's horse, causing him to fall.[19] After his accident Arcite's body sinks into a Saturnine decline: it blackens, swells with clotted blood, and fills with a corrupting poison that cannot be expelled. Arcite's subsequent death, caused by the combined actions of Saturn and the god of the underworld, leaves Palamon free to marry Emily. The gods in this poem are literal deities, the channels of astrological influences and allegorical figures for time, wrath, and concupiscence, but at the violent resolution of the question as to which knight will marry Emily, their influence is joined to demonic causation. In keeping with this sense of combined malign forces, a strong sense of human helplessness in the face of cosmological pressures pervades the whole narrative.[20]

The proliferation of late medieval popular scientific texts circulating in vernacular languages from the fourteenth century were designed in part to meet this anxiety about the place of human beings in the cosmos, as well as to instruct and entertain.[21] They outlined the nature and structure of the cosmos to newly literate audiences and described the effects that men and women could expect the celestial bodies to have on their lives. There is a minimum of theoretical explanations in this genre and an emphasis on dramatic personified cosmological threats. For example, a brief text devoted to the planet Saturn begins, "Wite you nat, Saturne es ye heyest planet and Wichedeste."[22] This text goes on to outline zodiac signs in which "he has moste powere to fulfille his malice." But the cosmological material in scientific, utilitarian, and instructional vernacular prose was also carefully Christianized, for example, by locating Christ in the empyrean heaven, emphasizing the capacity of human free will to overcome planetary influences and linking biblical persons and events to astrological, chronological, and cosmological divisions such as the zodiac signs, days of the week, or days of the moon.

The Middle English *Wise Book of Philosophy and Astronomy* was a popular and relatively typical work in this genre, in circulation from around 1400.[23] It also illustrates the kind of idiosyncratic thinking that can emerge from the popularization of complex cosmological ideas. In the middle of the treatise, a debate by two philosophers on predestination and free will draws the unusual and radical conclusion that the evil influences of the planets originated in the fact that they were corrupted by the original fall of the demons through the zodiac signs and the planetary and elemental spheres. "The tenth ordre & þe heighist of þe ten heuen, [of þe which order] Lucyffer was heighist next God, þorugh his pride fill doun with many legyons & his felawis þt hilden with hym into þe deppist pitte of helle; & euerych of hem aftir thay hadde synnyd, summe fill heigher summe fill lower, wher thorugh the signes, þe elements, & þe planetis ben infecte & corupte. And by this cause summe ben yvell & sume ben good aftir þe influence & multitude of þe spiritis þat at þat tyme fill doun of þe tenth heuene."

In this interpretation of the origins of planetary evil, then, the fall of the demons corrupted the cosmos, much as the fall of man infected the physical world. This absolves God of responsibility for the planets' evil influences but undermines the Aristotelian idea of a pure celestial realm and the theological idea of the planets acting as God's instruments.

Cosmology and Ritual Magic

When we turn to learned magic texts, we find diverse cosmologies that have drawn their influences from Greco-Roman, Islamic, and Judaic ideas, as well as from Christian thinking. In this chapter I focus on one late medieval group of Christian authors in particular, whom recent historiography has called "author-magicians."[24] Author-magicians take a more scholarly approach to magic than other (mainly earlier) Christian authors of magic texts, providing general theories and philosophical justifications and producing summae of texts and genres under their own names rather than assigning them a mythical authorship to figures like Hermes or Solomon. Although the texts of my four authors did not circulate widely, they are viewed by historians of magic as significant because the theoretical basis of their discussion of magic seems to have been acceptable to the authorities and, with one notable exception, neither they, nor their works was condemned.

In short, like the other authors of magic texts, their primary concern was to set out the powers in the universe and explain to the reader how to access them. The author-magicians are, however, all experts in astrology, and their cosmologies integrate an astrological understanding of the cosmos with Christian and non-Christian ideas about spirits. Thus, they provide another perspective on the question of how astrology and demonology map onto each other in Christian thinking about the universe.

Michael Scot was a translator of Arabic treatises in the early thirteenth century, a significant disseminator of Aristotelian science in the Latin West, and an astrologer at the Court of Frederick II by the late 1220s.[25] He is arguably the first significant medieval author-magician, although other authors may have contributed to surviving versions of his most substantial work, the *Liber introductorius* (ca. 1220–35).[26] The *Liber introductorius* introduces beginning students of astrology to cosmological and theological ideas and includes discussions of magical practices and the location, nature, and role of demons.[27] It has a vague and loose structure, and surviving medieval copies differ in length, organization, and detail of content, but in general it is clear that Michael guided students of astrology toward two main attitudes to magic. On the one hand he expresses a distaste for necromancy, the deliberate conjuring of evil spirits who had been imprisoned by God in the physical realm. On the other, certain kinds of magic, such as the making of astrological talismans, are viewed positively, and he refers to angels and demons inhabiting the celestial realm who are very wise and will respond to questions.[28]

In his *Liber introductorius* Michael describes the Aristotelian model of nested spheres, unpacks the astrological dynamics of the planets' movement through the twelve zodiac signs, and shows an awareness of popularizing analogies that compared the cosmos to an egg or onion. As agents within and of these cosmological structures and movements, angels and demons created possibilities and dangers for the student of the science of the stars. Michael divides this science into *astronomia fabulosa*, *astronomia superstitiosa*, and *astronomia ymaginaria*.[29] The first category refers to poets' use of narratives to reveal knowledge of the heavens, the second offers a critique of astrologers who are overconfident in their predictions, and the third concerns the science of things that are visible not to the senses but only to the intellect. Michael gives two examples for his final category: the lines mathematicians extend from east to west and south to north, and the evil spirits who inhabit the air around these cardinal points. The spirits in these regions belong to the order of angels. In the south are princes who rule over carnal love, and in the north, princes of hatred and other evils.[30]

It seems likely that mathematical and astrological projections were thought to indicate the locations of spirits because their particular characteristics and powers lead them to inhabit parts of the cosmos with similar properties. The demons of the four cardinal points appear relatively frequently in later medieval magic rituals, theoretical treatises, and works critical of magic.[31] Their notoriety is indicated by their appearance in the 1398 condemnation of magic at the University of Paris, which gives a detailed description of a magic ritual in which four demon kings are invoked, then cites as an error the view that there were demon "kings" of the east, west, north, and south.[32] Critics of magic wanted to detach demons from associations with mathematical and astrological projections, regarding this as a distraction from their fallen status.

In a further deviation from this status, the *Liber introductorius* locates some demons in the spheres above the moon, that is, in the perfect, incorruptible celestial realm. Michael divides the demons into nine orders and three kinds depending on the extent of their evil, although he emphasizes that none are able to redeem themselves and return to the empyrean heaven. In his first reference to their location, Michael states that the fallen angels can be found in all the elements under the sphere of the moon, including that of water.[33] Shortly afterward he comments that the bad angels are limited to the spheres of air or fire, worse angels are present in or near the earth, and the worst of all are imprisoned in hell.[34] However, in his final comment on this subject in the prologue, he places the worst in hell, and the next in evil in all the elemental spheres. The least bad category of demons—who are also the most wise and powerful—are now said to have remained in the ether (*remansit in ethere*) from the sphere of fire right up to the starry heaven.[35] This places demons in the celestial realm, though they are excluded from the empyrean heaven, whose perfection by comparison with the other celestial spheres is emphasized in Michael's commentary (ca. 1231–36) on the popular handbook of cosmology, the *De sphaera* of John de Sacrobosco.[36]

Elsewhere in the *Liber introductorius* Michael is more expansive about the nature of the fallen spirits who remained in the heavens. He locates demons in the constellations, which is significant given his view that all the star groups, not just the planets, influenced the physical world. Michael asserts that the wise demons (*demones sapientissimi*) who inhabit groups of stars will give answers if conjured correctly.[37] They can be found in the thirty-six decans, arcs of ten degrees in each zodiac sign, which together constituted the ecliptic (the apparent path of the sun relative to the stars). The decans had Egyptian origins and were introduced into Western Europe in Arabic magic texts, including the *Picatrix*.[38] In the *Liber particularis*, the location of the celestial demons (*spiritus maligni*) is extended to the figures of all forty-eight classical constellations, and Michael notes that if they are properly invoked, they will be effective for experiments relevant to their particular properties.[39] Although the demons' names are not given, Michael refers the reader to a *Liber Adam* for these. In another passage in the *Liber particularis*, the wise spirits in their images (*in faciem*) are assigned to certain malicious (*malignus*) works like lust and hatred;

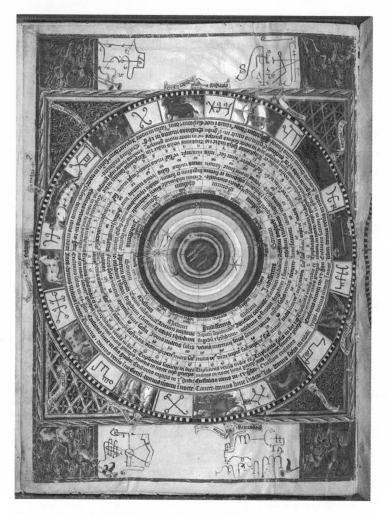

Fig. 9.2 Cosmological diagram with magical characers. Munich, Bayerische
Staatsbibliothek, ms Clm 826, fol. 1r. Photo: Bayerische Staatsbibliothek.

however, one of the three early fourteenth-century manuscripts of this text,
clearly uneasy with this characterization, replaces "malignus" with "magnus"
(great), thus softening the moral characterization of these spirits.[40] The celestial "images" in which demons are present are visualized as intricate magical
characters in a cosmological diagram from a fifteenth-century astrological
anthology (fig. 9.2) that belonged to Wenceslas IV, king of Bohemia, and contains an excerpt from the *Liber introductorius*.[41]

In Michael's *Liber de signis et imaginibus celi*, a description of the heavens
(all the constellations and planets), one constellation in particular is singled
out as the location of demons: Ara, also known as Putheus (the well) and as

Fig. 9.3 The constellation Putheus from Michael Scot's *Liber de signis et imaginibus celi*. Munich, Bayerische Staats-bibliothek, MS Clm 10268, fol. 83v. Photo: Bayerische Staatsbibliothek.

Sacrarius (the shrine) (fig. 9.3).[42] Illustrations of this constellation depict spirits emerging from it, clearly identifiable as demons in most manuscripts, although the text simply refers to them as very wise and cunning spirits (*spiritus*). Michael's commentary on the meaning of this constellation begins with its associations in ancient myth (*astrologia fabulosa*), then moves on to the role of its spirits in magic and divination (*astrologia ymaginaria*). Ara represents a place where the gods made sacrifices. According to Michael, perhaps with this ritual association in mind, the spirits inhabiting it are better than all others for conjuring, and they are called down by diviners (*vates*), practitioners of pyromancy (*pyromantia*), and necromancers (*nigromantici*). This commentary is typical of Michael's approach to images of the planets and constellations, which emphasized their astrological significance over their representation of classical myth.[43] The fiery altar with its connotations of pagan ritual made demons natural inhabitants of the constellation. At least two copyists felt uneasy enough about celestial demons to omit the depictions of spirits altogether, however, and when the physician and astrologer Louis de Langle used the *Liber de signis* as a model for his *De figura seu imagine mundi* (1456), he replaced the demons with angels.[44]

Michael's references to necromancy and divination were part of his intention to reveal hidden things in the cosmos rather than a sign of approval of this art, but later authors were more explicit in linking the location of spirits to advice on effective conjuring techniques. Our next author to consider the place of demons within cosmological structures and in relation to astrological rules was Francesco Stabili, better known as Cecco d'Ascoli, whose ideas about demons can be traced in his commentary on John de Sacrobosco's *De sphaera*. Like Michael Scot, Cecco's interest in demons and magic appears in the context of broader cosmological and astrological concerns. Cecco was also a professional and experienced astrologer, both in the sense of teaching astrology at the University of Bologna from 1322, and in his role as personal astrologer to Duke Charles of Calabria, lord of Florence (from 1326). Unlike the other authors discussed in this chapter, however, his writings brought him to the attention of the Inquisition, and he was burnt at the stake in 1327.[45] This has been seen by modern scholars as at least partly because of his construction of an astrological necromancy (or astrological nigromancy), that is, an unacceptable blending of the science of the stars and the conjuration of demons.

Cecco's demons are explicitly fallen spirits (intelligences outside the grace of God) who were expelled from heaven into the air and the spheres of the other elements.[46] In an approach similar to Michael Scot's *astronomia ymaginaria*, Cecco locates the fallen demons under significant astronomical and astrological divisions of the heavens and earth and links their activity to planetary movements.[47] He places incubi and succubi under the circles of the ecliptic and suggests that the activities of these demons intensify when there is a conjunction between the three superior planets in one of the two signs of the solstice (Cancer and Capricorn). Demons can also be found at the North and South Poles, and four superior spirits, each with twenty-five legions, under the four angular signs.[48]

The locations of demons in Cecco's commentary suggest that their natures have drawn them to astrologically appropriate parts of the cosmos, perhaps with the implication that they are able to manipulate celestial influences flowing down in these places, an idea that is more explicit in later writers on magic. Although surviving copies of Cecco's commentary refer only to demons below the sphere of the moon, his reference to demonic intelligences (a term normally reserved for an angelic order) and to the demon Floren as originating in the cherubim order and as having a most noble nature (*spiritus nobillissimus naturus*) seem to have led the Inquisition to suspect him of placing demons in heaven. The chronicler Giovanni Villani (d. 1348) states that the first error mentioned in Cecco's inquisitorial condemnation of 1324 was the proposition that evil spirits were generated in the celestial spheres (*spere de sopra*) and that these could be constrained by invocations made under appropriate constellations to do many wonders.[49] In fact, Cecco's ideas about the relationship between astrology and magic are not that different from the other authors I discuss, and it is possible that other reasons, such as his outspokenness or his drawing up of a nativity of Christ, led him to be the first university scholar to be condemned.

Antonio da Montolmo's *De occultis et manifestis* (On occult and manifest things) was influenced by Cecco's commentary on the *Sphere* of Sacrobosco, but in many ways his discussion of the demonic manipulation of celestial influences goes much further.[50] Like my other examples, Antonio had a background in astrology. He taught astrology and medicine at the University of Bologna from 1387 to 1392, and he was the author of an astrological text on nativities. Similarly to Cecco's commentary, but with a more serious agenda, Antonio da Montolmo's *De occultis et manifestis* seems to be a response to the complexity and oppressiveness of celestial influences in the Aristotelian cosmological model.[51] Like the other authors discussed above, he makes sense of these influences by linking them to demonic activity. But he also seeks more explicitly to empower men and women by explaining how the intelligences incline them to particular actions, and how they can use this knowledge for their own ends. Antonio's cosmological emphasis, like Cecco's, is primarily on vertical relationships between the heavens and earth. The good intelligences, which belong to the angelic order of powers, inhabit the planetary orbs. The intelligences deprived of divine grace inhabit the physical world but are defined by their relationships with particular parts of the heavens.

Antonio says that he wrote his treatise *De occultis et manifestis* to encourage his readers to contemplate (*contemplare*) and speculate upon (*speculare*) the highest and most significant things in nature that are knowable to humans, so their souls could strive for assimilation with the Prime Mover. The highest knowable things for Antonio were the intelligences, a category that included a subgroup of the fallen angels, which lived beneath the sphere of the moon but worked with the astral influxes (*influxus* or sometimes *radii*) of the celestial bodies. Antonio's second order of intelligences are "noble substances created with knowledge and nobility," fallen angels retaining many of their angelic faculties.[52] They are deceitful, quarrelsome, constrained by divine power, and full of malice. But, more unusually, they work with celestial influxes and thus (like the planets) have the power to incline the soul to good and evil. In Antonio's cosmology, the close relationship between these Intelligences and the celestial bodies was instituted by the devil, here called "the very wise first intelligence," who is knowledgeable and skilled at using the sacred influxes (*sacri influxus*) of the heavens.[53] In order to better deceive mankind, Antonio says, the first intelligence appointed some of his own princes to work with the celestial influences who were particularly suited to their own natural qualities.

Each prince dwells in the location where he can make best use of his constellation's astral influxes. When these influxes enter the bodies of created beings, the princes work with them to incline the soul to vice. For example, Fornifer, whose office is under the signs and stars of Venus, uses influxes from this part of the heavens to incline people to lust. In this case one could perhaps imagine a relationship between the planet and the terrestrially dwelling intelligence who is similar to that between the fallen angel Zephyr and the goddess Venus in the late medieval romance *Perceforest*.[54] The characters in this romance believe in the distant influence of Venus on their lives and loves. They pray to her for protection, celebrate her feasts, and give offerings at her temple. But it is the shapeshifting trickster spirit Zephyr who provides the supernatural assistance to enable lovers to come together, relationships to be consummated, and the line of noble rulers of England to be perpetuated. And, just as many of Zephyr's interventions appear to have positive outcomes for good governance, so Antonio suggests that the channeling of planetary influences may be used to provoke "honest love between two good people," as well as "concupiscent love."[55] The application of magic to both good and evil ends is typical of Arabic astral magic, on which these later author-magicians drew and in which the goal of the operation is the fitted to the planetary natures without reference to moral consequences.

An astrological approach to the celestial realm (as Antonio puts it, *celum secundum astrologos*) determines the location of the intelligences. Like Cecco d'Ascoli, Antonio situates four orders of intelligences in the four parts of the world (East, West, South, North), where they are placed under the four cardinal signs that divided heaven according to the astrologers (Aries, Libra, Capricorn, Cancer).[56] There are also intelligences standing beneath (*constitue*) each planet and an order of angels called "altitudes" located under every zodiac sign and whose power varies as the celestial bodies move toward and away from aspects with each other and as the sun travels through the zodiac.[57] The planetary intelligences have the power to cause actions appropriate to their planetary influxes, such as melancholy, treachery, and deceptions in the case of Saturn. Like William of Auvergne and Albertus Magnus before him, Antonio argues that the ancients worshipped these intelligences as their gods, a practice he says is reflected in the invocations and prayers recorded in astral magic texts. Most of Antonio's treatise is concerned with who can see, invoke, and constrain the intelligences and how worthy and knowledgeable practitioners can understand and manipulate the powers of both stars and spirits. Thus, the correspondences between star and spirit set in place by the devil to hide his machinations beneath the natural influxes of the heavens can also be used against him by those well trained in astrology and magic.

Giorgio Anselmi was a professor of medicine at the Universities of Parma and Bologna in 1448–49. His imposing treatise on magic, the *Opus de magia disciplina*, also gave demons a significant cosmological role.[58] Anselmi came to magic with a background in astrology and an interest in the making of images. Like Antonio da Montolmo he argued that magic (or *superstitio*, defined as the religious observance of superior things) should form part of the study of "the wise and good philosopher" who investigated nature's secrets for the advancement of mankind and in order to become to closer to God.[59] Anselmi's treatise gives a central but uncontroversial place to the influence of the motions of the celestial bodies on the inferior and corruptible world. What is radical, however, is that he gives a causal role to the four elemental spheres in his cosmology and assigns demonic movers to them.[60]

Anselmi's demonology incorporates ideas drawn from Platonic texts and astral magic but is grounded in mainstream Christian demonology. The influence of Apuleius's *De deo Socratis* and Calcidius's commentary on Plato's *Timaeus* is reflected in the fact that Anselmi's demons have passible natures, that is, they can suffer and some have the capacity for goodness. Like the other authors I have considered, he assigns the most power, wisdom, and capacity for goodness to the demons located highest in the cosmos. In Anselmi's cosmos, these are the demonic intelligences who rule the planetary bodies as subordinates to the angelic movers.[61] But there are also enough evocations of Christian demonology in Anselmi's text to give it a veneer of orthodoxy. His chapter on the names of demons begins by naming the most famous: "Satan or Satan the Transgressor, Lucifer, Temptator, Antichristus, Bahal, Bolgephor, Behel, Belzebuth, Belial, Behemoth, Lemathan."[62] His demons are rational, immortal beings, with exceptional knowledge and powers of movement and the ability to possess humans and deceive them with illusions and misleading dreams. Among diverse kinds of spirits, the worst are said to be evildoers, rebellious, impious, and polluted (*malefici et rebelles et impii et scelerati*), and all demons are distinguished from the blessed angels (*angeli benedicti*).[63]

Anselmi's demons are diverse in nature, and distinctions between them are often confusing, especially as he gives some subcategories of demons the nomenclature of "angels" (*angelus*), and it is not clear whether his demonic intelligences inhabit planetary orbs or simply manipulate their influence from the physical world. Anselmi divides demons into four types (celestial, ethereal, aerial, and those who are earthly or of a moist nature).[64] Sublunary demons may be good or evil: the airy kind love humans and elevate prayers, the moist kind are envious of humans and try to cause harm. Both can be invoked by humans in the art called the "greater theurgy." In Anselmi's cosmology the upper spheres are ruled by the traditional nine orders of angels, but the four elemental spheres and the four cardinal directions have their own spirits (*reges et principes*), who incline men to good or evil depending on their own nature. Demons also rule over the zodiac signs, planets, and Caput and Cauda draconis.

The planetary demons are particularly powerful: they have the power to introduce, take away, advance, and alter all things and events that fall under the nature of their planet.[65] These demons seem to be sublunary inhabitants who work with the celestial influxes. In his only specific example of planetary demons, Anselmi notes that the demon of Saturn and his army work principally in the parts of the world, the days and hours, the people and animals, and the things and events that partake of the nature of Saturn and are moved by its motions. Of course, Saturn was a particularly appropriate example to link to the activities of demons. Anselmi also suggested that the demons of a particular planet had power over men when this planet dominated their natal horoscope or the horoscope of the solar revolution (a horoscope drawn up on successive birthdays and compared with the natal chart).[66] Antonio da Montolmo had a similar proposal, namely, that every human being was allocated at birth an evil angel belonging to the order of altitudes (intelligences standing under the twelve zodiac signs). But his view was that men born under particularly impressive planetary aspects would be able to dominate the spirits.[67]

Anselmi and Montolmo were writing after the failure of "the angelic turn" in ritual magic (exemplified by magic texts like the *Ars notoria*, *Liber flores*, *Almandal*, and *Liber iuratus*) to convince the authorities that the ritual invocation of angels for particular ends was an acceptable form of Christian theurgy.[68] Although some angelic magic texts continued to circulate relatively widely, their frequent condemnation and, in particular, the 1323 burning of the Bene-

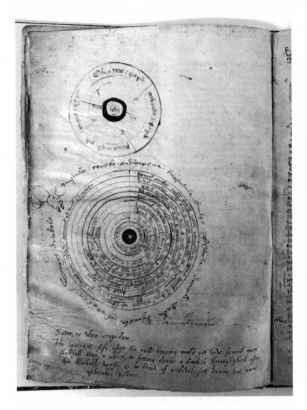

Fig. 9.4 Cosmological diagram (fifteenth century) with a
sixteenth-century drawing of a demon and demons' names
(Manstul, corebo, pudigopema, farantula, dalpo, perinela[?]
dunali, Balba, dymeta, Fardpeon, Snaye diabole) added
around a hypothetical "eighth sphere." University College
London, MS Lat. 12.

dictine John of Morigny's *Liber florum* (a revision of the *Ars notoria*) under-
mined the idea that they would eventually be accepted as orthodox mystical
technologies. In this context of condemnation, demons may have seemed a
more appropriate and malleable subject than angels for magic rituals, especially when a practitioner had astrological expertise and an idiosyncratic interpretation of the cosmos. It is not clear whether it was this impulse toward the
ritual exploitation of demons or the feeling of anxiety discussed earlier that led
a sixteenth-century scribe to draw a demon's head and write demons' names
around a hypothetical "eighth sphere" in a fifteenth-century cosmological diagram, pictorially locating them in heaven (fig. 9.4).

Conclusion

Diverse cosmological interpretations have been examined in this essay, including the ideas that demons moved, inhabited, or impersonated the planets, were helped by or worked with the stars, infected them as they fell through the spheres, or simply manipulated their influences from potent locations in the physical world. We can see these attempts to bring together celestial influences and demonic activities as a rationalization of the origins of evil and suffering that happened despite theologians' attempts to preserve the heavens as the creation and instrument of a good God. In the process of considering how the stars and demons combined to bring harm to humans, some authors suggested that the heavens were more corrupted than the mainstream cosmological model proposed, and others made the demons less evil. Two further conclusions are possible here. We can see these approaches to the Aristotelian model as reflecting and contributing to the increasing emphasis on demonic power, malice, and capacity to intervene in human life, an emphasis that can be tracked from the emergence of thirteenth-century demonology to the fifteenth-century coalescence of witchcraft mythologies. But we should also note that despite their sensitivity to cosmological pressures, magic texts on demons and the stars emphasized human agency. Higher spirits can be conjured so that they answer the practitioners' questions; astrological techniques are used to try to understand how, when, and where demons inclined people to good and evil; and knowledge of the cosmos can even be used to draw humans closer to God. Like the witchcraft mythologies, this positive approach to magic also had a future in the sixteenth century and beyond.

NOTES

1. On the universal potential for thinking cosmologically, see Edward Grant, *Planets, Stars, and Orbs: The Medieval Cosmos, 1200–1687* (Cambridge: Cambridge University Press, 1994), 40. I follow Grant's suggestion (p. 44) that to qualify as cosmological a text must discuss the operations of the celestial region.

2. See Grant, *Planets, Stars, and Orbs,* for a comprehensive discussion of the structure of the Aristotelian cosmos, which is presented in a simplified outline here.

3. The most significant biblical passage is Rev. 12:7–9.

4. For some scholastic debates about whether demons lived in the air or underground, see J. B. Russell, *Lucifer: The Devil in the Middle Ages* (Ithaca: Cornell University Press, 1984), 180.

5. On celestial influences, see Grant, *Planets, Stars, and Orbs,* 569–71, and on their relationship to astrology, see J. North, "Celestial influence—The Major Premise of Astrology," in *"Astrologi hallucinati": Stars and the End of the World in Luther's Time,* ed. P. Zambelli (Berlin: de Gruyter, 1986), 45–100.

6. A good overview of the dissemination of astrological texts and ideas in the Middle Ages can be found in Hilary Carey, "Astrology in the Middle Ages," *History Compass* 8 (2010):

888–902; on medieval critics of astrology, see Michael D. Bailey, *Fearful Spirits, Reasoned Follies: The Boundaries of Superstition in Late Medieval Europe* (Ithaca: Cornell University Press, 2013), chaps. 2 and 3.

7. The question of whether Aristotle's planetary movers could be reconciled with Christian angels was resolved in favor of this position by the end of the thirteenth century. See H. A. Wolfson, "The Problem of the Souls of the Spheres," *Dumbarton Oaks Papers* 16 (1962): 67–92; see also Grant, *Planets, Stars, and Orbs*, 469–87.

8. On astral magic, see especially Nicolas Weill-Parot, "Astral Magic and Intellectual Changes (Twelfth–Fifteenth Centuries): 'Astrological Images' and the Concept of 'Addressative Magic,'" in *The Metamorphosis of Magic: From Late Antiquity to the Early Modern Period*, ed. Jan N. Bremner and Jan R. Veenstra (Leuven: Peeters, 2003), 167–87.

9. William of Auvergne, *De universo* 2.3.8, in *Opera omnia*, 2 vols. (Aureliae: F. Hotot, 1674), 1:1033–34.

10. William of Auvergne, *De universo* 2.3.6, 1:1026.

11. William of Auvergne, *De universo* 1.1.46, 1:654–57. The chapter title is "Contra illos, qui dicunt planetas esse malos."

12. Pierre d'Ailly, *De legibus et sectis contra superstitiosos astronomos*, in *De imagine mundi* (Louvain, 1483), fol. 43r. See also fol. 44v, which focuses particularly on Saturn and Mars.

13. Albertus Magnus, *Super sententiarum*, in *Opera omnia*, ed. August Borgnet, vols. 25–30 (Paris: Louis Vives, 1893–94), lib. 2, dist. 7, art. 9, p. 158a.

14. Thomas Aquinas, *Summa theologica* 1.114.4.

15. Thomas Aquinas, *De malo*, ed. Brian Davis, trans. Richard Regan (Oxford: University Press, 2001). Question 16 updates Aquinas's previous comments on demons to present a full and original body of doctrine centered around twelve articles.

16. Ibid., q. 16, tenth article, proposition and answer 4.

17. Ibid., q. 16, tenth article, answer (pp. 936–37).

18. Alonso Tostado, *Commentary on the Gospel of Matthew*, q. 47 ("An homines portentur aliquando a diabolo per diversa loca"), in Joseph Hansen, ed., *Quellen und Untersuchungen zur Geschichte des Hexenwahns und der Hexenverfolgung in Mittelalter* (Bonn: Carl Georgi, 1901), vol. 2, no. 22, p. 106.

19. Chaucer, *Knight's Tale*, part 4, 1.2684. For the association of Pluto with Christian demonic hierarchies, see also Martianus Capella's suggestion that Pluto rules the air from the moon to the earth (*De nuptiis*, book 2) and Dante's location of Pluto in the seventh circle of hell (*Inferno* 7.1).

20. See especially Chaucer, *Knight's Tale*, part 3, ll. 1303–33 for a lament against the cruelty of the gods.

21. My research has so far focused on the Middle English material, for which see especially G. R. Keiser, ed., *A Manual of the Writings in Middle English, 1050–1500*, vol. 10, *Science and Information* (New Haven: Connecticut Academy of Arts and Science, 1998) and later supplements; L. Braswell, "Utilitarian and Scientific Prose," in *Middle English Prose: A Critical Guide to Major Authors and Genres*, ed. A. S. G. Edwards (New Brunswick: Rutgers University Press, 1984), 337–87; and L. E. Voigts, "Scientific and Medical Books," in *Book Production and Publishing in Britain 1375–1475*, ed. J. Griffiths and D. Pearsall (Cambridge: Cambridge University Press, 1989), 345–402.

22. Rules for the canicular days, London, British Library, MS Sloane 213 (ca. 1400), fol. 111v.

23. *The Middle English* Wise Book of Philosophy and Astronomy: *A Parallel-Text Edition*, ed. Carrie Griffin (Heidelberg: Universitätsverlag Winter, 2013). The *Wise Book* survives in two recensions and thirty-four manuscripts.

24. See Nicolas Weill-Parot, *"Images astrologiques" au Moyen Âge et a la Renaissance: Spéculations intellectuelles et pratiques magiques (XIIᵉ–XVᵉ siècle)* (Paris: Honoré Champion, 2002), 602–38; Jean-Patrice Boudet, *Entre science et nigromance: Astrologie, divination et*

magie dans l'occident médiéval, XIIᵉ-XVᵉ siècle (Paris: Publications de la Sorbonne, 2006), 393–408; and Julien Véronèse, "La notion d' 'auteur magicien' à la fin du Moyen Âge: Le cas de l'ermite Pelagius de Majorque (° v. 1480)," *Médiévales* 51 (2006): 119–38.

25. On Michael Scot, see especially see especially Charles Burnett, "Michael Scot and the Transmission of Scientific Culture from Toledo to Bologna via the Court of Frederick II Hohenstaufen," *Micrologus: Natura, scienze e società medievali* 2 (1994): 101–26, and Lynn Thorndike, *Michael Scot* (London: Thomas Nelson and Sons, 1965).

26. For a discussion of the difficulties relating to the authorship of this text, see Burnett, "Michael Scot."

27. The *Liber introductorius* comprises three books, the *Liber quattuor distinctionem*, the *Liber particularis*, and the *Liber physiognomie*. On the long and short versions of the *Liber introductorius*, see Glenn Michael Edwards, "The Two Redactions of Michael Scot's 'Liber introductorius,'" *Traditio* 41 (1985): 329–40. The *Liber particularis* is edited by Oleg Voskoboynikov in *Archives d'histoire doctrinale et littéraire du Moyen Âge* 81 (2014): 249–384. For the first two books, I have referred to the copy of the *Liber introductorius* in Munich, Bayerische Staatsbibliothek, Clm 10268.

28. On Michael's attitude to magic, see Paolo Lucentini, "L'ermetismo magico nel secolo XIII," in *Sic itur ad astra: Studien zur Geschichte der Mathematik und Naturwissenschaften; Festschrift für den Arabisten Paul Kunitzsch zum 70. Geburtstag*, ed. Menso Folkerts, Paul Kunitzsch, and Richard Lorch (Wiesbaden: Harrassowitz Verlag, 2000), 420–24, and Boudet, *Entre science et nigromance*, 181–86.

29. *Liber introductorius*, prologue. Clm 10268 fol. 17r.

30. Ibid.

31. Examples of magic texts are the Munich necromantic manual, the *De tribus figuris* and the *De quattuor anulis*. On these spirits, see Richard Kieckhefer, *Forbidden Rites: A Necromancer's Manual of the Fifteenth Century* (University Park: Pennsylvania State University Press, 1998), 155–56; J-P. Boudet, "Les condamnations de la magie a Paris en 1398," *Revue Mabillon* 12 (2001): 121–58; Nicolas Weill-Parot, "Dans le ciel ou sous le ciel? Les anges dans la magie astrale, XIIᵉ-XIVᵉ siècle," in *Les anges et la magie au Moyen Âge*, ed. Henri Bresc and Benoît Grévin (Rome: L'École française de Rome), 760–61.

32. This is in article 25 of the condemnation from the University of Paris, as described in Boudet, "Condemnations de la magie," 139.

33. *Liber introductorius*, prologue, Clm 10268 fol. 4v.

34. Ibid.

35. Ibid., fol. 13v (first column): "Et quod dicitur malum remansit in ethere ab igne supra usque ad orbem stellarum et hii sunt ceteris sapenciores in omni sciencia et potenciores ac minus mali noxa superbie."

36. Lynn Thorndike, ed., *The Sphere of Sacrobosco and Its Commentators* (Chicago: University of Chicago Press, 1949), lecture 4, p. 283.

37. *Liber introductorius*, prologue, Clm 10268 fol. 16v: "ymaginum dicit quia inter 12 signa conprobantur esse quedam ymagines numero 36 in quibus reperiuntur demones sapientissimi conmorari, et qui si rationaliter coniurentur dant responsa et multa reducunt ad conplementum eorum que sibi firmiter inponuntur, licet non omnia."

38. On decanic spirits, see D. Greenbaum, *The Daimon in Hellenistic Astrology: Origins and Influence* (Leiden: Brill, 2015), 213–22, and Benedek Láng, "Puissances ou démons? Les images décaniques dans le Picatrix de Cracovie," in *Images et magie: Picatrix entre Orient et Occident*, ed. Jean-Patrice Boudet, Anna Caiozzo, and Nicolas Weill-Parot (Paris: Honoré Champion, 2011), 137–48.

39. *Liber particularis*, chap. 34; p. 299 in the text edited by Voskoboynikov.

40. Ibid., prologue; p. 262 in the text edited by Voskoboynikov.

41. On this manuscript, see David Juste, *Les manuscrits astrologiques latins conservés à la Bayerische Staatsbibliothek de Munich* (Paris: CNRS Éditions, 2011), 86–87, and Eric Ramírez-

Weaver, "Creative Cosmologies in Late Gothic Bohemia: Illuminated Diagrams and Memory Tools for the Court of Wenceslas IV," *Manuscripta* 54, no. 1 (2010): 21–48.

42. Silke Ackermann, ed., *Sternstunden am Kaiserhof: Michael Scotus und sein Buch von den Bildern und Zeichen des Himmels* (Frankfurt am Main: Peter Lang, 2009), 234.

43. D. Blume, "Michael Scot, Giotto and New Images of the Planets," in *Images of the Pagan Gods: Papers of a Conference in Memory of Jean Seznec*, ed. R. Duits and F. Quiviger (London: Warburg Institute, 2009), 129–50.

44. See Kristen Lippencott's online "Saxl project" for a list of sixteen manuscripts of the text with illustrations of Ara. http://www.kristenlippincott.com/assets/Uploads/00-Ara-web -master-file-13-March-2016.pdf.

45. Thorndike, *Sphere*, 343–411. See also Nicolas Weill-Parot, "I demoni della Sfera: La Nigromanzia cosmologico-astrologica di Cecco d'Ascoli," in *Cecco d'Ascoli: Cultura, scienza e politica nell'Italia del Trecento; Atti del convegno di studio svoltosi in occasione della XVII edizione del Premio internazionale Ascoli Piceno* (Rome: Istituto storico italiano per il Medio Evo, 2007), 103–34.

46. Thorndike, *Sphere*, 39.

47. For a more detailed discussion of Cecco's references to demons, see Nicolas Weill-Parot, "Cecco d'Ascoli and Antonio da Montolmo: The Building of a 'Nigromantical' Cosmology and the Birth of the Author-Magician," in *Routledge History Handbook of Medieval Magic*, ed. S. Page and C. Rider (London: Routledge, forthcoming).

48. Thorndike, *Sphere*, chap. 2, p. 397.

49. Giovanni Villani, *Cronica*, ed. Giuseppe Porta (Parma: Guanda, 2007) book 11, chap. 41.

50. On Antonio da Montolmo, and on his influence by Cecco, see Nicolas Weill-Parot with Julien Véronèse, "Antonio da Montolmo's *De occultis et manifestis* or *Liber Intelligentiarum*: An Annotated Critical Edition with English Translation and Introduction," in *Invoking Angels: Theurgic Ideas and Practices from the Thirteenth to the Sixteenth Century*, ed. Claire Fanger (University Park: Pennsylvania State University Press, 2012), 219–93, and Weill-Parot, "Cecco d'Ascoli and Antonio da Montolmo."

51. On Antonio's knowledge of Cecco's commentary, see Weill-Parot, "Antonio da Montolmo's *De occultis*," 224–26.

52. *De occultis et manifestis*, prologue, 2: "Ipse equidem Intelligentie substantie nobiles in scientia ac nobilitate create consistent."

53. *De occultis et manifestis*, chap. 5.

54. *Perceforest*, ed. Gilles Roussineau, Cinquième Partie, 2 vols. (Droz: Geneva, 2012). Published in separate volumes between 1987 and 2014.

55. *De occultis et manifestis*, chap. 5, section 4: "amor honestus, qui est inter bonos, et amor concupiscentie."

56. *De occultis et manifestis*, chap. 1.

57. *De occultis et manifestis*, chap. 3.

58. This text survives in only one sixteenth-century manuscript in Florence, Biblioteca Medicea Laurenziana, MS Plut. 44, cod. 35 (1501–10). On Giorgio Anselmi de Parme, see especially Lynn Thorndike, *A History of Magic and Experimental Science* (New York: Columbia University Press, 1923), 4:242–46, 677–79; Charles Burnett, "The Scapulimancy of Giorgio Anselmi's 'Divinum opus de magia disciplina,'" in *Magic and Divination in the Middle Ages: Texts and Techniques in the Islamic and Christian Worlds* (Aldershot: Variorum, 1996), 63–79; and Weill-Parot, *Images astrologiques*, 622–38. I am grateful to Merlin Cox for sharing a copy of his excellent unpublished thesis on Giorgio Anselmi; see Merlin Cox, "Similar Stars and Strange Angels: Giorgio Anselmi's Astrological Magic" (master's thesis, Warburg Institute, 2016).

59. These ideas are found throughout the text but see especially the first part of the introduction (fols. 1–4).

60. *Divinum opus de magia disciplina*, fol. 37v and fol. 40v. The following discussion draws primarily on part 2 of this text (fols. 37–52), which examines the nature, substance, variety, numbers, and role of demons.

61. A "two-mover" model was considered by some scholastic authors; for example, Thomas Aquinas's commentary on the *Sentences* assigns two movers to each heaven—a conjoined mover (or soul) and a separated mover (or intelligence) (II, Sent. d. xiv, q. 1, a. 3).

62. *Divinum opus*, fol. 49v.

63. *Divinum opus*, fols. 44r and 49v.

64. *Divinum opus*, fol. 42v: "sunt eorum quidam celestes, alii etherei, aerii quidam, et alii humecti."

65. *Divinum opus*, fol. 47v: "hii qui planetis supposit sunt habent posse indando et auferendo et promovendo et alterando res omnes et accidentia quae natura sua planeta idem."

66. *Divinum opus*, fols. 47v–48.

67. *De occultis et manifestis*, chap. 3.

68. On angelic magic, see especially Fanger, *Invoking Angels*.

10

SCHOLASTICS, STARS, AND MAGI:
ALBERT THE GREAT ON MATTHEW 2

David J. Collins, S.J.

The thirteenth-century Schoolman Albert the Great had much to say about the wise men who appear in the second chapter of the Gospel according to Saint Matthew. His commentary runs about thirty-five times the length of the evangelist's own report. His enthusiasm is not unique. The story of wise men journeying from the East to Bethlehem and their adoration of the Christ Child has fascinated Christian believers from its first-century origins to the present day. The narrative has enticed readers not only by what it tells—of learned men from far away following a moving star that they knew to signal the birth of a great Jewish king—but also by what it does not. Details that Matthew did not clarify—such as what a magus was, how many they were, and where exactly in "the East" they hailed from—quickly piqued the curiosity of readers. The readers are further left on their own to conclude how the magi had become so learned, how they knew what the star meant, why they decided to follow it, and why this inspiration—this capacity to anticipate the birth of a new Judean king and the desire to give him homage—had been offered to them, and why indeed in such odd conjunction with a very different sort of person, the shepherds, as reported in another gospel. And yet another problem—one more vexing to a curious reader in eras earlier than our own, a reader whose familiarity with night skies, out of necessity and opportunity, made the usual movements of celestial bodies common knowledge—was the question of what kind of star could possibly move so unnaturally from south to north and then to south again, eventually to "stand over where the boy was" in Bethlehem.[1]

The author wishes to thank Georgetown University's Medieval Faculty Colloquium, where the chapter was presented in draft, and especially to his colleagues Tarmo Toom; G. Ronald Murphy, S.J.; Jo Ann Moran Cruz; and Sarah McNamer for their subsequent written comments. The author is also grateful for the comments of the press's anonymous readers.

By the time Albert turned to the passage, Christian believers—scholarly and ordinary—had had over a millennium to develop conventions of what needed clarifying, just as they had had time to speculate about explanations and allow various degrees of consensus to arise. The speculations, whose origins can often be traced back to the earliest Christian centuries, were commonly derivations from other biblical insinuations and were affirmed in the writings of Christian theologians as early and prominent as Tertullian (155–240) and Origen (184–253). That there were three magi and that they were kings, for example, were ideas of ancient origin and commonplaces in Albert's day. High medieval biblical commentaries repeated such answers, justifying them with reference to the other biblical passages and the authority of the church fathers. Albert's own commentary included many such appeals to earlier exegetical works, as when he explained the magi's Babylonian origin, named the Old Testament character Balaam as the source for the easterners' recognition of the star's significance, and offered a rationale for the three gifts.[2]

Just as the abundance of the accumulated interpolations provided later medieval commentators a resource to draw from in their own exegesis, it also constitutes a backdrop that can draw our own scholarly attention to the variations and novelties of particular commentators through the Middle Ages and beyond. A striking example of how divergence from convention can draw attention to original thought and ecclesiastical significance can be found in Bernard of Clairvaux's twelfth-century interpretation of the magi's three gifts to the Holy Family. The nearly unanimous patristic and medieval interpretation of the gifts—gold, frankincense, and myrrh—was figurative: gifts foreshadowed the Christ's royal, priestly, and sacrificial roles, respectively. In contrast, Bernard (1090–1153) proposed, after a dismissive wave of the hand toward the more theologically sophisticated explanations, that the magi may have offered gold because of the Holy Family's obvious poverty, myrrh because of the rough straw against the infant's delicate skin, and frankincense because of the stable's stench.[3]

Bernard's populist touch has no correlate in the life and work of Albert the Great, and their respective relationships with the burgeoning Aristotelian revolution in Western circles of learning could not be more different—think only of the contrast between Bernard's fearsome conflict with the twelfth-century's preeminent logician Abelard (1079–1142) and Albert's paternal cultivation of his protégé Thomas Aquinas (1225–1274). Exactly on this latter point—the development of Scholastism beyond established patristic and monastic traditions of theological and philosophical reasoning—we find divergences between Albert's insights into the story of the magi and Bernard's. I propose they are of two noteworthy sorts. The one set consists of formal aspects that distinguish

Albert's commentary from earlier patristic and monastic exegesis, as also from the Renaissance and Reformation exegesis to follow. These characteristics provide evidence of an approach to biblical commentary that correspond to stylistic developments typical in and around the thirteenth century and contribute to our understanding of a properly Scholastic mode of exegesis. The other set derives from distinctive scholarly interests of Albert's: more than that of his peers, his commentary is shaped by the latest concerns and tools of the natural philosopher, even as the commentary is still fundamentally theological. The two fields shared a common requirement that their arguments meet contemporary conventions of logical disputation derived from Aristotle; their crucial distinction resided in the philosopher's prohibition from appealing to the Bible as an authority and the theologian's obligation. Albert's work stands out in this respect. Careful examination of this aspect of his commentary enriches our appreciation of the breadth of larger issues that biblical commentary as a genre could be informed by as well as speak to.

One passage, which will be returned to, offers us a taste of Albert's approach as both characteristically Scholastic and distinctively natural philosophical. In introducing the magi as protagonists, he followed his predecessors in addressing the problem of whether the magi were sorcerers, not only in the sense of being expert at illicitly attaining hidden knowledge but also at manipulating the natural world to wicked ends. The well-established answer was, unsurprisingly, no; and Albert, also unsurprisingly, affirmed that conclusion. His exposition, however, includes a taxonomy of magical practitioners such as had not been so thoroughly or originally outlined since Isidore of Seville's seventh-century *Etymologies*. Albert brought magicians into relief with an emphasis on distinction and definition, modes of argument that could not be more characteristically Scholastic. His explication begins not with the typical direct assertion of what magi were but rather outlines and defines what they were *not*, that is, "not mathematicians, enchanters, sorcerers or necromancers, soothsayers, augurers, or diviners,"[4] a contrast that is finalized with reference to the natural sciences, which definitely distinguishes between what is superstitious and what is rational.

Staying attentive to the typically Scholastic and the uniquely "Albertine" contours of the commentary promises significant results: first, Scholastic biblical commentary remains an underexploited resource for the intellectual and cultural history of the Middle Ages and has been neglected in comparison to the greater excitement that the earlier patristic, monastic, and subsequent Renaissance and Reformation exegetes inspire in historians of the Bible. And second, Albert's approach represents an expansion to the customary "literal" approach to biblical exegesis. This literal sense of the Bible, as famously described in the seminal research of Henri de Lubac,[5] includes geographical, chronological, linguistic, and indeed sometimes natural-philosophical determinations of persons, objects, and events in the scriptures. Albert incisively deployed the most current natural learning, especially in the field of astronomy, to explain who the magi were, how they knew what they knew, and what this star they were following was.

This investigation into Albert's understanding of Matthew 2 proceeds in four steps. First, an assessment of the exegetical *status questionis*, in general and regarding Matthew 2, hangs the backdrop of precedent in front of which Albert's interpretations and rationales can be judged as typical or novel. Scholarship on the biblical commentaries in this central medieval period is incomplete. Thus, ascertaining trends in interests and approach is itself a worthwhile investigation regardless of Albert's continuities with and divergences from them. Second, I turn to Albert's commentary on Matthew 2 to verify its characteristic Scholastic aspect and its distinctively natural-philosophical one. Third, I sketch out its limited traces in subsequent commentaries, an exercise that is, nonetheless, consequential for sharpening our understanding of Scholastic exegesis. And fourth, I assess Albert's analysis for its implication for Western Christian thought on the natural world and the knowledge it contains. To be kept in mind throughout are the two fundamental characteristics I wish to impute to Albert's commentary: that it is distinctively Scholastic, and that it is unique in the kind and degree of its natural-philosophical concerns shaping it.

The Backdrop

Albert began composing his commentary on Matthew in 1257, the year he returned to Cologne for a period of lecturing at the Dominican priory. It will be recalled at least as a matter of coincidence that the archbishopric of Cologne had been in possession of the relics of the magi since Rainald of Dassel had forcibly brought them back from Milan in 1164. The building of the new cathedral, with the purpose of housing the new reliquary, had begun in 1248 and was underway as Albert wrote. By this time, interpretive commonplaces offered clarifications to the ambiguous points in the gospel narrative and interpolations to silent ones. Many of these commonplaces have histories that date to the earliest years of Christian reflection on the gospels. Here I will attempt to establish in two steps a rough, early thirteenth-century "standard" reading of Matthew 2 to serve as a benchmark against which to evaluate Albert's work. The first step looks to Aquinas's *Catena aurea* for an outline of patristic and monastic precedents; the second, to the commentaries on Matthew 2 composed in the two centuries leading up to Albert's day.[6]

Catenae were epitomes of scholarly work on a particular theme, and they were commonly composed to demonstrate mastery of the authoritative theological literature in a specific field. A scriptural catena is a verse-by-verse epitomization of earlier biblical commentaries. In turn, catenae could be pedagogically useful in reflecting scholarly precedent. Thomas's scriptural catena covers the four gospels and incorporates excerpts from nearly one hundred commentaries of both Greek and Latin origin. The two purposes—demonstrating mastery and facilitating learning—can be inferred from the origins of Thomas's own *Catena*, which he completed by 1264: he composed it while serving as the conventual lector at Orvieto, the office responsible for providing instruction to friars not destined for university training; and he presented it to Pope Urban IV that same year. Compiled above all for propaedeutic purposes by one of the era's leading theologians, the *Catena* offers a reliable overview of the patristic and early medieval monastic tradition of commentary on Matthew 2, as understood by thirteenth-century students of the Bible. Albert's commentary slightly antedates Aquinas's *Catena*; Thomas's close scholarly relationship with Albert implies that the interpretive world Thomas laid out in his *Catena* is the same one Albert had in mind as he composed his own commentary.

The *Catena aurea* proposes the following: citing the ninth-century monk and bishop of Mainz, Rabanus Maurus (780–856), it describes the magi as philosophers who inquired into nature rationally and were not *malefici*, that is, wicked practitioners of magic. It cites the *Glossa ordinaria* (which will be returned to below) in identifying the magi as kings but points out that identification of their number as three is a speculative derivation from the number of gifts. It cites the tenth-century monk Remigius of Auxerre (841–908) and others to indicate the ambiguous geographical origins of the magi, naming Chaldea and Persia as possibilities, and Pseudo-Chrysostom (fifth century?) to suggest they may have been the Priscilianists, adherents of an ascetical, prophetical movement originating on the Iberian Peninsula in the fourth century.[7] The magi's mode of travel, which could have included dromedaries and Arabian horses, and time of travel, which ranged from thirteen days to two years, are raised through quotations from Jerome (347–420) and Pseudo-Chrysostom.[8]

Many authors—Augustine (354–430) most of all—are excerpted in consideration of the nature and meaning of the star. An excerpt from the bishop of Hippo serves to remind that celestial signs cannot determine fate but might reflect divine will. A passage on the horoscopic significance of the star much quoted in other medieval commentaries comes from Pseudo-Chrysostom, namely, "The point of astrology [*astronomiae*] is not to learn from the stars who is born; but from the hour of their birth [*nativitatis*] to predict the future. These magi did not know the time of the birth so that they would know the future from it, but the converse: They said, 'we saw his star.'" In short, the magi's reading of the star's meaning was not future- but past-oriented and thus *not* astrological. Another passage from Pseudo-Chrysostom raises the question of whether the star really was a star. Several key attributes suggested it was not: it was visible in the day as well as at night, it moved along its own course from east to west, and it became irregularly invisible, as for example over Jerusalem long enough for the encounter with Herod.[9]

These interpretive passages attend to the literal sense of scripture, whose goal, as can be seen in the examples themselves, was the ascertaining of simple facts. Thomas as readily epitomized the more theological concerns from the earlier theology, or what de Lubac summarized as the spiritual senses of scripture: allegorical, linking testimony of the Old Testament to the New; tropological, providing moral guidelines; anagogical, foreshadowing the end-time. Along these lines, Thomas cited Gregory the Great, who had explained the distinction between the angel's verbal announcement of the Messiah's birth to the shepherds, understood to be Jewish, and the nonverbal sign, the star, offered the wise men, assumed to be gentile, by citing the Jews' more rational familiarity with God's revelation. A sentence from Leo the Great proposes that the many stars of the promise to Abraham foreshadowed the one star signaling the Christ to the pagans. A passage from the *Glossa ordinaria* explains that the magi lost sight of the star in Jerusalem because they turned to a lesser source—Herod and his Jewish scholars. Thomas presented the speculation over the three gifts at length, not only recounting the Christological interpretation described above but also elaborating it with Gregory's description of gold as typifying wisdom; frankincense, prayer; and myrrh, mortification.

The patristic and monastic tradition as sustained into the thirteenth century, through catenae but also through direct engagement with patristic and early monastic texts, struggled with a more precise identification of the magi—where they were from, the cause and purpose of their interest in the star and whom it signaled, the nature of the star itself, the knowledge it betrayed, and the ways that this knowledge could have been recognized. Theologians from the eleventh century through the thirteenth continued producing biblical commentaries on the gospels, as on all parts of the Bible. Though heavily informed by the earlier authors, these high medieval works belong unmistakably to another epoch. Scholasticism, as we now know it, is the form of philosophical inquiry characteristic of Western higher learning from the eleventh century to the sixteenth. Its principal characteristic is a confidence in dialectical reasoning (logic) as the foremost tool for interpreting texts, ascertaining truth, and resolving conflicting truth claims. The appeal of logic developed hand in hand with an exuberance for the thought of Aristotle as well as for interpretations of Aristotle that had developed in Muslim and Jewish centers of learning in the Mediterranean world. Scholasticism shaped all fields of learning in the medieval university, including both theology and the study of the natural world. Method is more characteristic of it than content, and what scholarship the Scholastics produced encompassed a wide range of opinions on specific questions and inspired several distinct and rival schools of thought. Renaissance humanists and sixteenth-century church reformers eventually dislodged Scholasticism from its position of dominance, objecting in various ways and for various reasons to the preeminence of dialectical analysis in learned discourse. Even to the extent that the commentaries of the High Middle Ages can be associated with Scholasticism, what can be said generally can be said in particular of biblical commentary: conclusions on matters of philosophical and theological importance have, as a rule, greater continuity than discontinuity with their antecedents. That is to say, high medieval thinkers, Scholastics included, can be counted on to have drawn heavily from and developed squarely upon earlier medieval thought rather than to have rejected it.

Despite the recognition that Scholasticism has enjoyed in modern scholarship as the keystone of high medieval thought and university life, its approach to biblical commentary has attracted little attention. The inattention, though not without exception, has several explanations. Patristic and Reformation exegetics, for example, have won closer scrutiny. The study of biblical commentaries emerged in departments of Christian theology, where the theological reflection of the church fathers—the earliest generations of theologians—has enjoyed universal preeminence and where historical exegetics were more the interest of Protestant theologians than Catholic ones. To the Protestant theologians, medieval theologizing of any sort was a diversion from the next preferred era of theological reflection initiated by the sixteenth-century Reformers; Catholic theologians considered Scholasticism's dogmatic theology and philosophy more momentous than its exegesis. Consequently, biblical commentaries produced from 800 to 1400 are among the least studied.

The state of research into high medieval exegesis benefits, nonetheless, from the groundwork laid out in the distinguished scholarship of Beryl Smalley and Henri de Lubac;[10] and many studies on particular texts, problems, and theologians put building blocks in place for understanding the exegesis of this period and a scholastic approach to the Bible.[11] This literature allows us to continue establishing the precedents for the interpretation of Matthew 2 by turning to three benchmark-setting expositions of the gospels:[12] the commentary in the

Glossa ordinaria by Ralph of Laon,[13] the *Enarrationes in Evangelium Sancti Matthaei* (of uncertain authorship),[14] and Peter Comester's *Historia Scholastica*.[15] All three writings emerged from the exegetical school of Laon. Laon's perspective is generally contrasted to that of its rival exegetical school, the Abbey of Saint-Victor, the former favoring the more literal interpretations of the scriptures, the later the more spiritual. Regardless of this key difference, the activities of the two schools intersected at many points: Saint-Victor's founder, William of Champeaux (1070–1121), had been a student of Laon's premier exegete Anselm (1050–1117); and leading biblical commentators in later generations, Hugh of Saint-Cher (1200–1263) and Nicholas of Lyra (1270–1349), drew deeply from both schools of exegesis.

Four sets of particular interests shape the three expositions and relate them to the earlier materials. All three attempt to specify who and what the magi were. They concur that the magi were three in number and were kings. These assertions necessitate appeal to other passages in the Bible outside of the gospels. Ralph of Laon elaborated little beyond that; the *Enarrationes* proceed to distinguish *magi* from *malefici*, describing the magi as *sapientes astrologi*, "authorities in the workings of the heavens" and surely not "sorcerers." Ralph associated the threesome with the sons of Noah; Peter Comester associated them with all the "peoples of the earth." References to peoples—Arabs, Chaldeans, Persians, and Sabeans—and geographical features such as the Sabean River and Mount Sinai suggest crudely a point of origin on the Persian Gulf or elsewhere in the Arabian south. Whereas a strict reading of Matthew 2 gives no direct indication of the magi's gentilism, no patristic or medieval commentator presumes otherwise.[16]

The second set of concerns, with attendant claims, pertains to the star. The star in Matthew 2 is reported as "appearing" at a certain point of time; it is deduced by the magi as giving indication of the birth of the new king of the Jews and thus gives the magi their motive to follow it first to Jerusalem and then to Bethlehem. The medieval authors share a common concern over when the star appeared relative to the birth. All reject the possibility that the star appeared before the birth, and they propose instead that the magi were able to arrive from southern Arabia in two weeks thanks to their Arabian horses and dromedaries. Indirectly, the authors further pondered how the star moved in the sky, a problem in the light of the day's astronomical convention that stars do not move relative to one another. Given the suggested route taken by the magi—from southern Arabia to Jerusalem, and then to Bethlehem—however, the commentators had to allow for the anomalous, even miraculous, movement of the star along the celestial orb, with an excuse that the text itself is ambiguous.

A third set of concerns, related to the second, can be categorized as epistemological: how did the magi know what they knew? Along these lines, there
are two central questions: How did they know what and whom the star signified, and why did they decide to follow the star? These questions find no explicit
answers in the gospel itself. The *Enarrationes* offers a magus's expertise in
reading the stars. Both other works sketch an appreciation that stars signify
prominence. Ralph of Laon explained to his readers axiomatically that new
stars make known new men.[17] Though their expertise made the magi suited to
reading the stars, the medieval commentators drew from precedent to explain
that the revelation of the Christ could be understood in the words of angels
to mere shepherds, but the lesser, mute star was required for the learned
magi. In an echo of Gregory the Great that Thomas repeated in his *Catena*,
angels reveal the birth *rationaliter*, the star does so *irrationaliter*. In any event,
with the angels' words and the star's silence, the revelation of the prophets, the
commentators observed, came to an end, and the further explanation is provided for the failure of Herod's scribes to discern the birth of the Savior from
the Jewish books and for the necessity for the magi to provide the details upon
their return through Jerusalem.[18]

Although it was clear to the Scholastic as to the earlier monastic and patristic authors that knowledge revealed through the star was good—how could
recognition of the Messiah be understood otherwise?—one more epistemological hurdle needed to be cleared: By what means did the magi come to that
knowledge, and was it moral? Medieval thinkers appreciated that certain truth,
about God as well as the natural world, could be hidden or obscured, and further that coming to the knowledge of hidden truths, though in principle good,
was also difficult. The possibility of demonic assistance was considered as wrong
as it was real. Practitioners of the mantic arts, and astrologers to the extent that
they sought knowledge through the study of celestial bodies and events, faced
this concern throughout the Middle Ages. Matthew 2 invited regular reflection
on the problem of knowledge gained from reading the stars. To this point the
Enarrationes addressed this point with the assertion that the nature of the Messiah's birth itself was beyond the capacity of demons, regardless of their usual
advantages over humans in such divination. The "kings" must have had prompting from another source.[19]

In the medieval literature, an interpretation of two parts emerged to explain
how the magi came to the knowledge of the star's significance. Usually the two
parts were presented in tandem, one leading to the other; sometimes only one
of the two parts was raised. One part began with a son of the first man Adam,
Seth, who traveled "east" with knowledge already then of a future Redeemer.
This knowledge was preserved through the generations by magi. The second

part turns to a different, post-Exilic character, Balaam, who appears in both the Old Testament and the New. He is introduced in the Book of Numbers.[20] Though a gentile, Balaam spoke as a prophet for the God of the Israelites. He lived east of the Jordan at the time when the Israelites were nearing the end of their wanderings out of Egypt. As they approached his native territory, a threatened king of Moab summoned Balaam to curse the Israelites. The king, Balac, made arrangements for the ritual cursing three times; and each time Balaam, responding to inspiration from the Israelite God, blessed them instead. In reaction to the king's increasing frustration, Balaam prophesied, "A star shall rise out of Jacob; and a scepter shall spring up from Israel, strike the chiefs of Moab, and waste all the children of Seth."[21] Although up to this point Balaam deserved later commentators' unequivocal admiration, he ultimately earns a mixed reputation by prompting Balac to connive to get the Israelites to curse themselves by encouraging their own debauchery and idolatry. The story concludes in Numbers: "Are not these they that deceived the children of Israel by the counsel of Balaam and made you transgress against the Lord by the sin of Phogor [idolatry], for which also the people was punished?"[22] The three references to Balaam later appearing in the New Testament draw on this negative image.[23] Regardless of the checkered scriptural testimony, medieval exegesis credited the wicked prophet with securing the messianic revelation and taking it with him to Arabia: Ralph of Laon wrote in the *Glossa* that the magi had heard of the future birth through the teachings of Balaam, drawing the connection between Balaam and the magi through Chaldea. The author of the *Enarrationes* remarked that Balaam's prophecy accounted for the initial movement of the star toward Jerusalem and then to Bethlehem.[24] And Peter Comestor added the detail that magi "were the successors of the teaching of Balaam, who knew the star through its wanderings, and the magi were so called for the greatness of their knowledge."[25]

Not only does the identification of Balaam as the source of the magi's knowledge absolve it of unwholesome origins, it also reinforces the star as an intended form of divine revelation to the gentiles. Whereas only the *Enarrationes* explicitly distinguish Balaam from *malefici*, all three works stress the distant geographical origins of the magi and impute to them status as gentiles. The purposefulness of the star as a sign of revelation to gentiles is further insinuated by the contrast sketched between the magi and the benighted scribes of Herod's court. It is emphasized once again at the moment of adoration in the stable when the commentators feel compelled to address Joseph's absence from the scene, as implied in the sentence "they found the child with Mary his mother" (Luke's account describes the shepherds going *cum festinatione* to find Mary and Joseph).[26] The *Glossa* and the *Enarrationes* explain his absence as preventing confusion to the gentiles over the baby's divine paternity.[27] Finally, the alien character of the magi is connoted by Peter Comester's lengthy elaboration of the names of the magi in Hebrew, in Greek, and in Latin.[28]

With the backdrop of extensive reliance on patristic interpolations to show that the magi's acquisition of this knowledge was moral and an intended revelation of the Christ to the gentiles, we can turn to Albert's own commentary on Matthew. His first step—after promising to respond to the six pertinent interrogatives *qui, quales, quanti, unde, ubi, qualiter* (who, what qualities, how many, whence, where, and what kind)—was to turn to a widely circulated patristic commentary on Matthew, the *Opus imperfectum*. Wrongly ascribed to John Chrysostom and likely penned by a fifth-century Arian, it proposes the magi's connection to the Magusaei, a Babylonian people.[29] Albert drew further from *Opus imperfectum* that Balaam's predictions and other prophetic writings, reputedly compiled by Adam and Eve's son Seth, were preserved by the Magusaei in a cave on Mount Victory. This knowledge was entrusted through the generations to the twelve most learned and respectable magi, who ultimately from the vantage of their highland retreat on Mount Victory spotted the star over the land of Jacob that marked the first step in the fulfillment of Balaam's prophecy.[30]

In turning to the magi themselves and what they were, Albert began as did his predecessors and contemporaries with the assertation that the magi were not sorcerers: *nec sunt magi malefici, sicut quidam male opinantur.*[31] But where other commentators moved on from that to other issues, Albert used the question of who and what these three magi are as an opportunity to explain at some length what magi in general are and are not: "Indeed magi, mathematicians, enchanters, sorcerers (or necromancers), soothsayers, augurers, and diviners are different from one another."[32] The mathematician, he continued, is of two sorts: one who studies "separation and abstraction" as is associated with the quadrivium,[33] and one who prophesies from the movement of celestial bodies. The former practice is "praiseworthy rather than objectionable." The latter is "sometimes good and sometimes bad," moral judgment being contingent on whether the prophecy was necessary or probable and on the nature of the knowledge's occultness: uncovering a maliciously placed poison would, of course, be always useful and good; but, he reminded the readers, predictions can also be the work of charlatans and quacks, and they require condemnation.[34] The caster of spells (*incantator*) uses animals, herbs, stones, and images to achieve his effects. The necromancer divines from the dead or from demons. The augurer divines from birds; the haruspex, from the entrails of sacrificed birds and animals. Albert addressed four mantic arts together: geo-, pyro-, hydro-, and aeromantics. Over and above these, there are soothsayers (*sortilegi*) and pythonic fortune tellers. None of these received revelation of the Christ Child, only the magi; and thus the moral status of the magi's learning and practices can be assumed, by contrast, to be good.

Albert's taxonomy, such as it is, warrants explanation: What are its sources, and how does it fit in the intellectual context that was intrigued by magic and concerned to classify it? The apparatus to the Cologne edition of Albert's works draws connections between Albert's classification, on the one side, and Jerome's commentary on Daniel and Isidore's *Etymologies*, on the other. It also points out passages in Albert's other works, such as his commentary on Isaiah and his *Metaphysics*, that define particular experts in the occult in similar ways.[35]

The most illustrative contrast is to Isidore's classifications in his early seventh-century encyclopedic work, *The Etymologies*. Isidore sketched his taxonomy under the heading "De Magis,"[36] and it offers both an overall organization and particular description of terms that Albert diverged from. First, Isidore developed a distinction between magicians whose functions are mainly ritual and those whose are divinatory, a distinction not maintained by Albert. Second, Isidore's taxonomy encompasses a wider field of magician than Albert's. Missing from Albert's list are the magicians of the Bible and classical literature, such as the Egyptian magicians, whom Moses battled, and Circe, the Greek goddess of magic. Isidore's explanations of the kinds of divination is also fuller: he includes for example *harioli*, whose knowledge, Isidore describes, comes from conjuring demons. Among astrologers, Isidore included not only *mathematici* and magi, but also made reference to *astrologi*, who read the stars, and *genethliaci*, who draft natal charts. *Horoscopi* distinguish themselves from the *genethliaci* by their comparative efforts at understanding the different fortunes of persons born at similar times. Third, Albert and Isidore defined several kinds of magician differently. Most relevant here, Isidore used "magi" as an umbrella term for all magicians and diviners, and he judged magi wicked by definition.

Given the influence of Isidore's work throughout the Middle Ages, his usages are striking where they diverge from ancient and late medieval consensus and especially where they do not correspond to legal definitions applied by spiritual and temporal authorities. The principal distinctions Isidore makes are between magicians, magical diviners, and diviners.[37] Isidore identifies three activities of magicians in ascending order of wickedness: those who perform illusions, such as Pharoah's magicians; those who raise the dead, such as the Witch of Endor; and those who engage in such evils as causing bad weather by agitating the elements, causing distress in men, and killing by the violence of their spells. Magical diviners include necromancers and hydromancers. Both straddle the fence between magician in the preceding sense and diviners. The efforts of the necromancer and the hydromancer aim at learning hidden knowledge—divination—but their divinatory methods are augmented by magical rituals, such as mixing the viscera of the dead with water while incanting. Isidore devoted considerable time to explaining the diviners, whose "magic" is the discovery of hidden knowledge through the interpretation of signs in natural objects. The distinction between the magician's manipulations and the diviner's interpretations is an important one to keep in mind, even as the historical agents in late antiquity and the middle ages were inconsistent. The moral quality of each of the two sets of practice warranted very different evaluations: the occult knowledge was there to be found, its uncovering was always in the first instance a matter of prudence and respect. Magic proper, however, was to effect something otherwise absent.

Finally, Isidore defined various practitioners differently. His organization already suggests different understandings of what some of the magical practitioners are. Albert, moreover, turned to drawing his taxonomy specifically to show how *the* magi are not magicians. For Isidore, however, magi ultimately belong to the third category of magicians—those who do evil. He explained, "magi are those who are popularly called evil-doers because of the magnitude of their crimes."[38] Later he touches on the discrepancy between the magi of the Bible and the magi in his taxonomy: "Now originally interpreters of the stars also used to be called magi, as we read of those who announced the birth of Christ in the Gospel; afterward they went only by the name *mathematici*. Knowledge of this art was permitted up to the time of the Gospel, so that after Christ had been born, no one ever again should interpret anyone's horoscope from heaven."[39]

The classicist William Klingshirn has concluded that Isidore maintained a distinction between diviners and magicians in his taxonomy that was becoming increasingly ambiguous in the early Middle Ages. Albert did not maintain the distinction six hundred years later. The distinct purposes of the writings explain part of the difference: Isidore was aspiring toward systematic classification, here on this subject as throughout the *Etymologies*. Albert, in the first instance, was explaining what the magi were with an eye to justifying what they knew and did as ipso facto good: a function of the unfolding revelation of the Christ Child. His first sentence of description underscores implicitly his purpose: the magi are not *malefici*.

In point of fact, Albert's terse beginning links him as much as it distinguishes him from Isidore. Isidore, after all, acknowledged the historical expertise of magi as astrologers before in effect ascribing to the term two meanings: a general meaning encompassing all magicians and diviners (and captured in the title of the section), and a specific term interchangeable with *malefici*. This tradition of signification had been handed down to Albert, who rejected it explicitly in his opening line. What follows is a meticulous distinguishing of magi from twelve other kinds of magician and diviner, whom Isidore had put under the umbrella term "magi." And third, Albert adopted the historical definition of "magi" that Isidore made reference to, but rejects the magi's degeneration over the centuries to magicians.

The object of a magus's study was also a matter of concern for the exegetes. In this regard, Albert was no exception. Albert identified five unusual characteristics of the star pursued by the magi. Each reveals links between natural knowledge, occult knowledge, and revealed knowledge of the natural world. First, regarding its "nature," this star was "perishable" (*corruptibilis*). It appeared and disappeared. Ancient and medieval astronomy understood stars to be permanent fixtures in the (outermost) celestial orb. Without a natural explanation, Albert explained the star's corruptibility theologically and symbolically: citing Paul's Epistle to the Corinthians, he pointed out that Christ himself was the light, thus rendering a new, permanent, natural star superfluous.[40]

Placement and motion were the next two irregularities. Placement (*situ*) refers to distance from earth; motion (*motu*) refers to its movement relative to other heavenly bodies. An ordinary star, by ancient and medieval reckoning, was affixed to the celestial sphere furthest from earth in the cosmos. Medieval Christian astronomers judged the Greek idea of celestial spheres compatible with biblical cosmology and used the biblical term "firmament" and the philosophical term "primum mobile" interchangeably. Affixed to this sphere, the stars did (and could) not move relative to one another. Astronomers following the geocentrist Ptolemy explained the movement of the stars en bloc with reference to the rotation of the primum mobile; Copernicus and other early heliocentrists explained this movement to the rotation of the earth. Both of these descriptions resulted in stars moving in arcs from east to west over the course of a day. But the star of Bethlehem moved, as Albert explained from the biblical text, in a straight line, first to the north (from Arabia to Jerusalem), then to the south (from Jerusalem to Bethlehem). Planets had earned a separate classification on account of celestial motion that, though regular, was not synchronous to the stars (or to one another). Each required its own celestial spheres to enable its distinctive wandering in the heavens. Retrograde motion—the occasional, apparent eastward motion of the planets—was the bane of geocentric astronomy: such reverse motion was a violation of the principle of unidirectional movement of celestial spheres, and Aristotelian physics could not support the mathematical solution of epicyclic movement as formalized by Ptolemy. But at least it could be mathematically described and thus predicted. By appearing and disappearing within a short timeframe and by not following a mathematically intelligible course, the star of Bethlehem corresponded to no known celestial body.

A hypothesis long circulated (and still does) that the star was in fact a comet. Comets attracted considerable attention in ancient, medieval, and early modern astronomy precisely because they seemed to appear and disappear according to no pattern.[41] Such irregularity insinuated that comets were atmospheric, sublunar phenomena; consequently, ancient and medieval astronomers treated comets more commonly in meteorological treatises than astronomical ones. Albert addressed these issues directly: the star of Bethlehem "was not at great heights with the other stars in the firmament. It was at a level closer to earth and within its atmosphere." Nonetheless, "it was not a comet," even though comets typically were understood to appear in conjunction with the birth and death of kings. The star of Bethlehem, by Albert's reckoning, needed to be understood as a divine intervention—something that the rest of his philosophical and theological work suggests should be very rare—and he cited images of God and light from the writings of Job and the prophets Malachi and Isaiah to explain himself.[42] In short, Albert argued, the star of Bethlehem was a star, but one that did not have the usual attributes of stars and thus had to be understood as a miracle.

After briefly celebrating the singular brightness (*claritas*) of the star, a characteristic that corresponded to the birth it signaled,[43] Albert turned to the star's fundamental import (*significatio*). Albert's lines are a reflection on the word "his," taken from the magi's answer to Herod that they came to Jerusalem because they have seen "his star" (*vidimus stellam eius*). In four respects, Albert wrote, the star is "His"—*efficienter*, because as God he created it; *figuraliter*, because everything about him radiates as a star; *obsequialiter*, because the pursuit of the star by the magi parallels the following that Christ is meant always to inspire; and *finaliter*, because the purpose of the star is only for Christ's praise and glory.

With these reflections, Albert turns from the astronomical to the theological. Up to this point, Albert had considered each characteristic of the star from a natural philosopher's perspective, grappling with the question of what this star was on the basis of its biblical description and with reference to what the state of astronomical science indicated should be the case. Albert admitted certain characteristics as rarities but explained how a correspondence to the accepted knowledge made sense of the rarity. Anomalies opened the opportunity for a more strictly theological consideration. His answers are a tour de force of medieval learning and take explicit advantage of his particular expertise in natural philosophy, giving his commentary at times a depth and vigor that one does not find in the earlier commentaries.[44]

As he discussed the *significatio* of the star, his analysis becomes more strictly theological. It is structured around, or rather creates, a web of connections between passages from the scriptures and Christian tenets that highlight the star's theological significance. Though a reading of this passage from the commentary does not resolve the vexing question of the balance between literal and spiritual interpretation as seen in the contrasting approaches developed by Beryl Smalley and Henri de Lubac, Albert's analysis of the star shifts here dramatically between a set of reflections (on nature, motion, and position) that are primarily literal readings, striking for their timely philosophical rigor and yet still with theological reference, to a pair of reflections (on clarity and meaning) that are decidedly spiritual.[45] The modes of interpretation favored in this passage are analogical and anagogical.

Finally, Albert's approach can be drawn into sharper focus with reference to four other commentaries, each representing a different aspect of later medieval exegetics, namely, those of the earlier, apocalyptic thinker Joachim of Fiore (1135–1202); of his student Thomas Aquinas; of Nicholas of Lyra (1270–1349), the author of the most widely circulated biblical commentary emerging from the later Middle Ages; and of Erasmus of Rotterdam (1466–1536), who, as a humanist, stood at the forefront of the movement to topple the theological Aristotelianism that the Scholastics, Albert the Great included, had succeeded in creating. All but Erasmus's obviously belong to the Scholastic tradition of commentary, but none of them exhibits the "literal," natural-philosophic precision or the interest in the natural-philosophical implications in the magi passage that Albert's does.

Joachim of Fiore ranks as the premier *prophetic* exegete in the Scholastic era.[46] His *Tractatus super quatuor Evangelia* covers the gospel story episodically, rather than verse by verse, but does indeed address the journey of the magi.[47] Joachim's interpretive insights distill to two. First, the magi and Herod contrast each other as humility and pride, and specifically in their ability (and inability) to recognize the significance of the star as knowledge and ignorance, the spiritual and the worldly, the true and the false, Christ and Anti-Christ. Second, a timespan for the Nativity episode is made analogous to, and thus supportive of, Joachim's epochal timeframe, the reputed twelve days separating Christ's birth from the magi's arrival (December 25 to January 6) corresponding to the twelve-hundred years separating the Nativity from Joachim's own day. Notably, the literal dimension of the scripture that occupied most patristic, monastic, and scholastic commentators—the geographical origin of the magi, the natural-philosophical and astronomical problems that had so attracted Albert's attention, and so forth—do not have a part in Joachim's reflections.

Thomas Aquinas, in addition to and after the *Catena aurea*, gave lectures on the Gospel according to Saint Matthew, likely in his second regency in Paris, 1268–1272. The title *lectura* suggests that trusted, note-taking auditors produced the *reportationes* from which a final text was produced. Thomas is not believed to have overseen the drafting of the final text. This method of transposition from lecture to text allows of course for differences, not easily detectible, between what was originally delivered and what we read today. In this particular case, Thomas's reputed commentary on the story of the magi is taken from the *reportatio* of Peter d'Andria.[48]

The *lectura* follows the *Catena* in relying on patristic commentators, but it also encompasses more of Thomas's own interpretation. His interpretive comments favor the literal and allegorical senses of the scriptures. On specific points: Aquinas dismissed the possibility that the magi had been sorcerers, asserting that in the East and in those times, magi were learned persons. He explained that the magi interpreted the significance of the star through ordinary and moral principles of astronomy, such as that the appearance of striking celestial phenomena can signify great terrestrial events, and that they benefitted from the insight brought to the East by Balaam, thus reaffirming the long-term connection of revelation through gentiles. Finally, Aquinas did indeed consider the nature of the star. It was, he had no doubt, a real star; but in order to account for its out-of-the-ordinary movements, he determined that it was of a different class from those created from the beginning: after all, it moved from north to south, moved without interruption, gave light even during the day, and could hover over a particular house. "Therefore it must be said that it was specially created in service of the Christ."[49] Of the three Scholastic exegetes examined here, Thomas spent more time considering the star from the perspective of astronomical knowledge, but he did so only in a derivative manner with reference to observations already made in other commentaries, and he came to the conclusion that the star was miraculous much more quickly than had his teacher Albert.[50]

The postils of Nicholas of Lyra were among the most widely distributed of the Middle Ages and printed through the end of the sixteenth century. Initially unaffected by the theological turmoil of Luther's Reformation, his postils enjoyed over one hundred printed editions between 1471 and 1600. Nicholas's interpretation is enhanced by his command of the Hebrew language and of Jewish commentary. His most popular work, the *Postilla litteralis*, covers nearly every verse of the Old and New Testaments and, as the title indicates, attends most closely to the literal sense of the Bible. *Postilla morales* (1339) followed. In the earlier work he addressed such issues of literal meaning as the nature of the star, the revelation it communicated, and the magi's ability to interpret it, but not from the expressly natural-philosophical or astronomical vantage that Albert had. Nicholas drew from the established patristic tradition that identified magi as men of learning, Balaam as the vehicle for ancient revelation's preservation "in the East," and the star as fundamentally a miraculous event.[51]

Though it is certainly important to avoid opposing Scholastics and humanists ham-handedly, Erasmus's *Paraphrase on the Gospel according to Matthew* offers a helpful point of contrast to the commentaries in the Scholastic style, and one especially opposed in style to Albert's. Drafted at the encouragement of the Swiss cardinal and leading humanist Matthäus Schiner (1465–1522) and published in Basel by Johannes Froben (1460–1527) in 1522, the *Paraphrase on Matthew* focuses on the Christological and soteriological implications of gospel passages. The spiritual senses of scripture appealed to Erasmus in their service to the change of heart that he understood as the transforming goal of the Bible. Mastery of the literal sense undergirded that higher purpose. Thus the mechanics of the star's movement, the magi's geographic origin and mode of travel, and the nature of their knowledge receive no explicit attention in the *Paraphrase*. Indeed Erasmus specified Balaam's role in the transfer of occult knowledge to the East only in the revised edition of 1534.[52] Instead, he intimated the incipient *philosophia Christi* to be found in the deportment of the magi over against Herod's arrogance and fear. Along these same lines, "simplicity" is the text's watchword, applied as it is to the devotion of the magi and the scene at the stable. In short, the fluid narrative style and heavy tropological emphases in Erasmus contrast with the style and interpretive lenses employed by the Scholastic exegetes and accordingly represent constitutive differences between humanist and Scholastic exegesis. Moreover, the absence of the natural-philosophical evaluation, such as was at the heart of Albert's commentary, in Erasmus's *Paraphrase* suggests yet another difference.[53]

The comparison of Albert's commentary to these others of the later Middle Ages adds to the contrast that exposes the continuities and novelties of his interpretation of Matthew 2. Albert hewed closely to standard interpretations—patristic, monastic, and scholastic—in understanding the theological significance of the magi's journey to and return from Bethlehem as an affirmation of God's revelation to the gentiles. The questions he brought to the text and the areas he identified as inviting freer speculations likewise corresponded to interpretive interests of commentators both before and after him. At the same time, his commentary cannot be confused with those of late Antiquity or the Renaissance. Most obviously, his manner of posing questions and offering definitions distinguished him from his predecessors, and his concern for the literal sense distinguished him starkly from the humanist commentaries like

Erasmus's that followed. Distinctive even among Scholastics, finally, was his advanced, naturalist approach to the literal sense of the passage. The star, whose workings had indeed attracted the interest of earlier Church Fathers, now became the opportunity for Albert to apply the newest understandings of how the heavens worked, shaped as they were in his century by the rediscovered natural-philosophical writings of Aristotle and the abundant further studies by Muslim and Jewish scholars in subsequent centuries. The striking contribution of Albert's commentary on the story of the magi is its highly advanced astronomical reflection on the star, its workings vis-à-vis the event it signaled, and the magi's ability to recognize that significance. He drew on the earlier interpretive traditions, rejecting them on no major point, yet exploited the gospel pericope with a set of scientific questions and insights that was particular to his era. These latest astronomical insights, or indeed more crucially the importance granted these insights for biblical commentary, gave Albert a way to produce new reflection on the questions of what the star was and how it worked as a mode of revelation. The goodness of the star's revelation, furthermore, provided Albert the opportunity to revisit the quandary of who practiced magic and how related practices should be distinguished and evaluated. The results give evidence of a Scholastic both typical in his exegesis and decidedly singular in his expertise.

NOTES

1. Albert's complete works can be found in Alberti Magni, *Opera omnia: Ad fidem codicum manuscriptorum edenda apparatu critico notis prolegomenis indicibus instruenda / curavit Institutum Alberti Magni Coloniense* (Münster: Aschendorff, 1951–). This is known as the Cologne edition, of which the *Super Matthaeum* is vol. 21, pts. 1 and 2. I will abbreviate this as Colon., followed by volume, part, page, and line number as required. Two other collected works cited in this chapter are the *Patrologiae cursus completus*, Series Graeca, ed. Jean-Paul Migne, 162 vols. (Paris, 1857–86), abbreviated as *PG*; and *Patrologiae cursus completus*, Series Latina, ed. Jean-Paul Migne, 217 vols. (Paris, 1844–64), abbreviated as *PL*.

2. Wilhelm August Schulze, "Zur Geschichte der Auslegung von Matth. 2, 1–12," *Theologische Zeitschrift* 31 (1975): 150–60; Michael Andrew Screech, "The Magi and the Star (Matthew 2)," in *Histoire de l'exégèse au XVIᵉ siècle*, ed. Olivier Fatio and Pierre Fraenkel (Geneva: Droz, 1978), 385–409; Richard C. Trexler, *The Journey of the Magi: Meanings in History of a Christian Story* (Princeton: Princeton University Press, 1997), 3–6; Tim Hegedus, "The Magi and the Star in the Gospel of Matthew and Early Christian Tradition," *Laval théologique et philosophique* 59 (2003): 81–95. Albert's commentary on Matt. 2 can be found at Colon. 21.1:44–65.

3. Bernhard of Clairvaux, *Sämtliche Werke*, ed. Gerhard B. Winkler, 10 vols. (Innsbruck: Tyrolia-Verlag, 1990–99), 4.15:11. The outward poverty of the Holy Family was often addressed to underscore the magi's estimation of Christ Child, whom, regardless of his poverty, they worshipped.

4. "Magus enim et mathematicus et incantator et maleficus sive nigromanticus et ariolus et haruspex et divinator differunt," ed. Colon. 21.1:46, lines 21–23.

5. Henri de Lubac, *Exégèse médiévale: Les quatre sens de l'Écriture*, ed. Faculté de théologie S.J. de Lyon-Fourvière, 2 vols., Théologie 41 (Paris: Aubier, 1959).

6. The section on Matt. 2 can be found in Thomas Aquinas, *Catena aurea in quatuor Evangelia*, ed. Bernard Marie de Rossi (Turin: Petrus Marietti, 1888–89), 1:26–41.

7. Tarmo Toom, "Was Priscillian a Modalist Monarchian?" *Harvard Theological Review* 107, no. 4 (2014): 470–84.

8. Thomas Aquinas, *Catena aurea* 1:26b–36a.

9. Ibid.

10. De Lubac, *Exégèse médiévale*, 41; Beryl Smalley, *The Study of the Bible in the Middle Ages*, 3rd ed. (Oxford: Basil Blackwell, 1983), 310; Smalley, *The Gospels in the Schools, c. 1100–c. 1280* (London: The Hambledon Press, 1985).

11. The following offers a sampling, however incomplete, of scholarship on biblical commentaries in the eleventh to fourteenth centuries: Marcia L. Colish, "Psalterium Scholasticorum: Peter Lombard and the Emergence of Scholastic Psalms Exegesis," *Speculum* 67 (1992): 531–48; Guy Lobrichon, "La Bible des maîtres du XIIᵉ siècles," in *Bernard de Clairvaux: Histoire, mentalités, spiritualité*, Sources Chrétiennes (Paris: Editions du Cerf, 1992), 209–36; E. Ann Matter, "The Church Fathers and the *Glossa ordinaria*," in *The Reception of the Church Fathers in the West: From the Carolingians to the Maurists*, ed. Irena Backus, 2 vols. (Leiden: Brill, 1997), 1:83–111; Frans van Liere, "The Literal Sense of the Books of Samuel and Kings: From Andrew of St Victor to Nicholas of Lyra," in *Nicholas of Lyra: The Senses of Scripture*, ed. Philip D. Krey and Lesley Smith (Leiden: Brill, 2000), 59–81; James R. Ginther, "The Scholastic Psalms' Commentary as a Textbook for Theology: The Case of Thomas Aquinas," in *Omnia disce—Medieval Studies in Memory of Leonard Boyle, O.P.*, ed. Anne J. Duggan, Joan Greatrex, and Brenda Bolton (Aldershot: Ashgate, 2005), 211–29; Thomas Prügl, "Thomas Aquinas as Interpreter of Scripture," in *The Theology of Thomas Aquinas*, ed. Rik Van Nieuwenhove and Joseph Wawrykow (Notre Dame: University of Notre Dame Press, 2005), 386–415; Robert J. Karris, "Nova et Vetera: Things New and Old in St. Bonaventure's Commentary on the Gospel of St. John," *Franciscan Studies* 65 (2007): 121–36; Ian Christopher Levy, "The Literal Sense of Scripture and the Search for Truth in the Late Middle Ages," *Revue d'histoire eccle'siastique* 104, no. 3–4 (2009): 783–827; Gilbert Dahan, "Exégèse et prédication au Moyen Age," *Revue des sciences philosophiques et theologiques* 95, no. 3 (2011): 557–79; Aleksander Horowski, "I Padri nell'opera esegetica di Alessandro d'Hales, O.F.M. (° 1245)," in *Les Réceptions des Pères de l'Eglise au Moyen Age*, ed. Berndt Rainer and Michel Fedou (Münster: Aschendorff Verlag, 2013), 465–91; Alexander André, "Trinitarian Theology in Commentaries on the Fourth Gospel from the School of Laon," in *In principio erat Verbum*, ed. Amerini Fabrizio (Münster: Aschendorff, 2014), 93–110; Franklin T. Harkins and Frans van Liere, eds., *Interpretation of Scripture: Theory*, Victorine Texts in Translation (Turnhout: Brepols, 2015); Lesley Smith, "Hugh of St. Cher and Medieval Collaboration," in *Transforming Relations*, ed. Franklin T. Harkins (Notre Dame: University of Notre Dame Press, 2010), 241–64.

12. Smalley, *Gospels in the Schools*, 11–35.

13. *PL* 114:63–178. Lesley Smith, *The* Glossa ordinaria: *The Making of a Medieval Bible Commentary* (Leiden: Brill, 2009), 2009.

14. *PL* 162:1228–500. On Matt. 2, 1253B–61B.

15. *PL* 198:1541–42. Mark Clark, "Peter Comestor and Stephen Langton: Master and Student, and Co-makers of the Historia scholastica," *Medioevo: Rivista di storia della filosofia medievale* 35 (2010): 123–44; J. H. Morey, "Peter Comestor, Biblical Paraphrase, and the Medieval Popular Bible: A Bibliographical Consolidation of the 'Historia scholastica' and Its Widespread Influence and Authority as a Pre-Reformation Vernacular Bible," *Speculum* 68 (1993): 6–35; Smalley, *Gospels in the Schools*, 37–83.

16. "Magos vero primitias gentium," *PL* 114:73C.

17. Ibid., 73B.

18. Ibid., 73C.

19. *PL* 162:1254B–C.

20. Num. 22–25 and 31:8, 16. Also in passing in Deut. 23:4–6; Josh. 13:22 and 24:9; Neh. 13:2; and Mic. 6:5.

21. Num. 24:17.

22. Num. 31:16.

23. 2 Pet. 2:15; Jude 1:11; Apoc. 2:14.

24. *PL* 162:1254A–B.

25. *PL* C148:1541C.

26. Matt. 2:11. Luke 3:16.

27. *PL* 114:75B; *PL* 162:1256D.

28. *PL* 198:1542C.

29. John Chrysostom (Pseudo), *Opus imperfectum in Matthaeum*, vol. 56 in PG. See Jean-Paul Bouhot, "Remarques sur l'histoire du texte de l'Opus Imperfectum in Matthaeum," *Vigiliae Christianae* 24 (1970): 197–209; Jean-Marie Salamito, "Christianisme antique et économie: Raisons et modalités d'une rencontre historique," *Antiquité Tardive* 14 (2006): 27–37; Fredric W. Schlatter, "The Author of the Opus imperfectum in Matthaeum," *Vigiliae Christianae* 42, no. 4 (1988): 364–75.

30. Sup. Matt. 2.1, ed. Colon. 45:63–46:11. Albertus Frederik Johannes Klijn, *Seth in Jewish, Christian and Gnostic Literature*, Supplements to Novum Testamentum (Leiden: Brill, 1977), 56–59.

31. Sup. Matt. 2.1, ed. Colon. 46:19–20.

32. "Magus enim et mathematicus et incantator et maleficus sive nigromanticus et ariolus et haruspex et divinator differunt" (46:21–23).

33. Sup. Matt. 2.1, ed. Colon. 46:28–29. Separability and abstraction were themes addressed by Aristotle in his epistemological engagement with Plato on mathematics.

34. Sup. Matt. 2.1, ed. Colon. 46:46–47.

35. Sup. Matt. 2.1, ed. Colon. 46:46, notes to lines 19 to 57.

36. Isidore of Seville, *The Etymologies of Isidore of Seville*, trans. and intro. Stephen A. Barney, W. J. Lewis, J. A. Beach, and Oliver Berghof (Cambridge: Cambridge University Press, 2006), book 8, chap. 9. The Latin critical edition of Isidore's text is W. M. Lindsay, ed., *Isidori Hispalensis Episcopi, Etymologiarum sive originum, Libri XX*, 2 vols. (Oxford: Oxford University Press, 1911). See also *PL* 82:310–14.

37. William E. Klingshirn, "Isidore of Seville's Taxonomy of Magicians and Diviners," *Traditio* 58 (2003): 66–67.

38. Isidore, *Etymologies*, 8.9.9.

39. Ibid., 8.9.25–28.

40. Sup. Matt. 2.2, ed. Colon. 48.28–37.

41. Isaac Newton verified the parabolic orbit of comets in 1680.

42. Sup. Matt. 2.2, ed. Colon. 48.38–67.

43. Sup. Matt. 2.2, ed. Colon. 48.68–74.

44. Sup. Matt. 2.2, ed. Colon. 48:49.

45. Sup. Matt. 2.2, ed. Colon. 48.75–49.19.

46. See, for example, Henri de Lubac, *La postérité spirituelle de Joachim de Flore* (The spiritual posterity of Joachim of Fiore), Collection Le Sycomore (Paris: Lethielleux, 1979); Kevin Madigan, *Olivi and the Interpretation of Matthew in the High Middle Ages* (Notre Dame: University of Notre Dame Press, 2003), 30–43; Gian Luca Potestà, "'Intelligentia Scripturarum' und Kritik des Prophetismus bei Joachim von Fiore," in *Neue Richtungen in der hoch- und spätmittelalterlichen Bibelexegese*, ed. Robert E. Lerner (Munich: R. Oldenbourg, 1996), 95. Contrast them with Beryl Smalley's retraction in her own words: "I dismissed Joachim of Fiore and Joachism as an attack of senile dementia in the spiritual exposition. The outflow of books and papers on the subject has made my metaphor look silly. I must change it and say that the spiritual exposition in its old age produced a thriving child, though not one that I should care to adopt. Certainly I buried it while it was still alive." Smalley, *Study of the Bible*, xiii.

47. Joachim of Fiore, *Tractatus super quatuor Evangelia*, ed. Ernesto Buonaiuti (Rome: Tipografia del Senato, 1930), 68–77.

48. Thomas Aquinas, *Super evangelium s. Matthaei lectura*, ed. Raphael Cai (Turin: Marietti, 1951). Regarding the *lectura*'s contested reception history, see Jeremy Holmes, "Aquinas' Lectura in Matthaeum," in *Aquinas on Scripture: An Introduction to His Biblical Commentaries*, ed. Thomas G. Weinandy, Daniel A. Keating, and John Yocum (London: T & T Clark International, 2005), 73–75.

49. Thomas Aquinas, *Super evangelium s. Matthaei lectura*, chap. 2.

50. See Holmes, "Aquinas' Lectura in Matthaeum," 78–80.

51. Philip D. W. Krey and Lesley Smith, *Nicholas of Lyra: The Senses of Scripture*, Studies in the History of Christian Thought (Leiden: Brill, 2000); Kevin Madigan, "Lyra on the Gospel of Matthew," in *Nicholas of Lyra*, ed. Philip D. W. Krey and Lesley Smith (Leiden: Brill, 2000), 195–249. The *Postilla litteralis* used here is the edition printed in Rome in ca. 1472, a copy of which is held in the Bayerische Staatsbibliothek, indexed in the BSB incunabula catalog as N-110 and in the Gesamtkatalog der Wiegendrucke (GW) as M26523. Volume 4 contains the commentary on the Gospels, and the commentary on the journey of the magi can be found on fols. 10r–12r.

52. Desiderius Erasmus, *Paraphrase on the Gospel According to Matthew*, ed. Dean Simpson and Robert D. Sider, trans. Dean Simpson, Collected Works of Erasmus (Toronto: University of Toronto Press, 2008), 14 n. 11.

53. Ibid., 45–53. The text in a Latin edition can be found in Erasmus, *Opera Omnia* (Leiden: Peter Vander, 1706), 7:8a–11b.

SELECTED BIBLIOGRAPHY

WORKS BY RICHARD KIECKHEFER

Kieckhefer, Richard. "Convention and Conversion: Patterns in Late Medieval Piety." *Church History* 67 (1998): 32–51.

———. "The Devil's Contemplatives: The *Liber iuratus*, the *Liber visionum* and Christian Appropriation of Jewish Occultism." In *Conjuring Spirits*, edited by Claire Fanger, 250–65. The Magic in History Series. University Park: Pennsylvania State University Press, 1998.

———. *European Witch Trials: Their Foundations in Popular and Learned Culture, 1300–1500*. Berkeley: University of California Press, 1976.

———. *Forbidden Rites: A Necromancer's Manual of the Fifteenth Century*. University Park: Pennsylvania State University Press, 1998.

———. "Holiness and the Culture of Devotion: Remarks on Some Late Medieval Male Saints." In *Images of Sainthood in Medieval Europe*, edited by Renate Blumenfeld-Kosinski and Timea Klara Szell, 288–305. Ithaca: Cornell University Press, 1991.

———. "The Holy and the Unholy: Sainthood, Witchcraft, and Magic in Late Medieval Europe." *Journal of Medieval and Renaissance Studies* 24 (1994): 355–85.

———. "Imitators of Christ: Sainthood in the Christian Tradition." In *Sainthood: Its Manifestations in World Religions*, edited by Richard Kieckhefer and George Doherty Bond, 1–42. Berkeley: University of California Press, 1988.

———. "Jacques Lefèvre d'Étaples and the Conception of Natural Magic." In *La magia nell'Europa moderna: Tra antica sapienza e filosofia naturale*, edited by Fabrizio Meroi and Elisabetta Scapparone, 63–77. Florence: Olschki, 2007.

———. "Magic and Its Hazards in the Late Medieval West." In *The Oxford Handbook of Witchcraft in Early Modern Europe and Colonial America*, edited by Brian P. Levack, 13–31. Oxford: Oxford University Press, 2013.

———. "Magic at Innsbruck: The Case of 1485 Reexamined." In *Religion und Magie in Ostmitteleuropa*, edited by Thomas Wünsch, 11–29. Münster: Lit, 2006.

———. *Magic in the Middle Ages*. Cambridge: Cambridge University Press, 2014.

———. "Mythologies of Witchcraft in the Fifteenth Century." *Magic, Ritual, and Witchcraft* 1 (2006): 79–108.

———. "The Office of Inquisition and Medieval Heresy: The Transition from Personal to Institutional Jurisdiction." *Journal of Ecclesiastical History* 46 (1995): 36–61.

———. *Repression of Heresy in Medieval Germany*. The Middle Ages Series. Philadelphia: University of Pennsylvania Press, 1979.

———. "The Specific Rationality of Medieval Magic." *American Historical Review* 99 (1994): 813–34.

———. *Theology in Stone: Church Architecture from Byzantium to Berkeley*. New York: Oxford University Press, 2004.

———. "Today's Shocks, Yesterday's Conventions." In "'Something Fearful': Medievalist Scholars on the Religious Turn," edited by Katherine Kerby-Fulton. Special issue, *Religion and Literature* 42 (2010): 253–78.

———. *Unquiet Souls: Fourteenth-Century Saints and Their Religious Milieu.* Chicago: University of Chicago Press, 1984.

———. "Witchcraft, Necromancy and Sorcery as Heresy." In *Chasses aux sorcières et démonologie: Entre discours et pratiques (XIVᵉ–XVIIᵉ siècles)*, edited by Martine Ostorero, Georg Modestin, and Kathrin Utz Tremp, 133–53. Florence: SISMEL, 2010.

OTHER SOURCES

Achelis, Hans. *Virgines subintroductae: Ein Beitrag zum VII Kapitel des I. Korintherbriefs.* Leipzig: J. C. Hinrichs, 1902.

Bailey, Michael D. "From Sorcery to Witchcraft: Clerical Conceptions of Magic in the Later Middle Ages." *Speculum* 76, no. 4 (2001): 960–90.

Barnes, John, and Paul Cattermole. *Wymondham Abbey.* Bury St. Edmunds: Miro Press, 2001.

Barone, Giulia. "Le due vite di Margherita Colonna." In *Esperienza religiosa e scritture femminili tra medioevo ed età moderna*, edited by Marilena Modica, 25–32. Acrireale: Bonnano, 1992.

———. "Margherita Colonna." In *Mein Herz schmiltzt wie Eis am Feuer: Die religiöse Frauenbewegung des Mittelalters in Porträts*, edited by Johannes Thiele, 136–45. Stuttgart: Kreuz Verlag, 1988. Translated by Larry F. Field as "Margherita Colonna: A Portrait." *Magistra* 21, no. 2 (2015): 81–91.

———. "Margherita Colonna e le Clarisse di S. Silvestro in Capite." In *Roma: Anno 1300. Atti della IV Settimana di Studi di storia dell'arte medievale dell'Università di Roma "La Sapienza" (19–24 maggio 1980)*, edited by Angiola Maria Romanini, 799–805. Rome: L'Erma di Bretschneider, 1983.

Boudet, J. P. *Entre science et nigromance: Astrologie, divination et magie dans l'occident médiéval, XIIᵉ–XVᵉ siècle.* Paris: Publications de la Sorbonne, 2006.

Boureau, Alain. *Satan the Heretic: The Birth of Demonology in the Medieval West.* Translated by Teresa Lavender Fagan. Chicago: University of Chicago Press, 2006.

Brentano, Robert. *Rome Before Avignon: A Social History of Thirteenth-Century Rome.* Berkeley: University of California Press, 1990.

Bresc, Henri, and Benoît Grévin, eds. *Les anges et la magie au Moyen Âge.* Rome: École française de Rome, 2002.

Caciola, Nancy. *Discerning Spirits: Divine and Demonic Possession in the Middle Ages.* Ithaca: Cornell University Press, 2003.

Clark, Elizabeth A. "John Chrysostom and the *Subintroductae.*" *Church History* 46 (1977): 171–85.

Corbin, Alain. *Village Bells: Sound and Meaning in the Nineteenth-Century French Countryside.* Translated by Martin Thom. New York: Columbia University Press, 1998.

Dalarun, Jacques, Michael Cusato, and Carla Salvati, eds. *The Stigmata of Francis of Assisi: New Studies, New Perspectives.* St. Bonaventure, N.Y.: Franciscan Institute, 2006.

Duffy, Eamon. *The Stripping of the Altars: Traditional Religion in England, c. 1400–1580.* 2nd ed. New Haven: Yale University Press, 2005.

Dunn, Caroline. *Stolen Women in Medieval England: Rape, Abduction, and Adultery, 1100–1500.* Cambridge: Cambridge University Press, 2013.

Elliott, Dyan. "The Physiology of Rapture and Female Spirituality." In *Medieval Theology and the Natural Body*, edited by Peter Biller and A. J. Minnis, 141–74. York: York Medieval Press, 1997.

Fanger, Claire. *Rewriting Magic: An Exegesis of the Visionary Autobiography of a Fourteenth-Century French Monk.* University Park: Pennsylvania State University Press, 2015.

French, Katherine. "Competing for Space: Medieval Religious Conflict in the Monastic-Parochial Church at Dunster." *Journal of Medieval and Early Modern Studies* 27, no. 2 (Spring 1997): 216–44.

———. *The People of the Parish*. Philadelphia: University of Pennsylvania Press, 2001.

Gougaud, Louis. "*Mulierum Consortia*: Étude sur le Syneisaktisme chez les Ascètes Celtiques." *Ériu* 9 (1923): 147–56.

Grant, Edward. *Planets, Stars, and Orbs: The Medieval Cosmos, 1200–1687*. Cambridge: Cambridge University Press, 1994.

Gravdal, Kathryn. *Ravishing Maidens: Writing Rape in Medieval French Literature and Law*. Philadelphia: University of Pennsylvania Press, 1991.

Grayzel, Solomon. "Popes, Jews, and Inquisition from 'Sicut' to 'Turbato.'" In *Essays on the Occasion of the Seventieth Anniversary of the Dropsie University*, edited by Abraham Katsh and Leon Nemoy, 151–88. Philadelphia: Dropsie University, 1979.

Grundmann, Herbert. *Religious Movements in the Middle Ages: The Historical Links Between Heresy, the Mendicant Orders, and the Women's Religious Movement in the Twelfth and Thirteenth Century, with the Historical Foundations of German Mysticism*. Translated by Steven Rowan. Introduction by Robert E. Lerner. Notre Dame: University of Notre Dame Press, 1995.

Heale, Martin V. "Monastic-Parochial Churches in Late Medieval England." In *The Parish in Late Medieval England: Proceedings from the 2002 Harlaxton Symposium*, vol. 14, edited by Clive Burgess and Eamon Duffy, 54–77. Donington: Paul Watkins, 2006.

Hegedus, Tim. "The Magi and the Star in the Gospel of Matthew and Early Christian Tradition." *Laval théologique et philosophique* 59 (2003): 81–95.

Heimann, Claudia. *Nicolaus Eymerich (vor 1320–1399)—Praedicator veridicus, inquisitor intrepidus, doctor egregius: Leben und Werk eines Inquisitors*. Münster: Aschendorff, 2001.

———. "*Quis proprie hereticus est?* Nicolaus Eymerichs Häresiebegriff und dessen Anwendung auf die Juden." In *Praedicatores, inquisitores*, vol. 1, *The Dominicans and the Mediaeval Inquisition*, edited by Wolfram Hoyer, 595–624. Rome: Istituto Storico Domenicano, 2004.

Hervieu-Léger, Danièle. *Religion as a Chain of Memory*. Translated by Simon Lee. New Brunswick: Rutgers University Press, 2000.

Kemp, Simon. *Medieval Psychology*. New York: Greenwood Press, 1990.

Klaassen, Frank. *The Transformations of Magic: Illicit Learned Magic in the Later Middle Ages and Renaissance*. University Park: Pennsylvania State University Press, 2013.

Kleinberg, Aviad. *The Sensual God: How the Senses Make the Almighty Senseless*. New York: Columbia University Press, 2015.

Knox, Lezlie S. *Creating Clare of Assisi: Female Franciscan Identities in Later Medieval Italy*. Leiden: Brill, 2008.

Labriolle, Pierre de. "Le 'mariage spirituel' dans l'antiquité chrétienne." *Revue historique* 137 (1921): 204–25.

Lopez, Bianca. "Between Court and Cloister: The Life and Lives of Margherita Colonna." *Church History* 82 (2013): 554–75.

Lubac, Henri de. *Medieval Exegesis*. 3 vols. Grand Rapids, Mich.: William B. Eerdmans, 1998.

McNamara, Jo Ann Kay. *Sisters in Arms: Catholic Nuns Through Two Millennia*. Cambridge: Harvard University Press, 1996.

Midelfort, H. C. Erik. *A History of Madness in Sixteenth-Century Germany*. Stanford: Stanford University Press, 1999.

Miller, Julie B. "Eroticized Violence in Medieval Women's Mystical Literature: A Call for a Feminist Critique." *Journal of Feminist Studies in Religion* 15, no. 2 (Fall 1999): 25–49.

Newman, Barbara. "Possessed by the Spirit: Devout Women, Demoniacs, and the Apostolic Life in the Thirteenth Century." *Speculum* 73 (1998): 733–70.

Nora, Pierre. *Realms of Memory: The Construction of the French Past*. Edited by Lawrence D. Kritzman. Translated by Arthur Goldhammer. New York: Columbia University Press, 1998.

North, John D. "Astronomy and Astrology." In *The Cambridge History of Science*, vol. 2, *Medieval Science*, edited by David C. Lindberg and Michael H. Shank, 456–84. Cambridge: Cambridge University Press, 2013.

Olden, T. "On the *Consortia* of the First Order of Irish Saints." *Proceedings of the Royal Irish Academy* 3 (1894): 415–20.

Olsan, Lea T. "Charms and Prayers in Medieval Medical Theory and Practice." *Social History of Medicine* 16, no. 3 (2003): 343–66.

Page, Sophie. *Magic in the Cloister: Pious Motives, Illicit Interests, and Occult Approaches to the Medieval Universe*. University Park: Pennsylvania State University Press, 2013.

Passenier, Anke. "The Life of Christina Mirabilis, Miracles and the Construction of Marginality." In *Women and Miracle Stories: A Multidisciplinary Exploration*, edited by Anne-Marie Korte, 145–79. Leiden: Brill, 2001.

Perarnau i Espelt, Josep. "El *Tractatus brevis super iurisdictione inquisitorum contra infideles fidem catholicam agitantes* de Nicolau Eimeric: Edició i estudi del text." *Arxiu de Textos Catalans Antics* 1 (1982): 79–126.

Pfau, Aleksandra. "Crimes of Passion: Emotions and Madness in French Remission Letters." In *Madness in Medieval Law and Custom*, edited by Wendy Turner, 97–122. Leiden: Brill, 2010.

Price, Betsy Barker. "Interpreting Albert the Great on Astronomy." In *A Companion to Albert the Great*, edited by Irven Michael Resnick, 397–436. Leiden: Brill, 2013.

Puig i Oliver, Jaume de. "El *Tractatus de haeresi et de infidelium incredulitate et de horum criminum iudice*, de Felip Ribot, O. Carm.: Edició i estudi." *Arxiu de Textos Catalans Antics* 1 (1982): 127–90.

Rader, Rosemary. *Breaking Boundaries: Male/Female Friendship in Early Christian Communities*. New York: Paulist Press, 1983.

Reynolds, Roger. "*Virgines subintroductae* in Celic Christianity." *Harvard Theological Review* 61 (1968): 547–68.

Rider, Catherine. "Demons and Mental Disorder in Late Medieval Medicine." In *Mental (Dis)Order in Later Medieval Europe*, edited by Sari Katajala-Peltomaa and Susanna Niiranen, 47–69. Leiden: Brill, 2014.

Rutkin, H. Darrel. "Astrology and Magic." In *A Companion to Albert the Great*, edited by Irven Michael Resnick, 451–505. Leiden: Brill, 2013.

Screech, Michael Andrew. "The Magi and the Star (Matthew 2)." In *Histoire de l'exégèse au XVIᵉ siècle*, edited by Olivier Fatio and Pierre Fraenkel, 385–409. Geneva: Droz, 1978.

Smalley, Beryl. *The Gospels in the Schools, c. 1100–c. 1280*. London: Hambledon, 1985.

Stannard, Jerry. "Magiferous Plants and Magic in Medieval Medical Botany." In *Herbs and Herbalism in the Middle Ages and Renaissance*, edited by Katherine Stannard and Richard Kay, 33–46. Aldershot: Ashgate, 1999.

Thiery, Daniel. *Polluting the Sacred: Violence, Faith and the "Civilizing" of Parishioners in Late Medieval England*. Leiden: Brill, 2009.

Thorndike, Lynn, ed. "*The Sphere*" *of Sacrobosco and Its Commentators*. Corpus of Mediaeval Scientific Texts 2. Chicago: University of Chicago Press, 1949.

Trexler, Richard C. *The Journey of the Magi: Meanings in History of a Christian Story*. Princeton: Princeton University Press, 1997.

———. "The Stigmatized Body of Francis of Assisi: Conceived, Processed, Disappeared." In *Frömmigkeit im Mittelalter: Politisch-soziale Kontexte, visuelle Praxis, körperliche Ausdrucksformen*, edited by Klaus Schreiner and Marc Müntz, 463–97. Paderborn: Fink, 2002.

Utz Tremp, Kathrin. *Von der Häresie zur Hexerei: "Wirkliche" und imaginäre Sekten im Spätmittelalter*. Hannover: Hansche Buchhandlung, 2008.

Vauchez, André. *Francis of Assisi.* Translated by Michael F. Cusato. New Haven: Yale University Press, 2012.

Voci, Federica. "La guérison du corps malade dans les miracles post mortem de Margherita Colonna." *Arzanà: Cahiers de littérature médiévale italienne* 18 (2016). https://arzana.revues.org/959/.

Weill-Parot, Nicolas, in collaboration with Julien Véronèse. "Antonio da Montolmo's *De occultis et manifestis* or *Liber Intelligentiarum*: An Annotated Critical Edition with English Translation and Introduction." In *Invoking Angels: Theurgic Ideas and Practices from the Thirteenth to the Sixteenth Century*, edited by Claire Fanger, 219–93. University Park: Pennsylvania State University Press, 2012.

CONTRIBUTORS

Michael D. Bailey earned his Ph.D. at Northwestern University, where he worked with Richard Kieckhefer. He is now a professor of history at Iowa State University. His research has focused on magic, witchcraft, and superstition, particularly in the later Middle Ages, as well as on heresy and religious reform. His most recent publications include *Fearful Spirits, Reasoned Follies: The Boundaries of Superstition in Late Medieval Europe* (2013) and *Magic: The Basics* (2018).

Kristi Woodward Bain is a senior REF impact coordinator in the Research Strategy Office at the University of Cambridge. She completed her Ph.D. in medieval and religious studies at Northwestern University in 2014 under the supervision of Richard Kieckhefer. She has published extensively on issues surrounding medieval parish churches in England, including conflict, collective memory, and cultural heritage. Her research has been funded by the Medieval Academy of America, the Mellon Foundation/Northwestern University Medieval Studies Cluster, and the German Academic Exchange Service (DAAD). She is an advisory board member of the Centre for Parish Churches Studies in Norwich, U.K., and a Trustee of Norwich Historic Churches Trust.

Maeve B. Callan is an associate professor of religion at Simpson College in Indianola, Iowa, and the author of *The Templars, the Witch, and the Wild Irish: Vengeance and Heresy in Medieval Ireland* (2015). She earned her doctorate in 2002 from Northwestern University, working under Richard Kieckhefer. Her work focuses on issues of sanctity, gender, heresy, and religious persecution in medieval Christianity. Her articles have appeared in *Journal of the History of Sexuality, Gender and History, Analecta Hibernica*, and *Proceedings of the Royal Irish Academy*, among other publications. Her current book project is *Sacred Sisters, Holy Isle: Medieval Ireland Through the Lens of Women's Lives*.

Elizabeth Casteen is an associate professor of history and a fellow of the Center for Medieval and Renaissance Studies at Binghamton University, SUNY.

She received her Ph.D. in medieval history from Northwestern University in 2009. Her research focuses on questions of gender and religion in medieval Europe during the High and late Middle Ages. She is the author of *From She-Wolf to Martyr: The Reign and Disputed Reputation of Johanna I of Naples* (2015). Her current research examines the problematic cultural, social, and legal contours of *raptus*—abduction, theft, seizure, or rape—in high- and late-medieval Europe.

David J. Collins, S.J., is an associate professor of history at Georgetown University (Washington, D.C.). He earned his doctorate in history at Northwestern University under Richard Kieckhefer in 2004. He has written extensively on the medieval cult of the saints, Renaissance humanism in Germany, and learned magic. He is the author of *Reforming Saints* (2008) and the editor of *The Cambridge History of Magic and Witchcraft* (2015). He is currently working on the legacy of scholastic understandings of magic, especially that of Albert the Great, from the High Middle Ages to the Enlightenment.

Claire Fanger is an associate professor of religion at Rice University whose research focuses on Latin Christianity in the later Middle Ages. She has written extensively on medieval magic, and especially angel magic in a Christian context. Her edited collections on this topic include *Conjuring Spirits* (1998) and *Invoking Angels* (2012). With Nicholas Watson, she edited John of Morigny's *Flowers of Heavenly Teaching*, and she discusses the implication of John's work in another book, *Rewriting Magic* (both 2015).

Sean L. Field received his Ph.D. in medieval history from Northwestern University in 2002. He is currently a professor of history at the University of Vermont. His books include *The Writings of Agnes of Harcourt* (2003), *Isabelle of France* (2006), *The Beguine, the Angel and the Inquisitor* (2012), and *The Rules of Isabelle of France* (2013). He is a coauthor of *Isabelle de France, soeur de Saint Louis* (2014) and a coeditor of *Marguerite Porete et Le miroir des simples âmes* (2013) and *The Sanctity of Louis IX* (2014). With Larry F. Field and Lezlie S. Knox, he has most recently completed a translation project for University of Notre Dame Press, entitled *Visions of Sainthood in Medieval Rome* (2017).

Anne M. Koenig is an assistant professor of history at the University of South Florida, where she teaches classes on medieval history, cultural and religious history, and the history of medicine and science. A recipient of numerous awards and fellowships, including a Fulbright Grant, the Dolores Zohrab Liebmann Fellowship, and the Northwestern University Presidential Fellowship,

Dr. Koenig researches the history of madness and is currently finishing a monograph entitled *Madness, Medicine and Society in Southeastern Germany from 1350 to 1500.*

Katelyn Mesler is a postdoctoral fellow at the Institut für Jüdische Studien at the Westfälische Wilhelms-Universität in Münster. She has previously held fellowships at the University of Pennsylvania and the Hebrew University of Jerusalem. She is also the editor, along with Elisheva Baumgarten and Ruth Mazo Karras, of *Entangled Histories: Knowledge, Authority, and Jewish Culture in the Thirteenth Century* (2017).

Sophie Page is a senior lecturer in the Department of History at University College London. Her research focuses on European medieval magic and astrology in the light of contemporary religious, philosophical, medical, and cosmological thought. Her publications include an edited collection, *The Unorthodox Imagination in Late Medieval Britain* (2010), and articles on learned magic, astrology, and the cultural history of animals. Her most recent book is *Magic in the Cloister: Pious Motives, Illicit Interests, and Occult Approaches to the Medieval Universe* (2013).

INDEX

abduction, 91, 95, 97–99, 105, 109

Abelard, Peter, 123, 128, 131
  See also Heloise

affect, 6, 77–78, 82, 85

Albert the Great, Saint, 12, 219–21, 238, 249, 257–61, 267–72, 274–75

Albertus Magnus. *See* Albert the Great

alchemy, 145, 147

Alverna, Mount, 31–33

amulet. *See* charm

animals
  animal spirit, 215, 221, 222
  and madness, 215, 220, 221
  and magic (*see* magic and animals)
  and the natural and mathematical sciences, 250
  and reason, 119, 215, 221, 222
  and temptation, 21

Arnulf, bishop of Lisieux, 54, 64

angels, 20, 35, 101, 105, 216–17, 235, 239, 242, 250–51, 262, 265
  fallen, 235–36, 243, 246–48.
  See also demons; intelligences; seraph

Anselmi, Giorgio, 249–50

Anthony of Egypt, Saint, 21

Antonio da Montolmo, 247–50

apocalypticism, 118–19

Aquinas, Thomas. *See* Thomas Aquinas, Saint

Aristotle, 11–12, 23–24, 236, 239, 259, 263, 275

asceticism, 17, 20, 22

astrology, 145, 147, 236, 238–39, 241–43, 246–47, 249, 251, 262, 265, 268–69
  texts of, 236, 238, 244, 247

astronomers, 239

astronomy, 11, 239, 260, 264, 270–71, 273, 275
  See also zodiac

Augustine of Hippo, Saint, 6, 152, 261

author-magicians, 241–42, 248
  See also magic, practitioners of

Avicenna, 218, 236

Balaam, 258, 266–67, 273–74

baptism, 164–65

Bartholomeo of Gallicano, 62

Beatrice of Provence (countess), 92–94, 108

beguines, 92–93, 101, 105, 107, 157

Benedictines, 64, 65n1, 71–72, 88n13, 89n14, 149, 217
  See also monasteries

Bernard of Clairvaux, Saint, 101, 133–34, 258

Bernardino of Siena, Saint, 149

Bethlehem, 12, 257, 264, 270, 274

bewitchment. *See* witchcraft, act of

Bible
  Albertine, 259, 267–72, 274–75
  commentaries of, 11, 258–65
  Jewish, 273
  monastic, 259, 261–62, 274
  patristic, 258–59, 261–63, 274
  Reformation, 259, 263
  Renaissance, 259, 274
  Scholastic, 259–60, 263, 265, 272–74
  See also New Testament, Old Testament

blessing, 26, 155–56

blood, 34, 103–4, 106–8
  menstrual, 219

body
  female, 91–110
  transformation of, 27, 35, 37–38

Bonaventure, Saint, 32–33

Byzantium, 147

Caesarius of Heisterbach, 101–2, 211–14, 223

canonization, 50, 53–54, 56–57, 59, 64
  trials, 96, 104–5, 109–11

Carthusian Order, 149, 157

Cassian, John, 43–45, 55–56, 64

Cathars, 151

Cecco d'Ascoli, 246–48

celibacy, 55, 118, 128

Charles, count of Anjou and Marne, 92–94, 108

Charles VI, king of France, 214

charm, 146–47, 149, 152, 214–15, 217–18, 242

chastity, 96, 103, 105, 118, 126, 129, 132–33

Chaucer, Geoffrey, 239–40